D0791662

THE LETTERS OF HART CRANE

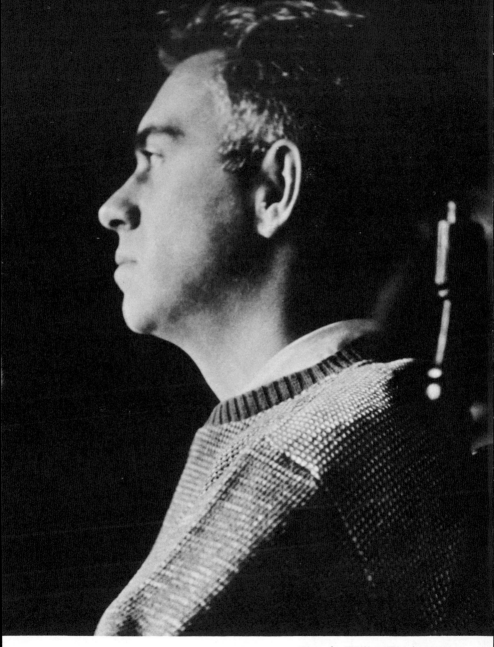
Photo by William Wright, 1931

816
C891L

Crane, Harold Hart

THE LETTERS OF

HART CRANE, 1899-1932,

1916-1932

EDITED BY BROM WEBER

The imaged Word, it is, that holds
Hushed willows anchored in its glow.
It is the unbetrayable reply
Whose accent no farewell can know.

928.1

52-12760

UNIVERSITY OF CALIFORNIA PRESS
Berkeley and Los Angeles 1965

COPYRIGHT, 1952, BY BROM WEBER

All rights reserved

First California Paper-bound Edition, 1965

MANUFACTURED IN THE UNITED STATES OF AMERICA

PREFACE

"Of the poets who came into prominence during the 1930's in America, none is more likely to achieve an immortality than Harold Hart Crane." So write Horace Gregory and Marya Zaturenska in their recent, authoritative *History of American Poetry*. The extraordinary quality of Crane's poetry and the tense drama of his brief life make such an observation valid and inevitable. It is amply supported in an indirect sense by the amount of devoted attention which Crane has received in the twenty years since his death by drowning in 1932. Waldo Frank's edition of the *Collected Poems* appeared in 1933. The first full-length book on Crane, Philip Horton's *Hart Crane,* came in 1937. Eleven years later, in 1948, the editor's *Hart Crane* was published. Meanwhile, magazines, anthologies, and critical volumes have given substantial space and consideration to the poet.

It seems fitting then, and necessary too, that the correspondence of this outstanding writer be presented now. Crane's letters exist in scattered condition: some in magazines, others in the appendices of books, still more in libraries and private collections. Many have already been lost, because of carelessness, wartime events, or other factors. But apart from such matters as preservation and compilation, there are the human revelations and literary merits which distinguish Crane's letters and make this collection desirable. Seldom has a man laid his heart bare as does Crane in these documents, seldom with the passion and skill which he so masterfully infused into his poetry as well. It seems undoubted that many of these letters will before long find their way into anthologies of great letters and prose.

The large quantity of letters written by Crane may be ascribed in part to the geographical gulf which separated him from those to whom he believed he could honestly announce his thoughts, emotions, and meaningful experiences. As soon as it became possible to

50821

enjoy closer contact with once-distant friends, he stopped writing to them. Thus scores of letters were sent to Gorham Munson from November 1919 to the early spring of 1923, at which time Crane joined Mr. and Mrs. Munson in New York. Thereafter, few letters were received by Mr. Munson, except in rare instances when either of the two men had left the city, or when Crane had an urgent need for communication which could not be satisfied with speech. In the case of friends like Slater Brown and Malcolm Cowley, where friendship was initiated and continued with social intercourse hardly ever broken by physical separation, only a handful of letters exist as a result.

As happens with some of us, many letters were the perfunctory expressions of a sense of obligation. An explanation of this character must often be assigned to a series of letters written to one person, or to a particular letter. It is as mundane sometimes as insistence by the poet's mother that he write her several times a week and make sure to send her a special delivery letter timed to reach her punctually each Sunday morning. In this class, too, must be placed those letters occasioned by Crane's failure to pay a debt, his desire to make amends for a squabble, and similar causes.

But far more compelling than distance or propriety as the dominant force behind Crane's prolific composition of letters was an emotional impulse which drove him to discharge so much expressive energy in a non-poetic form: his acquisitive need for sympathy, pity, understanding, affection . . . a need accompanied by the belief that these responses could be evoked with a persuasive explanation in words. Let us not confuse this poignant situation with dishonesty or a huckster's fraudulency. Crane was, after all, a poet to whom language was paramount. The outcome was that even those of his letters which had been intended as geographical bridges, or as duties, speedily found themselves converted into detailed and uninhibited recitations and exhortations. Examining the letters to his mother in this light, to choose one instance, we can understand why, despite the profound mutual misunderstanding of which each was aware, Crane persisted in alternately cajoling, threatening, and informing a basically-unresponsive correspondent.

The resultant rich character of Crane's letters, in terms of factual data and emotional subtleties, has enveloped them with a completeness calling for little amplification or clarification in the form of notes. These have consequently been held to a minimum. When Crane, for example, announces a decision, he bathes it in such a sea of rationalization and background that its origins, its validity, and its likely conclusion are all too evident to the reader. One is, indeed, encouraged to speculate whether the tremendous amount of energy involved in the production of so vast a profusion of details for even the most trivial of communications did not drain away some of the feeling and thought that might more happily have been incorporated in poems.

Strangely enough, however, it is apparent that the quantity and quality of Crane's letters were not negatively, but positively related to his poetic output. A correlation of the letters with the history of Crane's productivity reveals that it was precisely during periods of great poetic fertility and well-being that his most evocative and profound letters were composed. An illustration of this symbiotic relationship between the poetry and the prose, surely a phenomenon which demonstrates how organic and deep-seated was the urge for literary expression animating him, is the remarkable series of letters written to Gorham Munson between 1919 and 1923, when Crane perfected his control of a mature, individual language and music and composed some of his most striking lyrics. The highly-charged group of letters which Crane sent off to Waldo Frank from the Isle of Pines in 1926, while so feverishly engaged in molding several brilliant sections of *The Bridge,* is another relevant example.

The self-sufficiency of Crane's letters has made it less disappointing for the editor to be unable to include correspondence addressed to him, or to make extracts from it, as a complementary balance and check. Because of Crane's peripatetic career, letters he received were left behind in the boarding houses, steamship cabins, and hotels wherein he spent his days. A more drastic reduction in the number of remaining letters was apparently accomplished by his impetuous habit of destroying letters from people with whom he had severed relationships on an unfriendly note. Finally, the irregular and careless storing and handling of Crane's papers after his death has had its own inevitable results.

The responsibility to be exercised in the task of organizing the letters of a tempestuous and controversial man like Hart Crane, is as much a matter of human judgment as it is a familiarity with the canons of scholarship. Crane conformed less, overtly at least, to the dominant mores of his age than probably any of his contemporaries. The leitmotif was restless deviation—whether aesthetic, social, religious, or sexual. The record of his days vibrates with an explosive terror and repose—elated, wretched, violent, Rabelaisian—which find dynamic outlet in his letters. Insofar as Crane's letters will serve to develop a self-portrait and contribute toward an understanding of three decades of our American past, no harm can be accomplished by a forthright presentation.

The editor, therefore, has not suppressed any portions of Crane's letters which might disturb the genteel or excite the prurient. Those who have studied Crane's poetry with perception know how richly studded it is with the imagery, symbolism, and themes of love. As this preface was being put into final form, the editor received a copy of Dr. Paul Friedman's "The Bridge: A Study in Symbolism" (*The Psychoanalytic Quarterly*, Jan. 1952). After discussing such writers as Wilder and Kafka, Dr. Friedman, one of the few psychoanalysts who displays a genuine concern for literary values, goes on to say: "It implies no irreverence toward Crane's poetic sensibility to introduce these [psychological] concepts. The sexual imagery in his poetry is overt, undisguised." Of the "Voyages" series, Dr. Friedman writes: "Here the psychoanalyst could hardly be more explicit than Crane himself." Under no circumstances could the wealth of background experience and emotion which produced the alternately-pessimistic and ecstatic love poems of Crane conscientiously be omitted from a volume of his letters. One of the great love-poets of our time, few men have been so tyrannically governed by a chronic need to love and be loved. One need only observe in these letters how Crane's disinterest in poetry and his torpid creativity after 1929 were affected by a new and surprising love relationship. Miraculously rejuvenated, as it were, he wrote "The Broken Tower," one of his best poems.

The course of a man's life is inextricably linked with his fellows. For Crane in particular, relationships with other people were among the most weighty problems with which he had to cope. The letters uncover a pattern of tragic and repetitive failure which cannot help but influence our response to his statements about men and women. As one views the past with the advantage of hindsight, the fact is inescapable that almost everyone with whom Crane had close contact eventually became estranged from him in greater or lesser degree, though from a distance they may have continued to admire certain of his qualities. This held true for his literary as well as non-literary associates. All too often, it was Crane's vigorous egocentricity, his self-destructive behavior, which impelled a shocked and helpless friend to seek protective cover, to avoid Crane as gracefully as possible. Yet, far more frequently, those who drifted within Crane's orbit became the unwitting centers of emotional dramas in which fantasy was as powerful a constituent as reality. The fantastic dis-

tortion which blurred some people for Crane must be attributed to
his insecurity, his sexual inversion, his resentment against those who
could or did help him, his alcoholism, his paranoiac misrepresenta-
tion of motives and events, his hysterical existence . . . in short, to
the complex of neuroses which finally burgeoned forth during the
last year of his life into what was probably a full-scale psychopathic
state. Of course, this does not deny that Crane was probably also
the victim of envy, misunderstanding, and distaste for his poetry
and personality.

With these considerations as a guide, the editor has not thought it
necessary to delete those of Crane's comments which reflect un-
favorably upon the works or persons of artists or other public
figures, especially where such comments are balanced elsewhere in
the letters by favorable remarks. History, in any event, does not take
kindly to being expurgated or twisted for special purposes, no matter how laudable the intention. The editor has been encouraged in
his respect for honesty and frankness by Gorham Munson, Editor of
Hermitage House, who has interposed no stipulations although he
figures prominently in a variety of ways in the letters. The procedure has been different if it seemed that Crane's observations
would psychologically or socially harm any living person or the
close surviving relatives of a dead man. In such cases, and they have
been few, either the offensive material, or names and data which
might identify an individual, were omitted.

A few words of caution about some of the conclusions to be
drawn from the letters are in place. The editor has expanded space
and tried his publisher's spirit, in order to include every important
letter. But he has, of course, selected. Therefore, no ultimate conclusions, particularly those involving the personalities of Crane's
contemporaries or the nuances of relationships, are implied by the
arrangement which follows.

Further, the poetry of Hart Crane ought not to be hastily judged
by his life or letters, though the latter should no doubt be studied to
support an understanding and appreciation of the poetry. Art is not
subservient to the man; it has a life of its own which may be related but never subordinated. For example, the Brooklyn Bridge as
conception and poem will be seen to have occupied a compulsive
position in Crane's experience and thought. Granted that *The
Bridge* was a failure as a unified, major epic; this should not lead us
to conclude that Crane failed as a poet too, even though he did not
succeed as a latter-day Dante or Virgil. Various sections of *The
Bridge* are individually magnificent; in addition, Crane wrote other

poems before, during, and after his work on *The Bridge* which suffice to give him first rank among contemporary poets. Nor should we, at the same time, assume that Crane's poetic gift was gone because he said so, or because he didn't write much in his last years. "The Broken Tower" was completed little more than a month before he died in the Caribbean Sea. With only one such poem to his credit, a poet would deserve and gain the immortality predicted for Crane. Finally, Crane was admittedly not a thinker, rather a creative being who depended on sensation, intuition, taste. It would be unwise to characterize his poetry as valueless expression simply because he was neither a logician nor a pundit preoccupied, sensibly or otherwise, with questions of ideology and systematic knowledge. In his own valid and fruitful manner, Crane illuminated recesses of the human mind and heart with pregnant clarity.

The editor has prepared a chronology of Crane's life and works. The last chapter in the Crane biography occurred in 1947. On July 30th of that year, Mrs. Grace Hart Crane, the poet's mother, died in Teaneck, New Jersey. Before her death, she told Samuel Loveman that she wished to be cremated and her ashes to be cast into the East River from the Brooklyn Bridge. The necessary arrangements were made, and the editor was one of a small party which proceeded along Brooklyn Bridge on a windy, sunlit afternoon in Fall 1947. At intervals on the Bridge, there are signs warning pedestrians not to throw anything from the structure. By the time the party reached the center of the Bridge, considerable trepidation existed about the feasibility of respecting Mrs. Crane's last wishes. It remained at last for the editor to grasp the small, undecorated tin can and shake the ashes into the air, where they swirled about for a few moments and then fell mistily into the water below. Thus Crane's mother joined him in the element which had claimed him fifteen years earlier.

Crane's father had died in the Summer of 1931, bringing to an end a similarly complex relationship with his son. Though each bore a great and genuine love for the other, there is little doubt that the divorce of his parents in 1917 tended to separate father from son. Mrs. Crane's proximity, her emotional nature and her evaluation of her ex-husband's motives and actions, made it impossible for Crane to suspend himself impartially between both parents as he wished. Instead, he swam into the aura of his mother's beliefs and reactions. The resulting alienation from his father was not fully surmounted until almost a decade later, for it was not until then that each man grew reconciled to the other's personality and values. However, it seems unwarranted, if one can say so on the basis of their extensive correspondence, to perpetuate Crane's own misconceptions of the older man's values and attitudes in relation to his son prior to 1927. From an early date, the elder Crane was apparently profoundly interested in his son's choice of a literary career and anxious to have him prepare for it. During 1916 and 1917, for example, he pressed insistently for Hart to enter college, so that the latter might obtain the educational background expected to assist him in functioning as a writer. Although the elder Crane had only studied for a few years at Alleghany College, he had no contempt for education or culture such as marks some self-made practical men. When Hart refused to attend college, Mr. Crane recognized no realistic alternative for his son other than adjustment to the business world and development of his poetic life as an adjunct of his mercantile life. From a non-romantic point of view, Mr. Crane was unfortunately justified. Even in our advanced age, most full-time poets unsupported by private incomes, relatives, or philanthropic gifts either cease writing poetry at all or become embittered producers of occasional pieces. Perhaps Mr. Crane should have supported Hart from his adolescence onward with an allowance sufficient to enable him to write poetry and do nothing else. The moral and psychological results of such beneficence are mixed and problematical. In any event, his young son's early poetry did not yet reveal the merit which would have called forth a clamorous and effective acclaim to which Mr. Crane might have acceded; furthermore, Mr. Crane did not stem from a wealthy aristocracy to whom a life of cultured leisure is natural rather than phenomenal. Finally, the immediate outward signs of Mr. Crane's success were somewhat illusory; his business enterprises partook of the overblown quality of 1920-ish prosperity, and were underlaid with an insecurity not conducive to the assumption of a unique personal and financial responsibility. Once Mr. Crane recognized the impossibility of shaping his son's values, once he accepted the fact that Hart was (as he not unkindly wrote him) a poetic "vagabond," he generously supplied him with money to the best of his ability and understanding, continually offered him the security of his home, and ultimately left him a large cash bequest and an annual allowance that would have sustained his son under normal circumstances.

Crane was in great part responsible for creating the time-worn legend of a hard-hearted father. During the years from 1917 to 1925, less so afterward, he wrote or informed countless friends of the brutality of his father's behavior, his lack of kindness and generosity, and the suffering this caused. Yet it was during these years that

Crane was most uncompromising, patronizing, intransigent, prone to distortion of his father's image. The correspondence between them, not all of which is included here, is a tragic record of misunderstanding for which neither is to be adjudged guilty. It shows that they were temperamentally alike in many ways: in their humor, their warmth of spirit, their reckless pride, their strong need for freedom.

*   *   *

The letters have been assembled chiefly from original manuscripts, as well as microfilm and photostat copies, generously made available by their recipients, libraries, and collectors. Herbert Weinstock and William Wright furnished typed copies of letters to them; Samuel Loveman gave typed letters to William Sommer. The editor has been able to examine the papers of Crane and his mother; these provided Crane's own carbon copies of typewritten letters to his father, Otto H. Kahn, Yvor Winters, Edgell Rickword, Thomas Seltzer, and his stepmother . . . letters to his mother and grandmother . . . typed copies of several letters to his father and stepmother. Despite the hazards of transcribing manuscript, the editor has striven to attain maximum faithfulness to the original.

The major portion of the letters were obtained by the editor when he collected material for his book on Crane. Since then, he has made every reasonable effort to collect additional letters from people to whom Crane might have revealed himself fully and uniquely. The result is an edition which makes available the letters evoked by Crane's most important literary and personal relationships.

As a general rule, only those letters which are routine in nature, of little general interest, or which deal with subjects more intensively and significantly treated in other letters, were excluded. In this connection, it is pertinent to note that it was Crane's habit, when he wrote several people at about the same time, to write the same things in almost identical phraseology to each of his correspondents. This has made it necessary to delete portions of letters as repetitious. Another feature of Crane's letter-writing has required some editorial excision. Though he wrote lengthily and often, his letters were usually prefaced and closed with excuses for writing briefly and infrequently. These apologies are corollaries of his insatiable desire for affection and his fear of hostility. Though he acknowledges their psychological meaning, the editor has acted on the assumption that an excess of such material is bound to distract the reader from more valuable sections. He has accordingly deleted most of it, together with conventional greetings, regards, and other closes, though a few letters were left intact so that the flavor of Crane's apologetics might be communicated.

The editor has strengthened the punctuation, corrected obvious slips of the pen and the spelling of names and words when there seemed no advantage to letting them remain as Crane hastily set them down, supplied dates and addresses for letters which did not bear them or were incorrectly headed, italicized names of books and periodicals, enclosed titles of poems, etc., in quotation marks, and made a few insertions to supply missing words or to explain initials. Brackets indicate the editor's insertions; omissions of 1-25 words are shown with — — — —, omissions of over 25 words with —/—/; names deleted except for initials are given as J— —, though Crane often used initials himself. Recurrent details were reduced to uniformity by placing address and date on left and right respectively, allowing no indentations at the opening, and transferring all postscripts at top or side to the end.

The kindness of the following who assisted in the compilation of letters or furnished explanations of their contents is gratefully acknowledged: Eleanor Anderson, Peggy Baird, Slater Brown, Malcolm Cowley, Donald C. Gallup, Bessie M. Hise, Philip Horton, Philip Kaplan, Samuel Loveman, David Mann, Newberry Library, Norman Holmes Pearson, Katherine Anne Porter, Selden Rodman, Edwin Seaver, Isidor Schneider, David Swetland, F. Swetland, Robert Thompson, University of Chicago Library, Yale University Library, and Morton Dauwen Zabel. I am indebted to Richard Rychtarik and the late Charlotte Rychtarik for aid, friendship, and the 1920 photograph of Crane by Hervey Minns which serves as frontispiece, while to Horace Gregory, Marya Zaturenska, and Henri Peyre I owe gratitude for moral support of which they may not be aware. The interest and understanding of Gorham Munson and M. U. Sheldon has stimulated me to complete what began as a labor of love and was too quickly encumbered with depressing complications. I reiterate my thanks to those people and institutions earlier cited in the preface to my *Hart Crane;* their generous cooperation on that book made this one possible. Joseph Frank's name was inadvertently omitted from that group, as was that of Georgia O'Keeffe, Executrix, Alfred Stieglitz Estate; I thank them now. Martha Crossen helped with the manuscript at a crucial moment. Some of the editorial work was done at Yaddo, for which I am grateful to Louis Kronenberger, Elizabeth Ames, and the Yaddo Corporation. As always, my wife Nettie has done more than can here be listed.

BROM WEBER

CHRONOLOGY

Harold Hart Crane was born on July 21, 1899, in Garrettsville, Ohio, the only child of Clarence Arthur and Grace Hart Crane. In 1909, after a few years in Warren, Ohio, the family moved to Cleveland, Ohio. There Crane attended public high school, while his father developed a confectionery manufacturing and sales business. The boy also travelled with his family to the Isle of Pines, Cuba, and through parts of Western United States and Canada.

Crane's interest in writing and art evidenced itself at an early age. His first published poem ("C 33") appeared in *Bruno's Weekly* (N.Y.), Sept. 23, 1916, while his first prose, a letter, was printed in *The Pagan* (N.Y.), Oct. 1916. Thereafter, his devotion to poetry superseded any other concerns.

During 1916 and 1917, Crane's parents separated and were divorced. Symbolic of the effect on their son was his assumption of the maternal surname "Hart" as his own first name. In 1916, when the divorce actions were initiated, Crane left for New York City alone. There he soon became familiar with writers, artists, and editors. He remained in New York, despite a few return visits to Cleveland, until the late Fall of 1919.

At that time, he returned to Cleveland to work for his father and to live with his mother and maternal grandmother, both of whom had been Christian Scientists for many years. Dissatisfaction with his working and living arrangements led him, in 1921, to leave his father's employ and, in 1923, to move permanently to New York City.

By dint of night-school courses and practical experience, he had been able to earn his living in Cleveland during 1922 as an advertising copywriter. After a few months of this in New York, he resigned his job and left for Woodstock, New York. Thereafter, his periods of employment grew shorter until eventually he was generally without an income . . . his movements between country and city were frequent.

He had first conceived of his major poem, *The Bridge*, in February 1923, but was unable to work on it as he wished. Accordingly, his first book of poems, *White Buildings*, appeared late in 1926 without any sections of that poem. Fortunately, Otto H. Kahn granted him a sum of money to work on *The Bridge* during 1926, and Crane wrote much of the poem in Patterson, New York and on the Isle of Pines, Cuba. With his father's help, he wrote more in 1927; finally, in 1929, under the impetus of publication offered by Caresse and Harry Crosby, he completed the poem. It appeared early in 1930 in a Paris and a New York edition, and was generally acclaimed as one of the remarkable poetic achievements of our time.

In 1927 and 1928, Crane stayed in California as the companion of a wealthy invalid; in 1928, a bequest made available to him after his grandmother's death permitted him to travel in England and France. When he was awarded a Guggenheim Fellowship for creative writing in 1931, he left the United States for Mexico, where he hoped to write a never-initiated poem on Cortez.

With the exception of a brief return to the United States to attend his father's funeral, the remainder of his life was spent in Mexico City and its environs. On April 24th, 1932, he sailed for New York from Vera Cruz on the *S.S. Orizaba*. Three days later, on the 27th, he either jumped or fell into the Caribbean Sea and was drowned. His body was not recovered.

CONTENTS

PREFACE   v

CHRONOLOGY   xv

PART ONE   1
     OHIO (1916-1922)

PART TWO   111
     NEW YORK (1923-1925)

PART THREE   229
     WEST INDIES–EUROPE (1926-1930)

PART FOUR   361
     MEXICO (1931-1932)

LIST OF CORRESPONDENTS   413

INDEX   415

PART ONE

Ohio

(1916–1922)

1 9 1 6

1: To His Grandmother

[*Cleveland, Ohio*]   *Jan. 26, 1916*

My Dear Grandmother: Examination time is *on* now and I am kept completely occupied in the preparation for them. We had *English* today and Latin and Geometry are due tomorrow. They are my hoodooes and so I am not a little worried tonight about the outcome. I am invited over to G. Crane's for supper tonight as Aunt Bess is to be there on about a day's visit so Dora can go out early. As you already know, Father and Mother are in New York and I am running things alone now. The store was doing surprisingly well today when I was there owing perhaps to the balmy weather (almost summer) which we are having. Alice has been *very sick* and in response to my gift of some roses she sent me a beautiful note as soon as she was able to sit up. Your letters would augur a fairly favorable winter and good conditions on the island. So you rest as much as you can and enjoy the care-free feelings while you can whir around with the Wilcoxs in the machine. It is fine that you have found a group of such sympathetic thinkers and be sure and carry the *science*[1] as far as you can. I know of few better places to get a foothold in the faith than in the quiet and beauty of the island.

Mother left feeling fine for New York and suppose, tho busy, she is enjoying a splendid time. They will be back Sat. morn.

With the exception of a little sore throat I have felt fine myself lately. I think it is unnecessary to go to Mr. Ely.[2] My writing has suffered neglect lately due to study for examinations, but I will soon resume it with vehemence as I am intensely,—grippingly interested in a new ballad I am writing of six hundred lines. I have resolved to become a *good* student even if I have to sit up all night to become one. You will undoubtedly wink when you read this state declaration so often made but this time it is in earnest.

1. Christian Science.
2. A Christian Science practitioner.

2: TO HIS GRANDMOTHER

Cleveland Ohio   *Feb. 10, 1916*

My dear Grandmother: —/—/ I am now a Junior (capital) in high school and feel quite elated at having so passed my examinations. The present too, is more encouraging as fine marks have been in the great majority since my promotion. — — — —

I'll bet you were glad to be rid of that musty, fusty old preacher! Let him scramble the Andersons awhile with his talk. It is strange, in view of the fact that last winter I defended the desirability of northern winters to the expense of much discomfiture from other arguers, that the whole illusion has melted away and I have often this winter thought of the South with longing—yes, even Florida. My blood, I guess, has been thinner or digestion poorer. Some of these days have cut me thru and thru so that I have for the most part of the season been exquisitely uncomfortable, "Once south has spoilt me" as they say.

— — — — It is surely lonely for me here, eating alone and seldom seeing any one but in the darkness of morning or night. If you were here it would be different, but I am consoled amply by knowing of your comfort and welfare where you now are. I have been working hard lately at my writing but find it doubly hard with the task of conjoining it to my school work. They are so shallow over there at school I am more moved to disdain than anything else. Popularity is not my aim though it were easy to win it by laughing when they do at nothing and always making a general ass of oneself. There are about two out of the twelve hundred I would care to have as friends. —/—/

3: TO HIS FATHER

[New York City]   *Dec. 31, 1916*

My dear Father: I have just been out for a long ride up Fifth Ave. on an omnibus. It is very cold but clear, and the marble facades of the marvelous mansions shone like crystal in the sun. Carl [Schmitt] has been very good to me, giving hours of time to me, advising, helping me get a room, etc. The room I have now is a bit too small, so after my week is up, I shall seek out another place near here, for I like the neighborhood. The houses are so different here, that it seems most interesting, for a while at least, to live in one.

It is a great shock, but a good tonic, to come down here as I have and view the countless multitudes. It seems sometimes almost as though you had lost yourself, and were trying vainly to find somewhere in this sea of humanity, your lost identity.

Today, and the remainder of the week, I shall devote to serious efforts in my writing. If you will help me to the necessities, I think that within six months I shall be fairly able to stand on my own feet. Work is much easier here where I can concentrate. My full love to you, dear father. Write me often and soon.

1 9 1 7

4: To His Father

N.Y.C.   *Jan. 5, 1917*

My dear Father: — — — — It does me a great deal of good to hear from you often, and I hope you will continue to write me as often as you have lately done. While I am not home-sick, I yet am far from comfortable without letters, and often, from you.

Nearly every evening since my advent, has been spent in the companionship of Carl [Schmitt.] Last night we unpacked some furniture of his which had arrived from his home, and afterward talked until twelve, or after, behind our pipes. He has some very splendid ideas about artistic, and psychic balance, analysis, etc. I realize more entirely every day, that I am preparing for a fine life: that I have powers, which, if correctly balanced, will enable me to mount to extraordinary latitudes. There is constantly an inward struggle, but the time to worry is only when there is no inward debate, and consequently there is smooth sliding to the devil. There is only one harmony, that is the equilibrium maintained by two opposite forces, equally strong. When I perceive one emotion growing overpowering to a fact, or statement of reason, then the only manly, worthy, sensible thing to do, is build up the logical side, and attain balance, and in art,—formal expression. I intend this week to begin my studying—Latin, German, and philosophy, right here in my room. They will balance my emotional nature, and lead me to more exact expression. —/—/

5: To His Mother

N.Y.C.   *Jan. 26, 1917*

Dear Mother and Grandma: —/—/ Earl Biggers, the author of *Seven Keys to Baldpate,* was in for some grub, and I was shocked nearly off my feet by the quietness and un-worldliness of his behavior. He is a fine fellow however. I hear only pessimistic lines from Father, and hear from Erwin[1] (via, rather) that he is very unwell. The travel that he is planning, will straighten him out into better shape. We all needed to get away awhile.

I wouldn't be at all surprised to see Sullivan drop in any day, for his letters intimate such. He will be darn welcome, I can assure you, and promise you also that we shall have some fine times. You heard, I suppose, that I sent him a choice volume of Irish songs autographed by one of the principal literary figures in America today, Padraic Colum. I have invited Colum and his wife to dine with me tomorrow night at Gonfarones, an Italien eating-place, where the table d'hote costs only 60 cents per plate, and where the food is fine. Colum says I should have a volume of verse out in two years without any difficulty, and has offered to write a preface for it also. He has seen, as I said before, all my work,—nearly all, and admires it.

Every day I do my studying, and read a good bit also. The room I have been occupying has been too dark, and I shall change lodgings as soon as is possible. Friends of Carl have asked me out to dinners several times, and I have enjoyed as much of social life as I have ever cared for. When you move here, there is a fine bunch of friends waiting for you. O this is the place to live, at least for nine months of the year. —/—/

6: TO HIS MOTHER

N.Y.C.   *Feb. 19, 1917*

My dear, dear Mother: —/—/ Last night I took dinner with Harold Thomas and Carl in an Italien restaurant where you have to speak Italien to get anything at all to eat. They cook everything in olive-oil so that one has a good cathartic with his meal besides a splendid gratification of the palate. And this morning, it being Sunday, I took a long ride on an omnibus out into the Bronx and back, and saw all the fashion on Fifth Ave. When you see the display of wealth and beauty here, it will make you crawl. It is the most gorgeous city imaginable, besides being at present the richest and most active place in the world. The swarms of humanity of all classes inspire the most diverse of feelings; envy, hate, admiration and repulsion. But truly it is *the* place to live. —/—/

I wish above all other things that you could be here this week, for there are several big things that I have been invited to. The

1. Mr. Crane's employee.

initial exhibition of the choicest of Chase's pictures is to be privately
(by invitation) opened tomorrow afternoon from four until six. The
greatest painters of the day will attend. Carl having given me his
invitation, I am going to take Mr. Colum and perhaps his wife.
Then Mr. Colum has given me a ticket to the reading by Vachel
Lindsay of his own poems at the Princess Theater. Also, on Thursday, I shall attend the meeting of the Poetry Society of America,
which is quite exclusive. By the way, Mr. Colum intends to suggest me for membership. —/—/

7: To His Mother

N.Y.C.   *Feb. 22, 1917*

My dear Mother: Your good letter I have just read, and it cheered me
up a good deal. You know, I am working hard and see very few
people and even now haven't had more than a half-hour's talk with
anyone for over a week. My work, though, is coming along finely,
and I shall be published both in *Others* and again in *The Pagan*
this next month. Yesterday was a day of tremendous work. I turned
out, in some ways, the finest piece of work yet, besides writing a
shorter poem also.

Mother, you do not appreciate how much I love you. I can tell
by your letters that there exists a slight undercurrent of doubt, and
I do not want it there. If you could know how I long to see you
perhaps that might make some difference.

Now everything is in truth going splendidly, only I get terribly
lonesome often when I am through working. A man *must* wag his
tongue a little, or he'll lose his voice. Hurry, so that we can both wag!

8: To His Father

N.Y.C.   *August 8, 1917*

My dear Father: I am very, very sorry that things are going so badly
with Mother. I guess there is nothing for her to do but to get back
here as soon as is possible and try to re-instate herself in poise and
health. I look for her this week. At least I see no reason why she
should linger longer. But I have received no word from her and
am uncertain as to much of the true state of affairs with her. I only
hope you are avoiding any meetings as much as possible, for as I
said, it is now too early,—she is not yet established well enough to endure the strain which you know any contact causes. —/—/

I have been diabolically nervous ever since that shock out at the house, but Sunday Carl, Potapovitch and I went out to Long Beach, and lying in the sun did me some good. If you could shake responsibilities like this for a week or so, it would work inestimable good upon you. You cannot worry on such a beautiful beach with the sound of waves in your ears. We all get to thinking that our heads are really our bodies, and most of the time go floating around with only our brain conscious, forgetting that our bodies have requirements also.

I feel so near to you now that I do hope that nothing can ever again break the foundation of sincerity that has been established beneath our relations. Never has anyone been kinder than you were when I was last home. I want you to know that I appreciate it, and also your two fine letters.

9: TO HIS FATHER

[*New York City*]   *Sept. 18, '17*

My dear Father: Your good letter rec'd yesterday. From what Hazel says I presume this will find you back in Cleveland, and busy looking over what has happened while you have been away. I haven't written more because, as you can readily perceive, I haven't known your address most of the time, but once again you may expect my regular letters. This one thing though, I am going to ask of you. If, when you write me, you are thinking of Mother in a distasteful way, please conceal it, remaining silent on the subject. And if, in thinking of her, one kind thought should occur (as I know it does) express it. You remember that when I last was home, I said that I "was through."—That was possible with me for but one hour. My heart is still as responsive to both your loves, and more so, than ever. I have seen more tears than I ever expected in this world, and I have shed them through others' eyes, to say nothing of my own sorrow. And now, when I hear nothing but forgiveness, tenderness, mercy, and love from one side, how can [I] bear resentment and caustic words coming from the other without great pain? Happiness may some time come to me, I am sure it will. But please, my dear Father, do not make the present too hard,—too painful for one whose fatal weakness is to love two unfortunate people, by writing barbed words. I don't know how long we three shall dwell in purgatory. We may rise above, or sink below, but either way it may be, the third shall and must follow the others, and I leave myself in your hands. — — — —

10: TO HIS MOTHER

[*New York City*]   *Sept. 28, '17*

My dear sweet Mother: I have just read your letter and find it hard to express my rage and disgust at what you say concerning C. A. Crane's conduct. "Forget him," is all I can say. He is too low for consideration. I am only quietly waiting,—stifling my feelings in the realization that I might as well get as much money as possible out of him. Why be scrupulous in one's dealings with unscrupulous people, anyway? —/—/

Maxwell Bodenheim called the other evening, complimented my poetry excessively, and has taken several pieces to the editor of *The Seven Arts,* a personal friend of his. Bodenheim is at the top of American poetry today, and he says that after four years of absolute obscurity, he [is] succeeding in getting publication only through the adverse channels of flattery, friendships and "pull." It is all a strange business. Editors are generally disappointed writers who stifle any genius or originality as soon as it is found. They seldom even trouble to read over the manuscript of a "new man."

Bodenheim is a first-class critic though, and I am proud to have his admiration and encouragement. As soon as *Others* begins again this winter, he says I shall have an organ for all of my melodies, as he is one of the editors. Success seems imminent now more than ever. I am very encouraged, practically, at least. —/—/

11: TO HIS MOTHER

[*New York City*]   [*October 1, 1917*]

My dear Mother: —/—/ O if you knew how much I am learning! The realization of true freedom is slowly coming to me, and with it a sense of poise which is of inestimable value. My life, however it shall continue, shall have expression and form. Believe me when I tell you that I am fearless, that I am determined on a valorous future and something of a realization of life. The smallness of hitherto large things, and the largeness of hitherto small things is dawning. I am beginning to see the hope of standing entirely alone and to fathom Ibsen's statement that translated is, "The strongest man in the world is he who stands entirely alone." —/—/

12: TO HIS MOTHER

[*New York City*]   [*October 3, 1917*]

My own dear Mother: There is not much to tell you except that I am about to begin a novel. The plot is already thick in my head and tonight the first chapter will be written off, at least in rough draft. It is a story whose setting is to be Havana and the Isle of Pines. Walter Wilcox is to be the hero, and the heroine a N. Y. society maiden who is attending the races in Havana. More of this will doubtless bore you, now at least, so enough![1]

Grandma writes that you are succeeding beautifully. As soon as you found some active interests I knew you would improve in outlook and distinguish between a disgusting personality and the world in general.

These delightful autumn days, filled with cool sunshine, make me feel fine. I am alone a good deal of the time and am glad of it. My work will always demand solitude to a great extent in creative effort. Your son is improving every day, so don't worry one moment about me. — — — —

13: TO HIS MOTHER

[*New York City*]   [*October 31, 1917*]

Ma chere et charmante mere: Yesterday it poured rain all day, and I remained sheltered, studying French. But November is less evident now, and the sun is out again. I suppose that you are all right although I have had no letter since Sunday. Mrs. Walton[1] went off to the movies this morning, which makes me think again that it would be agreeable for you to enter them when you arrive.[2] After I mail this, I am going up to *The Little Review* office to have a talk with Margaret Anderson (and perhaps dispose of a poem). —/—/

    1. "My novel about the Isle of Pines has been somewhat blown to pieces by that blasting letter of yours. However I am busy thinking up plots for *Smart Set* stories. You see, I want to make my literary work bring me in a living by the time I reach twenty-five and one cannot begin too soon." (Letter to his mother, Oct. 6, 1917.)

    1. Crane's landlady. "Mrs. Walton and I are working out movie scenarios. She has had considerable experience and is of great help to me." (Letter to his mother, Oct. 8, 1917.)

    2. "Mother, when you arrive, I hope you will take up the Noyes dancing and enter the movies. You will find it fun I am sure, and I shall help you too. I am really getting a reputation for poetry and can find space now in at least two magazines for most of my better work." (Letter to his mother, Oct. 26, 1917.)

1 9 1 8

14: To William Wright

Cleveland, O.   *Aug. 12,'18*

Dear William: Your letter freshly "arriven." Your reference to ambulance service arouses me to protest. You will *not* be drafted—this year anyway, and I hope you won't become agitated so much as to rush into any kind of service. A word in the ear: I tried to enlist this morning and was not permitted even to enter the office. The guard at the door said to "look in the paper," which I did and found that all minors are to be excluded from "volunteering," and if drafted at all, will be apprenticed in machine shops, etc., during the war period. Anyhow, I think by the way things look at present, ambulance service, after the time necessary for training, transportation, etc., would be a little superfluous. (Some would call me a demon of the Huns for whispering this in your ear) I really believe the war isn't to last much longer.

Being destined, as you are, for Yale, you won't be drafted for anything. But you will have to undergo some discipline, as Mother, who visited no less than twelve Eastern colleges in her last expedition, states.

Let me clear myself. Heat and conditions at home (both of which you comprehend, I'm sure) drove me to the deed from which I was frustrated this morning. I take no credit for patriotism nor bravery. Neither was it an attempt to get into a uniform before the war is over for certain effects with the ladies. I am really sorry I couldn't get in, principally, I suppose, because I had made my mind up, and disposed of so many seductive distractions, such as, (well—) love, poetry, career, etc. Now the damned things come back again, sporting about me with all too much familiarity.

I may go to New York, I may remain here, I may explode, Lord knows. Thank your stars that you have a settled course to follow, and write soon.

15: To Charles C. Bubb

Cleveland, Ohio   *November 13,'18*

Dear Mr. Bubb: I hope I am not guilty of an officious presumption in approaching you with this meagre sheaf of poems. I am merely offering them to your consideration as being perhaps of enough in-

terest for you to publish them at the Church Head Press. As you
have published, much to the gratification of the few really interested
in poetry, some recent war-poems of Mr. Aldington, I know your
critical judgment to be of the highest standard, and while I am certain that you will be the first to detect any flaws and aberrations in
these lyrics, I know that you will also be alive to whatever beauty
they may contain.

These few poems are "gleanings," as it were, from my work of the
last few years, representing the best that I have done so far.—There
is still hope, as I am yet under twenty. They have been published
mostly in *The Pagan,* one in *The Little Review* of December last,
and while they are few in number, I thought that they might possibly be equal to the boundaries of a modest pamphlet. "Six Lyrics,"
or some such title might be used for the booklet. But anon for such
matters. . . .

I am at present engaged on the *Plain Dealer,* and am too much
occupied there for much of any personal "business." So, in lieu of
a real call on you at your residence, I am leaving these with Mr.
Laukhuff, as he says that you are a frequent visitor to his establishment.

May I again express my hope that I have not infringed upon your
generosity, and assure you that I shall welcome any opinion that
you might express regarding the poems themselves, or my suggestions.

1 9 1 9

16: TO HIS MOTHER

New York,   *Feb. 24,*

Dear Mother: I have just returned from a dinner and evening with
Mrs. Spencer. After the dishes were cleared away we sat before the
wood-fire and talked Science, and I played the piano while she
washed the dishes. She tells me some astounding stories about the
numerous demonstrations she has made. Pat [Spencer] is very deep
in it too, it seems, and has been twice saved in very dangerous falls
from over 500 feet which would otherwise have meant instant death.
It is convincing enough testimony that he is the only one living
of the ten instructors chosen for the position at the time of his appointment. I am to help Mrs. Spencer move some things from her
rooms over to Claire's [Spencer] apartment next Tuesday after-

noon. Mrs. Brooks has evaded all my efforts at a meeting today, but I hope to get to go to church with her tomorrow morning. —/—/

17: To His Mother

[New York City]   *March 7th,'19*

Dear Mother: The landlady has committed enough atrocities since writing you last to fill a book, and I have found another room which I expect to move into some time next week. In all truth she is quite insane. Mr. Brooks called me up three times the other day, and each time he asked for me was he told that there was no such person as Mr. Crane living here. Finally one of the roomers came to the rescue and took down his name and number, so that when I got in I was duly informed. Then in other ways she has been unbearable, coming up to my room several times, and vaguely pointing to some unseen object and inquiring, "Is that yours?" At other times she has come up and announced in a hushed voice, "It's down there." That would be all one could get out of her as to what was "down there"—letter, caller, or delivery man, and several times it has been nothing at all. —/—/ It has been very 'funny and very unpleasant, and I regret having to incur the expense of moving again. However, the room I have secured is better than the one I have—on the first floor, front, and much roomier. One of the fellows in the house here, a Harvard man and lieutenant just out of service, has roomed there before and swears to the complete sanity and integrity of the little Irish woman that runs the place. All these little trials have to be accepted in true sportsman-like fashion, in fact one might as well take them that way, or else get out of town.

—/—/ I am not sure, of course, but I feel quite certain that Mrs. Brooks is afflicted with consumption against which she is doubtless putting up a strenuous Scientific fight. I have noticed an incessant little cough that she has had on both my meetings with her since I arrived in town. She is quite thin, too, and without much colour. It must be due to a change of disposition within myself, but I find the Brooks's much more cordial and agreeable. That I, myself, am largely responsible is borne out by what Mrs. Spencer told me the other day. She said that Mr. Brooks had remarked about the astounding change in my manner and disposition, and said that I was now quite a delightful personality. I should blush to tell this on myself were it not such an interesting testimony to the influence of Science. —/—/

18: To His Mother

[New York City]   *March 11th, '19*

Dear Mother: Just a word to let you know that I am busy casting
about for a position somewhere. I have several ideas suggested by
friends as to where to find jobs as an ad-writer, etc., and am investigating the matter. I may make a call on Mr. Kennedy, the friend of
Grandmother's, if two or three other projects do not turn out well.
He runs a trade-journal, you know. Zell [Hart Deming] writes me
that she is to be here for two weeks next month, and if I am settled
by that time, I am positive that she will be able to get me in somewhere. You have no conception of the difficulties here in finding
work of any description just now. Every day a couple of troop-ships
dump a few thousand more unemployed men in the town, and
there really is danger of a general panic and much poverty as a result unless the government takes a hand to assist in the matter. I
know you are not worrying about me. As it happens, I am very
fortunately situated in comparison with the rest. I wrote Mr. Ely
yesterday, and so that is off my conscience. I would prefer that you
discontinued his treatment of me, as I feel quite able to stand on
my own feet and demonstrate the truth without assistance from
without. I shall probably not move from here for some time. I have
decided to make a demonstration over the landlady, and already
have noticed an improvement.

19: To His Mother

N.Y.C.   *March 26th '19*

Dear Mother: —/—/ At the recommendation of Colum, I am going to interview the publishing house of Boni and Liveright tomorrow in the effort to secure a job as proofreader, etc., with them.
I have been around to several Sunday Feature Syndicates today but
have found nothing there. I hope you aren't worrying,—for you
must realize that one cannot continue looking and looking as I am
doing without finding something in time. I have some interesting
news for you. I phoned up Alice Calhoun last night and find that
she is working in a newly-organized moving-picture production company here.—She is now engaged in her first big picture, and is very
busy, she tells me. How about writing a movie-story for her? It looks
as though there might be a chance for some of my work to get an
attentive reading after all. She can't see me this week, but we are
going to have a visit soon and I imagine it will be interesting. Alice

certainly is pretty enough for success in the movies, and young enough (only 18) to develop a good deal of dramatic talent. A telephone conversation is rather a slight thing to offer judgment from, but I was rather impressed with a decided improvement in Alice, both in manner and character. Byron's [Madden] letter arrived this morning. I think he is certainly a sincere well-wisher of mine. I hope to get into some sort of position in time to write him about it when I do write, because it "makes more to say," as it were. I'll write again in time for a Sunday delivery. The days are amazingly beautiful and the nights superb. Last night I took a long walk up Riverside Drive which is just around the corner from my room, and the Hudson was beautiful with the millions of tiny lights on the opposite shore. — — — —

20: To His Mother

New York City   *April 2nd, '19*

My dearest Mother: — — — — Yes, you do seem to be quite occupied with various engagements, pleasant and painful, as in the case of the dentistry, although I am very glad to hear of your having that duty performed as you have needed work and attention expended on your teeth for a long while back. I think you are holding the wrong and un-Scientific thought concerning me and my attitude toward Science. The fact that I do not talk and write about it continually is no sort of testimony that I am not as much interested as ever in it. You know that I am not and probably never will be one of those who make the matter a complete obsession, reducing every subject and thought and description to the technical language of the textbooks. I have met a number of Scientists who by such proceedure managed not only to bore me and others quite dreadfully, but also to leave one with the impression that they were scared to death about everything and found it necessary to maintain a continual combat against every aspect and manifestation of life in general. Perhaps it may serve as sufficient testimony to the efficacy of right thought, etc., that I am finding far less problems and fears that demand denial. I certainly have not felt quite so well or quite so clear-headed for several years, and that is, or ought to be enough to reassure you and alterate your somewhat morbidly anxious fears for me which have leaked into your last few letters. I again beg you to relax from such fears, etc., which seem to have you in their power enough to prompt you to such seemingly strenuous conflicts of resistance and denials. Your letters seem to be

prompted by some fear (I mean certain references in them) that
seems to me entirely un-Scientific. Please do not mistake me and
become hurt or offended. I only feel that you have not overcome,
not quite, what might be called "the fear of fear" which is an ultimate Scientific triumph. —/—/

21: TO WILLIAM WRIGHT

New York, New York   *May 2, 1919*

Dear William: Your letter came this morning, so you can't deny my
promptitude. Dash haberdashery! I hope you have more freedom in
writing your next letter,—the note of pain caused by the watchful
eye of the floor-walker was too evident. It was like a hurried lunch.
I felt your situation and rushed from line to line in trepidation of
the next moment. And then you asked such very vital questions
that you have set me thinking a good deal. No:—at present I am not
a Christian Scientist. I try to make my Mother think so because she
seems to depend on that hypocrisy as an additional support for her
own faith in it. So,—mum's the word to her. If it weren't very evident how very much good it has done her I should not persist in
such conduct,—lying to both Lord and Devil is no pleasure,—but as
I frankly was very much interested in Christian Science at the time
of my exit from home, I have not made any distinct denial of it to
her since, and for the aforementioned reasons. However, Bill, I have
unbounded faith in its efficacy. Not that a normal optimism will not
accomplish the same wonders,—it is a psychological attitude which
will prevail over almost anything, but as a religion, there is where I
balk. I recommend it to you if you are nervous, etc., though, as a
cure, and the best and only one to my knowledge. What it says in
regard to mental and nervous ailments is absolutely true. It is only
the total denial of the animal and organic world which I cannot
swallow.

I don't quite understand your criticism toward my "attitude of
mind," and sincerely wish you would particularize more in detail.
We have had so many good talks that I wish you were here right now
to tell me. But when you come to New York next autumn we shall
have an opportunity. I am laying many plans for your coming, and
you will enjoy meeting some of my friends here, I am sure. My advertising work for *The Little Review* is coming a little slower than I
expected. You have no idea how hard it is to even break into some of
these huge and ominous mechanisms, New York offices. It ought to
toughen me a little and perhaps that it what I need. It is a very

different matter when one approaches with the intent of selling, and selling the appealing article,—space. However, *The Little Review* has the possibility of affording me over four thousand per year on commissions if I can fill up the allowable space, and perhaps I am not wasting my time after all. —/—/

22: TO WILLIAM WRIGHT

New York, New York   *May 14, 1919*

Dear William: —/—/ At present I am under the spell of the first wave of rose fever! My reading lately has been rather diverse as is evident from any such list as Chaucer, D. H. Lawrence, Cervantes, Henry James, Plato, and Mark Twain.

Oh, by the way, I met Robert Frost's daughter at a theatre party the other evening, and had the pleasure of taking the very interesting and handsome young lady back to her Columbia dormitory. I am hoping to see more of her at a near date, as she is worth looking at.

23: TO HIS MOTHER

New York City   *Decoration Day,'19*

My dear Mother: I received your letter with check enclosed night-before-last, and hasten to thank you for them. Your letter was filled with the customary complaints about my not writing oftener. Now I admit that the last two weeks have been poorer in letters from me than usual, but you seem never to have realized, Mother, that there is absolutely nothing to fill up the three-or-four-letter-a-week pro-gram which I have been trying to conduct,—even were my days filled with tremendous action. A couple of letters a week will contain all the news worth telling, and whether you have appreciated that fact or not, the truth remains.

I see you are displeased at my having changed rooms, but I would like to ask you what you would have done faced with a like situation at the time I was. I felt indeed very fortunate to have located so successful a bargain as the two rooms here on the top floor of 24 West 16th St., for ten dollars per month. It only costs me that be-cause Hal Smith uses one of the rooms as a study separate from his apartment to come to for his writing, and so I have the use of his room as well as my bedroom. When I told Hal and Claire of my predicament, Claire rushed to the cupboard and the result was that a bed was bought for me and temporary bedding loaned. Hal also sent over other furnishings, etc., which has made the place livable and even comfortable for me. I see no reason for returning now to a rooming house, and shall probably remain here for sometime to come. I asked for the rugs because they would be simply an additional comfort, but if it's too much trouble for you to send them, or against your principles, it's all right with me to do without them.

What I wrote you about sending money still holds good. I have cashed the checks you sent as there is no use in my being foolish about such matters when I have only fifteen cents in my pocket and a very empty stomach. I do ask you for more, however. I am very much against your sending me money from your personal allowance. It seems to me that it would not be very much trouble to go down and see Sullivan for a half an hour for a few days and get sufficient results from the enactment of a perfectly just and practical contract so that I would not be due to hear within a few years the accusation of having made you economize and scrimp your own pleasures for my assistance during this trying time when I am making every possible effort to get started in something. You know, Mother, I have not yet forgotten your twitting me last summer at my not paying my board expenses when I was at home, and I don't welcome your generosity quite so much now on the possibility of a recurrence of such words at some future time. I don't want to fling accusations, etc., at anybody, but I think it's time you realized that for the last eight years my youth has been a rather bloody battleground for yours and father's sex life and troubles. With a smoother current around me I would now be well along in some college taking probably some course of study which would enable me upon leaving to light upon, far more readily than otherwise, some decent sort of employment. Do you realize that it's hard for me to find any work at all better than some manual labor, or literary work, which, as you understand, is not a very paying pursuit? My present job in connection with *The Little Review* possibly offers me an opportunity for experience in the advertising world, which is a good field for money,—but it's the hardest thing in the world to get worked up, especially with my complete inexperience in the work. I am looking for something else now every day,—anything that comes along,—with the intention of one way or another, establishing my independence from all outside assistance. In the meantime I am carrying on with this job, and should it give enough promise, will continue in it. I have found out recently what it is to be like a beggar in the streets, and also what good friends one occasionally runs across in this tangle of a world. For some time after your letter I was determined not to write rather than compromise with hypocrisy or hurt your feelings. If this letter has wounded you, then I am ready to beg your pardon in apology with the understanding that I write no more, for I have discovered that the only way to be true to others in the long run, is to be true to one's self.

24: TO WILLIAM WRIGHT

New York, New York   *June 17, 1919*

My dear William: I've just returned from several days in the country with Hal Smith and wife (Claire). They rent a little cottage out in New Jersey that is perfection itself and we go canoeing and play tennis and eat amazingly every time we go out there. I am, unfortunately, badly sunburned today,—rather a sight,—and am remaining in my room rather than shock my friends and enemies by exposing myself. It is fine (though) to get out of this crowded metropolis once in a while, and see the moon and stars and hear the frogs croak. We intend to go out again next Friday and stay until Monday, living in our bathing suits most of the time. From your last letter, you're in for quite a pleasant summer. I wish I could be in Cleveland when you are there. Hope you'll go out and see my mother if you get time, —she likes you very much and always asks about you in her letters. We have had some differences of late, but my fundamental feelings toward her are not in the least altered. If I can get enough money together I intend to take a short course in business and advertising out at Columbia this summer,—which might possibly be continued next fall when you will be there. I agree with you that for such as ourselves business life is not to be scorned. The commercial aspect is the most prominent characteristic of America and we all must bow to it sooner or later. I do not think, though, that this of necessity involves our complete surrender of everything else nobler and better in our aspirations. Illusions are falling away from everything I look at lately. At present the world takes on the look of a desert,—a devastation to my eyes, and I am finding it rather hard at best. Still there is something of a satisfaction in the development of one's consciousness even though it is painful. There is a certain freedom gained,—a lot of things pass out of one's concern that before mattered a great deal. One feels more freedom and the result is not by any means predominantly negative. To one in my situation N. Y. is a series of exposures intense and rather savage which never would be quite as available in Cleveland, etc. New York handles one roughly but presents also more remedial recess,—more entrancing vistas than any other American location I know of. When you come to Columbia you will not be apt to feel it because any college (less Col. than any other) enforces its own cloistral limitations which are the best things in the world while one is there. It will only be after you have left the place and lived and worked in the city (should you do so) that you will begin to feel what I mentioned. May I venture a personal criticism on your last letter? It's out of my habit to do so, and if I didn't care for you so much I wouldn't. Your remarks "about the ladies" really hurt me with a kind of ragtime vulgarity. It's hard to say in the limitations of a letter what I mean. You know I am very free from Puritanical preoccupations,—as much as from excessive elegance. What I lament is that gross attitude of the crowd that is really degrading and which is so easily forced upon us before we know it. You are far too sensitive to harbour it long, I know. It is only because I hate to see the slightest tarnish at all in you that I run the risk of offending you. I do hope you won't resent it. — — — —

25: TO HIS MOTHER

[New York City]   July 10, '19

My dear Mother: Your nice letter arrived this morning just a few minutes before the books, and I must thank you much for them and the check enclosed in the letter, which I have certainly sufficient use for as I need a haircut badly and a new set of razor blades besides being much in debt to Hal for this last week's meals. It has been rather humiliating to have to come to one person for absolutely everything, rent, food, and minute sundries and rather than do it I have several times gone for long periods without food. But Hal and Claire have been wonderfully thoughtful and I haven't had to ask,—evidences seemed to be enough and better than words. At last now, things seem to have lightened a little. I leave with them tomorrow for Brookhaven, Long Island, where Hal has rented a beautiful establishment for the rest of the summer. I am going along as their guest, although Hal lightened any embarrassment I might have felt at receiving such endless munificence at their hands by suggest[ing] an office for me as handy man about the place,—gardener, chauffeur, etc. —/—/ I can always find work in the machine shop and shipyard but cannot help avoiding them as a last resort, as they would merely suffice to keep breath in the body and get me nowhere in particular. I made no requests for assistance from C. A. [Crane] in regard to the Columbia summer course which began day before yesterday. In answer to his letter which announced his intention and *promise* to take an advertisement in *The Little Review*, I thanked him and told him that his payment would help me in taking a course in business advertising which I was hoping to take at Columbia this summer. That was all there was said about it. He didn't mention the matter in his next (and last) letter and has not even paid for the advertisement which he said he would do, as long as I was associated with the magazine, and he has heard nothing to the contrary, I am positive. Of course all my friends think his treatment of me is disgraceful and unaccountable. My own opinion is hardly less reserved, as you know, but I try my best to turn my thoughts to other channels as much as possible. It is only when hunger and humiliation are upon me that suddenly I feel outraged. —/—/

26: To His Mother

Brookhaven, [Long Island]   *July 30th, '19*

My dear Mother: Your letter dated the 8th has just come, and in answer, I of course will not need to repeat the contents of yesterday's note. At best I think your words are a little unkind and very inconsiderate. I will not attempt again to reckon with your misunderstanding, etc., of the part you and I together, and as individuals, have played in relation to C.A. You either have a very poor memory, or are very confused when you think you have a right to accuse me of either a wrong or a right attitude toward him,—an unfriendly or a friendly one,—after the continually opposite statements and accusations you have made to me for the last four years yourself. At one time you have recommended a course of diplomacy toward a veritable devil, and five minutes later a blow in the face and scorn of any relationship whatever. And now you suggest a wily and conniving attitude toward a character which you claim as fundamentally good. With such inconsistencies in memory I fail to see how you have adequate reasons for "accusing" me of a "wrong" attitude toward him, whatever position I might have taken. It has all been very hard, I know. Probably the truth consists more moderately in the estimate of him as a person of as many good inclinations as bad ones. Your feelings as a woman lover were bound to be dangerous in diverting you from an impersonal justice, and, however much I may have been blinded by my own relationship with him, I cannot deny having been influenced by your sufferings and outcries. There are reasons for acts and prejudices which cannot always be justified at the turn of the moment, but look hard enough, and substantial roots will be found.

I returned to Brookhaven last night after a very satisfactory interview with Mr. Rheinthal, of the firm of Rheinthal and Newman, which handles the Parrish prints. I shall begin work there in the

order department early in September, until which time I'll be out
here with Hal and Claire. My note of yesterday was expressive
enough of the satisfaction I am feeling about the matter without
repetition here. Everything is pointing toward very friendly relations
with C. A. in the future, which good turn is greatly due to the interest of the New York office. People change in their attitude either
from enlightenment of the understanding or change of impulse. In
the case of father toward me I think a revival of interest was seconded by a more adequate understanding of my motives, interests,
character and position which the office supplied. Also, a certain
pride (now that his wealth begins to assume rather large dimensions)
in the position of his only son, was equally responsible. —/—/

27: To Gorham Munson[1]

[New York City]   *[August 22, 1919]*

Have been back in town for last 2 weeks very busy at my new job.
Glad to know you are enjoying yourself. Look me up as soon as
you return! Haven't been over to see *The Modernist* but suppose
it is racing along as usual.

28: To Charmion Wiegand

N.Y.C.   *Nov. 5th,'19*

Dear Charmion: Here are the rest of your poems; I think they are
all there. *The Modernist* took one of the Egyptian sonnets, I cannot
remember the exact name of it, and hopes you will send more soon.

I leave for Cleveland tomorrow night, and am very anxious to get
off. Packing all the truck I have accumulated here has proved a de-
lirious task. Let me thank you and Hermann [Habicht] again for
the evening last week and the many other treats of the summer.

Let's write occasionally and be as metropolitan as possible. You
know I'm now out in those great expanses of cornfields so much
talked about and sung, and you can't very well dispense with me
even though you do live "in the big city." I am beginning something in an entirely new vein with the luscious title: "My Grandmother's Love Letters." I don't want to make the dear old lady too
sweet or too naughty, and balancing on the fine line between these
two qualities is going to be fun. I hope that living close to her in
the same house won't spoil it all.

1. Postcard. On the reverse side, over a photograph of Brooklyn Bridge, Crane
wrote: "Knowing your predilection for bridges, I send you this!

P.S. Much to my surprise I got yesterday a very friendly letter from Sherwood Anderson thanking me for the *Pagan* art[ic]le.

29: To Gorham Munson

[*Cleveland*]   *Nov. 13, 1919*

My dear Gorham: It begins to look as though my work was to be confined to the hours between midnight and dawn,—that is, in writing. I go to Akron, O., next week to take up a position in my father's new store there and my own hours are to be from six in the morning until eleven at night. I was down there with him yesterday, and find that he has a wonderful establishment,—better than anything of its kind in New York. It's too bad to waste it all on Akron, but there seems to be a lot of money there that the rubber tire people have made. The place is burgeoning with fresh growth. A hell of a place. The streets are full of the debris from old buildings that are being torn down to replace factories, etc. It looks, I imagine, something like the western scenes of some of Bret Harte's stories. I saw about as many Slavs and Jews on the streets as on Sixth Ave. Indeed the main and show street of the place looks something like Sixth Ave. without the elevated.

The size of my father's business has surprised me much. Things are whizzing, and I don't know how many millions he will be worth before he gets through growing. If I work hard enough I suppose I am due to get a goodly share of it, and as I told you, it seems to me the wisest thing to do just now to join him. He is much pleasanter than I expected him to be, and perhaps will get around after awhile to be truly magnanimous.

You evidently were not consulted about the Josephson mss., as I saw one of them returned the day I left N. Y. I haven't been able to locate a single copy of *The Modernist* anywhere in Cleveland, and I suggest that Richard Laukhuff, 40 Taylor Arcade, would be a good one to send it to. He handles most of the radical stuff, and *The Pagan,* he tells me, is getting too tame. He also says that *The Little Review* has suffered neglect since the last Baroness [Freytag-Loringhoven] contribution. The B. is a little strong for Cleveland.

I don't know when I shall get time or the proper mood to work more on the Grandame poem. Contact with the dear lady, as I told you I feared, has made all progress in it at present impossible.

Rec'd a letter from Sherwood Anderson this morning in which he tells me about early business experiences in Cleveland and Elyria.

The latter is about as unpleasant as Akron, so I guess I needn't despair. My mother and grandmother are going to Cuba this winter and close up the house, so I fear that our visiting plans will have to be postponed a while. I won't be in Akron long. After that it may be Kansas City, Frisco, or even New York. The business is simply enormous now and growing so that I expect I will have a real job in time. I like to think that I can keep on writing a little, at least, of good quality, until,—someday when I shall start up a magazine that will be an eye-opener. I feel in a Billy Sunday mood this evening, and am very much in haste, so I hope you will not consider this letter as anything other than a scrap-heap of petty news. — — — —

30: To Gorham Munson

[*Akron, Ohio*]   *Nov. 22nd*

My dear Gorham: —/—/ If business were to continue so slow behind my counter at the drug store as it has thus far, I could get a good deal of reading done. As it *has* been, *Pavannes & Divisions*, T. S. Eliot, Maupassant and *The L. R.* have been my steady companions. I have to be on the job about 14 hours every day, and when the Christmas rush begins I fancy I will be indeed well tired out at night. However, I don't expect to remain here very long after that date on account of a probable promotion, when my evenings, at least, will be free. And, after all, that is about all I ask for.

Josephson wrote me a fascinating letter last week enclosing a poem of his own and two translations from Jules Romains. If you two continue to keep me warm, I am not at all pessimistic about my interest waning in les arts. Josephson's opinions of *The Modernist* will more than match your own, I think. Fawcett sent me a copy of *The Modernist,* and having time to peruse it, I was quite astonished by the amount of literary rubbish he had managed to get into its confines. There was hardly a gleam of promise through it all. Your three poems were practically the best things in it, and I am not complimenting you thereby. For a time I was sorry for you and for me. I wanted to write a letter withdrawing my contributions. But a certain resignation to fatality dissuaded me from the effort . . . . — — — is a poor ignorant bastard of some kind. His comments on history and government are not even in a class with the *Evening Journal.* The rest of the sheet seems like a confused, indiscriminate jelly-like mass. . . . But, ah, well-a-day, the time must come when we can do more than groan and hoot.

I have thought for some time that your connection with it resulted mostly in a waste of time. I may send them more stuff simply to have it published and also on account of a kind of dumb-animal affection that I have for Waldo [Fawcett]. How furious he would be to hear this!!

I am liable to break forth in song most any time, but nothing has happened as yet. I wrote a short affair last night that I may hammer into shape. Grandma and her love letters are too steep climbing for hurried moments, so I don't know when I shall work on that again. As it is, I have a good beginning, and I don't want any anti-climax effect. If I cannot carry it any further, I may simply add a few finishing lines and leave it simply as a mood touched upon. New theories are filling my head every day.—Have you given the poems of Wallace Stevens in the Oct. *Poetry* any attention. There is a man whose work makes most of the rest of us quail. His technical subtleties alone provide a great amount of interest. Note the novel rhyme and rhythm effects.

Josephson sends me a list of names for reading that you might be interested in. Marlowe is one of his favorites, John Webster, and Donne; the last is a wonder speaking from my own experience. I've got to rush back to work now so this is all. — — — —

31: To Gorham Munson

Akron   *Friday*

Dear Gorham: Have been up to Cleveland for over Thanksgiving, and rushed back again at dawn today and spent the day as usual. I enjoyed your letter with its encouragement to Grandma and am sending you a record of her behaviour to date. She would get very fretful and peevish at times, and at other times, hysterical and sentimental, and I have been obliged to handle her in the rather discouraging way that my words attest. However, I think that something has been said, after all, although the poem hasn't turned out as long as I had expected. Tell me, pray, how you like it.

Have you read *The Young Visitors* by Daisy Ashford (alias Sir James Barrie) yet? I don't know when I have been more delighted. Subtle satire par excellence!

I shall try to get hold of your article in *The Smart Set* and see how you have got up in the world, according to Joe Kling.

I hear a little gossip even here in Akron. There is a bookseller here who is well known far and wide as a character. I had known him years ago in Cleveland, but our acquaintance has recently come to more ripeness here. I just missed dining with Alfred Knopf who came here to see him the other day. Knopf tells him that Mencken is about to publish a book with him of which the title I forget, but the last scene is laid in the Sultan's bed. The S. having a very large and luxurious one. This bookseller also gave me the enclosed booklet which was written by Mark Twain in one of his ribald moments. You will enjoy it, I know, and it gives me a stronger light on some of the reasons for Mencken's enthusiasm for the writer. The grand ejaculatory climacteric speech of Queen Bess is magnificent. You will regard the book as quite a treasure. I don't know where else on earth it could be procured.—/—/

32: To GORHAM MUNSON

[*Akron*]   *Dec. 13th, '19*

My dear Gorham: I think you are wrong about *1601*. The bookseller friend who gave me the book you have, informs me that that is just another name for the same piece. So you see it is even more scarce and valuable than you thought. Will you ever forget that sentence of Raleigh's where he says he was but clearing his nether throat!? I must get another one and send it to Josephson, who, by the way, has just written me about my "Grandmother." He has some of the same complaints to make of her as yourself, and many others, but he ends up by calling it the best thing I have written, and, what is more flattering, begs to keep the copy I sent him. He says he has had a falling out with Amy Lowell, but a falling in with T.S. Eliot by way of compensation. His letters are charming with a peculiar and very definite flavor to them, and buck me up a good deal. I have lately begun to feel some wear from my surroundings and work, and to make it worse, have embarked on a love affair, (of all places unexpected, here in Akron!), that keeps me broken in pieces most of the time, so that my interest in the arts has sunk to a rather low station. Now that Christmas is coming on with its usual inhuman rush in candy selling, I shall not have a moment for anything but business and sleep. My life is quite barbarous and the only thing to do is recognize the situation and temporarily bow to it.

Waldo Frank's book IS a pessimistic analysis! The worst of it is, he has hit on the truth so many times. I am glad to see such justice done to Sherwood Anderson, but this extreme national consciousness troubles me. I cannot make myself think that these men like Dreiser, Anderson, Frost, etc., could have gone so far creatively had they read this book in their early days. After all, has not their success been achieved more through natural unconsciousness combined with great sensitiveness than with a mind so thoroughly logical or propagandistic (is the word right?) as Frank's? But Frank has done a wonderful thing to limn the characters of Lincoln and Mark Twain as he has,—the first satisfactory words I have heard about either of them. The book will never be allowed to get dusty on the library shelves unless he has failed to give us the darkest shadows in his book,—and I don't think he has. I notice that Marsden Hartley is mentioned, but how does it come that "our Caesar" [Zwaska] is omitted!?

This last makes me think of *The Little Review,* and how terrible their last issue, November's, is. I have sent them my poem, but have heard no answer as yet. If *The Dial* goes on as you announced in your letter, perhaps they would care to print it. I am thoroughly confident about the thing itself since it has got by the particular, hierarchic Josephson, and I won't blush to show it to almost anyone now.

If *The Modernist* is not already in the mails for me, please do not forget that I am anxious for a copy. I wrote Fawcett a long time ago, but he hasn't responded. My last letter from Anderson urges me to make him a visit, and I am hoping that sometime next summer such a thing will be possible. He calls the poem beautiful, but says that it is not as much poetry to him as "the flesh and bone" of my letters. He and Josephson are opposite poles. J. classic, hard and glossy,— Anderson, crowd-bound, with a smell of the sod about him, uncouth. Somewhere between them is Hart Crane with a kind of wistful indetermination, still much puzzled.

33: To GORHAM MUNSON

Akron, Ohio   *Dec. 27, 1919*

My dear Gorham: — / — / My stand in the drug store has not proved exactly a success, although my father is good enough to admit that I am not to blame in any way. The principal reason that it will be discontinued is that no one can be found to work there without a quite exorbitant salary, and the location is too poor to afford that. So many things have happened lately with the rush of Christmas, etc., that I am tired out and very much depressed today. This "affair" that I have been having has been the most intense and satisfactory one of my whole life, and I am all broken up at the thought of leav-

ing him. Yes, the last word will jolt you. I have never had devotion
returned before like this, nor ever found a soul, mind, and body so
worthy of devotion. Probably I never shall again. Perhaps we can
meet occasionally in Cleveland, if I am not sent miles away from
there, but everything is so damned dubious as far as such conjectures
lead. You, of course, will consider my mention of this as unmention-
able to anyone else.

Sherwood Anderson is coming to N. Y. this week, he writes, and
perhaps it would be possible for you to meet him. Vide *The Little
Review* for information as to his whereabouts. He says that Van
Wyck Brooks has given in Doran's hands for publication a book well
named,—*The Ordeal of Mark Twain,* which, I imagine, will follow
on something the same line of direction that Waldo Frank suggests
in his book. Hackett's review of the latter is a bit severe, although
he touches the weak points in every instance. The work *is* too rhap-
sodical, and I noticed frequent lapses in plain grammar, not to mention diction. But the meat is there anyway, and the book is stimulating, even though a bit pathetic. Anderson says he respects the mind
of Brooks more. Brooks and Hackett belong, both, to a harder and
more formal species. Therefore Hackett's critique is quite consistent
with his characteristics.

I have been reading Masters' latest, *Starved Rock,* and must mention to you my enthusiasm for "Spring Lake," the best thing he has
written since the *Spoon River* elegies. "The Dream of Tasso" has a
few splendid passages free from rhetoric, and there are others, a few,
that satisfy. More and more am I turning toward Pound and Eliot
and the minor Elizabethans for values. I have not written anything
for a month, but I feel, somehow or other, as though progress were
being made. Your estimates of Djuna Barnes and Ida Rauh are interesting and true. I have been instructed recently not to read behind my counter and so, working twelve hours per day, have not had
time to do much reading. I want to get at your *New Republic* reviews, if possible, tomorrow. The booklet, *1601,* is your own to keep.
I can get another, I think, any day for the asking. My write-up in the
paper was silly enough, but forced upon me, and misquotations as
well. However, I took it as an agreeable joke and an anachronism in
Akron. But the pater was furious, at the headlines in particular, and
I spent a nervous day yesterday with him in explanations, etc. Sic
semper. Akron has afforded me one purple evening, however. I got
dreadfully drunk on dreadful raisin brew, smoked one of the cigars
made especially for the Czar, defunct, of Russia, and puked all over
a boarding house. You will believe me an ox when I tell you that I

was on the job again next morning, and carried the day through with flying colours. I enclose an opus by Eugene Field,—very exclusive,—which you will copy if you wish, and then return. Do not let Burleson or your father see it, as it is quite strong. I think you will more than smile. — / — /

Yes,—Edgar Saltus *is* gone. I remember reading him and a rare and wonderfully complete edition of Catullus on the night of the debauch. However,—I hope you will not think that my companion on that occasion was the one I mention early in the letter. This fellow of the raisin brew is another poor soul like myself, in Akron exile from N.Y. A very sophisticated and erudite fellow to whom I was introduced by my bookseller.

1 9 2 0

34: TO GORHAM MUNSON

[*Akron*]   *Jan. 9th, '20*

My dear Gorham: What a good job Somerset Maugham does in his *Moon and Sixpence!* Have just finished reading it at a single sitting. Pray take the time to read it if you haven't already. How far it follows the facts biographical to Gauguin, I am not able to say, but from what little I do know, it touches his case at many angles. Your letter coming this morning calls echoes in my ears of many such moods familiar to me during my times in N. Y. and I know how you feel. The mentioned book, I suggest as a tonic for hardness,—we all need how much more of it!

Complaining of a headache this morning I was excused from my duties for the day, and so have had time for reading, etc. I have not had to serve at the soda fountain as yet, and as a matter of fact, have not had much of anything to do,—my duty seeming to be a kind of marking *time* until I shall be occupied in the addition to the store, —a restaurant,—or am sent up to Cleveland to fly about in a Dodge car, selling. I have a kind of tacit quarrel with everyone at the store, in spite of smiles, etc., but am becoming accustomed to the atmosphere, and suffer considerably less. Akron has, after all, afforded me more than N. Y. would under present circumstances and time, and, odd as it may seem, I have almost no desire for an immediate return there. Of course, I suppose my "affair" may have a great deal to do with my attitude. And I have also made two very delightful friendships, one,—the fellow I mentioned as my companion in the raisin

brew debauch (Candee), and a more recent acquaintance with a
filthy old man,—a marvelous photographer [Minns], the only one in
this country to hold the Dresden and Munich awards, and who has
several times been "written up" in the *International Studio*. Authorities rank him with Coburn and Hoppé of London, and there is no
one in New York who compares with him. He used to read *The Little
Review*, knows Marsden Hartley,—and lives in a tumble down old
house in the center of the city. I expect the pictures of me that he
takes to be wonders. He refused to take the "rubber-king," F. H.
Seiberling, for love nor money, simply because he thought his face
without interest. He confided in me yesterday that he was an anarch-
ist, and I picture with some pain the contrast in his circumstances
here with what acclaim he would achieve in a place like London. He
has always been afraid of N.Y.—and wisely,—for probably he would
have long since starved there.

I was suddenly surprised last evening (Candee and I have been
in the habit of talking until two and three in the morning) to hear
him mention the Baroness. It seems he knows her very well. Knew
her before she came to the village and Margaret Anderson got hold
of her at all, and believe me he had some surprising tales to tell. He
goes on for hours telling of exotic friends of his and strange experiences. He know[s] Europe well, English country house parties, and
Washington society,—prizefighters, cardinals, poets and sculptors,
etc., etc., and the wonderful thing is to find him here in Akron,
forced to earn his living as secretary for some wheezing philanthropist.

Your anecdote of New Year's Eve was interesting,—who knows,—
perhaps someday you will fall too. Prenez garde!

35: TO GORHAM MUNSON

Cleveland, O.   *[January 15]*

Dear Gorham: Your play presents simple difficulties of criticism as
far as particular details. Of course you cannot take it seriously as a
work of art after the first page. It is stark propaganda, however much
in the right direction it may be. For types like ourselves it should
hold no deep interest, as it begins and ends with the universally-
obvious understanding between the artist and what is supposed to be
his "audience." The Comstock raps are good, but not well enough,—
humorously enough, placed to be sufficiently amusing or effective.
Humor is the artist's only weapon against the proletariat. Mark
Twain knew this, and used it effectively enough, take *1601* for example. Mencken knows it too. And so did Rabelais. I think that *The*

Liberator would be likely to take it, but I cannot imagine it presented on a stage. You have a sense of humor and I cannot see how you allowed some lines of it to pass your pencil. I have marked a few. You're too damned serious. You victimize your hero. Your aristocrat is much more vital and admirable than the polyphonic God, chosen to symbolize the artist. And anyway,—it's sentimentality to talk the way he does. The modern artist has got to harden himself, and the walls of an ivory tower are too delicate and brittle a coat of mail for substitute. The keen[est] and most sensitive edges will result from this "hardening" process. If you will pardon a more personal approach, I think that you would do better to think less about aesthetics in the abstract,—in fact, forget all about aesthetics, and apply yourself closely to a conscious observation of the details of existence, plain psychology, etc. If you ARE an artist then, you will create spontaneously. But I pray for both of us,—let us be keen and humorous scientists anyway. And I would rather act my little tragedy without tears, although I would insist upon a tortured countenance and all sleekness pared off the muscles.

My love affair is affording me new treasures all the time. Our holidays are spent together here in Cleveland, and I have discovered new satisfactions at each occasion. The terrible old grind at the factory is much relieved by this. I live from Saturday to Saturday. Gold and purple. Antinoüs at Yale. So the wind blows, and whatever might happen, I am sure of a pool of wonderful memories. Perhaps this is the romance of my life,—it is wonderful to find the realization of one's dreams in flesh, form, laughter and intelligence,—all in one person. I am not giddy or blind, but steadier and keener than I've ever been before. The daily grind prevents me from doing anything productive. Here is something enclosed on which I would like your opinion, as frank and unmerciful as mine has been of your play.[1] — — — —

36: TO GORHAM MUNSON

Cleveland, O.   *Jan. 28th, —20*

My dear Gorham: Well, I hope that Kling will be able to sell out for the price of dinner anyway,—but most of all that he sells out, and rids his own arms, as well as the public's, of that fetid corpse, *The Pagan*. The last issue is the worst ever, and I don't think there are lower levels to be reached. Joe doesn't properly belong in an editor's chair,—hasn't taste or discrimination, and that's all there is to it. He

1. "Garden Abstract"; see Brom Weber, *Hart Crane* (New York: Bodley Press, 1948), p. 76.

can make just as good money a thousand other ways,—most Jews can.

I am enraged at Mencken and Nathan for satisfying the public and insulting their admirers so grossly with that cheap and banal play,—*Heliogabolus.* Any one who has read even Saltus' *Imperial Purple* knows that there is not a vestige of historical truth in the setting or dialogue,—and that character, Heliogabolus, the most dissolute minion of decadent Rome, portrayed as I thought our authors were about to do,—so truthfully that a limited edition hastily gathered up would be the only possible method of presentation in America,—that delusion induced me to part with two good dollars. Instead we have a senile Al Jolson, farting the usual bedroom-farce calamities. If you want to read up on Heliogabolus, read some of Dio Cassius, if you can procure the old scribe,—at least this is what my Akron man-of-the-world prescribes. He agrees with me about the book, and writes thus: "I confess I was terribly disappointed. When I think of that slim child of seventeen with his hair powdered with diamond dust and gold, his half oriental eyes all but closed, dressed in the costume of a priest of Baal, offering his hand covered with jewels, to a gladiator who has fallen at his feet with the words,—'Hail, Lord,' and answering him,—'Call me not Lord, for I am thy Lady,' and then read of the senile, doddering creature with twelve wives as he is pictured by the joint authors, I have to laugh."

Your N. Y. notes of the journalese, artists, etc., keeps me awake during these days of trial at the factory. I am packing cases and moving heavy cases of chocolate, barrels of sugar, etc., for my living at present, but even this is better than a station behind the soda counter. My father is just as impossibly tedious and "hard" as ever, and still as insistent on starvation wages. I'll be glad when my mother returns from the south and the house and my own room are open to me again, and living will be a little less expensive. Then, too,—I am beginning to discover that I enjoy her society,—I have worked over her for three years painfully,—and the result is a woman of more interest than I had dared to hope for.—/—/ I'm still in love, too, so I have much to be sad about.

37: TO WILLIAM WRIGHT

Cleveland, Ohio   *Feb. 5th, —'20*

Dear William: — / — / But I have cheering news to tell you. "My Grandmother's Loveletters" tempted *The Dial* to part with ten dollars, my first "litry" money,—the seduction was complete,—and you may begin to look for outrageous exposures next month or the next, in that magazine. I cannot write much now, cramped in this rooming house room, but when my mother returns from the tropics next month and I am re-installed in my own room with my little Victrola, I hope to revive my intimacy with la Muse. Just now I am deep in Baudelaire's *Fleurs du Mal,* and won't brook anything healthful or cheery about the place.

38: To William Wright

Cleveland, Ohio   *Feb. 24, 1920*

My dear William: — / — / Take a layman's word of advice and remain in your present surroundings as long as possible and extract the full amount of enjoyment from them while they last. It is not very exciting to arise and essay forth to ten hours dull and exasperating labor every morning at five-thirty and return home at night with a head like a wet muffin afterward. And that is the routine that I am enmeshed in at present, to say nothing of trying to exist on starvation wages. It's the old bunko stuff about "working from the bottom up" and "earning an honest dollar" in practice, and if there are not some enlivening changes in it soon, I am liable to walk into the office and tell the amused and comfortable and rich and thriving spectator that "the joke's up." Catullus uses somewhere in his epigrams about a man that he was "——ed flat," meaning I suppose a reference to emaciated thighs, etc., but the phrase is none too vivid for me to use at present in reference to my nervous and intellectual state. Add to this, an uncomfortable room, cold, etc., and a routine of hasty and inadequate meals snatched from chance lunch counters and there is further evidence for the state o'things. — / — /

39: To Gorham Munson

[Cleveland]   *March 6th, —'20*

My dear Gorham: Well,—my mother is at length returned and the house open again. At present, however, the domestic vista appears a desolate prospect to me,—a violent contrast to the warm pictures that the former rooming-house room had conjured up as anticipations. I wrote you a while ago that I had gotten 'round to enjoy my mother's companionship. That illusion, at least for the present, seems to be dispelled. She left here two months ago, a rather (for her) ductile and seductive woman with a certain aura of romance about her. She comes back now, satisfied, shallow, unemotional, insistent on talking food receipts and household details during meals. The weight of this terrible Christian Science satisfaction I feel growing heavier and heavier on my neck. Tonight I am distraught after a two-hour's effort at camaraderie and amusement with her. "Dutiful son," "sage parent,"—"that's nice,"—and a pat on the back and the habitual "goodnight kiss." I give up evenings to her to hear advice about details in business affairs which she knows nothing about. Mon Dieu!!! And there is Grandmother in a loud background to add to the confusion. Exhausted as one may be from an inhuman day, one must beam out the dinner and evening in proper style or there are exclamations culminating in excruciating tears. However, I mind it most when I am alive, like tonight,—not tired, stupid, mild, as on "week nights."

Well, anyway, last night was made enjoyable by the spectacle of a good prize-fight. I have been to a number lately as guest of a newspaper man who lived over at the rooming house. Of course many matches are boresome, but provide two sublime machines of human muscle-play in the vivid light of a "ring,"—stark darkness all around with yells from all sides and countless eyes gleaming, centered on the circle,—and I get a real satisfaction and stimulant. I get very heated, and shout loudly, jump from my seat, etc., and get more interested every time I go. Really, you must attend a bout or two in N.Y. where a real knock-out is permitted. Along with liquor, that aristocratic assertion has disappeared here. There is something about the atmosphere of a ring show that I have for long wanted to capture into the snares of a poem. I shall not rest easy until I do, I fear. To describe it to you,—what I mean,—would be to accomplish my purpose. A kind of patent leather gloss, an extreme freshness that has nothing to do with the traditional "dew-on-the-grass" variety conveys something suggestive of my aim. T. S. Eliot does it often, —once merely with the name "Sweeney," and Sherwood Anderson, though with quite different method in a story of his in *The Smart Set*, some time ago, called "I Want to Know Why," one of the greatest stories I ever expect to read,—better even than most of the *Winesburg* chapters. This brings me to your story in *The Plowshare*. What there was of it was well done. But it seems to me that the humor and satire of this kind of theme depends on a continued heaping-up and heaping-up of absurd detail, etc., until a climacteric of either bitterness or farce is reached. For example,—have you read Gogol's "The Cloak," ever? I don't know what Hervey White did to it,—but I would mistrust him of any improvement on it after reading his comments on Frank's *Our America*. — — — — I am as anti-Semitic as they make 'em, but Frank's comments cannot afford to be ignored merely because of race prejudice. White is just an ordinary ass, though, and can easily be disposed of. I don't understand, though, how you can consent to such "operations" in your mss.

I'm very glad you sent the poem. It begins well,—dramatically, and sustains itself well until the last two lines. They are an appendix which I'd remove—merely repetition of better phrases in the beginning. Why not divide up the second verse into two equal parts and have three quartet-line verses? Another thing,—the "shoot-the-chutes" image jars,—one wants to laugh,—and one shouldn't—something else there would be better. Also, why use a French title? I know it's "done in the best families," but there seems a touch of servility,—inadequacy about it to me. I'd send it to *The Dial* if I had it, and be quite proud of it whether taken or not.

Josephson writes me that *The Dial* is causing a great stir, but that clique favoritism, the old familiar and usual magazine [pattern?], is beginning to become evident. J's letters are charming, and a recent love affair of his, a disappointment, has added seasoning to his observations. I only hope that you, he, and Anderson continue to keep me awake with occasional mail.

I had a long and hypocritical conference with my father today, and succeeded to the extent of a five dollar per week raise in salary, —this makes existence at least possible.

I don't know, G., whether I'm strong and hardened or not. I know that I am forced to be very flexible to get along at all under present conditions. I contrive to humanize my work to some extent by much camaraderie with the other employees and this is my salvation there. Of course I am utterly alone,—want to be,—and am beginning to rather enjoy the slippery scales-of-the-fish, continual escape, attitude. The few people that I can give myself to are out of physical reach, and so I can only write where I would like to talk, gesture, and dine. The most revolting sensation I experience is the feeling of having placed myself in a position of quiescence or momentary surrender to the contact & possession of the insensitive fingers of my neighbors here. I am learning, just beginning to learn,—the technique of escape, and too often yet, I betray myself by some enthusiasm or other.

My Akron friend has not been able to see me for some five [?] weeks, and I am in need of a balm, spiritual and fleshly. I hope next Sunday something can be arranged. — — — —

40: To Matthew Josephson

Cleveland   *March 15th-'20*

Dear Matty: Your praise of *Parsifal* reminded me to buy a certain Victrola reproduction,—*The Processional,*—that I have long wanted, and I have found it an incessant pleasure ever since. I read the *Times* often enough to realize that music is the only extra stimulus that N.Y. has to offer above Cleveland in these dry days. As I've said before, I don't especially long for N.Y. as of yore, except once in awhile when an overwhelming disgust with my work afflicts me and I want to lose myself in the chill vastness of the old place. (I should better have said "find myself," for I play a business part so much and so painfully, that the effort wears.) The little "iridescent bubbles" of poems that you suggest as fortnightly events simply refuse to come to the surface, and as I get so much of regularity in my daily routine,—time-clock ringing, etc., and rushing,—I won't even worry about it. I cannot commit the old atrocities,—and I have not time at present for new adventures. At any rate, in the slow silence my taste is not suffering. There are still Rabelais, Villon, Apuleius and Eliot to snatch at occasionally. In my limited surroundings I grow to derive exceptional pleasures from little things such as a small Gauguin I have on the wall, Japanese prints, and Russian records on the Victrola, in fact, the seclusion of my room. My mother is able to offer me only the usual "comforts of home" combined with stolid, bourgeois ultimatums and judgments which I am learning how to accept gracefully. So, if you are bored and spleenful, we have much in common, though you are less impulsive and emotional than myself, and take it, I am sure, more lightly. Your suggestion of a flight to the walks of Chelsea or the Mediterranean tempts me exceedingly. I should like to be rash. I assure you that if I were in your position I should do just such a thing, but I feel too much bound by responsibilities in connection with my Mother's fate, to more than dream of it. However, I wish we could get together for a while next summer. Perhaps you could make me a visit here. I will be badly in need of your conversation for a tonic by that time, and perhaps you will consider it. I can offer you no woodland retreat or metropolitan carnival,—only a very middle-class house and dull conversation,—but the time we had to ourselves would be very interesting to me, at least.

The last *Dial* was interesting, mainly on account of a story of Anderson's and "Mrs. Maecenas." Burke can write at least very cleverly. I was entertained. The hero, I cannot help remarking, touches resemblance to you in several intellectual instances. Physically,—I never saw you broken out with a rash, or gawky,—but Burke has known you longer.—Is there an understanding between you about it? . . . . My opus comes out in the April issue, and you will remark a couple of salutary changes,—omissions.

It's late, and those who arise at five must get sleep, so I'll barbarically acquiesce. My poem, the phallic theme, was a highly concentrated piece of symbolism, image wound within image.[1] You were only too right in your judgment of it. When I get some time I'll work more on it. What you saw was fresh and unshodden enough.

41: To Gorham Munson

Cleveland, Ohio.   *April 14th, '20*

My dear Gorham: —/—/ Yes,—the Grandmother poem came out very nicely. You notice, of course, that I cut it in several places, which improved it, I am sure. It is the only thing I've done that satisfies me at all now,—whether I can even equal it in the future remains to be seen. I've recently been at work on something that I enclose for your verdict.[1] As usual I am much at sea about its qualities and faults. It is interesting to me,—but do I succeed in making it of interest to others? Please slam and bang your best about it,— pro or con. I have much faith in your critical powers. Much remains to be done on it yet, but enough is done with it at present to detect the main current of it, which is principally all that worries me. My daily routine tends to benumb my faculties so much that at times I feel an infantile awe before any attempt whatever, critical or creative. This piece was simply a mood which rose and spilled over in a slightly cruder form than what you see. It happens to be autobiographic, which makes any personal estimate of it all the more dangerous.

I like Marianne Moore in a certain way. She is so prosaic that the extremity of her detachment touches, or seems to touch, a kind of inspiration. But she is too much of a precieuse for my adulation. Of this latter class even give me Wallace Stevens, and the fastidious Williams in preference. Is there anything more fastidious in poetry than these lines of his in a recent *Little Review* . . .? —/—/ ["To a Friend Concerning Several Ladies," ll. 1–7.]

The Bynner poems and translations were fine. Vildrac is the one who set me on the track of the Grandmother mood, and it is odd that our poems should have come out in the same number.

Have not heard from Josephson for some time. His last letter told of splenetic days following his post-graduation from Columbia, and an urge to ramble toward the continent via a stewardship on some vessel. Perhaps, for all I know, he has left our shores. Anderson

1. "Garden Abstract."
1. "Episode of Hands"; see Weber, *op. cit.*, p. 384.

writes me often from his Alabama bower. He is enthusiastic about the Negroes and their life, and will probably write something, sooner or later, on the subject.

The prospect of Easter spent at home was too much for me, and so I went to visit an Akron friend armed with two bottles of dago red. That didn't seem to suffice after we got started, and a quart of raisin jack was divided between us with the result that the day proper (after the night before) was spent very quietly, watered and Bromo-Seltzered, with amusing anecdotes occasionally sprouting from towelled head to towelled head. The bath in the unconscious did me good, though, and was much better than the stilted parade and heavy dinner that my home neighborhood offered. Since then I have been beset by two terrible occasions,—a Crane-grandparent— golden-wedding celebration, and a collegiate ball. The terrors of the first were alleviated by some real champagne, but the second was aggravated by auto trouble on the way home with two hysterical, extremely young and innocent females under my care at three in the morning. I am just getting over it.

Well, this is all for tonight. I have no youths to put to bed,—otherwise perhaps my correspondence might suffer. I'm afraid I wouldn't do in your position at all. But enough! I read in the paper that John Barrymore is going to appear before the movie public in *Dorian Gray!!* Mercy me!! Poor Oscar's ghost upon the screen!! I wonder what will be done with the part.

42: To Gorham Munson

[*Cleveland*]   *April 26, '20*

Dear Gorham: Thank you "muchly" for your speedy response to the plea for a critique. I was very anxious for your words, and they proved very valuable. You are right in every particular, except in so far as the understanding of my personal motive of interest in the poem. I realize that it is only my failure in the realization (concretely) which has permitted you this possibility. The poem fails, not because of questions, propagandistic and economic, which you mentioned, but because of that synthetic conviction of form & creation, which it lacks. It is all too complicated an explanation to attempt least wise on paper at this time of the night,—but perhaps you will miraculously be able to penetrate through to my meaning. As it stands, there are only a few fragments scattered thru it to build on,—but I may make something of it in time. However,—if it does evolve into something,—it will be too elusive for you to attach sociological arguments to, at least in the matter of most of the details you have mentioned. At present,—I feel apathetic about it,—but there is, of course, no telling when I will take it up again. The "Garden Abstract" has got hold of me now—and I venture that you would not recognize it. It is carrying me on with all the adventuresome interest that "Grandmother's Love Letters" did, and I am very hopeful. Later, when I am further advanced with it and surer, I'll send it to you. Also, I am "working up" the "Aunty Climax" which you will remember,—and a new piece in conventional form about a child hearing his parents quarreling in the next room at midnight,—a rather Blake-ian theme, I fear.

I have gone through a good deal lately,—seen love go down through lust to indifference, etc., and am also, not very well. This, I blame mostly to overwork. In fact the most of last week I spent at home mending an incipient rupture caused by the incessant heavy lifting at the factory. The possibility of such a thing made me furious with resentment against all those concerned in the circumstances of its cause. But I am quieter now that the affair has not been as serious as I at first suspected. I am back at it again today,—but shall in the future take more precautions against strenuosity. Your letter breathed an equanimity which it seems is more possible in your late surroundings. The change must be doing you good.

43: To Gorham Munson

[*Cleveland*]   *May 25th, '20*

Dear Gorham: —/—/ Your story in *The Plowshare* was good and in the right direction, I think. Somewhat in the Chekhov tradition,— but a little too slight to leave many foot-marks. Work up to a few more complications in plot and treatment, and you will give us more of a chance for a grip. But the main point for praise strikes me in the evident fact that you have attained an hygienic attitude ("naturalism," or what you will, but the only foundation left for serious and interesting modern work). I'm, I fear, a little obscure, but I need a conversation with you to get at the root of the matter.

I am plugging along in a very sodden way, planning as much as I dare on a chance to work a little in the New York office for a few weeks this summer by way of a change. After a recent conversation with my father the move seems rather more probable than before,— so, it may be that I shall see you within six weeks from now of a hot evening. Have been reading Stendhal's *Chartreuse de Parma, Noa Noa, Way of All Flesh,* and Landor's *Conversations,*—a strange mix-

ture. Anderson wrote me very much the same criticism of my "Episode of Hands" poem that you did. I haven't done anything more
with it in spite of frequent attempts. The new version of "Garden
Abstract" I enclose for your criticism. *The Dial* has rejected it, but
that doesn't mean much to me after reading in their last number
that vacant lyric of Alter Brody's.

This "business life" is getting me in a terrible way,—and I am beginning to feel that I must contrive a jolt for myself soon. If it were
only myself concerned in the "jolt" I wouldn't have delaying qualms,
—but,—perhaps I am fated to a life of parental absorptions. My interests are as keen as ever, though, and so I suppose I need not worry
about myself,—as long as I keep worrying.

44: TO GORHAM MUNSON

Cleveland,   *June 8th, '20*

Dear Gorham: —/—/ I've just read your critique in *The Freeman,*
and while I have never been to a Provincetown performance, I
should certainly want to after this of yours. *The F.* rejected my "Garden Abstract" along with *The N. Rep.* and *The Dial,* and I'm at a
loss to understand such things in the light of some of the mediocre
effects that are more-or-less the rule in the columns of the first two.
Of course the theme was pure pantheistic aestheticism,—and I suppose they would say that it was too detached from life, etc. I'm
started on a set of sketches connected with Akron life now, and enclose a sample.[1] Maybe I shall be able to do something in New York
in the mornings, the best time for such work, but as you know, plans
for that kind of thing can never be made. — — — —

45: TO GORHAM MUNSON

[Cleveland]   *July 30th, —'20*

Dear Gorham: —/—/ I have been promised the territory around
Washington, D. C., Norfolk, Richmond, Va., etc., as a hunting
ground for "selling," beginning about the second week in September
when I shall embark for Washington as headquarters. This last
named place strikes me as interesting in the extreme,—even better
than N.Y. which I know so well anyway. I shall more or less freely
govern my own operations, rise and retire at later hours, and have

1. "Porphyro in Akron," together with the comment: "The last is so far the
only satisfactory part. I include the first two sections merely as hints for direction
of the theme." See Weber, *op. cit.,* pp. 89-90.

a drawing account at the bank at my own disposal in addition to a good percentage commission on everything I sell. I must admit a happy surprise at my father's recent appreciation of my efforts here during the last six months. He even made the unhoped-for concession of mentioning that he had chosen this territory for me on account of the better sort of business type that is in Washington and also on account of Washington's "literary and journalistic associations." Well, it will be much better than this smug atmosphere around here, and I rather tend to expect a moment or two of revived inspiration. Before closing, I must mention my enthusiasm for our Henry James. I have read recently his *American,* an early novel, and a group of tales in his "middle manner" collected in a book called *The Better Sort,* also I have been at his letters which I bought riskily but wisely, after all. — — — —

46: To Gorham Munson

[Cleveland]   *August 18th—'20*

Dear Gorham: I am delighted to hear about your sudden appreciation of D'Annunzio's novels. In fact, I get a picture of you running with them under your arm, (one arm, I should say,—the other being occupied with other cargo,—) away from the, as usual, glaring M. Schopenhauer who stands in the doorway of your erstwhile quiet ivory tower waving his arms and shaking fists at you. I would rather, and more truthfully, I think,—think of you thusly than as another picture, more common to humanity, that always obtrudes upon me when anyone announces "an engagement"—"The Storm" . . . . You will remember seeing it in a thousand "art store" windows:—a curly youth partly in a bearskin trotting amiably with a barefooted flaxen lady away from something that evidently hasn't taken the starch out, as yet, from a rag that they are dragging along above them. It is all "too lovely" and pink. I am sure there is more of a "rouge et noir" cast to your surrender. Well,—betrayal brings memories and wisdom (to the male, anyway), and so I congratulate you on your splash even though I suffer from unaccustomed silence. One word before we close the subject, though:—you must not expect me to read D'Annunzio.

Did I tell you that I have been enjoying the letters of Henry James? Also, Aldous Huxley's "Limbo," and the Noh plays of Fenollosa and Pound. Conrad's *Nigger of the Narcissus* seems to me all polyphonic prose, plus the usual quality of Conrad characterization, etc. Then I've read most of the tales in James' *Better Sort* vol. and

that is about all I've been able to cram into the exhausted evening
hours since New York. I'll chuck in a page of the Akron poem that
I struck off the other evening just because I want an opinion on it
from you.[1] Hustle back to the ivory tower and put on your specks
for a minute, please, and tell me what you think of this uncouth
trifle, sir. In view of my attitude toward what Akron so strongly
represents, I have been thinking that it might be amusing to call the
whole series "Porphyro in Akron." I don't much care whether anyone will care for it or not. What I seem to want to do more and
more as time goes on, is to preserve a record of a few thoughts and
reactions that I've had in as accurate colors as possible for at least
private satisfaction. —/—/

47: TO GORHAM MUNSON

Washington, D. C.   *Sept. 13th, '20*

Dear Gorham: — — — — Here I am after a three-days search for a
room in an unexceptional maison in a row of other rooming houses.
There are charming places in Washington, but it takes time and information to get at them, and as I haven't either, and had to give
the Cleveland office "an address" very quickly, I shall remain here
for three weeks yet, anyway. Your last came just before I left home.
You ought to thank your stars for such a summer as you have had.
I haven't any idea yet how much I shall like Washington. There is a
certain easiness about it, and geographically it is, I should judge, the
nearest like Paris of any American city. An endless number of parks
and monuments, and all the streets are lined with trees. At least it
is more elegant than any other American city and with a very different psychology than N.Y., Cleveland or Akron. This last name
reminds me that I sent "Porphyro" to *The Dial* with some additions and subtractions from the version you read, before leaving
home. I dread this tramping around trying to sell Crane's candy, but
this week will see me started in it, and my affection for Washington
will largely depend upon how well I get on. At present I feel a terrible vacuity about me and within me and a nostalgia for Cleveland.
— — — — I share your enthusiasm for Cowley's poem in *The L.R.*

48: TO GORHAM MUNSON

[Washington]   *Sept. 24th,—'20*

Dear Gorham: — — — — I've been running around talking, talking,
talking and waiting for the proper persons to arrive at their offices,

1. See Weber, *op. cit.,* pp. 91-92.

etc., etc., etc., all week, and have succeeded to the mild extent of inaugurating two new accounts for the firm. Fortunately, people here don't seem to arrive at their offices until after ten, and so I have the opportunity to sleep more than I did in Cleveland where the requirements commanded my resurrection at five A.M. My Akron friend, Mr. Candee, gave me an introduction to a poet friend of his who has charge of all the official communications, etc., that come into the State Department. He has proved a charming person, and has introduced me to several other interesting people. He is one of the few who is cognizant of what is going on abroad, knows some things weeks in advance of the newspapers and, of course, a great many things that never come out. His opinion of most of Europe, especially the greedy tactics of some of the freshly hatched nationalities, is below cynicism. I have not yet heard from *The Dial* about "Porphyro," or at any rate he has [not] been redirected to me. I am beginning to feel that he is my lost soul, and will be a long time in returning. This simply means that I haven't had a creative impulse for so long that I am even getting not to miss it. I am not in the type of Washington life that offers material or incentive for writing. The diplomatic circles have all kinds of scandals waving around which I generally hear a whisper of from the fringes, but there is really no cafe life here or factory or shop life worth mentioning. Thousands of clerks pour out of government offices at night and eat and go to the movies. The streets are beautiful with many parks, etc., but it is all rather dead. I am really more interested in the soldiers and sailors that one meets than anything else. They have a strange psychology of their own that is new to me. This sounds bad, and perhaps it is so,—but what should one do with the reported example of our new VICE — — — — scenting the air as it does. From what I'm hearing, about every other person in the government service and diplomatic service are enlarged editions of Lord Douglas. Amusing Household! as Rimbaud would say. I shall look for *The Rainbow* in Brentano's here, and hope that it may be interesting. — — — —

49: TO GORHAM MUNSON

[*Washington*]   *Oct. 13th '20*

Dear Gorham: —/—/ New York seems to be set for a fine musical and dramatic season. I took in *Footloose* here last week and enjoyed it in spite of many obvious impossibilities of situation, etc. Emily Stevens did well in it—I suppose it would have failed without her. *Stepping Stones* is here this week and I may go to see it. — — — —

What think you of this Aldous Huxley's "Leda" poems? They strike me as dry and very clever,—but is real poetry so obviously clever? Modern life and its vacuity seems to me to be responsible for such work. There is only a lime or a lemon to squeeze or a pepper-pot left to shake. All the same I admire his work very much. He comes in the line of Eliot and Sitwell. Eliot's influence threatens to predominate the new English.

50: TO GORHAM MUNSON

Washington, D.C.   *Oct. 20th,—'20*

Dear Gorham: —/—/ Your letter that arrived this morning had the true rage of the celibate unwilling in it. I sympathize with you. . . . My nights are uneasy also. But you ought to pity me more than yourself,—my satisfactions are far more remote and dangerous than yours, and my temptations frequent, alas!

I have just been reading your Pollard article, and on bringing it to the attention of my friend Wilbur Underwood here, was delighted to find that U. knew Pollard very well, the latter having been enthusiastic about the two vols. of verse that Underwood brought out in England a long time ago. What pathos there is in these sudden flashes on forgotten people, forgotten achievements and encounters! Here is this man, Underwood, with the beauty and promise of his life all dried and withered by the daily grind he has had to go through year after year in the State Dept. with a meagre salary. A better critic and more interesting person one seldom meets, yet the routine of uninteresting work has probably killed forever his creative predispositions. A very few friends is all that life holds for him. Yes, Pound is right in what he says in his "The Rest,"—"O helpless few in my country, O remnant enslaved! . . . . You who cannot wear yourselves out by persisting to successes."

U. has a very fine collection of rare translations, etc., from antiquity, and I have just been enjoying to the full his copy of the *Satyricon* of Petronius (Arbiter), a rare and completely unexpurgated Paris edition, purported to have been translated by Oscar Wilde, although it seems to me too fine a job for what I imagine Wilde's scholarship to have been. Also, I am enjoying *The Golden Asse* of Apuleius, and some Saltus vols. that he has.

I went to see Hampden in *The Merchant of Venice* recently here. The way it was done, setting, costumes, speech, gestures,—everything was sickening. Hampden, in one scene only,—the tantrum with Tubal,—was good, everywhere else his acting was indifferent. I cannot understand how a man of his intelligence,—for I remember his Hamlet as being quite good,—will venture forth with such a cast of burlesque queens, (his Portia!!!) and bitches. The worst examples of antiquated theatricality, and mouthing of words! And the audience was ample and enthusiastic,—a true barometer of the American stage at present. —/—/

I shall be glad to get back to Cleveland for a while, if only to see the copies of Vildrac, Rimbaud, and Laforgue that have arrived from Paris since my leaving. I expect to return to W. later, in Jan. when the "season" here is on. I find agreement from my father that my lack of results here has not been so much a matter of personal inadequacy as the weather and general slowness of business here at this particular time. . . . I shall certainly be in an ungodly rush, though, all the time I am at the factory, as the holiday season orders will be coming in and things become perfectly maddening there for two months. However, anything will be better than the maddening experience I have been having here of clawing the air day after day without getting any but the most meagre results. —/—/

51: To Gorham Munson

Cleveland,   *Nov. 9th—'20*

Dear Gorham: — — — — Yes, "Jurgen" has been breathing his *native* Ohio air for two weeks now, and is elbow and knee-deep in shipping and packing at the factory. The Christmas rush has already begun and I'm tired to death tonight after a rush since five this morning. But in spite of all it has been better to get out of the ghostly time I was having in Washington, back into the usual smoky and tawdry thoroughfares. Does one really get so used to such things as, in time, to miss them, if absent? I am sure I should not miss factory whistles in Pisa or Morocco, but I frankly did miss them in Washington. Anyway, they were more enlivening (and the people they claim) than anything or anyone that I saw in W., which seemed to me the most elegantly restricted and bigoted community I ever ventured into. They say it has changed a lot since the war, and prohibition, of course, smothered its last way out.—I almost hope I will not have the opportunity of returning there in Jan., as expected. But you've heard most of this before.—

I have written Margaret Anderson to find out the *L.R.* situation. Probably what you have heard is only too true. There is no use expressing familiar resentments about such proceedings, and anyway one grows rather calloused and numb in time. There is that danger with me,—of relaxing into an indifference more comfortable than an interest in the arts nowadays and here, allows. I suppose the Minns pictures, my poems, etc., are smothered,—at least I've reconciled myself to it peacefully. I'm sorrier about the Minns pictures than anything else, as it meant a great deal of trouble to bring their reproduction about. Perhaps they'll print them again, I don't know yet. My great wonder is that M.C.A. and j.h. keep persisting as they do.

When you get a chance see the new monograph on Jacob Epstein including fifty photos of his works. He seems to be much better than most of Rodin, and I'm enthusiastic almost to the point of silliness. I'm reading *The Possessed* at your suggestion. Dostoievsky is a stranger to me beyond *Crime and Punishment* which caught me by the throat. He *does* give one more life than my mundane world supplies,—and stimulates. He makes you forget yourself (should I better say, lose) in the life of his characters for days at a time. And how few writers can do that! You see this record of my temper at present,—I'm tired, with every evidence of it. — — — —

52: TO GORHAM MUNSON

[*Cleveland*]   *11/23/20*

My dear Gorham: Your letter has just come, and I'm sorry to know you are having such an ordeal of "nerves." Of course, being thrown back violently again on celibacy after your Woodstock freedom would naturally tend to bring about such a result, and it is only a pity that you cannot find anything near you of sufficient temporary interest to relieve your situation. Of course, I realize, that the puritanical taboos of a typical boys' school are what stands in the way most of all, and then you might possibly resent and refuse sheer sensuality after having experienced what I imagine has been offered you. I don't believe in the "sublimation" theory at all so far as it applies to my own experience. Beauty has most often appeared to me in moments of penitence and even sometimes, distraction and worry. Lately my continence has brought me nothing in the creative way,— it has only tended to create a confidence in me along lines of action,— business, execution, etc. There is not love enough in me at present to do a thing. This sounds romantic and silly,—you understand that I mean and refer to the strongest incentive to the imagination, or, at least, the strongest in my particular case. So I have nothing to offer you for reading and judgment. Mart Anderson writes me that the next *L.R.* will be out the twenty-fifth,—96 pgs., and will contain my poem, etc., and a publication of the J. Joyce trial and proceedings which she says are interesting. It ought to be a rich number with John Quinn and Burleson throwing epithets at each other. I stopped in the middle of *The Possessed* to read *Poor White,* but am again on the Russian trail. What marvelous psychology!!! A careful reading of "Dosty" ought to prepare one's mind to handle any human situation comfortably that ever might arise. . . . You will like the Anderson book. It fascinated me as much as *Winesburg* and this in spite of a great fear I had of disappointment. There is a woman in it something like jh although too removed to do anything but suggest her. I wish, after you have read it, that we could have a fireside hour over the book. We might agree perhaps on the exquisite work of such scenes as the description of the murderer-saddlemaker sitting by the pond and rocking gently to and fro (the simplicity of A's great power of suggestion is most mocking to the analyst)—and the scene where the sex-awakening girl hears the men in the barn in speaking of her, say,—"the sap is mounting into the tree." Nature is so strong in all the work of Anderson—and he describes it as one so willingly and happily surrendered to it, that it colors his work with the most surprising grasp of what "innocence" and "holiness" ought to mean. Also, his uncanny intuition into the feelings of women (a number of women have remarked to me about this) is very unusual. I have an absurd prejudice against Frank's *Dark Mother* merely on account of what I read of it in a copy of *The Dial.* There it seemed to me too exclamatory, Semitic, and too much in the style of David Pinski, whose stuff I somehow am terribly bored with. So I probably shall never read it, as I probably shall never read more than the three pages of W. D. Howells that I once attempted. Frankly, you see, I admit to a taste for certain affectations and ornamental [c]ommissions. I wish I could follow your finger guide to the advice of Brooks in *The Freeman* about "outside interests" for the fallow seasons between poems. I had read the article and agree with it in many ways. But with me, there are no poems for "doldrums" to lag between, and no time, literally, for poems, to say nothing of energy. The fact is last week I ran gait at the factory at the rate of fourteen hours straight per day of rushed and heavy and confusing labor, and as it will probably continue that way until very near Christmas, I have all I can do to think of getting enough sleep to begin the rush again next day. Of course I am becoming very morose and irritable under this pressure of exertion, not to mention disgust and boredom, and yesterday, my first day of a chance to sit down and think a minute, I found myself in a rather serious state of indigestion and neurotic fever. So it goes. Our age tries hard enough to kill us, but I begin to feel a pleasure in sheer stubbornness, and will possibly turn in time into some sort of a beautiful crank. Pax vobiscum!!!!

53: TO GORHAM MUNSON

[*Cleveland*]   *Sunday, Dec. 5th,—'20*

Dear Gorham: Your article in *The Plowshare* was so late as to have arrived only a few days ago,—the "Pascal" came yesterday. In almost every way, I think, the latter work is superior, and to me, more suggestive, but this is probably because we agreed pretty well over most of the contents of "Cafe St. Beuve" last summer in my parlours at the Prince George and so it was familiar material to me. I have never read Pascal and so can't speak beyond telling you that I like your handling of the theme and it seemed to me that your style was richer than I have noticed before. I am filled with a kind of bleakness of mind and spirit lately, so that even this answer to your appreciated interest in my bland career is somehow an unsatisfactory effort. I should like to be able to see and talk to you,—the mere technical mechanics of writing have become so foreign to me from long neglect, that I feel awkward at best. Again I am very much at sea about everything that personally concerns me. —/—/ I am not sure about remaining in Cleveland much after the first of the year, as there is a possibility of my being sent out on the road again as salesman. On the other hand, it seems to me that it will be about as much as I can endure to remain at my present work in the shipping dept. until Christmas is over without a clean and final break with my father and his company, owing to various humiliations he seems interested in either forcing or countenancing others about the place to force, on me. As soon as my mother is off the scene I shall feel freer to do more as I please. I have practically no money and as employment is hard to find now, she is very much worried for fear I shall do something rash and suffer for it. About the only course I see is to save for all I am worth for two years or so, and then embark once and for all for foreign lands, Italy or Russia or Paris, and not come back until I want to. Literature and art be hanged!—even ordinary existence isn't worth the candle in these States now. I enclose Matty Josephson's last letter to me with his plans. They make my mouth water.

I wish I had three poems to send to *The Nation,* but I shall have to desist from a lack of "numbers." *The Possessed* was one of the most tremendous books I've ever read, I think, and I am planning on reading *The Brothers Karamazov* as soon as time permits. At present I dip into Seutonius' *History of the Caesars,* which is easy to recognize as one of Saltus' principal authorities and sources for his *Imperial Purple.* — — — —

54: To SHERWOOD ANDERSON

[*Cleveland*]   *12/8/20*

Dear Anderson: Your mention of a possible trip East soon makes me hope very much that you will care to stop off at Cleveland here (a few hours at least) and see me. I shall not be living at home at the time as my mother expects to leave for her place in Cuba very soon, closing the house, but if you come alone I can accommodate you at my room wherever it may be. I want very much to talk with you and hope you can "make it" this time. Better look me up at the factory at 208 St. Clair Ave. if you arrive between 8 A.M. and 5 P.M. You don't know how much I appreciate the encouragement your letters give me. Although I am not at present doing anything creatively, I have not sunk too much into despair or indifference to hope.

Do come,—won't you!

55: To — —

[*Cleveland*]   [*Dec. 22, 1920*]

Dear — —: NEWS! News! NEWS!—The "golden halo" has widened, —descended upon me (or "us") and I've been blind with happiness and beauty for the last full week! Joking aside, I am too happy not to fear a great deal, but I believe in, or have found God again. It seems vulgar to rush out with my feelings to anyone so, but you know by this time whether I am vulgar or not (I don't) and it may please you, as it often might have helped me so, to know that something beautiful can be found or can "occur" once in awhile, and so unexpectedly. Not the brief and limited sensual thing alone, but something infinitely more thrilling and inclusive. I foolishly keep wondering,—"How can this be?—How did it occur?" How my life might be changed could this continue, but I scarcely dare to hope. I feel like weeping most of the time, and I have become reconciled, strangely reconciled, to many aggravations. Of course it is the return of devotion which astounds me so, and the real certainty that, at least for the time, it is perfectly honest. It makes me feel very unworthy,—and yet what pleasure the emotion under such circumstances provides. I have so much now to reverence, discovering more and more beauty every day,—beauty of character, manner, and body, that I am for the time, completely changed.—But why aren't you here to talk with me about it! How I wish you were here.

I have written you this way (typewriter) because, as you have discovered, my writing is hard deciphering. I have given up trying to improve it, and don't try any more. You have probably got the candy and hymn by this time,—neither amount to much, but I wanted to send them. I don't understand — — — —'s silence,—but certainly hope that I have not been relinquished as one of Akron's temporary "makeshifts" or "reliefs." It would really hurt. I have told you all that has happened. This rest would merely be to mention details of ungodly strain and hours of "Christmas rush" at the factory,—seventeen hours a stretch sometimes. When I have had time I have spent it with Dostoievsky's *Les Freres Karamazov* which I like even better than *The Possessed*. The beautiful young Alyosha, and Father Zossima! Dostoievsky seems to me to represent the nearest type to the "return of Christ" that there is record of,—I think the greatest of novelists. But I am forgetting Frank Harris, who, you know, comes second to the "woman taken in adultery." —/—/

1 9 2 1

56: To GORHAM MUNSON

[*Cleveland*]   *1/14/21*

Dear Gorham: —/—/ I'm slightly disabled today with a touch of la grippe and am remaining away from the factory. A talk with my father last week settled things more definitely for me than many months have afforded. I shall remain in my present capacity at the factory indefinitely until I find a job at some more "literary" work, when my father and I will more-or-less conclusively part hands so far as a business connection is concerned. At last he seems, after questioning various mutual friends as to my interests, etc., to have been forced into this much recognition of my persistence in artistic directions,—and it was gratifying to observe as gracious a surrender as he offered me. You see I have not said anything to him about my

personal interests for almost two years, leaving him only what details of indifference to business as naturally revealed themselves
throughout my association with him, to judge from. I long ago
"gave up" talking over such sores with him,—and it has amused me
vastly to find that at last the attitude aroused him to seek such indirect solutions to the "enigma." Now I can hope to get a little reading and writing done before spring here in some sort of tranquillity.
Before the summer is over I may have found me a journalistic job,—
but the main point under either drudgery is that I accomplish
some real writing. But this is the usual ante-room soliloquy, and I
won't bore you further with more of it.

I am just as glad for you that you didn't start your magazine,—
and with the same considerations in mind that you gave as your
reasons against it. Italy will do you infinitely more good,—why waste
your good money on what is, after all, an indifferent public. It is bad
enough to waste brains and time—but not money!!! I haven't seen
Contact yet, but will try to get 'round to send for a copy soon. Williams has a very fine poem in the last *Poetry* and also there is a
beauty by Padraic Colum. By the way, I hope you saw Colum's write-
up of Ezra Pound's *Instigations* in a not very recent *New Republic.*
It was the best appreciation of Pound on his own grounds that I've
ever read.

Your last letter, although very brief and fragmentary, did bring
a whiff from you of revived sensibilities. N.Y. does that to one always
after any period of provincial stiffness. What are you writing now?
Of course I shall send you whatever I do,—but the waiting is longer,
by far, for me than for you. I'm caught dead tight in a new affair
de coeur that at least keeps me stirred up in some ways. I don't know
how much blood I pay for these predicaments,—but I seem to live
more during them than otherwise. They give the ego a rest. I may
sound like an utter profligate,—but there is much sincerity, too painfully much, for me to laugh.

57: To Matthew Josephson

Cleveland, O.   *1/14/21*

Dear Matty: —/—/ What you say about the Akron suite is very true.
I have only one point of disagreement with you,—crudeness of form.
This was deliberate, and you have got to convince me that such a
treatment of such a mood and subject is inconsistent before we can
pick asphodels together again on the slopes of Parnassus. By the way,
—do you care for my "Garden Abstract" in its final form in *The L.R.?*

I think that the version I sent you was an earlier and poorer experiment. I must bestir myself soon and write something new. My main difficulty is at present a kind of critical structure that won't permit me the expression of the old asininities, *and* (as you say) the poverty of society in these "provinces." Your suggestion about the trade paper work is alluring. However, I am bound not to break away from my father's concern until spring, when there may be a little striving and stirring up of the dust,—I hope.

Are you still planning on Italy? Why not the island of Capri? I hear there is interesting company about there,—D. H. Lawrence and Mackenzie musing and moping around the baths and arcades of Tiberius. . . . I don't long so much for change of surroundings as time, TIME which I never seem to get to read or write or amuse myself. I hear [that] "New York" has gone mad about "Dada" and that a most exotic and worthless review is being concocted by Man Ray and Duchamp, billets in a bag printed backwards, on rubber deluxe, etc. What next! This is worse than The Baroness [Freytag-Loringhoven]. By the way I like the way the discovery has suddenly been made that she has all along been, unconsciously, a Dadaist. I cannot figure out just what Dadaism is beyond an insane jumble of the four winds, the six senses, and plum pudding. But if the Baroness is to be a keystone for it,—then I think I can possibly know when it is coming and avoid it.

58: TO GORHAM MUNSON

[Cleveland]   *1/28/21*

Dear Gorham: Your N.Y. bulletin interested me immensely. Last Sunday I went down to Akron to see Minns after a four months' separation. I read him the opinions of Man Ray, whereat he flew into a holy rage. "There is no sense in the theory of interesting 'accidents,' " and I am with Minns in that. There is little to [be] gained in any art so far as I can see, except with much *conscious* effort. If he doesn't watch his lenses, M. Ray will allow the Dada theories and other flamdoodle of his section run him off his track. He seems to have done much good work so far, but it has been in spite of his ideas. If he is just recently infected, it's too bad, because there is less chance of him containing his qualities under such theories—But so much for photography.

—/—/ When I get "Dosty" more cleared out of the way, I intend to get more poetry reading again, but just now he is all-absorbing, and somehow his offering is such a distinct type of itself that one

doesn't want to mix any other kind of reading with it. Here is my sum poetic output for the last three months—two lines—
> "The everlasting eyes of Pierrot
> And of Gargantua,—the laughter."

Maybe it is my epitaph, it is contradictory and wide enough to be. But I hope soon to make it into a poem and thereby, like Lazarus, return.

59: To Gorham Munson

[*Cleveland*]   *2/11/21*

Dear Gorham: Yes, my writing is quite Dada,—very Dada (I like the term as applied) and yet you must put up with it again as my machine has suffered another relapse.

I was very much amused and interested by the *Contact* that arrived about a week ago. Thank you, as always, dear old bean, for being so thoughtful. You are always sending me something to make my eyes blink delightedly and arouse me from the general stupor of these parts. How fine the Wallace Stevens were! And some of Williams' talk was good—but how horrid that the room had to be splashed with the wet-dream explosions of Virgil Jordan and McAlmon. Their talk is all right—but what is true of it has been said adequately before,—and all they can seem to add is a putrid remnant or two. Perhaps I am on the downward grade, but when I come to such stuff as theirs I can only say "Excuse me." I will be glad to receive stimulation from the sky or a foetid chamber or maybe a piss-pot but as far as I can make out they have wound their *phalli* around their throats in a frantic and vain effort to squeeze out an idea. In fact they seem very "Dada" in more sense than one. But enough!!!

Don't disown me,—but I have done literally no writing to give you. The fact is that I am entirely engrossed in personal erotic experience lately that nothing seems possible in that way. O if you had ever seen the very Soul of Pierrot (in soul and incarnate) you would at least admire. Never, though, has such beauty and happy-pain been given me before—which is to say that my love is at least somewhat requited. You and one other are the only ones to know now or later of this, so do not think me silly or vulgar to tell you. Well, you have felt the fire somewhat yourself so you may appreciate my mood. Never have I suffered so, or reached such moods of ecstasy. . . .

What do you think of *Poor White?* It certainly has made Anderson one of the most talked-of artists there are. I wrote you my opinion some time past. I'm still on "Dosty"—a very fine biography and estimate and analysis by J. Middleton Murry.

You will please forgive this letter. I have been perhaps a little too personal,—perhaps vulgar. But if anything's to blame it's the Subconscious rioting out through gates that only alcohol has the power to open. —/—/

60: To GORHAM MUNSON

[*Cleveland*]   2/24

Dear Gorham: Your article on education, etc., in the last *Freeman* delights me. Remarkably courageous and true. I hope it may do at least a little good concretely,—but at least it will serve as an accentuation mark in the minds of a good many like myself who have felt with you along that line for some time.

Two new pictures just arrived from Minns that I wish you could see. One,—an old man's head that is as good as a Rembrandt, and at the opposite pole, a young girl's head that brings Pound's sonnet lines persistently into my head,—"No, go from me. I have left her lately. I will not spoil my shield with lesser brightness.—" You know how it goes. I intend to send the old man's head to *The Dial* for publication, but scarcely hope they will accept it after the mediocrities they have lately staged there. Really,—I flatter myself, you see,—I have more doubts about their accepting a poem I recently wrote and sent them, which I enclose.[1] You see, my present job allows me more time while "at work," and I may even do more,—for better or worse, according as you feel about it.

This is all now until I hear from you and have more to build on. You know there is precious little for me to build on here, and so you must not too much mind if my letters have a predominance of what must seem banality to you. If so, forgive me,—and when you get tired of vainly tugging at your end of the line, let me know, and I'll take it philosophically.

61: To GORHAM MUNSON

[*Cleveland*]   *April 10th*

Dear Gorham: — — — — For me here—the same old jog-trot except that I have lately run across an artist here whose work seems to carry the most astonishing marks of genius that have passed before my eyes in original form, that is,—I mean present-day work. And I am saying much I think when I say that I prefer Sommer's work to most of Brzeska and Boardman Robinson. A man of 55 or so—works in

1. "Black Tambourine"; see Weber, *op. cit.*, pp. 95-6.

a lithograph factory—spent most of his life until the last seven years
in the rut of conventional forms—liberated suddenly by sparks from
Gauguin, Van Gogh, Picasso and Wyndham Lewis, etc. I have taken
it upon myself to send out some of his work for publication, an idea
that seems oddly, never to have occurred to him. —/— I enclose an
incipient effort of mine of recent date.[1]

62: To Gorham Munson

[*Cleveland*]   *April 20th*

Dear Gorham: Your letter did me good, and has left a good hangover for me for the last few ungenerous days. I left my father's employ yesterday *for good*—nothing, I think, will ever bring me back.
The last insult was too much. I've been treated like a dog now for
two years,—and only am sorry that it took me so long to find out the
simple impossibility of ever doing anything with him or for him.

It will take me many months, I fear, to erase from memory
the image of his overbearing head leaning over me like a gargoyle.
I think he had got to think I couldn't live without his aid. At least
he was, I am told, furious at my departure. Whatever comes now is
much better than the past. I shall learn to be somewhere near free
again,—at least free from the hatred that has corroded me into illness.

Of course I won't be able to get to N.Y. now for any summer vacation. You know what a privation that means to me. I have nothing
in sight in the way of employment,—and as times are so bad,—I don't
know when I shall. A job as copy-writer for an advertising house will
probably be open to me about June 1st. And there is a new newspaper
opening out here soon,—perhaps that may yield me something. I
have a roof over my head and food, anyway—here at home—and maybe I shall write something. The best thing is that the cloud of my
father is beginning to move from the horizon now, you have never
known me when it has not been there—and in time we *both* may
discover some new things in me. *Bridges burn't behind!*

Glad you like "Estador." I'm beginning to myself. I cannot quite
accept your word changes although I'm far from satisfied with it. But
the more I work over it the less I seem likely to be,—so I'm going to
try it on *The Dial.*—Anything for some money now.

63: To Gorham Munson

[*Cleveland*]   *May 3rd 21*

My dear Gorham: —/—/ I feel sure S[ommer]'s work is as important
as any contemporary work anywhere, and I'm very interested to hear

1. "The Bridge of Estador"; see Weber, *op. cit.*, p. 385.

what you will think. I wish I were better trained for analysis of this kind of work,—but as it is I can only "feel" the power of it. I may send you a few of his drawings at any time,—and later if you have time around N.Y. after school is out, you might care to show some of them to people who could give him a chance perhaps, of exhibition somewhere. —/—/

I agree with you about your distinction between the earlier and later Anderson. I have never got hold of *Windy McPherson's Son,* but I never could clap very loudly for *Marching Men,* although I imagine that it is an improvement on the former. He, I understand, is anxious for these two books' extinction. They will probably never be issued by the publisher again. I'm anxious to read his "Out of Nowhere into Nothing" that *The Dial* announces for three summer issues. By the way, a new book of essays by my acquaintance, Charles S. Brooks, has a chapter in it, "A Modern Poet," which is a burlesque on me, the Baroness, and my rooms over *The Little Review* on 16th Street. His effort is all the funnier for the especial lack of comprehension he has for *The L.R.* and "modern poetry." I promise you a laugh or two anyway. The Yale Press has just got it out,—its title is *Hints to Pilgrims.* Brooks lives a few houses down the street from me here, but at that time he was a New Yorker, and used to be very hospitable to me with theatres and dinner at his apartment on 10th St. —/—/

64: To GORHAM MUNSON

[*Cleveland*]   *May 16th, '21*

Dear Gorham: I am delighted that you have found so much to hold your interest in Sommer's work. Some later things that he had recently shown me only confirm my convictions the more. I'll send you more of his work as soon as I can assemble what I want to. Sent two watercolours to *The Dial* again last week, which I don't see how they can let pass by—but all things are possible to them. —/—/ There is a French-Swiss artist here just eight months from Paris,—doing very interesting work with a peculiar sharp diabolism in it. Willy E. Lescaze. His work at a local exhibition here recently caused a terrible furor, being in company with Burchfield's, the only work worth looking at. It amuses me to see Lescaze praise Sommer's work—there [are] all the differences between them that distinguish Baudelaire from Rabelais. I recently sent some of L's work to *The Little Review* along with S's—but what ever keeps Margaret Anderson so impolitely silent I cannot figure out. Do what I will, I can't seem to get a word out of her. I begin to despair. At least I hope she will return the drawings someday. If you want more to take about with you, you might call on her when you next are in town and find out if she wants them. If not you will find some interesting additions to add to your bundle. I cannot but feel that there is an audience in N.Y. ready for such work. Sommer has tried Cleveland people and found them so indifferent that he didn't even send one canvas or sheet to this last exhibition here. In one way, a mistake, I think. Before I forget your request,—*William Sommer* is as completely as he signs himself.

Went yesterday to see the first movie for a long time. Did you see it—*Deception*—the foreign picture of the affairs of Henry VIII and Anne Boleyn? It really was stimulating. I could wish for more of such fare, even though it should (horrid thought!) impoverish our native celluloid manufactories. There were mob scenes in it, perfect in every detail, that only the screen can produce. And the old sensualist king was well acted.

Am still without work. There is absolutely nothing doing here. Things are at such a standstill that I hate to think of it. I am practically on my mother's hands here at home,—and you can believe me that such a situation is far from a pleasant one for me who have been used to paying my own way now for some time. If only that promise I have for a job with a local advertising house fulfills itself next month I shall be all right. But most friends and friendly offers have proved themselves such slippery fish! Two years thrown away at the feet of my father without the gain of a jot of experience at anything but peon duties in a shipping room! I can never forgive him, nor my own foolishness. Just now I am too uneasy to concentrate on any writing. Have got to prepare myself for some kind of practical activity—and so I do not even read much but advertising books and business folders! Roger Fry's *Vision and Design,* a large tome beautifully illustrated, is good to unloosen one's tongue about such work as Sommer's. He brought it around one evening, and I have enjoyed it. Haven't read *Main Street* or *Moon Calf* yet, nor *Miss Lulu Bett.* I am beginning to feel rather distinguished about it all.

65: To Gorham Munson

Cleveland   *May 21st*

Dear Gorham: I'm glad to say that my tension is less acute at present than when I last wrote you. An improvement of the weather with opportunities for tennis and getting out and around more helps me work off surplus energies generated by my "change of life." And you are, of course, very much right in urging me not to be ridiculously bourgeois in accepting bourgeois standards.

I'm very glad you like "A Persuasion." Perhaps it seems a bit tame to me on account of having used several phrases coined some years ago in it. I was much pleased this week to get word from *Double Dealer* accepting "Black Tambourine" for publication and urging me to send them some prose. They claim they are much in need of some. Haven't you some to offer them? I might write something on Joyce or Anderson—but I don't know. I always feel singularly lacking in ideas about these people excepting to blindly enthuse or refute some ridiculous criticism of them. Their ("*D.D's*") check has not arrived yet but they promise it soon—before the June number when they expect to use the poem. It surprises me to find such a Baudelairesque thing acceptable *anywhere* in U.S. I sent it out as a kind of hopeless protest—not expecting to see it printed at all. I'm beginning to lose interest in it now—it cannot be as good as I had thought it. —/—/

66: To GORHAM MUNSON

Cleveland,   *Friday*

Dear Gorham: —/—/ Excuse my apparent evasion of your request for an explanation about "Black Tambourine." The Word "midkingdom" is perhaps the key word to what ideas there are in it. The poem is a description and bundle of insinuations, suggestions bearing on the Negro's place somewhere between man and beast. That is why Aesop is brought in, etc.,—the popular conception of Negro romance, the tambourine on the wall. The value of the poem is only, to me, in what a painter would call its "tactile" quality,—an entirely aesthetic feature. A propagandist for either side of the Negro question could find anything he wanted to in it. My only declaration in it is that I find the Negro (in the popular mind) sentimentally or brutally "placed" in this midkingdom, etc. Tell me if I have made it plain or not to you.

67: To GORHAM MUNSON

Cleveland,   *June 12th '21*

Dear Gorham: —/—/ Sommer said you had something in a very recent *Freeman* which I've been trying to get, but guess I'm too late. Sometimes I get so exasperated with the "intellectual" attitudes of these papers like *The Freeman, New Rep., Nation,* etc., where everything is all jumbled together,—politics, literature, painting, birth control, etc., etc., etc., that I ignore them for a time and probably miss some good things. It's the way they are served that I object to. I'm beginning to be somewhat pained by this "Intelligentsia" mood when it comes upon me. This probably indicates that I am not a very responsible individual—and truth is—I'm not. How tired I am of the perpetual ferment of *The New Rep.* Those fellows are playing a canster game nonsense. Does anything they ever say have any concrete effect? Old Washington goes on just the same on the old rotten paths. These gentlemen are merely clever at earning their livelihood in clean cuffs. But hear me rant on!!! I don't care twopence for the whole earth & heavens and least of all for politics. It's only when the political gentlemen (Irish potatobeds) obstruct my view of my petunias and hollyhocks that I'm thus aroused,—and even that is a small complaint in the long list of larger ones I have. −/−/

No job in sight even now! I'm about convinced of the hopelessness of the advertising plan. Business gets worse and worse and they haven't enough to do to keep a new man busy.

Oh well!—I manage to get drunk once a week on delicious wine served out by a friend of mine here and I have an evening a week with Sommer when we do all kinds of stunts from Chopin Ballades and Heine lyrics to sparring with an old set of gloves I have. Wish I could think of something entertaining to write—but, at present I'm mostly trying to regain a mental and spiritual status that has been lost to me for over a year. What I want to do is gather up the threads again and go on, to put it stale-ly.

I have reached such blind alleys and found no way out of them that there is nothing at present for me to do but laugh a little and *endure*—which I hope to do. −/−/

Did I tell you I'd been drawing and painting some? I find it a tremendous stimulation—and you begin to see so many more things than before wherever you look. My drawings are original, at least, and Sommer professes to see much in 'em. −/−/

68: To GORHAM MUNSON

Cleveland   *June 16th '21*

Hail! Citizen of the world! −/−/ No work here except what I've lately been making myself. This has all been occasioned by a very cordial letter from the editor of *The Double-Dealer,* Basil Thompson, who urged me to write something for them on Anderson. This has been done (to the extent of 2000 words which, if taken, means $20.00) and dispatched. In my present mood it seems to have been a good job. Also, I got up courage and erudition enough to "do" a Vildrac translation for them which in the original at least is fine.

I was very disappointed to find quite a bad typographical error in "Black Tambourine." "Mingle" instead of "mingl*ing*"—last line 2nd verse. How foolish it makes me feel that way! It quite destroys the sense of the thing.

They pay .30 per line of verse & 1 cent per prose word and want prose badly. As I need money worse, I may do something in the short story way for them if they fancy the Anderson thing. This last little effort has rewarded me much already merely in getting my mind to working a little again. I don't dare hope for an ultimate success as a "free lance" but am beginning to think that this writing game offers a chance to augment one's savings a little now and then at least.

69: To Gorham Munson

[*Cleveland*]   *Saturday midnight*

Dear Gorham: Well. It has been a day I shall not soon forget. I have just a little time since returned from my first visit to the Sommer farm and studio—about half way between here and Akron in a beautiful untrodden valley. He has an old old-fashioned schoolhouse for his studio—the walls all white and hung with such an array of things as you never have seen. Forgive my enthusiasm—I have been so dazzled for the last 8 hours that I may seem somewhat incoherent in my expression. I have brought home with me a considerable number of water-colours and drawings which I am going to send on to you within a few days. These are representative of his *best* in this medium and I think you will be enthusiastic about them. I could picture a dozen N.Y. picture dealers in that studio today—radical or pedantical—all tearing each other's hair for the first chance of exhibiting such stuff. I feel convinced now that all that needs be done is to get some samples of this work before them,—and if they have any sense at all—either artistic or commercial—they will seize upon it. —/—/

"Dynamism" is the splendid & fitting word for Sommer—the word I had been looking for and got only as far as the adjectival use. —/—/

70: To Gorham Munson

Cleveland,   *July 8th*

Dear Gorham: —/—/ The weather has been terrifically hot here, making motion and thought alike impossible,—but I am slowly try-

ing to labor out in the suitable style for *Shadowland* an article on
Ezra [Pound] which may bring me in a little money. This magazine
is popular and in some ways becoming more interesting than *Vanity
Fair*. I would like a foothold in it if it is possible. It seems evident
enough that I have accomplished something in the estimation of the
editors of *The D.D.* as they have incorporated me in their list of
contributors on their stationery. I got word the other day that they
will bring out my Anderson article in this July issue. I haven't got
my check yet but it ought to be twenty dollars or so.

I have a query for you. What would you think of a play on or
around the figure of John Brown? There is plenty of material, but
the only trouble I see is the issue of slavery, North and South, etc.,
which might kill it. I am reading a fine biography of the man by
Villard. As I am principally interested in this idea for mere commercial reasons the possibility of popularity is the largest factor. I
tend to think the subject, in this light, too forbidding.

— — — — I always seem to choose the wrong moment for my letters,
when the ice-man is hammering at the door or the family is waiting
to be driven to town, so my letters are more like bulletins and telegrams than anything else. Things pan out the same way when I
start on an essay, article or poem,—but I hope for better days. —/—/

71: TO GORHAM MUNSON

Cleveland,   *July 14th, '21*

Dear Gorham: This is the kind of note I got yesterday from JH of
The Little Review, returning some mss.,—"Found this as I was going
through Mart's files. She's crazy. The drawings are fine but we
haven't any hope of printing them for ages, so I sent them back.—jh."
So it looks as though *The L.R.* was done for, and perhaps poor Mart.
Doesn't the way jh puts it makes you feel rather uneasy. I wish I
knew more details,—whether it is a mere — — — — rumpus that is all
the matter, or whether Mart Anderson has worn herself out in vain
assaults against the decision against her in the Joyce trial. I wish I
could get in touch with her direct, but as she hasn't answered any
letter for the last six weeks she probably cannot write. I happen
to know from Mart's friends too much inside information on the
two women's mutual relationships to feel certain of any direct truth
about Mart from jh. If you hear anything about them or their plans
please let me know. You know my admiration and (yes) affection for
Margaret Anderson is very strong, and I detest nothing more than
such a brutal squib as this thing that jh just sent. —/—/

The cover for the July *Double Dealer* gives me the shivers, but my Anderson article is all there. Write me what you think of it now that you have read him more or less completely. I enclose a letter of introduction [to Anderson]. My Pound article is a far more difficult thing and progresses slowly, but I am bent now on making as much money writing as I can, and I'm going to get it published one place or another. Your encouragement anent the John Brown adventure is very gratifying. This is a long winded matter, but I think I shall go ahead with it, hoping by the time you get back from Europe to have something to show you. By the way, when you are in Paris there is one place you must go. Joyce's *Ulysses* is to be brought out complete in Paris this fall. I enclose a subscription blank with address, etc. I have already subscribed for it. $-/-/$

72: To Gorham Munson

Cleveland   *July 22nd, '21*

Dear Gorham: The "march of events" has brought upon us Cleveland's 125th anniversary with all its fussy & futile inanities and advertisements to make hideous the streets. Blocked, and obliged to wait while the initial "pee-rade" went by today, I spent two hours of painful rumination ending with such disgust at America and everything in it, that I more than ever envy you your egress to foreign parts. No place but America could relish & applaud anything so stupid & drab as that parade—led by the most notable and richest grafter of the place decked out in Colonial rags as the founder of the city Moses C. Ah—the Baroness, lunatic that she is, is right. Our people have no *atom* of a conception of beauty—and don't want it. One thing almost brought tears to my eyes (and I hope you do not think me too silly in mentioning it)—the handful of Chinese who came along in some native and antique vestments & liveries to prostitute themselves in the medley of trash around them. To see them passing the (inevitable) Soldier's Monument ablaze with their aristocratic barbarity of silk, gold and embroideries *was* an anachronism that could occur *only* in America. And the last of their "section" brought a float with a large "melting pot"—its significance was blazoned in letters *on* it!! All I can say is—it's a gay old world! If ever I felt alone it has been today. But I must encounter fireworks, bawling "choruses" and more "pee-rades" for 7 more days—as the community believes in celebrations that are productive of business.

Your letter came this morning, and I agree largely with what you have to say about the Anderson article. A friend of mine here,

Lescaze the painter, who is an excellent literary critic as well, told me that reading it gave him the impression of a young man inflating and playing with a series of variously-colored balloons in the boredom of his chambre—which in an imagistic way singularly seems to agree with the substance of your opinion on it. Well,—this is true & rather painfully so—I must admit. My only justification is the singularly inadequate surroundings I have here for any kind of concentration. My one hope is to do better with more practice at such work and relieved somewhat of the haste that the pressing necessities for money presently force upon me. I struggle with the Pound article still,—but the subject itself is so complex and (I fancy) the audience interested so small, that I may be forced to give it up.

You are right about *The D.D.'s* exceedingly uneven quality. To my mind almost every issue has been largely filled with utter weakness and banality. Will some one tell me how as (often) a good poet as Haniel Long can bring himself to allow to be printed such *stuff* as he has signed himself to in *The D.D.?* As a matter of fact I am continually being more and more horrified at what names we had always been accustomed to hoping rather much of,—are rushing into print with, and obviously out of the urgent need or desire of more money. *Shadowland,* especially the August number with Babette Deutsch's list of American poets! Alas—what Fletcher wrote on the artist's conscience in *The Freeman* (July 12th or so) makes me think a good deal. Living *is* at last becoming quite impossible, at least here,—when you get to Italy I advise a permanent residence there for you. Later, perhaps I'll come over and join you. In time there may be only D. H. Lawrence, the rainbow, and Capri left. I shall (with my millions acquired by that time in flattering biographies of rich businessmen)—I shall rejuvenate the baths and temple there of Tiberius and we shall live in state,—waited on by the only fair and unsullied youths & maidens then procurable in Europe. —/—/

73: To Gorham Munson

Cleveland, O.   *Aug. 9th '21*

Dear Gorham: —/—/ My unemployment lingers. I learn a Scriabin Prelude,—make a drawing,—stroke my black cat (a recent acquisition) and read intermittently. Lately I had a good letter from Colum, who likes my "Black Tambourine," and yesterday a long letter from Matthew Josephson, the first word for almost a year. He is up in Maine with Carl Springhorn and Kenneth Burke in a kind of camp. (Also his wife.) They both expect to sail for Italy six weeks from now, to stay two years or more. I don't know their proposed localities, but hope you will meet. — — — —

74: TO CHARMION WIEGAND

Cleveland, Ohio   *August 13, '21*

Dear Charmion: —/—/ I am very glad to know that you have been keeping up the writing,—whether prose, poetry, or drama doesn't so much matter. The point about it all is that it serves to keep you alert and alive much more than any other activity I know of,—and especially anything as warm as a "Byzantine drama of blood" sounds interesting. The historical drama seems to me as legitimate as any other provided it has enough organic life of its own and doesn't depend merely on the fame, etc., of the protagonists for effect. Have you read Stendhal's *Chartreuse de Parma?* So far as I know it has never been dramatized, and there is much good material in it. I find Stendhal, incidentally, one of the few men who wear deeper with familiarity. You probably have read his *Rouge et Noir.* —/—/

75: TO GORHAM MUNSON

Cleveland, Ohio   *Sept. 19th '21*

My dear Gorham: —/—/ *The L. R.,* I was informed on a card from j.h. the other day, is recovering, will shortly re-appear as a quarterly under Pound, Picabia, etc., 24 illustrations and 96 pgs! Mart Anderson also recovering "sanity," etc. — — — — I sold them [*The Dial*] the poem you read just before leaving, "Pastorale"—which will come out soon. I also sold one, "Persuasion," to *The Measure*—and "Porphyro in Akron" came out in the last *Double Dealer* in first place.

The result of all this is that I am "sold out" and will have to rush rhymes and rhythms together to supply my enthusastic "public" as fast as I can. But the family is all upset about my unemployment and money *is* needed. I am too uneasy to accomplish a thing, but hammer out a translation of de Gourmont's marginalia on Poe & Baudelaire for *The D.D.* I have projects and a few lines started on poems,—but nothing "comes through"—it is at times discouraging. I do not expect to hear from Josephson again. He wrote me several letters full of brilliant criticism and suggestions—but we do not exactly agree on theory and he has become so complex—that the lack of sympathy my last letter offered him will bring no response from [him] I'm quite sure—especially now after an unusually long interstice. But this extremity of hair splitting palls on one after awhile. A little is interesting—but goes a long ways. He seems afraid to use any emotion in his poetry,—merely observation and sensation,—and because I call such work apt to become thin, he thinks me sloppy and stupid,—as no doubt I am. But after all,—I recognize him as in many ways the most *acute* critic of poetry I know of—the only trouble is that he tries to force his theories into the creative process,—and the result, to me, is too tame a thing. —/—/

76: TO GORHAM MUNSON

Cleveland   *Oct. 1, '21*

Dear Gorham: My terrible hay fever days are over, and the fine autumn weather that I like the best of the year has arrived to console me. My mood is neither happy nor desperately sad. It will best be conveyed to you by the quotation of a new poem, "Chaplinesque" —only started (if I can help it) as yet: —/—/[1]

And I must tell you that my greatest dramatic treat since seeing Garden in *The Love of Three Kings* two winters ago, was recently enjoyed when Charlie Chaplin's *The Kid* was shown here. Comedy, I may say, has never reached a higher level in this country before. We have (I cannot be too sure of this for my own satisfaction) in Chaplin a dramatic genius that truly approaches the fabulous sort. I could write pages on the overtones and brilliant subtleties of this picture, for which nobody but Chaplin can be responsible, as he wrote it, directed it,—and I am quite sure had much to do with the settings which are unusually fine. If you have not already seen it in N. Y., it may now be in Paris. It was a year late in arriving in Cleveland, I understand, on account of objections from the state board of censors!!!! What they could have possibly objected to, I cannot imagine. It must have been some superstition aroused against good acting! But they will always release any sickening and false melodrama of high life and sex, lost virginities, etc., at the first glance. Well, I am thankful to get even what their paws have mauled of the Chaplin and *Caligari* sort. My poem is a sympathetic attempt to put in words some of the Chaplin pantomime, so beautiful, and so full of eloquence, and so modern.

—/—/ It will be time for me to raise my voice in praise of Anderson soon, as his new book *The Triumph of the Egg*, and other stories, is on the market. This also includes the serial "Out of Nowhere into Nothing," recently completed in *The Dial*. I would lay

1. See Weber, *op. cit.*, pp. 108-9.

a bet on it that long after Zona Gale, Lewis, etc., are forgotten, Sherwood will hold his own. There are lots of things I want to read but haven't the money to buy, like Hecht's first novel, a great success they say, *Erik Dorn,* recently out. I wrote you how much I enjoyed Shaw's *Back to Methuselah,* a review of which I wrote for *The D.D.*

I am taking a course in advertising two nights of every week until next May which is very good and ought to help me get started. It has the advantage, at any rate, of giving one a diploma which, I understand, has a real value. I am now pretty sure of making advertising my real route to bread and butter, and have a strong notion that as a copy writer I will eventually make a "whiz." —/—/

77: To GORHAM MUNSON

Cleveland,   *Oct. 6th,'21*

Dear Gorham: Here you are with the rest of the Chaplin poem. I know not if you will like it,—but to me it has a real appeal. I have made that "infinitely gentle, infinitely suffering thing" of Eliot's into the symbol of the kitten. I feel that, from my standpoint, the pantomime of Charlie represents fairly well the futile gesture of the poet in U.S.A. today, perhaps elsewhere too. And yet, the heart lives on. . . .

Maybe this is because I myself feel so particularly futile just now that I feel this pathos, (or is it bathos?). Je ne sais pas.

Yesterday I worked my first day foreman-ing three men on a distribution job, and walked untold miles of city blocks. I am stiff,— but the exercise did me much good. No work today,—perhaps tomorrow. At this work the most I can hope to get before spring is $30.00 per week. Yesterday brought me $2.50. Needless to say, I will look for something better as soon as I can get hands on it.

A new light and friend of my friend, the Swiss-French painter, Willy Lescaze, has arrived in town,—Jean Binet, teacher of Eurythmics in our very alive Cleveland School of Music which Ernest Bloch heads. I am to meet him tonight and with some anticipations, as I am told he is a remarkable and inspired amateur pianist, playing Erik Satie, Ravel, etc., to perfection. Lescaze has proved an inspiration to me. Knowing intimately the work of Marcel Proust, Salmon, Gide, and a host of other French moderns, he is able to see so much better than anyone else around here, the aims I have in my own work. We have had great times discussing the merits of mutual favorites like Joyce, Donne, Eliot, Pound, de Gourmont, Gordon

Craig, Nietzsche, etc., ad infinitum. After this it goes without saying that I never found a more stimulating individual in N. Y.

78: TO WILLIAM WRIGHT

Cleveland, O.   *Oct. 17, 1921*

Dear William: I can come half way with you about Edna Millay,—but I fear not much further. She really has genius in a limited sense, and is much better than Sara Teasdale, Marguerite Wilkinson, Lady Speyer, etc., to mention a few drops in the bucket of feminine lushness that forms a kind of milky way in the poetic firmament of the time (likewise all times);—indeed I think she is every bit as good as Elizabeth Browning. And here it will be probably evident that most of her most earnest devotees could not ask for more. I can only say that I also do not greatly care for Mme. Browning. And on top of my dislike for this lady, Tennyson, Thompson, Chatterton, Byron, Moore, Milton, and several more, I have the apparent brassiness to call myself a person of rather catholic admirations. But you will also notice that I *do* run joyfully toward Messrs. Poe, Whitman, Shakespeare, Keats, Shelley, Coleridge, John Donne!!!, John Webster!!!, Marlowe, Baudelaire, Laforgue, Dante, Cavalcanti, Li Po, and a host of others. Oh I wish we had an evening to talk over poetic creeds,—it is ridiculous to attempt it in a letter. I can only apologize by saying that if my work seems needlessly sophisticated it is because I am only interested in adding what seems to me something really *new* to what *has* been written. Unless one has some new, intensely personal viewpoint to record, say on the eternal feelings of love, and the suitable personal idiom to employ in the act, I say, why write about it? Nine chances out of ten, if you know where in the past to look, you will find words already written in the more-or-less exact tongue of your soul. And the complaint to be made against nine out of ten poets is just this,—that you are apt to find their sentiments much better expressed perhaps four hundred years past. And it is not that Miss Millay fails entirely, but that I often am made to hear too many echoes in her things, that I cannot like her as well as you do. With her equipment Edna Millay is bound to succeed to the appreciative applause of a fairly large audience. And for you, who I rather suppose have not gone into this branch of literature with as much enthusiasm as myself, she is a creditable heroine.

I admit to a slight leaning toward the esoteric, and am perhaps not to be taken seriously. I am fond of things of great fragility, and also and especially of the kind of poetry John Donne represents, a dark musky, brooding, speculative vintage, at once sensual and spiritual, and singing rather the beauty of experience than innocence.

As you did not "get" my idiom in "Chaplinesque," I feel rather like doing my best to explain myself. I am moved to put Chaplin with the poets (of today); hence the "we." In other words, he, especially in *The Kid,* made me feel myself, as a poet, as being "in the same boat" with him. Poetry, the human feelings, "the kitten," is so crowded out of the humdrum, rushing, mechanical scramble of today that the man who would preserve them must duck and camouflage for dear life to keep them or keep himself from annihilation. I have since learned that I am by no means alone in seeing these things in the buffooneries of the tragedian, Chaplin, (if you want to read the opinions of the London and Paris presses, see *Literary Digest,* Oct. 8th) and in the poem I have tried to express these "social sympathies" in words corresponding somewhat to the antics of the actor. I may have failed, as only a small number of those I have shown it to have responded with any clear answer,—but on the other hand, I realize that the audience for my work will always be quite small. I freely admit to a liking for the thing, myself,—in fact I have to like something of my own once in a while being so hard to please anyway.

The job I mentioned lasted just one day. I took the men out and carried the thing through to success, sore feet, and numb limbses,—but,—there was no work to be done next day, nor the next,—and I got tired of trailing around hoping for only $2.50 for a fortune, and don't care whether there is little or much awaiting me there now, having hit the employment trail again toward other fields. When I once get pastured again, I'll praise even Edna Millay—may even buy her *Second April* (if it is in Season) and not bore you so much with long diatribes on Poetry. Just now, though, that is all I have. Can't even buy the books I long to read, like *Three Soldiers, Erik Dorn,* and the new *Little Review* (Quarterly—AND $2.00). Write me soon and cheer me up. Just for fun, look up the poems of Donne in the Library and read some of the short lyrics like "The Apparition," "A Jet Ring Sent," "The Prohibition," "The Ecstasy," and some of the longer things like "The Progress of the Soul," etc., if you feel intrigued.

79: To GORHAM MUNSON

Cleveland   *Nov. 1st, '21*

Dear Gorham: —/—/ Yes,—I much wish I could share your horizons, —instead of retracing day after day a few familiar circles of routine·

& thought. Keep on writing me your bright kindly letters. They are
a lantern of hope and a warmth to the heart. I sometimes wonder if,
without you, I should have kept writing so long.

Just read *Erik Dorn* and am shy a little of criticizing it. Undoubtedly it is a fine piece of work,—and an odd addition to Am.
literature. Almost European in viewpoint. I cannot, though, yet
make sure whether Hecht has his tongue in his cheek part of the
time or not. Hecht is a virtuoso, and arouses suspicions that one
would never feel for Dreiser or Anderson. One sees an influence of
Joyce in the book,—diluted or "rationalized" just enough to be
more pleasing to the public taste. Carl Sandburg and Anderson are
given parts in the scenery in an interesting way. —/—/

80: TO GORHAM MUNSON

[*Cleveland*]   *Nov. 3rd, '21*

Dear Gorham: —/—/ You are very right about the poems. I can't
blame you for not seeing as much in "Chaplinesque" as myself
because I realize that the technique of the thing is virtuosic and
open to all kinds of misinterpretations. Maybe, though, since you
have seen *The Kid* which "inspired" it, you have got nearer to my
meaning. For me, it holds double the interest of "Pastorale" which
is more perfectly done, but to me, not so rich. Chaplin may be a
sentimentalist, after all, but he carries the theme with such power
and universal portent that sentimentality is made to transcend itself into a new kind of tragedy, eccentric, homely and yet brilliant.
It is because I feel that I have captured the arrested climaxes and
evasive victories of his gestures in words, somehow, that I like the
poem as much as anything I have done. But we will see. My mind
changes sometimes sooner than I plan. I was much surprised that
Sherwood Anderson should like it, who is not prone to care for complicated expressions. He was, further, more or less in agreement with
you about the sea poem.[1] —/—/

Further time and thought on *Erik Dorn* lessen my opinion of it.
It hangs somewhere between the prose symphonies of Huysmans and
the poetic symphonies of Aiken. Impressionistic. However, there is
little character. As long as we have *Ulysses* and *Tarr* to praise we
need not spend too much breath on it, recognizing it, nevertheless,
as a hopeful sign, not much more. One misses any actual sincerity,—
and somehow the issue or accusation of meretriciousness creeps in.

1. "The Bottom of the Sea Is Cruel." Sent to Munson, Oct. 1, 1921.

It brings back to me something about Hecht that Saphier once told me:—"A brilliant fellow," he said. "He can sit down to a typewriter and reel off that stuff by the yard. Has three or four of them (short stories) on hand at once." This was apropos of the really fine little things of his that were appearing in *The L.R.* then. In fact I am moved into sympathy with Seldes' review of it in the Oct. *Dial* which you will have read by this time. —/—/

Tonight I attend the weekly "salon" that Lescaze gives to his friends. There will be banter and chatter enough to be tiresome. Somehow, when there are women present (the kind one has around here) no conversation can be had uninterrupted by little compliments, concessions to them, etc. They insist upon being the center of attention irrespective of their ability to take part in any argument. Consequently there are interminable innuendoes and clucking and puffings that never terminate anywhere. One of the few women who would carefully avoid this kind of thing is Margaret Anderson. Hommage to Margaret!!

The Dada dramas are tres amusant,—but—well—alright56789——*!!

81: To GORHAM MUNSON

Cleveland,   *Nov. 21st.*

Your letter about the *Gargoyle* plan has just come and as I haven't written you for some time, I'm giving some kind of answer, however unworthy. These enclosed poems you are welcome to use if you care to. — — — — *The L. R.* has it ["Chaplinesque"] in hand now, but I shall probably not hear from them about it for months and should they decide to take it,—I cannot see that its publication in France should complicate matters any. The same applies to "Black Tambourine" which came out misprinted in *The D.D.* last July. I would like to see it printed right sometime and it occurs to me that this may be an opportunity. I am doing nothing new worth while, so I can't send you anything else. If you get the names your letter mentions together as contributors you will have something worth while. Burke's contribution to the new *L.R.* quarterly just out is about the only good thing in it. I don't need to go on about it, as you have probably seen it in Paris by this time. About the only thing to be gathered from Pound's article on Brancusi is that Pound wishes to avoid being obvious at the cost of no matter what else. For myself—I [have] just finished a week's trial at selling real estate—of which, of course, I didn't sell any. Trying now to get into a bookstore to help out during the Christmas rush.

There is nothing but gall and disgust in me,—and there is nothing
more for me to tell you but familiar, all-too-familiar complaints. I
wish I could cultivate a more graceful mask against all this. —/—/

82: To GORHAM MUNSON

Cleveland   *Nov. 26th, '21*

Dear Gorham: —/—/ I've been having a wonderful time diving into
Ben Jonson, so you see I haven't been so far off, after all. After one
has read *Bartholomew Fair* it isn't so hard to see where Synge got
his start,—a start toward a husky folk-element in the drama. I can
see myself from now rapidly joining Josephson in a kind of Eliza-
bethan fanaticism. You have doubtless known my long-standing
friendship with Donne, Webster, and Marlowe. Now I have another
Mermaid "conjugal" to strengthen the tie. The fact is, I can find
nothing in modern work to come up to the verbal richness, irony
and emotion of these folks, and I would like to let them influence
me as much as they can in the interpretation of modern moods,—
somewhat as Eliot has so beautifully done. There are parts of his
"Gerontion" that you can find almost bodily in Webster and Jonson.
Certain Elizabethans and Laforgue have played a tremendous part
in Eliot's work, and you catch hints of his great study of these writers
in his *Sacred Grove*. I don't want to imitate Eliot, of course,—but I
have come to the stage now where I want to carefully choose my
most congenial influences and, in a way, "cultivate" their influence.
I can say with J[osephson] that the problem of form becomes harder
and harder for me every day. I am not at all satisfied with anything
I have thus far done, mere shadowings, and too slight to satisfy me.
I have never, so far, been able to present a vital, living and tangible,—a positive emotion to my satisfaction. For as soon as I attempt such an act I either grow obvious or ordinary, and abandon
the thing at the second line. Oh! it is hard! One must be drenched
in words, literally soaked with them to have the right ones form
themselves into the proper pattern at the right moment. When they
come, as they did in "Pastorale" (thin, but rather good), they come
as things in themselves; it is a matter of felicitous juggling!; and no
amount of will or emotion can help the thing a bit. So you see I believe with Sommer that the "Ding an Sich" method is ultimately the
only satisfactory creative principle to follow. But I also find that
J[osephson] stirred up a hornet's nest in me this summer with his
words about getting away from current formulae, from Heine to
Wallace Stevens, by experimentation in original models, etc., and

my reaction to this stimulation is to work away from the current impressionism as much as possible. I mean such "impressionism" as the
Cocteau poem (trans.) in *The Little Review,* which you have probably seen. Dada (maybe I am wrong, but you will correct me) is
nothing more to me than the dying agonies of this movement, mal-
adie moderne. I may be even carried back into "rime and rhythm"
before I get through, provided I can carry these encumbrances as
deftly and un-selfconsciously as, say, Edward Thomas sometimes did.
I grow to like my "Black Tambourine" more, for this reason, than
before. It becomes to my mind a kind of diminutive model of ambition, simply pointing a direction. S'much for this endless tirade,
but write as usual and keep me cheered and momentarily thrilled.

Maybe J[osephson] has already started on his novel, burlesquing
the Americans in the Quartier, that he intended. Tell him to send
me some poetry, anything he is writing. It's sure to be better than
anything the magazines offer here.

83: To Gorham Munson

Cleveland   *December the tenth*

Dear Gorham: Your letter in French (which innovation I like)
reached me yesterday, a welcome evening stimulant after the day's
work. For I am, in a way, very glad to announce that I've been busy
for the last two weeks at selling books in a store here during the seasonal "rush." This is, in all probability, entirely a temporary tent
for me,—but it has enabled me, though intensely occupied, to get
free of the money complex that had simply reduced me to ashes.
This item added to a total lack of any sex life for a long period had
left me so empty that I gave up insulting you with a mere heap of
stones for a letter, and though I haven't more to offer you now, I
have sufficient interest again in the activity of writing to make my
meagreness seem less obvious. Erotic experience is stumbled upon
occasionally by accident, and the other evening I was quite nicely
entertained, in *my* usual way, of course. And thus the spell is broken!
I can't help remarking also that this "breaker of the spell" is one
very familiar with your present haunts, "La Rotonde," etc., etc.,
only of a few years back. You see, then, that one may enjoy a few
Parisian sophistications even in Cleveland!

The *Ulysses* situation is terrible to think on. I shall be eternally
grateful to you if you can manage to smuggle my already-subscribed-

for copy home with you. If this will in any chance be possible, please let me send you the cash for purchase, etc., at the proper time. I *must* have this book!

De Gourmont's *Une Coeur Virginal* has just been published here, (trans. by Aldous Huxley), and I have snatched it up against its imminent suppression along with *Jurgen* and other masterpieces. If this is a fair sample of its author, and it's supposed to be, I cannot see how his *Physique d'Amour,* translated by Pound and to be published by Boni & Liveright, will ever get beyond the printers' hands. Yet how mellow and kindly is the light from de Gourmont! One hates to see him on the tables with Zane Grey and Rex Beach. Maybe, after all (and since I have procured my volume), it will not be so heart-rending to see the "destruction" of the jealous Puritan at work again. Two weeks of book-service to the "demands of the public" in a store have bred curious changes of attitude toward the value of popularity (of the slightest sort) in my mind. The curious "unread" that slumber lengthily on the shelves, and whose names are never called, are much nearer my envy than I had once thought they might be from the mere standpoint of neglect. This pawing over of gift-book classics in tooled leather bindings, etc., etc., is a sight to never forget. Poor dear Emerson must slumber badly. Aristocratic is Whitman, though—no one ever calls for that "democrat" any more than for Landor or Donne. And Edgar Guest and Service, death's-heads both, are rampant.

Of course you have heard of Anderson's winning of *The Dial* prize. I was quite certain of it anyway, but intensely gratified at the fact nonetheless. He will probably go to Mexico now as money was all he needed. He wrote me an answer recently to my criticism of *Erik Dorn,* praising parts of it much and damning others. The book still puzzles me, which makes me dislike it a little more than ever. As a whole it is deficient, but I have always admitted certain parts good. But when one compares it with such a book as Anderson's *Triumph of the Egg,* it fades out terribly. This latter is an anthology of recent short stories of Anderson and re-reading them together I get the most violent reaction. He has written of ghastly desolations which are only too evident in my own experience and on every hand. I am more enthusiastic than ever in my praise for him although I feel in an odd way, that he has, like a diver, touched bottom in a certain sense, and that his future work must manifest certain changes of a more positive character than the bare statement of reality, or conclude his promise. —/—/

84: TO GORHAM MUNSON

[*Cleveland*]   *Dec. 25th, '21*

Dear Gorham: Your letter arriving a few days ago, of the 5th, and the note of the seventh announcing my presence on the boulevards (in Chaplinesque attire) have provided me with rich materials for a kind of Christmas tree, at least as thrilling as any of remotest childhood memories. Names and presences glitter and fascinate with all kinds of exotic suggestions on the branches. I can be grateful to you for the best of Christmas donations, as I can thank you for the main part of my mental and imaginative sustenance of the last six months, weary and tormented as they have been. And now things seem, at least, to look a little better for me. I have been asked to remain on for a brief period in the capacity of book-clerk, and there is a possibility in sight of my gaining a very promising position soon in a very high-class advertising house here that has the attraction of the best connections with the largest agencies in New York and elsewhere. At least my interview with the "authorities" there today proved favorable to me, and if I can only manage to write them the proper kind of letter and "sell myself" as they ridiculously put it, I may secure myself something profitable. Leastwise, however, I have paid off an obligation that worried me and had a little change to spend during the last few weeks which has worked unbelievable miracles on my spirit. My work has been so hectic during the last month that I have not had time to write you, much less poems, but I have a feeling that now that the rush is over and the New Year started, I shall again do something. You see I am promising again.

You cannot imagine how interesting to me have been your opinions of the personalities you have come in contact with. Your opportunities in this direction have far exceeded my happiest anticipations for you. It strikes me that you have met about all the personalities in the younger left-wing at all worth while. —/—/

It has been very gratifying, also, to hear of your amiable progress with Josephson. His "tightening and hardening" effect on one is exactly the compliment I owe to him. In a way he is cold as ice, having a most astonishing faculty for depersonization,—and on the other hand, you have no doubt found a certain affectionate propensity in his nature that is doubly pleasant against the rather frigidly intellectual relief of the rest of him. He likes you much, and wrote me so, also sending me some poems to submit to *The D.D.* which I cannot fancy as having a ghost of a show in such an uneven corner. But he needs money, and I shall be glad to do anything in my power to help him along,—not worrying, however, very, very much, as he has a flexibility and resourcefulness that I envy.

—/—/ If I were only in N.Y. I would see to it that S[ommer]'s work were given its due,—but that time will have to wait. Meanwhile he shows not the slightest inclination to wilt. As I said, his achievements present one gorgeous surprise after another. A mutual friend of ours here recently died, a Nietzschean and thorough appreciator of all the best, who has pursued his lonely way in America since the age of fifteen when he left his family in Norway on account of religious differences. Bill and I were among the pallbearers at this funeral, where there were only a few others present, although all appreciative of what the man was. I can't go into detail, but the affair was tremendous, especially the finale at the crematorium. It was beautiful, but left me emotionally bankrupt last Sunday, the day following. That funeral was one of the few beautiful things that have happened to me in Cleveland.

Now for a brief résumé of American literature. It is, in a way, hopefully significant that Anderson's *Winesburg* has been issued by Boni and Liveright in their Modern Library with a very fine introduction by Ernest Boyd which gives much praise to *The L. R.* for having had the acumen to introduce Anderson to the world. —/—/

The Dial for December has a fine article in it on American painting by Rosenfeld, singling out Hartley for extra and very intelligent praise. It also includes a fairly good poem by Malcolm Cowley, a rather disappointing article on Flaubert by Middleton Murry, and an atrocious piece of dull nonsense by Bodenheim. The new *Shadowland* is [as] far from thrilling as those tepid baths it did offer last summer, and the *Ladies Home Journal* and the *Atlantic* are as bouncing as ever.

This is all for tonight. We have a houseful of indiscriminate relatives and it has been hard to collect myself for even this potpourri, but I have more to say when I can get to it. I need time (a natural requirement with me for all writing or thought) to sit Buddha-like for a couple of hours every day and let things sift themselves into some semblance of order in my brain. But I haven't' had the opportunity for such operations for weeks, and may never,—until which time I pray you to be contented as you can by such thrusts in haste as this letter.

Your figure haunts me like a kind of affectionate caress through all sorts of difficulties. You are always my final and satisfactory "court of appeal," and it is useless to attempt to tell you how much this means to me. So believe me when I tell you that I love you, and plan and plan for the glorious day when we shall get knees under the table and talk, and talk, and talk. The inefficacy of my letters to you always troubles me.

1 9 2 2

85: To Sherwood Anderson

Cleveland   *Jan. 10th*

Dear Anderson: Waiting on shoppers in a book store during the holiday hurricane deferred my answer to your letter. I was glad to get any kind of work, however, after my empty-pocketed summer and fall. Now I am working as a copy-writer for the Corday and Gross Co. here which you may have heard of. I like this better than any bread-and-butter work I've ever done. You were right about the real estate job. Ogling poor people for small investments against their will didn't appeal to me very long. I had given it up before you wrote.

If I can satisfy the requirements of my position here, I shall feel a little hope returning for the satisfaction of a few aims again. I mean, of course, to turn out a little verse or prose this winter. When out of work I am not able to rid myself of worries enough to accomplish anything. Some pecuniary assurances seem necessary to me to any opening of the creative channels. Now things begin to look a little better for me.

I saw your story "The Contract" in the last *Broom,* and would like to offer a criticism. It may be an infraction, but if it is I want to ask your forgiveness. This story in some ways strikes me as inferior to the intensity and beauty of your other recent work, and I have an idea that it is something you wrote quite a while ago. Coming from anyone else, I would think, "This is good; but this fellow is trying to imitate Anderson and can't quite do it."

I wouldn't attempt any suggestions nor try to point out any places. Your work is always too much a composite whole for that critical sort of prodding to yield anything. I only felt this story as somehow an anti-climax to the amazing sense of beauty I recently got in re-reading the short stories you have done during the last few years that are collected together in the *Egg* volume. Please pardon me for this doubtless unnecessary comment. It is only in the light of my own desires and feeling in such circumstances that I have ventured it.

In my own work I find the problem of style and form becoming more and more difficult as time goes on. I imagine that I am interested in this style of writing much more than you are. Perhaps, though, we include the same features under different terms. In verse this feature can become a preoccupation, to be enjoyed for its own sake. I do not think you will sympathize with me very strongly on this point, but, of course, if you got as much pleasure out of finding instances of it in other writers as I do, you would see what I mean. For instance, when I come to such a line as the following from John Donne,—I am thrilled — — — — ["Of the Progresse of the Soule, The Second Anniversary," ll. 296-98]. Or take another, called "The Expiration": —/—/ [ll. 1-12]. What I want to get is just what is so beautifully done in this poem,—an "interior" form, a form that is so thorough and intense as to dye the words themselves with a peculiarity of meaning, slightly different maybe from the ordinary definition of them separate from the poem. If you remember my "Black Tambourine" you will perhaps agree with me that I have at least accomplished this idea once. My aims make writing slow for me, and so far I have done practically nothing,—but I can wait for slow improvements rather more easily than I can let a lot of stuff loose that doesn't satisfy me. There is plenty of that in the publishing houses and magazines every day to amuse the folks that like it. This may very well be a tiresome ranting for you, but I think you will like the quotation anyway.

What are you going to do this winter: go to Mexico as you had thought of? I was all ready to scrape around for money enough to start for Europe when this job came along, and I thought I had better take it. Two friends of mine, however, have been in Paris for some time, writing me letters that made me foam at my moorings, and the desire to break loose has been strong.

If you aren't too busy write me. A friend of mine, Lescaze, was in N. Y. over Christmas and says he had a very pleasant talk with you one evening at Paul Rosenfeld's.

86: TO GORHAM MUNSON

[Cleveland]   Jan. 23rd, '22

Dear Gorham: I come to my first evening, free and alone, in some time, and recognize quite plainly that I have neglected you. There are so many rather interesting people around this winter that there is always something or other doing. A concert to go to, a soirée,— and then since I have been writing ads a certain amount of hang-

over work to be done evenings sometimes,—that altogether I don't
like it. But I like my work and am wonderfully treated at the office.
Never guessed a commercial institution could be organized on such
a decent basis. And they actually will come of their own accord and
tell you that they are pleased with the work you are doing for
them!!!!!!!!!! I pass my goggle-eyed father on the streets now without
a tremor! I go on mad carouses with Bill Sommer wherein we begin
with pigs' feet and sauerkraut and end with Debussy's "Gradus ad
Parnassum" in the "ivory tower." Around Ernest Bloch at the Institute of Music here are gathered some interesting folks from all
over everywhere. There is even a French restaurant here where the
proprietress stands at the cashier's desk reading *La Nouvelle Revue
Francaise* and where wonderful steaks with mushrooms are served—
alas, everything, including real garçons, except vin. The place looks
like a sentence without any punctuation, or, if you prefer, this letter.

And now, mon cher, willy-nilly as it all may be, we come to your
magazine. I don't want to hurt you at all, but I must confess to little
or no enthusiasm at the prospect of another small magazine, full of
compressed dynamite as yours might well be. Unless one has half a
million or so, what's the use of adding to the other little repercus-
sions that dwindle out after a few issues!? Don't waste your time
with it all, is my advice. Much better sit down and pound on your
typewriter, or go toting mss. around to stolid editors. Listen,—
there is now *some* kind of magazine that will print one's work however bad or good it is. The "arty" book stores bulge and sob with
them all. I pray you invest your hard-earned money in neckties,
theatre tickets or something else good for the belly or the soul,—
but don't throw it away in paper and inefficient typography. Don't
come home three months sooner for the prospects of that rainbow.

No one will especially appreciate it — — — —. By all this you must
not think that I have joined the Right Wing to such an extent that
I am rollicking in F. Scott Fitzgerald. No,—but by the straight and
narrow path swinging to the south of the village DADA I have
arrived at a somewhat and abashed posture of reverence before the
statues of Ben Jonson, Michael Drayton, Chaucer, sundry others
already mentioned. The precious rages of dear Matty [Josephson]
somehow don't seem to swerve me from this position. He is, it
strikes me, altogether unsteady. Of course, since Mallarmé and
Huysmans were elegant weepers it is up to the following generation
to haw-haw gloriously! Even dear old Buddha-face de Gourmont
is passé. Well, I suppose it is up to one in Paris to do as the Romans
do, but it all looks too easy to me from Cleveland, Cuyhoga County,

God's country. But Matty will always glitter when he walks provided the man in front of him has not sparkled,—which we hope he never does, of course,—and so I am happy to hear from him always about his latest change of mind. Quite seriously Matty is thrilling, in prose especially. His performance is always agreeable despite my inability to sympathize with his theories. Paris seems to be a good place for him to work and I suppose he will stay there at least until his contes are published. —/—/

87: To William Wright

Cleveland, O.   *February 11, 1922*

Dear Bill: Don't let me keep on worrying. Your visit was a great pleasure to me, resulting in the renewal of old contacts and the discoveries of many new ones. I am so much interested in you now, that I am in danger of pestering you with all kinds of advice and admonitions. One of these is: not to let the caprices of any unmellow ladies result in your unbalance or extreme discomfiture. Even the best of them, at times, know not and care not what they do. They have the faculty of producing very debilitating and thoroughly unprofitable effects on gentlemen who put themselves too much in their hands. Woman was not meant to occupy this position. It was only the Roman Catholic Church who gave it to her. Greeks, Romans, and Egyptians knew better how to handle her. I suggest your reading De Gourmont's *Virgin Heart* for a delicate dissection of this kind of problem. De Gourmont was something more than a purely "literary critic," you know. He was one of the most thorough students of physiology and psychology of the modern world. He was an adept scientist of the emotions. Stendhal was another, but less clear.

All this suffering is quite romantic and beautiful, you know, but you pay a stupid price for it. I can't help saying these things because of my interest and because I saw you go away in ominous style. I hope you haven't been ill, and that you have merely forgotten to write me.

I have been through two or three of these cataclysms myself, harder than yours because of their unusual and unsympathetic situations. Maybe I have gained something by them, I don't know,— but it is certain that I lost a great deal too.

88: To Gorham Munson

[Cleveland?]   *Feb. 25"—'22*

Dear Gorham: Arrived yesterday the new *Gargoyle*. Altogether not such a poor issue as Matty predicted in one of his letters of last month. Your translations amuse me without interesting me as thoroughly as your nicely administered spanking of McAlmon. Maybe your translations (or rather selections) would excite me somewhat if I weren't somehow so hopelessly tired of Art and theories about Art lately. I can't quite account for it—never having suffered from indigestion like this before. It is, after all, I suppose, because I have nothing of my own to "give," and therefore feel so little at stake in all the deluge of production and argument that I grow either bewildered or else indifferent. I am going through a difficult readjustment right now, besides meeting a period in my so-called "creative life" where neither my conscious self nor my unconscious self can get enough "co-operation" from the other to do anything worth while. I wrote something recently which I thought, on the moment, was good. Today I have faced it as a hopeless failure, disjointed and ugly and vain. I am only momentarily depressed by these facts, however, as I am kept so busy with my ad writing that I haven't time to think much about it. −/−/

89: TO WILLIAM WRIGHT

Jamestown, New York   *March 2, 1922*

Dear Bill: This is my second excursion to this place, no doubt somewhat familiar to you,—having been here part of last week. It's a matter of business for the Co. ("investigation of the product," in ad. lingo) and I rather enjoy getting out of Cleveland for a day or so. I've been getting out a catalog for the Art Metal folks here and puzzling my head over blue prints and figures until I have become somewhat dull. −/−/

By this time I suppose you are back again and full tilt in your customary carousels. I was glad to know that the trouble with you was only "physiological." By this time you have probably read some of De Gourmont's observations on that sort of thing, and, wise man!, were fully experienced to appreciate them. What an awful lot of novel forms there are! The novel is the most flexible literary form there is. It permits the freest and completest expression. Have you read Louis Hemon's *Maria Chapdelaine* yet? The young French emigrant who wrote it died shortly afterward, but for what it intends it is one of the most finished things one could hope for. Human emotion in it is like delicate pastel tinted flowers on a background of midnight black. The black terrific power of the forest and winter threatens continually behind every word in the action. But I am nowhere near so enthused about this book as I am about Gogol's

Taras Bulba that I read on the train recently. I think someone has called it the Russian *Iliad*. It is certainly not secondary to *The Iliad* in many ways. That sting and tang of those Cossack adventures are something I won't forget, and the hero, old Taras, is altogether memorable. This is something you *must* read.

I don't want to go any further without thanking you for your "Ballade." I find so much that is good in it that I am tempted beyond the proper respect for your very dégagé gesture of presentation in your letter, and want to risk the impropriety of some criticism of it. The main faults of it are faults inherent with the form you used. I do not, as you know, insist by any means on vers libre forms. But it is just when I see such a thing as your ballade with the (unavoidable) tiresome repetitions of sound or rhyme, that I am most moved to applaud even the slouchy vers libre work that seems to "get over" its meaning or lack of meaning at least without that mechanical insistence of certain formal patterns that can sometimes infuriate me. For instance, after "sweet, feet, deceit, conceit, and fleet" have all successively pecked at the ear, along comes "discreet retreat"!!, giving the whole poem at the point a tone of the neatest mean-ness. And that sort of tone is exactly what you do not want,—at least not along with some of your quite exquisite imagery that speaks in largeness of a full heart.

The first verse, the first four lines especially, is fine, and the idea behind that "discreet retreat behind sophistications of bread and meat" is good. It would be improved by using another and richer word than "sophistications" just to *improve* the sophistication a little, however. I feel this way,—that however you wrote this poem,— in jest, literary exercise, or emotionally,—it proves distinct poetic possibilities in you, which, whether you care to follow or not, are still there. Why don't you work this poem into an easier form or perhaps into a vers libre form? I could do it to show you what I mean, but that would take all the fun out of it for you. Forms as strict as the ballade, can, in my opinion, be used satisfactorily for only very artificial subjects, or abstract themes.

I've been doing something myself, but don't feel satisfied enough with it yet to send it.

90: To Gorham Munson

[*Cleveland*]   *March 2 '22*

Dear Gorham: —/—/ Just now, I apologize for it, I am so much worried by family finances that it's hard for me to do anything more than my work. My mother's alimony has reached its limited time and she is preparing (at 45 yrs. of age!) to go out into the world to learn to make her living!

I, naturally, shall henceforward be called upon not only to "keep" myself, but to lend as much of a helping hand as is possible in this predicament. So, it's hard work for some time ahead for me, I guess. My present wages just suffice for my own limited requirements. My pater is too much of a cad to really do anything for his former wife except what the agreement between them says. The fact that this was made when she was partially out of mind and very ill, makes no difference to him.

However, I shall not resign myself to the proverbial and sentimental fate of the "might-have-been" artist without a few more strenuosities. I will have to expect a certain tardiness of gait, however.

I have just read Aldous Huxley's latest, *Crome Yellow*, one of those things that evokes much quiet laughter and holds delightful savours, at least for a contemporary, between its covers. — — —

As no good plays ever get to Cleveland, and the Chicago opera not at all this year, my outside entertainment has been meagre. Only a symphony concert every other week, and little new there.

Ernest Bloch, however, conducted two weeks ago his *Trois Poèmes Juifs* which were magnificent enough for Solomon to have marched & sung to. I occasionally pass him on the streets or in the aisles of the auditorium, and realize that genius, after all, may walk in Cleveland. — — — —

91: TO GORHAM MUNSON

[Cleveland]   *March 24th*

Dear Gorham: —/—/ You know I shall talk it [*Secession*] up,—but the worst is that most of my acquaintances are totally unfitted for enthusiasms of this sort. The indifference you will encounter when you return to these States you must be prepared to face. Every one is suddenly and enormously *busy*—making money, attending teas, motoring, starving—God knows what all. It makes me reel! Life is too scattered for me to savor it any more. Probably this is only on account of my present work which demands the most frequent jerks of the imagination from one thing to another, still—the war certainly has changed things a bit here. The question in my mind is, how much less vertigo are we going to suffer in the latter whirl than we did in the first blows and commotion. If I am drifting into nonsense, it must be because I'm getting no time lately for anything but work.

If you come home in May—one of the first things you must do is to make me a good visit. You will be free to come, whereas there is a considerable doubt now about my coming east at all this summer. Here in my tower-study, rimmed with Sommer paintings and grey cracked paper, you will have a good chance to focus your recent observations — — — —. Besides,—you have never seen any of the midwest, and it ought to be part of your education. —/—/

92: TO GORHAM MUNSON

[*Cleveland*]   *March 29th,'22*

Dear Gorham: —/—/ With the banal arrival of spring and weeks of rain and cloudy skies, I have again fallen in love! I guess I might about as well take up quarters at La Rotonde—and be done with it. However, *something* must be indulged in to make Cleveland interesting.

93: TO WILLIAM WRIGHT

Cleveland, O.   *April 2nd*

Dear Bill: Your prose is much better than your verse. I don't know how to explain—perhaps if I saw more of your poetry I might,— but certainly the story you recently sent me makes me quite certain of it. The poem has the tepid and pubescent steam in it that always seems to issue from the environs of a college campus. It is college adolescence in only a slight advance from the ordinary. It has enough in it to "get by" on the first reading with a rather pleasing effect. But the second discovers much to be criticized. It's not in the technique but in the attitude that I blame you for this. You have a real flair for phrasing, and two years ago I should have probably praised you for the poem.

But now let's turn to the story. It is vital and well told. Nobody can imitate Anderson, of course, but that is not what we want anyway. Your story stands on its own feet quite well. In some places it is too accented. I say this in spite of my realization of the intent of it and also via recommending the very effective literary device of under-accentuation in just the right place to produce "overtones" of overwhelming effect. Then you could afford to be more sparing of adjectives! But I won't rail any further! You certainly are displaying evidence and promises of a hopeful career. If you don't get too engrossed in commerce after you leave college the break will do you good, I think. No matter how "free" one may be in college, the campus world with its idols and codes is very different from the world outside. Don't think, please, that I'm decrying education, it's only a mention that things are somehow harder and a little "scarey." "Practical people" suddenly surround one, and they have such an insistence about being listened to. —/—/

The more speed I develop in ad-writing the more occasion I'm given to use it, and I seem to need to keep in touch with so many people that the hours spent at home are too few. This hankering for continual conversational excitement is one of my weaknesses. What I *should* be doing is working. Truly, on this gay Sunday afternoon, my conscience is weighted.

94: TO GORHAM MUNSON

[Cleveland]   *April 19"—'22*

Dear Gorham: —/—/ The two copies of *Secession* reached me yesterday. Of course they were immediately and doubly devoured. But right here I ought to stop—I have so many things to say about it. —/—/

I find I have many, at least several disagreements with you. I can't say nearly so much for Matty's poem as you do—I mean the Café phallicus. The Tzara poem is perfectly flat. The Cowley poem is encouraging, although dreadfully alike something he had published in one of the last *L.R's.* The Aragon prose is, in its odd way, a quite beautiful thing. But what has happened to Matty!?! And,—just *why* is Apollinaire so portentous a god? Will radios, flying machines, and cinemas have such a great effect on poetry in the end? All this talk of Matty's is quite stimulating, but it's like coffee—twenty-four hours afterward not much remains to work with. It is metallic and pointillistic—not derogatory terms to my mind at all, but somehow thin,— a little too slender and "smart"—after all.

O Matty must be amusing himself perfectly in Paris. And so he took you to be a real, honest-to-God disreputable and commercial editor! Serve you right, you bad boy, following the primrose path of the magazines! —/—/

95: TO CHARMION WIEGAND

Cleveland, Ohio   *May 6th,'22*

Dear Charmion: —/—/ You must put me in direct touch with Emil Reeck, however, as soon as possible. I have just written Anderson all about the plan, and shall rush the answer to you as soon as possible. But letters take such a dreadfully long time to get back and forth and

you say you are leaving Berlin just about a month from now!! I somehow feel as though I were rushing to catch a train!

I very much agree with you that Germany would be really appreciative of Anderson, and they ought to have him. However, as Huebsch, Anderson's publisher, is himself a German and very much in
touch with Berlin, I suspect that already translation arrangements
may have been started. Anderson is having a great enough vogue
here at present to turn the head of anyone but a pessimist like
Anderson. He is, I understand, very much made of by *The Nouvelle
Revue Francaise* Group (headed by Jacques Copeau) and has been
translated into French. His trip to Europe last summer put him in
direct touch with all the younger crowd in France. However, we'll
see about Germany. There is still a chance.

Did I tell you that our friend, Gorham Munson, has been in Europe all this time? He is the one we went with to that meeting
against prohibition, restricted speech, or something at some church
on Central Park W. one night. Gilbert Cannan spoke, etc. Munson
has been quite a bit in Berlin, and from Vienna has started a new
literary magazine of his own, *Secession,* which is (first number) just
seeping into this country. Munson must have just arrived in New
York again, is due to anyway. He expects to print his magazine in
Vienna right along as he can get it done there so much cheaper. His
magazine is filled with quite ultra things by EE Cummings, Marianne Moore, Slater Brown, Matthew Josephson, Malcolm Cowley,
etc., all of whom were with him in Paris last fall and winter when the
inception of the magazine took place. I am sceptical about all such
dear, darling and courageous and brief attempts, but shall do my
best to make his magazine a success, despite my literary and philosophical differences with him in this project. —/—/

Thinking it might interest Chaplin to read the poem I wrote
about him, I sent it to him,—and with the result that today I've received a most delightful acknowledgment of the same. . . . You
know I worship Chaplin's work. Think he is the greatest living actor
I've seen, and the prime interpreter of the soul imposed upon by
modern civilization. —/—/

You asked about French books. I have not been reading much
modern work, but I am in touch with a good deal of it through a
French-Swiss painter friend of mine here who has modern tastes and
is in touch with Europe and the best of it all the time. —/—/

Any of the works of Andre Gide are good, same of older ones like
Rimbaud, Laforgue (Jules) and Guillaume Apollinaire. The latter's
Calligrammes and *Alcools* (poems) are just being talked about in

this country. I am mad about Laforgue, but he is hard to translate and very acid.

There is a wild bird and fashionable, Jean Cocteau, who writes plays, poetry and novelties that I understand is the present king of les boulevards, but I haven't read him. The scene in France today is, I judge, about as scattered as the Genoa Conference. Everybody is being intensely clever, and everybody is also worried about what new standard tomorrow may erect. However, I have tried to name people here who have already been more-or-less settled and accepted, or who bid fair to be.

The people I am closest to in English are Yeats, Eliot, Pound, and the dear great Elizabethans like Marlowe, Webster, Donne and Drayton, whom I never weary of. I've lately been enjoying Melville's *Moby Dick,* however. —/—/

I'll write to you as soon as I hear from Anderson. If you come across any good monograph on Cezanne in Germany I would be glad to pay you for it as soon as you get back. Otherwise—with the exception of a good book illustrating Greek Vases well, I can't think of anything.

96: TO GORHAM MUNSON

[*Cleveland*]					*May 16th '22*

Hooray Whoop La! That little note on the back of the envelope meant a lot to me. And I somehow feel good that you are once more with me on the same stretch of land! Jump right on the train, old dear, and I'll meet you at the station. I'm very anxious to see you. I want you to meet this *great* Bill Sommer—and tell me all about all you have done and seen. I have the assurance now that you'll come as soon as you can get the money, and it makes me quite happy.

Your rough & tedious transition back to the States gave you a good chance to prepare for the surprises of New York—there must have been some new aspects of the place awaiting you. I know that even a few months in the West Indies and Canada open your eyes to new things on your return. Of course there will be only too evident all the old aggravations,—but from occasional references in your letters I judge that you have more than once been touched by these same things during the last six months. The world is fast becoming standardized,—and who knows but what our American scene will be the most intricate and absorbing one in fifty years or so?

Something is happening. Some kind of aristocracy of taste is being established,—there is more of it evidenced every year. People like you, Matty and I belong here. Especially Matty, who was doing better work last summer before he got in touch with the Paris crowd than I suspect since. —/—/ His present crazes are, frankly, beyond my understanding. They are so much so that I have still a great deal of confidence that no matter how wild and eccentric he becomes, it's just a phase which will be a practical benefit in the end. But, on the other hand, if one denies all emotional suffering the result is a rather frigid (however "gay") type of work. Let us watch & pray! —/—/

97: TO GORHAM MUNSON

[Cleveland]   *Same evening (May 16")*

Dear Gorham: I forgot to mention that the art books reached me and how pleased I am. Derain is one of my favorites—more even than Matisse & Picasso—and Vlaminck I have long admired. Marie Laurencin is amusing—but no more than any febrile female. Have you seen the amazing satires of (Georg?) Grosz and the beautiful metaphysics of Chirico? My friend Lescaze has put me in touch with a lot of moderns that I fear, off here in Cleveland, I should otherwise never have heard of.

I'm at work on a metaphysical attempt of my own—again I mention the familiar "Faustus & Helen" affair which has received a little stimulus lately. The trouble is—I get so little *expanse* of time undisturbed for it, that it's hopelessly fragmentary so far. Here is a tentative beginning. — — — — [See Weber, *op. cit.,* p. 175]

I wish you would tell me how you like my translations from Laforgue's "Locutions des Pierrots" in the current *Double Dealer.*

You will notice below them a very interesting poem by Allen Tate. This poem interested me so much that I wrote him a letter and his answer reached me along with yours today. —/—/

98: TO ALLEN TATE

Cleveland   *May 16th '22*

Dear Allen Tate: Being born in '99, I too, have a little toe-nail in the last century. You are not alone in all your youth and disgrace! But perhaps the umbilical cord made a clean margin of it with you, for I am reminded that it is 1922 and there is a chance of that. I popped on the scene shortly after Independence Day! and consequently have always had a dread of firecrackers.

Despite all this desperate imminence, I want to thank you for your answer to my letter. It has thrown me clear off the advertising copy work I brought home with me (yes, I'm one of the band!) as I feel more like putting that off until tomorrow, than this. But on the other hand there are so many things I want to say that I don't know where to begin. Letters are sometimes worse than nothing, especially for introductions, so if I am chatty and autobiographical you must pardon it.

Certain educated friends of mine have lamented my scant education, not in the academic sense, but as regards my acceptance and enthusiasm about some modern French work without having placed it in relation to most of the older "classics," which I haven't read. I have offered apologies, but continued to accept fate, which seems to limit me continually in some directions. Nevertheless, my affection for Laforgue is none the less genuine for being led to him through Pound and T. S. Eliot than it would have been through Baudelaire. There are always people to class one's admirations and enthusiasms illegitimate, and though I still have to have the dictionary close by when I take up a French book, a certain sympathy with Laforgue's attitude made me an easier translator of the three poems in *The D.D.* than perhaps an accomplished linguist might have been. However, no one ought to be particularly happy about a successful translation. I did them for fun, and it finally occurred to me that I might as well be paid for them.

As I said before, it is because your poem seemed so much in line with the kind of thing I am wanting to do, that I felt almost compelled to write you. While I am always interested in the latest developments in poetry I am inveterately devoted to certain English old fellows that are a constant challenge. I refer to Donne, Webster, Jonson, Marlowe, Vaughan, Blake, etc. More "modernly," have you read and admired Yeats (later poems), Ezra Pound, T. S. Eliot, Edward Thomas, Wallace Stevens? I am missing a few, but I like all these people.

I am interested greatly in seeing your poems in *The Fugitive*. It occurs to me that my friend, Gorham Munson, editor of *Secession*, would possibly be interested in publishing some of your things, although he can't pay anything yet for mss. Notice and N.Y. address of his magazine are in the back pages of the current *D.D.* I am trying to give him something myself, but I write so little that I simply haven't anything. The last went to *The Dial* and ought to be out next month.

Don't tell me you like the enclosed poems unless you really do. You may have seen them in different places, but I'm in the dark as to that.

P.S. Robinson is very interesting—his work is real and permanent, yet it is also a tragedy—one of the tragedies of Puritanism, materialism, America and the last century. Wm. Vaughn Moody's beautiful tonality suffered in a kind of vacuum, too. We are more fortunate today, despite Amy Lowell!

The poetry of negation is beautiful—alas, too dangerously so for one of my mind. But I am trying to break away from it. Perhaps this is useless, perhaps it is silly—but one *does* have joys. The vocabulary of damnations and prostrations has been developed at the expense of these other moods, however, so that it is hard to dance in proper measure. Let us invent an idiom for the proper transposition of jazz into words! Something clean, sparkling, elusive!

99: TO GORHAM MUNSON

[Cleveland]   *June 4th '22*

Dear Gorham: — — — — I probably should not be here at the Corona were it not that I want you to see the new coin from the mint enclosed herewith.

I have been at it for the last 24 hours and it may be subjected to a few changes and additions, but as I see it now in the red light of the womb it seems to me like a work of youth and magic.

At any rate, it is something entirely new in English poetry, so far as I know. The jazz rhythms in that first verse are something I have been impotently wishing to "do" for many a day. It is the second part of the (three section) "Marriage of Faustus and Helen" that I must have tired you with mentioning. The other parts are entirely unlike it, and God knows when they will be done. The first part is just begun. However, I have considerable ambitions in this opus, as I have told you. Please let me know your sentiments regarding the enclosed.

The reassurance of your projected visit here makes me happy in spite of rose-fever cyclones. What talks we shall have! and there are three others here who have heard so much about you that they are anxious to meet you too. Bill Sommer has moved to his country

place where the charming schoolhouse-studio is located. We shall
have to spend a week-end there among the gay canvasses that line its
walls.

100: TO ALLEN TATE

Cleveland   *June 12th*

Dear Allen: So you are in love with the dear Duchess of Malfi also!
How lovely she speaks in that one matchless passage: —/—/[1] Exquisite pride surrendering to love! And it was this that faced all the
brutality of circumstance in those hideous and gorgeous final scenes
of the play! The old betrayals of life, and yet they are worth something—from a distance, afterward.

What you say about Eliot does not surprise me,—but you will re-
cover from the shock. No one ever says the last word, and it is a
good thing for you, (notice how I congratulate myself!) to have been
faced with him as early as possible. I have been facing him for *four*
years,—and while I haven't discovered a weak spot yet in his armour,
I flatter myself a little lately that I have discovered a safe tangent to
strike which, if I can possibly explain the position,—goes *through*
him toward a *different goal.* You see it is such a fearful temptation
to imitate him that at times I have been almost distracted. He is, you
have now discovered, far more profound than Huxley (whom I like)
or any others obviously under his influence. You will profit by reading him again and again. I must have read "Prufrock" twenty-five
times and things like the "Preludes" more often. His work will lead
you back to some of the Elizabethans and point out the best in them.
And there is Henry James, Laforgue, Blake and a dozen others in
his work. He wrote most of this verse between 22 and 25, and is now,
I understand, dying piecemeal as a clerk in a London bank! In his
own realm Eliot presents us with an absolute *impasse,* yet oddly
enough, he can be utilized to lead us to, intelligently point to, other
positions and "pastures new." Having absorbed him enough we can
trust ourselves as never before, in the air or on the sea. I, for instance,
would like to leave a few of his "negations" behind me, risk the
realm of the obvious more, in quest of new sensations, *humeurs.*
These theories and manoeuvres are interesting and consolatory,—
but of course, when it comes right down to the act itself,—I have to
depend on intuition, "inspiration" or what you will to fill up the
page. Let us not be too much disturbed, antagonized or influenced
by the *fait accompli.* For in the words of our divine object of "envy"

1. John Webster, *The Duchess of Malfi,* III, ii, 66-70.

("Reflections on Contemporary Poetry," *Egoist,* London, '19–): "Admiration leads most often to imitation; we can seldom long remain unconscious of our imitating another, and the awareness of our imitation naturally leads us to hatred of the object imitated. If we stand toward a writer in this other relation of which I speak we do not imitate him, and though we are quite as [. . . .][1]

101: TO GORHAM MUNSON

[Cleveland]   *[ca. June 18]*

Dear Gorham: I have been in a house up in "Little Italy," a section of Sicilian immigrants very near our house where one can get good three-year Chianti,—and incidentally am feeling very fine as Sunday evenings go. *There* is the place to enjoy oneself, in the family parlour of a pickslinger's family with chromos on the walls that are right in style of Derain and Vlaminck. Bitch dogs and the rest of the family wander in while the bottle is still half empty and some of the family offspring. *Tristram Shandy* read to a friend with a Spanish Bolero going on the Victrola sounds good in such a milieu! I never should live without wine! When you come here we shall make many visits to this charming family. You will like my classic, puritan, inhibited friend Sam Loveman who translates Baudelaire charmingly! It is hard to get him to do anything outside the imagination,—but he is charming and has just given me a most charming work on Greek Vases (made in Deutschland) in which satyrs with great erections prance to the ceremonies of Dionysios with all the fervour of de Gourmont's descriptions of sexual sacrifice in *Physique de L'Amour,* which I am lately reading in trans.

I am glad you like Lescaze's portrait of me. He *has* an athletic style. Your criticism of painting et al strikes me as very exact and appreciative—at least, as far as I am able to justly criticize it. He hates Cleveland with all the awareness of the recent description of this place accorded in the last *Masses* or *Liberator,* as I understand. Just now I am in too banal a mood to give sympathy to anything. At times, dear Gorham, I feel an enormous power in me—that seems almost supernatural. If this power is not too dissipated in aggravation and discouragement I may amount to something sometime. I can say this now with perfect equanimity because I am notoriously drunk and the Victrola is still going with that glorious "Bolero." Did I tell you of that thrilling experience this last winter in the dentist's chair when under the influence of aether and *amnesia* my mind spiraled

1. The rest of this letter has been lost.

to a kind of seventh heaven of consciousness and egoistic dance among the seven spheres—and something like an objective voice kept saying to me—"You have the higher consciousness—you have the higher consciousness. This is something that very few have. This is what is called genius."? A happiness, ecstatic such as I have known only twice in "inspirations" came over me. I felt the two worlds. And at once. As the bore went into my tooth I was able to follow its every revolution as detached as a spectator at a funeral. O Gorham, I have known moments in eternity. I tell you this as one who is a brother. I want you to know me as I feel myself to be sometimes. I don't want you to feel that I am conceited. But since this adventure in the dentist's chair, I feel a new confidence in myself. At least I had none of the ordinary hallucinations common to this operation. Even that means something. You know I live for work,—for poetry. I shall do my best work later on when I am about 35 or 40. The imagination is the only thing worth a damn. Lately I have grown terribly isolated, and very egoist. One has to do it [in] Cleveland. I rush home from work to my room hung with the creations of Sommer and Lescaze— and fiddle through the evenings. If I could afford wine *every* evening I might do more. But I am slow anyway. However, today I have made a good start on the first part of "Faustus & Helen." I am, needless to say, delighted that you like the second part so well. The other two parts are to be quite different. But, as yet, I am dubious about the successful eventuation of the poem as a *whole*. Certainly it is the most ambitious thing I have ever attempted and in it I am attempting to evolve a conscious pseudo-symphonic construction toward an abstract beauty that has not been done before in English—at least directly. If I can get this done in the way I hope—I might get some consideration for *The Dial* prize. Perhaps I'm a fool for such hopes— sooner or later I expect to get that yearly donation. —/—/

I am not going to read this over in the clear sober light of the dawn. Take it for what it is worth tonight when I seal the envelope— *if* you can read it!

102: TO GORHAM MUNSON

[*Cleveland*]   *June 22nd*

Dear Gorham: —/—/ This is just rushed off between jobs. I must have insulted you to the limit with that letter of Sunday night,—but when I am filled up I am feeling too good to be taken seriously, so please don't mind.[1] Your applause of the "Faustus and Helen II" has

1. "Glad you really like my Silenus letter." (Letter to Munson, June 28, 1922.)

heartened me, although I am having a terrible time with the first part of it. The best way for me to speed up, I guess, is to forget all about time and be quite indifferent. −/−/

103: To − −

[*Cleveland*]   *4th of July*

Dear − −: −/−/ I am sorry to disappoint you about my "Praise." There were no accouchements there at all. Not even temptations in that direction. It is, or was, entirely "platonic." Nelson was a Norwegian who rebelled against the religious restrictions of home and came to America when a mere kid. Went to art school in Washington and won some kind of distinguished medal there. As soon as he was through school, an aunt of his in America who had been paying his tuition abruptly withdrew all her help and forced him into the prostitution of all his ideals and a cheap lithographic work that he was never able to pull out of afterward. He wrote several good poems published in *Scribner's* & *Century* a long time ago, got married, and I finally met him here in Cleveland where he had been living in seclusion for a number of years. One of the best-read people I ever met, wonderful kindliness and tolerance and a true Nietzschean. He was one of many broken against the stupidity of American life in such places as here. I think he has had a lasting influence on me. −/−/

104: To Allen Tate

[*Cleveland*]   *July 19th, '22*

Dear Allen: − − − − Let me salute you again. "Bored to Choresis" is as good as "Euthanasia,"−if not better. You do the trick here. Your vocabulary is exceedingly interesting−you have a way of meticulously accenting certain things in a quiet, yet withal so sharp a note, that the effect is greater than as though you roared. "Tribal library," "Her rhythms are reptilian and religious," etc., are excellent. And then, of course, I like your lunge at the bourgeois literary biographical interests. No one has ever put it better than you have.

You see what is good about this poem is over and above the merely personal sketches and digs that Robinson has been getting you into. Here you come into something larger, as you did in "Euthanasia," where you hit all humanity a few slaps, but in so interesting a way! In other words,−this poem is *creative* where the ordinary "character" portrait is merely analytic and, generally, unimportant (at least in poetry). You needn't be afraid of running too squarely into Eliot with work like this.

I would like to see you follow out the directions indicated in this poem—not their downward slant (interesting enough), but (if you get what I mean) their upward slant into something broadly human. Launch into praise. *You* are one who can give praise an edge and beauty, Allen. You have done so well in a couple of damnations, that I feel confident in you.

I must close. Bosses brush near my shoulder, and poetry isn't exactly encouraged around here. Munson is strong for you with this new poem. I think he would like it for *Secession* if *The Dial* does not take it. He asks me to inform you that no particular "jargon" is necessary for *Secession* contributors. Be your own language—in so pure a way that it will be noticeable, and you will do well enough.

My hay fever temporarily passes. I peer again on the world with subsiding eyes. It's a pleasure to think you of down in the clear valleys, and feeling so top-spinning! Marriage! Well, it sounds ominous. Think well, beforehand. Are you easily satisfied? That's the main danger.

105: To — —

[*Cleveland*]　　　　　　　　　　　　　　　　　*July 27th, '22*

Dear — —: —/—/ I feel like shouting *EUREKA!* When Munson went yesterday after a two weeks visit, he left my copy of *Ulysses,* a huge tome printed on Verge d'arche paper. But do you know—since reading it partially, I do not think I will care to trust it to any bookbinder I know of. It sounds ridiculous, but the book is so strong in its marvelous oaths and blasphemies, that I wouldn't have an easy moment while it was out of the house. You will pardon my strength of opinion on the thing, but it appears to me easily the epic of the age. It is as great a thing as Goethe's *Faust* to which it has a distinct resemblance in many ways. The sharp beauty and sensitivity of the thing! The matchless details! I DO HOPE you get a copy, but from what Munson says there is little hope unless you can get some friend of yours in Europe to smuggle it in in his trunk. It has been barred from England. It is quite likely I have one of two or three copies west of New York. *The Dial* ordered six and has only been able to get one so far, etc., etc. Munson, who met Joyce several times in Paris last summer, tells me that the Man Ray photo of J. in the recent *Vanity Fair* is really not a good resemblance. The face is not so puffy-looking, nor the odd ocular expression. Man Ray, you know, has his

own individual temperament to express! Ah, these interesting pho-
tographers. Joyce dresses quietly and neatly. Is very quiet in manner,
and, Anderson says, does not seem to have read anything contemporary for years. His book is steeped in the Elizabethans, his early
love, and Latin Church, and some Greek;—but the man rarely talks
about books. I rather like him for that. —/—/

Joyce is still very poor. Recently some French writers headed by
Valery Larbaud, gave a dinner and reading for his benefit. It is my
opinion that some fanatic will kill Joyce sometime soon for the
wonderful things said in *Ulysses*. Joyce is too big for chit-chat, so
I hope I haven't offended you with the above details about him. He
is the one above all others I should like to talk to.

I have been very quiet while Munson has been here. Tonight,
however, I break out into fresh violences. —/—/ And thanks, dear
————, for the newspaper bundle. In the *Times* I enjoyed Colum's
account of Joyce's early Dublin days, although he told me the story
of the Yeats encounter several years ago. —/—/

106: TO GORHAM MUNSON

[Cleveland]   *Aug. 7th, '22*

Dear Gorham: I sent 27 Sommer things off to Anderson last Saturday, feeling very much as though I were delivering Plato into the
hands of the Philistines. Anderson has been very nasty besides being
"just another fool." I have been shocked, sensation very rare with
me, with the contents of your letter relating his manoeuvres. He is
evidently none too sure of the quality of his work so highly praised
by Rosenfeld. I realize that he insulted me while he was here—it
wasn't necessary to tell fibs to avoid my company—but I shall beam
on until all hope of his getting Bill an audience has vanished. In
that event, I judge by your letter that we can depend fairly certainly
on Frank, and Stieglitz, perhaps. I haven't much hope in Anderson's
interest in anything connected with us now, after disgracing himself
the way he has. Encore, regardez, mon ami,—don't let kittens out of
the bag before they have claws again if you want to be an effective
iconoclast. —/—/

Why haven't I received *Secession* #2 yet? Your letter of last week
mentions it, and I am anxious to get at it. I got the new *Broom* with
your Epstein trans. in it and Matty's very clever translations and
criticisms. Delightful "Blahs" and "blagues," too! Matty has developed a "high hand" attitude in criticism that is (to anyone ignorant of his subject matter, direct contact with his authors, etc.) as

effective and compelling as Pound's. I am beginning to see little
Caesarian laurels sprouting on his brow. His (anti-Zwaska) Caesarian
attitude is not a little pleasing. Matty and Julius! Surely they have
both gone into Gaul with somewhat the same stones, though Matty
will have to wait until he gets back to the good old U.S.A. to be
divided into three parts!

I am glad Frank took so well to your book. I have since wanted
to read it over again, say fresh in the morning to better absorb its
many compact and rich allusions toward your esthétique. Stupid
and hasty as this letter is—I hope you won't think I am satisfied with
it. I've got so much on my mind that you must bear with me until
a cool day comes when I shall not be so tired at night, nor the
garret study be so hot as it is this evening. I enclose some poetry.[1]
I think the first part of "Faustus" is about right now. Tell me what
you think of the thing as a whole. Read it entirely over from the
first so as to judge better of my graduation from the quotidian into
the abstract, and tell me frankly what you think about it. I have
been so close to the thing for so long a time that at present I cannot
judge it *synthetically* at all. The third part has not been even started
yet. The other evening I had a hint for the speed that I wanted in
something like the following [four] lines: — — — —[1] But I have found
nothing yet to satisfy me at all. It must be a dramatic comment done
somewhat in a new idiom. I have got to search awhile yet for it.
Meanwhile I have a homely and gay thing to show you that I did
yesterday out of sheer joy, "Thinking of Bill——", etc.[2] — — — —

Joyce is being savoured slowly—with steady pleasure. Meanwhile
I find *Enormous Room* a stimulating article. It has taught me to
better appreciate Cummings' poetry—although the things in the
last *Broom* of his are, I think, boresome. *Since Cezanne* by Bell has
interested me a good deal.

Dominick! O yes! I think we both were bored with the climacteric
after your departure. I have not seen him since!

"The Bottom of the Sea" is too deep for me to model yet as I
want it. I haven't forgotten it though.

107: TO CHARMION WIEGAND

Cleveland, O.   *Aug. 15th, '22*

Dear Charmion: You will be delighted to know, I'm sure, that the
Anderson trans. matter has been settled. I got a letter from Huebsch

1. See Weber, *op. cit.*, p. 176.
2. "Sunday Morning Apples."

last week saying that he had given Herr Reeck the rights—so *some* letters got across the waters anyway! This suggests the mention that Anderson was here about six weeks ago while Munson was visiting me, and came out to the house for an evening. The man's personal charm supported the impressions his letters had given me (we had never actually met before) but I have been very disappointed in him since he went down to N. Y. afterward and stirred up a petty rumpus in *The Dial* office, about something that Munson told him [in Cleveland] on the subject of Rosenfeld's position as a critic, etc. The story is not worth going into, but it showed Anderson to be surprisingly petty and malignant, not to say untactful. La-La! Well,— he hasn't yet destroyed my taste for some of his work yet—despite that most of my friends don't value his work above a Russian rouble.

"Pandora's Box" is a good piece of "general" criticism. It is more social than literary and is the kind of thing, above all, that Americans need to read. I hope you find a good market for it. You must let me know where and when your things are published so I can look for them and get them.

Since Munson brought me my copy of *Ulysses* I have been having high times. A book that in many ways surpasses anything I have ever read. 800 pgs! You must read E. E. Cummings' *Enormous Room* for a real inspiration in language and humanity.

The first issue of *Secession* does not come up to the second, now out. You should get it somewhere there in N. Y. and read Cowley's two poems and Josephson's story. "The Oblate." —/—/

108: To Gorham Munson

[*Cleveland*]   *Friday night*

Dear Gorham: — — — — My enthusiasms, the hot weather, the onset of hay fever, the infinite and distasteful detail work I have been doing at the office, and the suspense of finding another position, etc., etc., have brought me very near the ground. In fact, for several days this week I have been unable to retain food and have [thought] that at any moment something would snap and I would go into a million pieces. I haven't felt as "dangerously" for several years. But I am picking up today—since I have got the job matter settled and informed the office that I shall not be with them after the first of September. This bit of news I had the wonderful pleasure of delivering to them just as my boss was starting in on a series of gentle reprimands, etc., and so instead of ever hearing the end of that rigmarole—I was begged to remain at a higher salary. Where I am going however, I shall have complete charge of the copy work and shall receive ten dollars a week more to start with and a considerable raise within sixty days. I was literally urged to come with them—a new agency—which was a unique pleasure for me!

Well,—we heard from Anderson! Rosenfeld's remarks along with those of several other artists present at the time of the "trial" were quoted in effect that S[ommer] was not a notable man at all—had no personal vision—his work a mixture of half-a-dozen modern influences—and *couldn't draw a head on man, woman or animal!* Anderson was very sorry he had had anything to do with any adverse criticism, etc., etc. So much for that. Dear G., let us create our own little vicious circle! Let us erect it on the remains of such as Paul Rosenfeld. But enough of this for now.

Of course I'm enthusiastic about "Faustus and Helen" now! Who wouldn't be after your comments. However,—when it comes to the last section—I think I shall not attempt to make it the paragon of SPEED that I thought of. I think it needs more sheer weight than such a motive would provide. Beyond this I have only the surety that it is, of course, to include a comment on the world war—and be Promethean in mood. What made the first part of my poem so good was the extreme amount of time, work and thought put on it. The following is my beginning of the last part—at present: —/—/ How neatly here is violence clothed in pathos! —/—/

109: To GORHAM MUNSON

[*Cleveland*]   *Thursday*

Dear Gorham: —/—/ My vacation has given me the time to read *Rahab* and finish *Ulysses*. *Rahab* is a beautiful book. It has a synthetic beauty that is more evident than the lyric note behind *Ulysses*. It contains beautiful language—Frank is a real artist—no doubt about that and of course way beyond Anderson when it comes to craft. My only doubt about *Rahab* comes in with the question, as yet undecided, as to whether or not there isn't a slight touch of sentimentality attached to Frank's "mysticism." Certainly the man is not a *realist*—certainly he is sincere. There is also this question— Fanny's later development, so far as I can see, does not put her far enough beyond her initial appreciation of life at the time she is deserted by her husband to warrant the stress on that thesis which Frank evidently intends as the *motif* of the book. As a picture of crucifixion the book is superb—but, after all, what tangible gain has Fanny got out of it except an attitude that Butler outlines in some such words as I believe I have repeated to you: "No one has ever begun to really appreciate life, or lived, until he has recognized the background of life as essentially Tragedy." It is from this platform of perception that I conceive every artist as beginning his work. Does Frank consider Fanny's course as complete where he leaves her at the end of *Rahab*—or isn't there still something more to be said? The reason I pose this question is because Stephen Daedalus has already gone as far as Fanny before *Ulysses* begins. The *Portrait* took him beyond where Fanny sits at the end of *Rahab*. Of course it would stretch reality a great deal, probably, to take Fanny Dirk any further—but, in my mind, it is just this stubborn impossibility (however nonresponsible Frank may be) that makes my judgment of *Rahab* suffer in the light of *Ulysses*. Perhaps I am unfair and "all off." Both books, however, have a strong ethical and Nietzschean basis and reading them at the same time as I have, I am irresistibly drawn into comparisons. Frank is so young that he has lots of time to benefit by Joyce and even go further—although I doubt if such will will be done for a hundred years or more. The point is—after all—I am interested in Frank and thank you for putting me out of prejudice. As an American today he is certainly in the front line—no doubt about that at all. —/—/

110: TO GORHAM MUNSON

[*Cleveland*]   *Monday*

Dear Gorham: I'm glad that Burke meets you in approving the "sea" poem,[1] and I'm sorry that it is, or at least appears to be beyond me to make changes in it. Of course you know I have never been very enthusiastic about it. Its only value in my mind rests in its approach to the "advertisement" form that I am contemplating and, I think, spoke to you about. It is a kind of poster,—in fact, you might name it "Poster" if the idea hits you. There is nothing more profound in it than a "stop, look and listen" sign. And it is this conception of the poem that makes me like the last line as I do—merely bold and unambitious like a skull & cross-bones insignia. —/—/

111: TO GORHAM MUNSON

[*Cleveland*]   *Tuesday*

Dear Gorham: —/—/ God! I wish I were on the New York scene, what with the items of your last letter. I was especially thrilled at

1. "The Bottom of the Sea Is Cruel."

the Damon book on Blake. You know how much Blake has always interested me. I've always thought Damon a very capable figure, and hope you get the Vers-Libre histoire for *Secession*. Sam [Loveman] was telling me today that he had seen some notice of issue #3 of that notable sheet in Sunday's [N. Y.] *Times,* with a mention specific of Matty too.

I answered jh last Saturday, with a slight reprimand for the impotence of her "kick" at you in *The L. R.* I should rather like to see her aggravated a little longer, which is pretty sure to occur. I, as you know, have a certain admiration for Cuthbert Wright, but I felt his anti-DADA article in *The D. D.* was rather weak. I'm so tired of seeing the *young* turn their heads and wag them despairingly at every modern manifestation. They don't need to accept them all, —but it's so uninspiring to see them turn back to Greece and quote some Meleager lyric as the paragon of all time. This gesture from Wright was a little disappointing to me. Allen Tate writes me that he has returned to Nashville and joined the Ransom crowd there again. Your rejection of "Choresis" I presume was largely responsible for this return to the native.

I'm about fed up on furnaces and hot water heaters. I've been very attentive to the little ad. stories now for quite awhile. It's about time that I did something about "F and Helen" again. To make things better or worse (I don't know which yet) I've almost fallen in love. I may add, an object more than usually responsive this time. —/—/

112: TO GORHAM MUNSON

[*Cleveland*]   *Sept. 29th, 1922*

Dear Gorham: What would you think of my using the first part of "F and H" alone? Calling it just "For the Marriage of," etc. This would seem rather disappointing, I know, but I feel that it is fate. This conviction comes after much thought and especially after writing one added verse (originally intended for part 3) to be inserted as the next-last, coming just before the "eye motif." I feel that with this added the first part becomes an intensity that is definitely developed and closed,—and that further additions such as part 2 are irrelevant—at least anti-climactic by position. And as for the third part, I am interested enough in the aeroplane, war—speed idea but I think it would be better developed under a different sky. Let me know what you think of the idea;—what you think of the additional verse also.

"The Springs of Guilty Song," or former part 2, would do very well, I think, to send to *Broom*. Of course, I want to try *Dial* on "F and H," before it goes anywhere else. Its present length will slightly overlap two pages.

I am glad to have the *Secession* program in advance. You're travelling right along it seems. I wish I could spare an erection, as suggested, but I have to save them all for Seiberling Tires, Furnaces, etc. I have a widening interest, you see, in filling the public mind with my ideas of excellence. Frankly, I'm tired to death. The new job has been beyond expectations in many ways, but it simply keeps my imagination tied down more than ever. I have so much to do.

Allen Tate is in Cincinnati visiting his brother and may come up here for a couple of days. I really enjoy admonishing him—Matty is not the only one who has "disciples." By the way,—I guess that latter gent got peeved again at my last letter. I preface every letter now, you know, with the prediction that its contents will absolutely disgust him beyond the desire to answer—someday, perhaps already, that prophecy will be fulfilled.

I can't spare the money to put into reproductions of Bill's [Sommer] pictures for some time. It will cost over twenty dollars just for six. It will be two months before I even break clear from the dentist and hay fever bills of the year,—so I guess we can't send Loeb anything yet. —/—/

113: TO CHARMION WIEGAND

[*Cleveland*]   *Oct. 9th, '22*

My dear Charmion: —/—/ I've changed jobs only to find myself completely imprisoned now, there's so much more to do. It's copy work (as before) only now I have about *all* of it to write. I haven't had time to think about poetry for weeks and letters have to wait. There are birth pangs to go through with, even in so staid a thing as advertising copy and ideas. I hammer my forehead for hours some days trying to get an idea that will be read, and loosen purse strings. —/—/

About *Ulysses*—I paid $20.00 for mine, that being the original subscription price (1 ½) years ago when I ordered it. But I should never have got it past the censors and customs had Munson not brought it all the way from Paris in the bottom of his trunk. I know that already it is bringing such prices as $200.00—$300.00 (depending on binding and paper) in some places. Certainly I should never part with mine for any price. I feel quite luxurious!

I got a beautiful German monograph on Etruscan art the other day. But the art books I ordered months ago from Halim (Bremen) haven't yet arrived. God knows,—I suppose the postoffice found something "obscene" in the Japanese landscapes somewhere, or the Chinese temples—or the Egyptian monuments!! —/—/

114: To Gorham Munson

[*Cleveland*]   *Oct. 12, '22*

Dear Gorham: —/—/ Today also brought me the most prodigious book on Egyptian sculpture that I've ever seen. Of course it's German,—one of the books I ordered from Halim (Bremen) months ago. I shall gloat over it many hours.

Looking it over gives one the impression that the children of the Nile completed every possibility of sculpture long before the Greeks began to work. The latter added some architectural features, in figures they only added a few rondures and a certain humanity that is less evident in the African forms. It's largely the spacious austerity of Egyptian art that particularly hits me. —/—/

Williams wrote Bill [Sommer] a memorable letter accompanying his check (for $25.00) in which he said that Bill got under his underdrawers!—and went on to say that he was potentially greater than Marin. It has heartened Bill wonderfully. Such a letter was worth more than the plaudits of a hundred Rosenfelds. I'd like to meet Williams! (Repeating this statement so many times won't do any good I suppose, but there's that directness about the man that I know I'd find cleansing.)

I'm sending off "F. & H." to *The Dial* today. I'm impatient for the money—besides that I feel that it is complete and might as well be out and aired. Having it around stagnates new ideas for me.

Allen Tate sends me a good poem, acknowledges myself and Eliot as his models—calls me mature and perfect—so that now (with a grain of salt) I feel vastly superior to Matty. I feel quite jolly tonight! — — — —

O Hell! what can you expect with a gallon of sherry gone since Sunday! It's as smooth as Prufrock and is only supposed to be sold to *rabbis* for religious purposes. Rabbi Crane! What strange conversions there are.

I've been reading Rebecca West's *Judge* with much delight. She's the best exponent of the old novel form I know, and she has fine pathos and a certain cleanliness that is more than neatness. "Codes" are interesting after all. As a rabbi and upholder of document and tradition, I applaud. — — — —

115: TO GORHAM MUNSON

[*Cleveland*]   *Oct. 25th,'22*

Dear Gorham: —/—/ You should see me in my luxurious new coat.
Light brown with wide cross-stripes in orange! My progress down
the avenue is attended with awesome gazes, to say the least. From
now on, having broken the spell of modesty and bashfulness, I shall
wear what I want to—providing I can afford it. But I just got a
raise,—so maybe I stand a better chance in the future. —/—/

116: TO GORHAM MUNSON

[*Cleveland*]   *Nov. 7th,'22*

Dear Gorham: "F and H" came back from *The Dial* on Monday. Evidently Mr. Watson, Jr., has something to say about things as Seldes
mentioned that he was obliged to keep it over time in order to show
it to Mr. Watson, concluding with, "Regrettably, we cannot use it."
Now it is on its way to *Broom* along with "The Springs of Guilty
Song" (former part II). I would like to make a vow, if I felt capable
of keeping it, not to send anything again to *The Dial* for two years.
But, of course, I am merely cutting off my own nose with such
tactics.

Matty wrote me quite a long letter from the *Broom* office in Berlin, arriving last week. After dissecting the copy of "Guilty Song"
that I had sent him last summer as a sample of what I was doing, he
came forth with the statement that there was damned little stuff
of this calibre being written these days. So I am presuming that he
will be glad to publish that poem, whether or not he fancies "F and
H." This latter he will probably find too emotional or old fashioned
to praise, but I thought I'd submit it anyway.[1] If you care to, show
it to Burke. In case of its second rejection—I am assuming your continued interest—you might care to use it in *Secession*. *The Dial*
seems to have abandoned all interest in publishing American things,
or anything, in fact, that comes to them unheralded by years of
established reputation. Certainly, if the remaining installments of
Anderson's *Many Marriages* are equal in stupidity and banality to
the first installment, they are going to make pretty fools of themselves. Anderson's "naiveté" or what-you-will, becomes very aggravating.

I am strong with you in my admiration for Burke. I repeat for the

1. It was accepted by Josephson.

eleventh time, I wish I could be in New York to talk to him, especially lately do I feel an intense need for contact and conversation with the right sort of people. I have rather missed Lescaze's stimulation since he left, while Loveman, the only other person left here, becomes more incoherent every day. I am, really, suffering a great deal these days, and the worst is that I have almost no impulse toward writing. This wholesale "fertilization" of America by such half-baked people as the Algonquin gang is one of the most depressing features of all, because it is without any sense of values. Ben Hecht and Eliot get equal honors in such company. But at any rate I can rival you in some ways. Where you have Untermeyer, I can trot out Braithwaite. A letter from Braithwaite came last week inviting or rather soliciting my "Praise for an Urn" for the 1922 *Anthology*. At last I shall rub shoulders with Florence [sic] Wilkinson!

Allen Tate was a week later than expected in getting to N. Y., but you have probably met him by this time. I am rather looking forward to his two days here—he has enthusiasm and brains, however undeveloped his style may be. Matty's trans. from Soupault in the last *Broom* are undoubtedly clever, but I don't see how he can rave so about this man's conceptions. Matty mentions his recent love for Francis Jammes and Vielé-Griffin, the latter as being much abler than Laforgue. Where is he headed for, anyway? His Joyce article was amazing in its lack of recognition of the great elements in Joyce. I look forward to his final suicide with Frank. But, after all,—Matty will always keep his head up, and sniff ominously. —/—/

117: To Gorham Munson

[*Cleveland*]   *Nov. 20th,'22*

Dear Gorham: I am immersed totally in a rush job and will be for a week or so more. These campaigns are taxing affairs and very confining, so I can't write much. But I do want to assure you of my enthusiastic desire to both write the jacket for your *Frank Study* and also write a communication to the Double Skull[1] (delightful name) about it. As regards the latter,—it will necessarily be very short, as they once returned a reasonably-sized review I had written on Shaw's *Back to Methuselah* on the argument that it was too long for the comparative importance of the book! Please send me the proofs as soon as they are out and I'll begin.

1. *The Double Dealer.*

I hope you enjoyed — — — —. I took the liberty of writing him to look you up because you had once mentioned a certain interest in him incurred in Pollard's *Their Day in Court*. — — — — is delightful company, whether he goes in for post-Beardsley attitudes or not. The episodes of the *Satyricon* are mild as compared to his usual exploits in N. Y. during vacations. —/—/

Are you continuing with the advertising instructions? What do you think of Eliot's *The Wasteland*? I was rather disappointed. It was good, of course, but so damned dead. Neither does it, in my opinion, add anything important to Eliot's achievement.

I like the admonitions you offered on Macy, etc., in *The New Republic*. You are developing a tightened hold on criticism that is a favorable opposite to Mr. Rosenfeld's rapturous Turner-sunset technique.

118: TO GORHAM MUNSON

[*Cleveland*]   *Thanksgiving Day '22*

Dear Gorham: —/—/ I have not seen Sommer for weeks and weeks. He is very peculiar, never looks you up, never phones or manifests the slightest interest. I have got tired of ever-lastingly tagging after him and shall wait until I have some important news for him before I crash into his cosmos again. I don't think he ever so much as replied with a note of thanks to Williams for his purchase and beautiful, generous tribute of praise. I can't understand it. But it is perhaps good to become impersonal in the admiration of art.

Poor — — — —! I feared you would not like him very much. My affection for him is based on a certain community of taste and pursuit we have which you will understand. Because he has been mewed up so long with unpleasant work — — — — in a city where conversation and letters never existed—he has, out of sheer ennui, been forced to find entertainment in ways which have taken the best of him to feed what has become a sort of obsession. His creative impulse was never very strong, but in his letters and on his favorite topic you get as strong a satire as Petronius! Life has tamed him terribly,—yet he has lived a great deal if the senses mean anything.

I haven't had time to read all of #3.[1] But I can well understand your dismay at Matty. With all his boasted time and leisure he ought to have made a better job of it. And that silly slant at Joyce—putting him along with Cabell! Matty's "gay intellectualism" will eventually expose him to the jibes of a psychoanalyst if he continues in such

1. *Secession*.

loose estimates as his article in *Broom* on advertising displays. Some things he says may be true,—but how damned vulgar his rhapsodies become! I would rather be on the side of "sacred art" with Underwood than admit that a great art is inherent in the tinsel of the billboards. Technique there is, of course, but such gross materialism has nothing to do with art. Artistry and fancy will be Matty's limit as long as he is not willing to admit the power and beauty of emotional intensity—which he has proved he hasn't got.

Burke has an Egyptian quality of hard and solid speculation. Egyptian literature is, of course, not my comparison,—but in looking at the sculpture of that nation one gets the same impression, the same austerity. I have decided, perhaps I repeat myself, that no advance in sculpture has been made since the Egyptians so far as essential plastique is concerned. This after looking at the 200 or so photographs in a modern German book on the subject that I got recently.

Sam Loveman didn't like your Saltus review. Said it was scattered, etc. I haven't read it. His book on the man and his works is progressing, he says. I think it will probably be very bad. He is the kind of "critic" that feels it needful to damn every one else in order to praise. He made the terrible assertion that "while Saltus was steadily working, neglected in obscurity, Henry James was applauded in two countries for his *puking.*" James never did that, whatever else you may say about him. Ridiculous. Of course I don't take Sam seriously in any criticism. The man *Rychtarik* and his wife are really the best company I have now. (Note the spelling of his name, correct this time.) His initials are W. R. I mention this because it would be sad to get his name wrong for that cover. He was pleased greatly by your acceptance and praise. —/—/

119: TO WALDO FRANK

[Cleveland]   *Nov. 30th '22*

Dear Waldo Frank: I have heard through Munson that you care for some of my poems. Let me take the occasion of *Secession #3* to tell you how powerfully I think you can write in such a story or episode as "Hope." This is so fine that I cannot keep [from] writing you.

I never read prose before that flowed with such lyricism and intensity.—I suppose there are sure to be shocked cries, but the beautiful manipulation of symbolism in the thing has made your daring (if it took any) infinitely worth while. Writing like this is a real legacy, and nothing could be cleaner!

You may be interested in seeing six reproductions of work by Wm. Sommer that I sent Gorham today. In that case, anyway, this outburst may have served some purpose.

120: To GORHAM MUNSON

[Cleveland]   *Dec. 7th,'22*

Dear Gorham: Frank's "Hope" struck me so strongly that I wrote him a few encomiums. I also wrote Fisher, ordering a copy of the Kuniyoshi monograph. His reply included mention that he failed to get to New York last week but expected to see you this week; that he would not be able to publish anything of Sommer's for some time in any case until he got some monetary returns from his recent collections, etc. I hope Stieglitz likes them.

I haven't heard anything whatever from Tate, not even a rumor. He must be quite ill, deranged or something. If, by any chance, he is sore at me, I cannot account for a reason.

Untermeyer's article was at least decent, it was a non-insulting sort of bulletin and one of the better sort of things that could happen to *Secession* and its group. I was quite surprised that this parodist and facile assessor could so gracefully rise to the occasion of a new attitude. Whether we like him or not, his "position" in the American scene carries some weight, so I rather hope to see him continue his interest —/—/

121: To — —

Cleveland   *December 10th,'22*

My dear — —: My mother will not tolerate wine at the house—so I am rebelling. I am thinking seriously of moving into permanent private quarters where one need not be questioned about every detail of life and where one can be free of the description of one's food and its contents and manner of preparation while it is eaten at the table. To this end I am at present staying for a few days at a hotel. Maybe I shall move out as above indicated, or maybe I shall go back; it all depends on the course she takes. Because I dread to leave her on account of the position it puts her in I hope she will be more lenient with me. I don't ask much, and the little wine I succeed in getting has never resulted in embarrassing her. I never "carry on" at the house or annoy her. The fact of wine, alone, is what infuriates her puritanical instincts. All this is tedious and maudlin stuff to write, but that very fact makes it in some measure an excuse for my present dull outlook on things. Life is hard enough, God knows, without having to put up with a hundred extra restrictions in order to just have a room and a bed! —/—/

How *do* you manage such exquisite delights every time you journey to the Metropolis?! Your letter was superb. I can understand, also, how you failed to "mix" with Munson and his friends. You are so much of the Nineties that it was scarcely to be expected. You had the same reactions as H — — would have had to such a meeting. I am not saying that there is any single attitude toward art that is final. I do contend, however, that Munson, Burke, Cummings and Waldo Frank all have something new and fine to offer. And whether or not you agree with their critical "lingo" you will nevertheless find their creative results interesting and vital. In last week's *New Republic* there was an article on the group by Louis Untermeyer, non-committal but intelligent, on *Secession* and its contributors in which I was mentioned casually. We are all of us quite different. Our differences from the attitude of the present generation-in-power are in each case individual. I shall probably never amount to anything—but the others that I have just mentioned will do things of considerable importance. Frank, in *Rahab,* and Burke in his criticisms and in a number of short ideographic stories, have already established places in contemporary letters. —/—/

I am quite disrupted. Family affairs and "fusses" have been my destruction since I was eight years old when my father and mother began to quarrel. That phase only ended recently, and the slightest disturbance now tends to recall with consummate force all the past and its horrid memories on pretext of the slightest derangement of equilibrium. As I write I am ensconced at my office. Everybody else is away, for it is Sunday. Yet, in forgetfulness someone was very kind in leaving a gallon of delicious sherry. I have already had two good glasses of it without permission. I shall probably have two more before I go to see Isadora Duncan this evening and go back to the uninteresting room at the hotel. For without my books around me and my pictures and my Victrola with its Ravel, Debussy, Strauss and Wagner records—I am desolate, I find. I have grown accustomed to an "ivory tower" sort of existence. I am succeeding very well in my advertising writing. Salary raised and promises of more and decent people to work with who enjoy Joyce, Cabell, Pater and the best things of life. Yet even so—Life is meagre with me. I am unsatisfied and left always begging for beauty. I am tied to the stake—

a little more wastefully burnt every day of my life while all America is saying, "every day I am growing better and better in every way," and Dr. Coué makes his millions!

I am just enough filled with wine at the time of this letter to make confessions that will bore you. Yet, oddly enough, it is at such times that I feel most like writing you and H— —. He is floating under the shades of bamboos up the rivers of China under the dragon stars. You and I are in offices—seeking the same things—but my gift of humor has left me today. —/—/

122: To Gorham Munson

[Cleveland]   *Tuesday, Dec. 12th*

Dear Gorham: You, as well as some of my local friends, must share in my excitement at seeing Isadora Duncan dance on Sunday night. She gave the same program (All Tschaikowsky) that she gave in Moscow for the Soviet celebration and, I think, you saw it in New York recently. It was glorious beyond words, and sad beyond words too, from the rude and careless reception she got here. It was like a wave of life, a flaming gale that passed over the heads of the nine thousand in the audience without evoking response other than silence and some maddening cat-calls. After the first movement of the *Pathétique* she came to the fore of the stage, her hands extended. Silence,—the most awful silence! I started clapping furiously until she disappeared behind the draperies. At least one tiny sound should follow her from all that audience. She continued through the performance with utter indifference for the audience and with such intensity of gesture and such plastique grace as I have never seen, although the music was sometimes almost drowned out by the noises from the hall. I felt like rushing to the stage, but I was stimulated almost beyond the power to walk straight. When it was all over she came to the fore-stage again in the little red dress that had so shocked Boston, as she stated, and among other things told the people to go home and take from the bookshelf the works of Walt Whitman, and turn to the section called "Calamus." Ninety-nine percent of them had never heard of Whitman, of course, but that was part of the beauty of her gesture. Glorious to see her there with her right breast and nipple quite exposed, telling the audience that the truth was not pretty, that it was really indecent, and telling them (boobs!) about Beethoven, Tschaikowsky, and Scriabin. She is now on her way back to Moscow, so I understand, where someone will give her some roses for her pains.

I am in great ferment, and have been staying at a hotel for several days until I talk to my mother about some things that will determine whether or not I shall continue to live out at the house any more. They are little things, mostly, but such little things accumulate almost into a complex that [is] too much for me to work under. There is no use in discussing them here, but just the constant restraint necessary in living with others, you may appreciate, is a deadening thing. Unless something happens to release me from such annoyances I give up hope of doing any satisfactory writing. — — — —

123: To WILLIAM WRIGHT

Cleveland, O.   *December 24, 1922*

Dear William: However much boredom you may find in Warren—I assure you, it will not be as strenuous as the hot water I am stewing in. The Pittsburgh Water Heater surely has been on my mind the last three weeks, and the burden is still unshifted. I am growing bald trying to scratch up new ideas in housekeeping and personal hygiene—to tell people why they need more and quicker hot water. Last night I got drunk on some sherry. Even in that wild orgy my mind was still enchained by the hot water complex,—and I sat down and reeled off the best lines written so far in my handling of the campaign. All of my poems in the future will attest this sterilizing influence of HOT WATER!

Nothing happens here, either. I am grateful only for wine. I have neither women or song. Cleveland street car rides twice a day take out all hope of these latter elements. I think of New York and next summer when the present is too sharp (or is it dull!). But the main faults are not of our city, alone. They are of the age. A period that is loose at all ends, without apparent direction of any sort. In some ways the most amazing age there ever was. Appalling and dull at the same time. —/—/

PART TWO

New York

(1923–1925)

1 9 2 3

124: To Gorham Munson

[*Cleveland*]   *Jan. 5th, '23*

Dear Gorham: I cannot remember a more hectic month than the last unless I recall some of the old bivouacs of New York days, when I ricochet-ed "from roof to roof" without intermission. Two rush campaigns to write, gifts and remembrances to buy and send to far too many people—suppers, parties and evenings—much tossing of the pot,—"prison, palace and reverberation"! That is why I've been so slow in writing.

At present I'm flabbergasted and dull. But my carousing on New Year's Eve had one good outcome; it started the third part of "Faustus and Helen" with more gusto than before. When I catch my next breath I hope to carry it on to the end. —/—/

Waldo Frank wrote me a very cordial letter in answer to my written praise of "Hope." I should like to be in New York now and hear his lectures at the Rand School. I am hoping to make my visit along in May or June when the weather is mild and some of the shows are still going. I shall appear with a new cane that was given me for Christmas. Despite my objections to cane-carrying last summer, I find it very pleasant. Puce-colored gloves complete the proper touch.

I notice that *Broom* has been consistently weak in poetry. Cowley's things have been by far the best—but (with all due modesty) I think that my "F. and H." will be an improvement over their past offerings. Matty appears to rest in clover and periwinkles, what with the Guggenheim millions and the international sweep of editorial authority. (In accepting my poems he merely mentioned that he thought Loeb also liked them!) What do you think of his *Broom* ad in the Dec. number? He asked my opinion on the grounds that literary ads were generally the flattest in the world. It seems "attractive" enough to me—but the prize-subscription offer I balk at as a matter of policy in such a type of magazine.

Stieglitz voiced an old feeling of mine about Bill's [Sommer] work —the lack of finish evident in so much of it. This has always pained me. As a whole, his comments seem very just. But I tend to differ with him on one point in common with other critics who are so obsessed with the importance of current developments in art that they fail to recognize certain positive and timeless qualities.

I refer to the quality of line in Sommer's work. That has, in particular, nothing more to do with modern work than the draughtsmanship of Michelangelo. It is something that may not distinguish a man as a great innovator or personality—but it is, for all that, a rare and wondrous quality. From what you write Stieglitz has the sense to recognize this quality and to value it. But a person like Georgia O'Keeffe, who has so distinctly her own horn to play, is scornful of everything short of evolution and revolution.

It is a relief once in awhile to detach one's judgment from such considerations as hers, and to look at a piece of work as totally detached from time and fashion, and then judge it entirely on its individual appeal. I think that in Sommer's case, you, Williams and myself are appreciators of this kind. I can enjoy Bill's things regardless of their descent, evident or otherwise, from French or German artists of the last generation. He has certain perfections which many of the most lauded were lacking in. God DAMN this constant nostalgia for something always "new." This disdain for anything with a trace of the past in it!!! This kind of criticism is like a newspaper, always with its dernier cri. It breeds its own swift decay because its whole theory is built on an hysterical sort of evolution theory. I shall probably always enjoy El Greco and Goya. I still like to look at the things Sommer makes, because many of them are filled with a solid and clear beauty.

I have frequently wondered why you were so laggard in your interest in Eliot. Your recent announcement brings me much pleasure of anticipation. Please let [me] know what you find in Eliot. With your head knocked against Burke's over such a topic there ought to be some fine illuminations. You already know, I think, that my work for the past two years (those meagre drops!) has been more influenced by Eliot than any other modern. He has been a very good counter-balance to Matty's shifting morale and violent urgings. My amusement at Matty's acceptance of "F and H" considerably heightened by the memory of several sly hints against Eliot which some of his more recent letters had contained.

There is no one writing in English who can command so much respect, to my mind, as Eliot. However, I take Eliot as a point of departure toward an almost complete reverse of direction. His pessimism is amply justified, in his own case. But I would apply as much of his erudition and technique as I can absorb and assemble toward a more positive, or (if [I] must put it so in a sceptical age) ecstatic goal. I should not think of this if a kind of rhythm and ecstasy were not (at odd moments, and rare!) a very real thing to me. I feel that Eliot ignores certain spiritual events and possibilities as real and powerful now as, say, in the time of Blake. Certainly the man has dug the ground and buried hope as deep and direfully as it can ever be done. He has outclassed Baudelaire with a devastating humor that the earlier poet lacked.

After this perfection of death—nothing is possible in motion but a resurrection of some kind. Or else, as everyone persists in announcing in the deep and dirgeful *Dial*, the fruits of civilization are entirely harvested. Everyone, of course, wants to die as soon and as painlessly as possible! Now is the time for humor, and the Dance of Death. All I know through very much suffering and dullness (somehow I seem to twinge more all the time) is that it interests me to still affirm certain things. That will be the persisting theme of the last part of "F and H" as it has been all along. —/—/

125: To GORHAM MUNSON

[*Cleveland*]   *Jan. 10th, '23*

Dear Gorham: Your *Study* came day before yesterday. So far I have only had time for a single reading, but am ready to offer wholehearted congratulations. It IS much improved from the fragment I read last summer, and I think you have made a criticism that, besides being quite exact and fair, is dramatic—and very constructive beyond the actual boundaries of the man and subject concerned. I shall go over it again this evening. By early next week I hope to have some words for the jacket written,—later a review for the Double-Skull. I'll send them both to you as soon as they are ready, for suggestions or "corrections." By this time, according to a recent letter of yours, you will be something of a "copy" critic also.

Sommer's gratitude to you for your interest and success in helping him will never reach the frenzied pitch of a letter,—but I know that he feels quite deeply grateful. As I am his official and unofficial secretary in other matters I include mention of his sentiments here. I must admit that I personally got a greater "thrill" out of the news than any personal acceptances have given me for many a day.[1] — — — —

1. Sommer's work was accepted by *The Dial*.

126: To Gorham Munson

[*Cleveland*]   *Jan. 14th '23*

Dear Gorham: This (enclosed)[1] may, or may not yet be finished. Anyway, I think it is rounded enough as it is to be somewhat enjoyed.

Some things about it surprise and satisfy me. It has a bit of Dionysian splendor, perhaps an overtone of some of our evenings together last summer. It is so packed with tangential slants, interwoven symbolisms, that I'm not sure whether or not it will [be] understood. However, I am sure that it perfectly consorts with the other two parts of the poem as I intend them:

> Part I
> Meditation, Evocation, Love, Beauty
>
> Part II
> Dance, Humor, Satisfaction
>
> Part III
> Tragedy, War (the eternal soldier), Résumé, Ecstasy, Final
> Declaration

There is an organization and symphonic rhythm to III that I did not think I could do. The last three evenings have been wonderful for me, anyway! A kind of ecstasy and power for WORK.

III doesn't seem half long enough to me now—but I'm too much with and in it to know.

127: To Charmion Wiegand

[*Cleveland*]   *Jan. 20th, '23*

My dear Charmion: It didn't take me long to decide that Buschor's *Graechische Vasenmalerei* is a book that I shall always carry about with me, even though it has taken me an unforgivably long time to tell you so. You and Hermann [Habicht] have my sincerest gratitude for such an unexpected and beautiful holiday present.

With a few exceptions I prefer Egyptian sculpture to the Greek, and this book makes me feel that the Greeks had more to express in line and design than they had in the third dimension. In pottery you get the less ambitious and less "cosmopolitan" aspiration and expression of these people. There is an intimacy and rusticity to the pottery which especially appeals to the literary instinct. The famous

1. "Faustus and Helen" III.

Nike of Samothrace always left me somewhat cool. Lady Milo is a bit imposing (Jove's too near around the corner) and these idealized human dolls all stand too much on their dignity. O I know how they prostrated Heine and Pater et al., and I do respect them—but give me these lovely vase intaglios and arabesques—and maids and naughty satyrs with their rank lustful lives and leaves and brine and wine!

—/—/ I think it is a credit to Munson's platform and writing that so much attention has already been proffered *Secession.* I was very lukewarm in the beginning and urged him not to "waste his time" on any magazine project. But after his visit here last summer I quickly switched about, especially as *S* has contained such new and suggestive material as the last 2 numbers included. *Secession* gets away from the "temperamental" editorial attitude of *The Little Review* (good in many ways as this has been) and bases its judgment on more tradition while at the same time being far more daring in its experiments than such magazines as *The Dial.* It has been discouraging to see how very "safe" *The Dial* plays sometimes, despite its protests to the contrary.

I find that I have derived considerable stimulation from *Secession.* Without it there would be only the vague hope that the steady pessimism which pervades *The Dial* since Eliot and others have announced that happiness and beauty dwell only in memory—might sometimes lift. I cry for a positive attitude! When you see the first two parts of my "Faustus & Helen" that comes out in *Broom* in Feb. or March, you will see better what I mean. I've about finished the third and last part now, and am pleased at the finale. —/—/

I'm rather worn out with the incessant activities of the last two weeks—last *month,* in fact. I can't stand much "society" even with interesting people, and my acquaintance in Cleveland has somehow increased so extensively during the last two years that with work, reading, writing, etc., things are becoming entirely too febrile. You'll excuse my mention of such "ailments" I hope, as part of my excuse for delay in writing. But I have already probably exhausted you beyond "resentments" of such nature by this lengthy gust. — — — —

128: To Gorham Munson

[*Cleveland*]   *Jan. 24 '23*

Dear Gorham: I'll wait for your next letter before sending any other versions of "F. & H. III" The last two days have been occupied with the enclosed strange psychoanalytic thing. I can't quite justify the title in words, but it came to me quite freely as *the* right thing. Let me know how you like it.[1] —/—/

129: To GORHAM MUNSON

[Cleveland]   *Feb. 6" '23*

Dear Gorham: Everyone writes me such encouraging notes about "F and H" that I am doubly sorry that I ever sent any to *Broom* for publication. Frank wrote me a very shrewd appreciation of Part II which he probably repeated to you. Untermeyer's mention of me among the New Patricians prompted me to send him a copy after reading his article on Eliot in a recent *Freeman*. I disagreed with him openly on many points, but the substance of his last paragraph made me think he would be interested in reading the poem. I was rather foolish to follow such an impulse, but his answer was quite decent. He made the charge of a new type of "rhetoric," however, which is just what Frank took pains to mention as fully absent. Untermeyer comes here for a lecture on March 11th and says he wants to have a talk with me if possible. This is all right, but I am not keen about argument. Allen Tate writes me the most glowing praises possible, calls me the greatest contemporary American poet, etc., etc., so I feel about ready to deliver myself of my memoirs and expire in roses. And then, your appreciation has especially been enjoyed. You "get" the form and arrangement of the "Stark Major" poem much better than Frank does, but he is right about the second paragraph being too complicated and vague and you are wrong about the last verse being redundant. When I get the second verse worked out to suit me I'll send you another copy. In the meantime I am ruminating on a new longish poem under the title of *The Bridge* which carries on further the tendencies manifest in "F and H." It will be exceedingly difficult to accomplish it as I see it now, so much time will be wasted in thinking about it. Your news about *Broom* is discouraging in view of the fact that I had just sent part III of "F and H" to Matty last week. Everything has been bungled all the way through. I hope I can get enough material together during the next few months for a small volume where things can be arranged in proper order. I am so deadly sick of manipulating things with magazines, *The Dial* included. This latter refuses my "F and H" and then takes such a silly thing as that Apleton or what's-'ername woman contained this month in its covers. I have been so rushed around with too much society that I have not yet got at the

1. "Stark Major."

review for your study, but it will be done within two weeks anyway. It was much easier to rap out this enclosed review for Fitts. Let me know what you like or don't like about it. I am very awkward at reviews, mainly, I suppose, because the procedure is strange to me. I am through doing things for Sommer until he cooperates better. He has received notice and photographs from *The Dial* I learn from second hand. Ten days ago this was. I had especially asked him to phone me as soon as he heard anything definite from them, certainly a small task, but he never peeps or comes near. I shall not send back the photographs to you to show to anyone until he returns them to me. He knows I paid twenty dollars for them and that I want to keep them circulating, etc. He knew that I would be the one to write to *The Dial* and blow 'em up if they failed to keep their word on the reproductions, and naturally want to know the facts of the situation, yet he keeps his stolid distance. What's the use? It's too much trouble with all the rest I have to do, though I'd be only too glad to keep it up indefinitely if he'd show a little interest.—/—/

130: TO ALLEN TATE

[*Cleveland*]   *Feb. 6th, '23*

Dear Allen: I can't seem to get around to write you a decent consideration of your recent poems, "Yellow River," etc. When I get time to write, as now at the office, they are not by me, and you have already had evidence of my state of mind at other odd moments. Meanwhile, do not think me indifferent, please.

I'm afraid you will have to postpone your kind proclamations in regard to "F and H" until the three parts appear in book form and in proper sequence. The inadvertency of "The Springs of Guilty Song" in the *Broom* is too complicated to explain fully. Josephson is most unscrupulous in his editorship, and it takes so long to get word back and forth that I shall probably not send anything more to *Broom* even if they finish "F and H" with the other two parts. This is quite unlikely as Munson writes me doleful presages about its financial straits. Two more issues and it will probably expire. However, in case they do print the third part which I sent about two weeks ago, it will include a note at the bottom of the page explaining the sequence, etc., and correcting the misnomer "The Springs of Guilty Song." In regard to this latter I had a very fine appreciation from Waldo Frank who was quite astonished at it. Then with your fine praise and Munson's I feel more encouraged than ever about my work. I'm already started on a new poem, *The*

Bridge, which continues the tendencies that are evident in "Faustus and Helen," but it's too vague and nebulous yet to talk about.

In the next S_4N I have an amusing parody of Cummings and have asked Fitts, the editor, to send you a copy. Don't be puzzled by the name of this magazine, it's taken from the insignia of a mosquito fleet during the war, I think. I wish I could partake of the genuine Tatian Theory, but it's not so universal in its application, I fear, as it used to be. Sherry and bad Port are about all one succeeds in safely absorbing around here. When am I to expect that promised portrait of you?

131: TO WALDO FRANK

Cleveland, Ohio   *Feb. 7th, '23*

Dear Waldo Frank: I have not been so stimulated for a long time as I was with your letter and its exact appreciation of the very things I wanted to put into the second part of "For the Marriage of Faustus and Helen" or its misnomer, "The Springs of Guilty Song." The fact that its intention was completely evident to you without any explanations or "notes" from me, has renewed my confidence and made me quite happy. It has also made me doubly anxious that you should have a copy of the entire poem to read. This is enclosed, and, of course, is yours to keep if you want it. It has been very discouraging the way *Broom* has handled the publication of this poem. The mails are slow and unreliable, and Josephson is hasty, to say the least, in his methods. At best now, it will come out in broken sequence, and a final Note with part III cannot much repair the situation. I want at least a few of my friends to have the thing in decent shape.

A few planks of the scaffolding may interest you, so I'll roughly indicate a few of my intentions. Part I starts out from the quotidian, rises to evocation, ecstasy and statement. The whole poem is a kind of fusion of our own time with the past. Almost every symbol of current significance is matched by a correlative, suggested or actually stated, "of ancient days." Helen, the symbol of this abstract "sense of beauty," Faustus the symbol of myself, the poetic or imaginative man of all times. The street car device is the most concrete symbol I could find for the transition of the imagination from quotidian details to the universal consideration of beauty,—the body still "centered in traffic," the imagination eluding its daily nets and self consciousness. Symbolically, also, and in relation to Homer, this first part has significance of the rape of Helen by Paris. In one word, however, Part I stands simply for the EVOCATION of beauty.

Part II is, of course, the DANCE and sensual culmination. It is also an acceleration of the ecstasy of PART III. This last part begins with *catharsis,* the acceptance of tragedy through destruction (The Fall of Troy, etc., also in it). It is Dionysian in its attitude, the creator and the eternal destroyer dance arm in arm, etc., all ending in a restatement of the imagination as in Part I. You would probably get all these things without my crude and hasty mention of them, but to me, the entire poem is so packed with cross-currents and multiple suggestions that I am anxious that you should see the thing as I do, even though I have perhaps not succeeded in "putting over" all the points which I think I have. If you feel like severe criticism in any cases I shall certainly welcome it. Certainly I was not "hurt" by the very accurate criticisms you offered in your last letter.

"Nuances" in Part II takes the American pronunciation, that is, the "es" is voiced. You were quite right about the second verse in "Stark Major." I have never been satisfied with it as to clarity, and it will undergo revision before publication anywhere. −/−/

132: To Gorham Munson

[*Cleveland*]   *Feb. 9th, '23*

Dear Gorham: You don't deserve my pains in copying these two charming things of Allen Tate's until you send back that much belabored poem of Harris's, but these being yours to keep or throw away, I submit them casually, as possible material for *Secession.* Tate sent them to me this week, and seems to have written them in a mood of amusement with no idea of their publication anywhere. I shall not say anything at all to him about above considerations unless you should happen to want one or both of them. Tate has a whole lot to offer when he finds his way out of the Eliot idiom, which as you know, is natural to him, and was before he ever heard of Eliot. These things are certainly not imitative of anyone to [any] noticeable extent. They certainly beat Gerty Stein on her own ground—that is from the standpoint of her announced desire to break up poetry into an idiom corresponding to cubism, etc. Tate has much more precision, while giving the same broken effect. Not that I care a damn about such theories beyond their being merely interesting, but that may be because from now on I feel that personal problems of my own, extenuating from the experience in writing "F and H," will be enough to interest myself.

I am in a very unfavorable mood, and just after having congratulated myself strongly on security against future outbreaks of the affections. You see, for two or three years I have not been attacked in this way. A recent evening at a concert some glances of such a very stirring response and beauty threw me into such an hour of agony as I supposed I was beyond feeling ever again. The mere senses can be handled without such effects, but I discover I am as powerless as ever against those higher and certainly hopeless manifestations of the flesh. O God that I should have to live within these American restrictions forever, where one cannot whisper a word, not at least exchange a few words! In such cases they almost suffice, you know. Passions of this kind completely derail me from anything creative for days,—and that's the worst of it.

Tate wrote me a charming old fashioned sonnet on my picture that I recently sent him. Because, in a loose way, it is so clairvoyant, I confide it to you, an act which would be almost immodest in other circumstances.

133: TO ALLEN TATE

[Cleveland]   *Feb. 12th '23*

Dear Allen: Let me congratulate you on the "Tercets of the Triad," however mockingly intended. It is among your very best results, as is, also, the "Pins and Needles." O I shall not soon forget "grandfather's knees," etc., etc. The interweaving of the lines is very cunning. I think you display a great amount of cleverness also in the "Pins and Needles"—although I'm not sure that I applaud the name for this. There might be others more apropos. To my mind you beat "Gerty" Stein on her own race track. That is, you succeed much better than she in accomplishing what is her avowed aim—to split up lyrical or picture-word sequences into pieces in the same way that Cubists do in painting. She is entertaining only at the expense of all coherence, whereas you break things up into sharp impressions and also preserve the outlines of the scattered pieces. This comparison, now that I see it written, is aimless, because your directions and temperaments are so entirely different. Yet its record here may amuse you as an idea that immediately came to my mind when I read your poem.

Odd paradoxes occur. These things which you claim to have written for amusement only, seem to carry through so far as completeness of form is concerned better than "Yellow River" and "Quality of Mercy" where your "seriousness" was, if anything, too evident. You won't misunderstand me on this, I hope. I simply mean that your

satirical leanings are very strong . . . that their astringency frequently breaks up your lyrical passages and at other times overloads
them to the point of obscurity. In an indifferent or gay mood you
escape these encumbrances, as well as [the] slight tendency that such
endowments always carry with them—the danger of occasional lapses
into sentimentality. Do not be abashed. The same was true of no less
a man than Jules Laforgue, who was like you in many ways and who
naturally had far less temptations in Paris and Berlin than you and
I, Allen and Hart in Kentucky and Ohio (U.S.A.) respectively. If I
can find it I'll send you a scrap of De Gourmont's essay on Laforgue
that I translated last summer. This is more illuminating than anything I could offer.

I think you need to cultivate greater simplicity of statement in
your more emotional things,—however well your present facility suits
the more ornamented and artificial congruities of satire or brilliant
impressionism. In "Yellow River" there are many lines that are too
noble to be wasted,—some of great penetration and beauty. So all this
makes me wish you would devote some extra effort into perfecting
this poem, willfully extracting the more obvious echoes of Eliot. You
are certainly rich enough to get along without them. Don't let your
interest in *The Fugitive* woo too many things into too sudden print.
Forgive my pedantic bass and lifted finger, but I think you are inclined to too hasty mss. dispatches sometimes.

The ads are calling, so Addios. I feel like quoting the first verse
of *The Bridge* for a snappy close:—

> Macadam, gun grey as the tunny's pelt,
> Leaps from Far Rockaway to Golden Gate,
> For first it was the road, the road only
> We heeded in joint piracy and pushed.

134: To Allen Tate

[*Cleveland*]   *Feb. 15th, '23*

Dear Allen: —/—/ I enclose a note from James Daly, whose poetry
you may have sampled in *Broom*. He was here last Fall visiting a
mutual friend, and I think I showed him some of your verse. After
you have seen what "some others" think of you, please return the
enclosed. *Broom,* by the way, has busted; N. Y. office closed last
Saturday; March issue, the last, to be distributed from Berlin while
the tent-stakes are being pulled up. I rejoice in a way. At least they
won't get a chance to murder my "F and H" any more. *Secession*
will publish the three parts together probably sometime next sum-

mer. (There is no use in my sending anything more to *The Dial;* they just rejected my "Stark Major," and it is plain that their interest in helping American letters is very incidental. Note the predominance given to translations of the older generation of Germans, etc., who have absolutely nothing to give us but a certain ante-bellum "refinement." They aren't printing the younger crowd of any country.) All this should convince you, as well as myself, of the real place and necessity for *Secession.* Of course I'm sorry now that I fooled around sending "F and H" anywhere else at all. *Dial* had a chance at that, too, you know.

You may be indisposed to Waldo Frank, but I must recommend to you *City Block* as the richest in content of any "fiction" that has appeared in the American 20th century. Frank has the real mystic's vision. His apprehensions astonish one. I have also enjoyed reading Ouspensky's *Tertium Organum* lately. Its corroboration of several experiences in consciousness that I have had gave it particular interest.

135: TO GORHAM MUNSON

[Cleveland]   *Feb. 18th, '23*

Dear Gorham: — — — — Your summary of praises for "F and H" was such a fine tribute that it might account for my backache and confinement to the bed yesterday. But the more probable cause for *that,* however, is liquor and the cogitations and cerebral excitements it threw me into regarding my new enterprise, *The Bridge,* on the evening precedent. I am too much interested in this *Bridge* thing lately to write letters, ads, or anything. It is just beginning to take the least outline,—and the more outline the conception of the thing takes,—the more its final difficulties appal me. All this preliminary thought has to result, of course, in some channel forms or mould into which I throw myself at white heat. Very roughly, it concerns a mystical synthesis of "America." History and fact, location, etc., all have to be transfigured into abstract form that would almost function independently of its subject matter. The initial impulses of "our people" will have to be gathered up toward the climax·of the bridge, symbol of our constructive future, our unique identity, in which is included also our scientific hopes and achievements of the future. The mystic portent of all this is already flocking through my mind (when I say this I should say "the mystic possibilities," but that is all that's worth announcing, anyway) but the actual statement of the thing, the marshalling of the forces, will take me months, at best; and I may have to give it up entirely before that; it may be too impossible an ambition. But if I do succeed, such a waving of banners, such ascent of towers, such dancing, etc., will never before have been put down on paper! The form will be symphonic, something like "F and H" with its treatment of varied content, and it will probably approximate the same length in lines. It is perhaps rather silly to go on this way before more than a dozen lines have been written, but at any rate it serves to excuse my possible deficiencies in correspondence in the near future, should the obsession carry me much further. I hate to have to go to work every day! When I get *The Bridge* done, or something of equal length, I think it will be time to try Liveright or Huebsch or Knopf for a collected publication. Just now I have hardly enough of even quality and tone to satisfy me. Of course I'm glad to know that Wheeler and Wescott are interested in me, especially as I am led to respect their standards, but I might as well relinquish my mss. to the desk drawer as to offer its publication to Wheeler, at least so far as I know. Did he publish Turbyfill in Chicago? or was it Berlin? You will naturally see my reasons for at least attempting the more standard publishers first, I'm sure. And until I have the extra and necessary amount to add, there is no use committing myself to any arrangements at all. In passing I do want to thank you, Gorham, for your constant interest in interpreting me to others whose added interest all makes me confident that I have more to offer than I once supposed. And I am even more grateful for your very rich suggestions best stated in your *Frank Study* on the treatment of mechanical manifestations of today as subject for lyrical, dramatic, and even epic poetry. You must already notice that influence in "F and H." It is to figure even larger in *The Bridge*. The field of possibilities literally glitters all around one with the perception and vocabulary to pick out significant details and digest them into something emotional.

Your visit to Amy Lowell was a characteristic literary experience in American letters of the day, a baptism, as it were, from the Episcopal font, endowing you with the proper blessing and chastisement necessary for the younger generation. All hail to Amy's poetry propaganda! but I should not enjoy talking to her.

I think you discovered the weak points in my review pretty well. However, I think Wheelwright's recent letter about *Secession* in *The Freeman* displayed very little evidence as prose workmanship, even of the most fundamental nature. He certainly sustained himself much better as "Dorian Abbott." In the letter his partis pris emotionalism was too evident to convince his readers properly. In this sense, a course in advertising would be good for him, which reminds me that I'll soon send you one of my campaigns that not only "went over big" but is theoretically a good piece of work. Are you still studying this modern science?

It must be rather hellish reading through so many books every week that your eyes pop out. Truly, you must look for some editorial post, copywriting job, or something that will relieve you of such strains. I think you will probably find things much smoother in your new apartment which I'm delighted to think of. Is it in the Village? I can't quite place it. When I come down in June, I'll probably plan on staying with you and Elizabeth [Mrs. Munson].

Just now, it's Vulcan back to the Furnace! The "bowels" poem comes out in the next *S4N*, which bunch Tate writes that he has just joined through my communications. He has submitted "Pins and Needles," which I imagine Fitts will use. I'm waiting now for *The Dial* to send back my "Stark Major." Just sent a caricature of Paul Rosenfeld to *The Little Review*, telling them to publish it, if they cared to, "along with the rest of my inadvertent correspondence." It is called "Anointment of our Well Dressed Critic," or "Why Waste the Eggs?"—Three-dimensional Vista, by Hart Crane. Allons!

136: To — —

[*Cleveland*]   [*Feb. 20*]

Dear — —: Those who have wept in the darkness sometimes are rewarded with stray leaves blown inadvertently. Since your last I have [had] one of those few experiences that come,—ever, but which are almost sufficient in their very incompleteness. This was only last evening in a vaudeville show with — — — —. — — — — has manifested charming traits before, but there has always been an older brother around. Last night—it sounds silly enough to tell (but not in view of his real beauty)—O, it was only a matter of light affectionate stray touches—and half-hinted speech. But these were genuine and in that sense among the few things I can remember happily. With — — — — you must think of someone mildly sober, with a face not too thin, but with faun precision of line and feature. Crisp ears, a little pointed, fine and docile hair almost golden, yet darker,—eyes that are a little heavy—but wide apart and usually a little narrowed,— aristocratic (English) jaws, and a mouth that [is] just mobile enough to suggest voluptuousness. A strong rather slender figure, negligently carried, that is perfect from flanks that hold an easy persistence to shoulders that are soft yet full and hard. A smooth and rather olive skin that is cool—at first.

Excuse this long catalog—I admit it is mainly for my own satisfaction, and I am drunk now and in such state my satisfactions are always lengthy. When I see you ask me to tell you more about him for he is worth more and better words, I assure you. O yes, I shall see him again soon. The climax will be all too easily reached,—But my gratitude is enduring—if only for that *once,* at least, something beautiful approached me and as though it were the most natural thing in the world, enclosed me in his arm and pulled me to him without my slightest bid. And we who create must endure—must hold to spirit not by the mind, the intellect alone. These have no mystic possibilities. O flesh damned to hate and scorn! I have felt my cheek pressed on the desert these days and months too much. How old I am! Yet, oddly now this sense [of] age—not at all in my senses—is gaining me altogether unique love and happiness. I feel I have been thru much of this again and again before. I long to go to India and stay always. Meditation on the sun is all there is. Not that this isn't enough! I mean I find my imagination more sufficient all the time. The work of the workaday world is what I dislike. I spend my evenings in music and sometimes ecstasy. I've been writing a lot lately. —/—/ I'm bringing much into contemporary verse that is new. I'm on a synthesis of America and its structural identity now, called *The Bridge.* —/—/

137: TO WALDO FRANK

Cleveland, O.   *Feb. 27th '23*

Dear Waldo Frank: Such major criticism as both you and Gorham have given my "Faustus and Helen" is the most sensitizing influence I have ever encountered. It is a new feeling, and a glorious one, to have one's inmost delicate intentions so fully recognized as your last letter to me attested. I can feel a calmness on the sidewalk—where before I felt a defiance only. And better than all—I am certain that a number of us at last have some kind of community of interest. And with this communion will come something better than a mere clique. It is a consciousness of something more vital than stylistic questions and "taste," it is vision, and a vision alone that not only America needs, but the whole world. We are not sure where this will lead, but after the complete renunciation symbolized in *The Wasteland* and, though less, in *Ulysses* we have sensed some new vitality. Whether I am in that current remains to be seen,—but I am enough

in it at least to be sure that you are definitely in it already. What
delights me almost beyond words is that my natural idiom (which I
have unavoidably stuck to in spite of nearly everybody's nodding,
querulous head) has reached and carried to you so completely the
very blood and bone of me. There is only one way of saying what
comes to one in ecstasy. One works and works over it to finish and
organize it perfectly—but fundamentally that doesn't affect one's
way of saying it. The enclosed poem will evidence enough meaning
of that, I fear, in certain flaws and weaknesses that, so far, I've not
had the grace to change. The norm of accuracy in such things is,
however, at best so far from second-reader penetration, that bad as
it is, I can't resist sending it to you now.

Please do not feel it necessary to answer me until you are perfectly free from other preoccupations. I know what such things cost,
and knew before your last letter exactly why you delayed. (Now that
I see this written, it sounds all-too presumptuous; however, my appreciation was "prematurely ripe," for that idea did occur.)

Munson's *Study* came to me today. I think Liveright did a very
good job, better than I expected. The photograph seconded an impression I remembered of you several years ago in New York. I
may be repeating myself when I mention that you came into Brown's
Chop House one evening and greeted some friends near a table where
Harrison Smith and myself were dining;—only, of course this
Stieglitz portrait gives me a much deeper impression.—/—/

138: To Gorham Munson

[*Cleveland*]   *March 2nd, '23*

Dear Gorham: —/—/ The last several days have been equally among
the most intense in my life. The annoyance comes in only on the
swing of a repressive *fate*. To be stimulated to the nth degree with
your head burgeoning with ideas and conceptions of the most baffling interest and lure—and then to have to munch ideas on water
heaters (I am writing another book for house fraus!) has been a real
cruelty this time, however temporary. The more I think about my
Bridge poem the more thrilling its symbolical possibilities become,
and since my reading of you and Frank (I recently bought *City
Block*) I begin to feel myself directly connected with Whitman. I
feel myself in currents that are positively awesome in their extent
and possibilities. "Faustus and Helen" was only a beginning—but in
it I struck new *timbres* that suggest dozens more, all unique, yet
poignant and expressive of our epoch. Modern music almost drives

me crazy! I went to hear D'Indy's *II Symphony* last night and my hair stood on end at its revelations. To get those, and others of men like Strauss, Ravel, Scriabin, and Bloch into *words,* one needs to *ransack* the vocabularies of Shakespeare, Jonson, Webster (for theirs were the richest) and add our scientific, street and counter, and psychological terms, etc. Yet, I claim that such things can be done! The modern artist needs gigantic assimilative capacities, emotion,—and the greatest of *all—vision.* "Striated with nuances, nervosities, that we are heir to"—is more than a casual observation for me. And then—structure! What pleased me greatly about Frank's comment was the notice of great structural evidence in "F and H." Potentially I feel myself quite fit to become a suitable *Pindar* for the dawn of the machine age, so called. I have lost the last shreds of philosophical pessimism during the last few months. O yes, the "background of life"—and all that is still there, but that is only three-dimensional. It is to the pulse of a greater dynamism that my work must revolve. Something terribly fierce and yet gentle.

You have no doubt wondered why I have behaved so strangely about the review for your *Study.* It is coming sometime. At present I have developed a chronic hesitation against it which must seem almost pathological. I am so enthused about it that I can't seem to adopt a level-headed, conventionally-critical attitude about it. Also, the space for such considerations as I would like to [get] into is too restricted in the Double-Skull to permit much more than either a screed, ineffective or broken, or mere jacket type of advertisement. I hope you won't misinterpret my delay at any rate. As I said in my last note, the typography, paper, cover, photograph—everything in fact, is of the best taste and distinction. This book is bound to do you as much good as Frank. The latter is shown by Stieglitz's picture to be an extremely mystic type. Don't think me silly when I call the head and the eyes extremely beautiful. Frank has done me a world of good by his last letter (which promised another soon including further points on "F. & H.") and, as I wrote him, now I feel I can walk calmly along the sidewalk whereas before I felt only defiance. He gripped the mystical content of the poem so thoroughly that I despair of ever finding a more satisfying enthusiast.

And now to your question about passing the good word along. I discover that I have been all-too-easy all along in letting out announcements of my sexual predilections. Not that anything unpleasant has happened or is imminent. But it does put me into obligatory relations to a certain extent with "those who know," and this irks me to think of sometimes. After all, when you're dead it doesn't matter, and this statement alone proves my immunity from any "shame" about it. But I find the ordinary business of earning a living entirely too stringent to want to add any prejudices against me *of that nature* in the minds of any publicans and sinners. Such things have such a wholesale way of leaking out! Everyone knows now about B — —, H — — and others—the list too long to bother with. I am all-too-free with my tongue and doubtless always shall be—but I'm going to ask you to advise and work me better with a more discreet behavior. —/—/

139: TO CHARLOTTE AND RICHARD RYCHTARIK

[*New York City*]   *Sunday* [*March*]

Dear Lotte and Richard: —/—/ I am quite happy. A long walk this afternoon in salt air and clear sunlight. Everyone carrying canes and wearing bright clothes. Lunch tomorrow with Waldo Frank. Munson is enthusiastic about my staying with them. They have a fresh and charming apartment with room enough for me, so everything is FINE.

I sat a long while thinking about how beautiful you both were when I left you last night. Yes,—of course, Life is very beautiful when there are such people to meet and love as I love you both. Be very happy. Along with me. I never felt better before.

140: TO WALDO FRANK

[*New York City*]   *Easter*

Dear Waldo: —/—/ I don't need to mention that it was great to shake hands and talk with you. This I must mention, however,—that we have not yet had a real meeting. My mind has been packed with things that must be talked over with you when conditions are opportune. I am not intending mysterious words. But I am looking forward to the time—perhaps the time*s*—that we shall get together and (in the wonderful slang phrase) "spark." Since reading *City Block* I have not wavered in an enthusiastic conviction that yours is the most vital consciousness in America, and that potentially I have responses which might prove interesting, even valuable to us both. My statements are awkward, and I really do not know how to proceed about such conversations: they "usually," as you know, "just happen." All this leads to a very simple suggestion, however,—and that is that I hope you will let me know when you are next in town when we can lunch or dine together. — — — —

141: TO CHARLOTTE RYCHTARIK

New York City   *April 13th, '23*

Dear Lotte: I am glad that you can use the smock. Richard's illustration of you using it is very effective, and the "covers the earth" drawing is exemplary and inspirational indeed. —/—/

I am glad that you like *Our America*. Frank says some very wonderful things in that book. It is coming out again next year and with new additions. This time, as I understand him, he intends to mention my work in it. Meeting some of the older poets and writers down here is an odd experience. Most of them are very disagreeable, and don't talk the same language as we do, they are not concerned with the same problems. I read "Faustus and Helen" to a group of people last evening, and very few of them, of course understood anything that I was talking about. If it weren't for the praise and understanding I have received from people like Frank and Munson and Allen Tate, etc., I would begin to feel that I might be to blame. But this "new consciousness" is something that takes a long while to "put across." I want Richard to meet my friends, the Habichts, who have their apartment filled with lovely things to touch and look at, and who serve wonderful sherry and Benedictine. I have too many invitations to really enjoy. Your friends quickly turn into enemies here, unless you limit the time you give for social affairs. —/—/

142: TO ALFRED STIEGLITZ

[*New York City*]   *April 15th, '23*

Dear great and good man, Alfred Stieglitz: I don't know whether or not I mentioned to you yesterday that I intend to include my short verbal definition of your work and aims in a fairly comprehensive essay on your work. I had not thought of doing this until you so thoroughly confirmed my conjectures as being the only absolutely correct statement that you had thus far heard concerning your photographs. That moment was a tremendous one in my life because I was able to share all the truth toward which I am working in my own medium, poetry, with another man who had manifestly taken many steps in that same direction in *his* work. Since we seem, then, already so well acquainted I have a request to make of you regarding the kernel of my essay, which I am quoting below as you requested. Until I can get the rest of my essay on your work into form, I would prefer that you keep my statement in strict confidence. I would like to give it a fresh presentation with other amplifications and details concerning what I consider your position as a scientist, philosopher or whatever wonder you are. You know the world better than I do, but we probably would agree on certain reticences and their safe-guarding from inaccurate hands. I shall be up to see you probably very soon, and we can talk again. The reason for my not accompanying Mr. Munson this afternoon, however, is that I want to get into certain explanations of your photographs about which, now, I feel a certain proud responsibility.

*   *   *

"The camera has been well proved the instrument of personal perception in a number of living hands, but in the hands of Alfred Stieglitz it becomes the instrument of something more specially vital —apprehension. The eerie speed of the shutter is more adequate than the human eye to remember, catching even the transition of the mist-mote into the cloud, the thought that is jetted from the eye to leave it instantly forever. Speed is at the bottom of it all—the hundredth of a second caught so precisely that the motion is continued from the picture infinitely: the moment made eternal.

"This baffling capture is an end in itself. It even seems to get at the motion and emotion of so-called inanimate life. It is the passivity of the camera coupled with the unbounded respect of this photographer for its mechanical perfectibility which permits nature and all life to mirror itself so intimately and so unexpectedly that we are thrown into ultimate harmonies by looking at these stationary, yet strangely moving pictures.

"If the essences of things were in their mass and bulk we should not need the clairvoyance of Stieglitz's photography to arrest them for examination and appreciation. But they are suspended on the invisible dimension whose vibrance has been denied the human eye at all times save in the intuition of ecstasy. Alfred Stieglitz can say to us today what William Blake said to as baffled a world more than a hundred years ago in his 'To the Christians':

'I give you the end of a golden string:
    Only wind it into a ball,—
It will lead you in at Heaven's gate,
    Built in Jerusalem's wall.' "

143: To CHARLOTTE RYCHTARIK

[*New York City*]   [*ca. May 7*]

My dear Lotte: —/—/ R[ichard Rychtarik] wanted me to ask Frank about the privilege of translating some of the stories in *City Block*.

I got an answer from Frank this morning, suggesting that Richard translate the book if I thought him able. Well,—translating is difficult, and especially Waldo Frank is hard to translate, I am sure. I think it would be fine if Richard went ahead with the stories. But before any are published I think it would be wise to try them out on some other people who do Czech trans. from *Czech into English* and see how true the original style has been preserved. You are going to be angry with me for all this fuss, I am sure, but you see I have no way of judging how well Richard understands English as a literary language. I don't want to misrepresent Richard to Frank either. Please let me know what you think of my plan. I shall send you back the copy of *City Block* that R. brought. It is your copy *to keep;* Frank is going to send me another for myself.

I am going over to the office of *The Dial* now to leave Richard's drawings, etc., for their consideration. We can't expect to hear anything about them for two or three weeks. I'll let you know as soon as I do. −/−/

144: TO WILLIAM SOMMER

N. Y. C.   *May 9th, '23*

Dear Bill: At LAST a letter from you!!! And let me mention that it was one of the most beautiful I ever got from anyone. AND I am expecting more. I read it the second and third times during my meal last night down in one of the Italian restaurants on the lower East Side. There you get a bottle of wine (fine, too!) and a good meal (that delights the eyes as well as the stomach) for about $1. And such service! The waiters all beam and are really interested in pleasing you. As Rychtarik said when he was here last week, it's just like Europe. I don't know where I should have been by this time, however, had it not been for three or four fine people,—Gorham and his wife, and Slater Brown (the friend of Cummings, "B" in *The Enormous Room*) who, in spite of knowing me only a couple of weeks, has put me up nights in his room during the recent spell of grippe in the Munson household, and who has kept me in funds, poured wine into me, and taken me to the greatest burlesque shows down on the lower east side that you ever imagined. We went to one last night, and I so wished you were along. (They do everything but the Act itself right on the stage, marvelous jazz songs, jokes, etc., and really the best entertainment there is in N. Y. at present.) I have bids in for jobs at two very good agencies. The thing is a farce, however, the way you are kept waiting to know the outcome of one interview after another with various executives. J. Walter Thompson have had me on the string for three weeks, and a letter this morning tells me that within the next few days I must drag myself up there again for another interview with one more Thompson executive. It is the same way at Batten's. I shall have to cast about for anything available from stevedoring to table-waiting pretty soon if they don't get a move on.

Of course I have been rushing around to a lot of other agencies, too, but the ones I just mentioned are the only ones who have anything to offer me at the present time. I am very glad that you reminded me about the cost of the photographs as I certainly can use as much of that money as you can afford to send me at the present time. Hill charged me $20.00 for the six reproductions. I can't cash any check here, so if you can send me whatever portion of this amount in currency through the mail (I enclose an addressed envelope) I'll be immensely grateful. There is, you realize, no use whatever in my thinking about returning to Cleveland. I should simply have to go through the same process there of looking around for work, and under embarrassing conditions. You need me HERE, now, more than *there,* too, Bill, as I want to do everything I can to get your pictures shown around and maybe bought. And also, in almost every way, N.Y. is getting to be a really stupendous place. It is the center of the world today, as Alexandria became the nucleus of another older civilization. The wealthier and upper parts of the city have their own beauty, but I prefer as a steady thing the wonderful streets of this lower section, crowded with life, packed with movement and drama, children, kind and drab-looking women, elbows braced on window ledges, and rows of vegetables lining the streets that you would love to paint. Life is possible here at greater intensity than probably any other place in the world today, and I hope and pray that you will be able to slip down here for a week or so during the summer. You must plan on it. Later on I shall probably take a small apartment with Brown, and then there will be plenty of room for you to stay with us at no expense at all. —/—/

145: To Charlotte and Richard Rychtarik

[*New York City*]   *June 5th, '23*

Dear Charlotte and Richard: If you have seen or heard from my mother lately you know already that I am all fixed up in my own room and as happy as a bug in a rug! I wish you could see it for it is very pleasant. Two windows opposite each other so there is almost always a breeze, square high ceiling, newly-painted light-grey walls, black floor and white ceiling, and all black furniture very plain but plentiful. I have a fine large table to write on. When my luck turned it seemed to turn equally favorably in every direction. I am not having to live in any rooming house with an inquisitive land-lady always looking through the keyhole. A friend of my friend, Slater Brown, who has just left for a long trip in Europe, has let me take his room with all his own furniture and all for a very low price in comparison with the high rents everywhere around here. It's also right in the neighborhood where most of my friends are living. Add to this good fortune a fine new Victrola, and you see I am all ready to begin on *The Bridge* again. It would not have been possible to have done this if you had not been so generous and helped me out so much,—but I can't tell you how fine I feel to get my feet on the ground again and put my nose up into the sky again for a few minutes with the *Meistersinger* Overture.

New York has been like a blazing furnace for the last two days, but I shall be glad to stay here all summer working at my job and writ-ing. I feel that I am getting now just where I have longed to be for so long. I can have absolute quiet and seclusion when I want it, wine when I need it, and the intense and interesting spectacle of the streets and all the various people. —/—/

146: TO HIS MOTHER

[*New York City*]   *June 10th '23*

Dear Grace: —/—/ Really, I'm having the finest time in my life. There's no use trying to describe the people I go round with. Not that there are so many—there could easily be, but I'm always cutting down on all but the few I like the most. Last night marketing with Sue [Jenkins] and Bill Brown down in the Italian section (where everyone looks so happy!) was a perfect circus. We carried pots and pans, spinach, asparagus, etc., etc., from place to place—only buying one kind of thing in each store—jostling with the crowds, etc. I've never been with young people I enjoyed so much, and they, of course, have had real lives. Then there is Kenneth Burke up at the *Dial* office, Matty Josephson (who has suddenly been moved to value me highly), Edward Nagle, Gaston Lachaise, Malcolm Cowley—but what's the use going on with so many mere names. You can see how much fun I am having—and all the more because I have a job and a totally different world to live in half the time. Did I write you that I am getting quite a reputation with my "Faustus & Helen" poem?

Although it is only now being printed in Florence, those critics and writers who have seen it are acclaiming me with real gusto. Waldo Frank asked me to luncheon with him recently and said I was the greatest contemporary American poet with that piece alone. And John Cowper Powys, whose *Suspended Judgments* and *Visions and Revisions* you have read, is very enthusiastic. Since I got presented with my Victrola I am ready to start again on *The Bridge*. Waldo Frank is very anxious for me to have that finished, as he intends to take me up to his publisher (Boni & Liveright), and have me published in volume form. But, of course, such things *can't* be rushed as he understands.

I have not seen or heard from Miss Spencer since I made her my initial bow. She spoke of finding me something but evidently didn't sprain herself in the attempt. That's all right, however. There was little reason why she should have. I didn't *ask* her, anyway. I shan't see her again, as she is your friend and we have nothing special in common anyway. Waldo Frank, Alyse Gregory & others used some influence in getting me my job with *J. Walter Thompson* (get the name right this time!), but I never would have got it if my samples and conversation had not convinced them. I begin to see N. Y. very much more intimately since I've been working. It makes living here far more pleasant than ever before. Such color and style (on men, too) I've never seen before—no two alike. That's what is so interesting— the perfect freedom of wearing what you want to, walking the gait you like (I have a much less hurried gait than you're familiar with) and nobody bothering you.

I don't know many at the office yet. It's too immense and I'm confined to a highly specializing dept., but I've already been invited out to tea by the personnel secretary. They employ a lot of real writers as copywriters at Thompson's, and have an entirely different feeling about art & business than you encounter any place west of N.Y. In fact it's a feather in your cap if you know a little more than you're "supposed to" here. I think I've gained immeasurably by coming here now instead of dragging along in Cleveland month after month. —/—/

147: TO RICHARD RYCHTARIK

[*New York City*]   *June 21st, '23*

Dear Richard: —/—/ Dr. Watson, President of *The Dial* (Magazine), has seen your drawings, etc., and wants me to ask you if you would care to sell him "one" of them, and the rights for reproduction for *two* others in *The Dial*. He is offering the same price and terms to you that he made to Sommer,—$25.00 for the original, and the reproduction rights without any payment. So will you kindly let me know what you think about the matter very soon?

I don't know what selections he has made yet, and will probably have no time to see him for weeks, as I have office hours and he is seldom at *The Dial* offices,—but regardless of these details, I think that it would be wisdom for you to accept the terms, however modest, in view of the amount of prestige it will possibly give you, in the first place to be "hanging in his house," and in the second place to have your work shown to about 18,000 people through the pages of the magazine. Of course, I am *very* happy that he has liked your work so well. This makes *Two* artists' work that I have had a hand in getting exhibited,—both from my "home town." —/—/

148: To Alfred Stieglitz

[New York City]   *Fourth of July*

Dear STIEGLITZ: Your letter was the most welcome thing that has come to me in these last two weeks since you left, however late and partial my response may seem to be. You should have heard from me much before this if I hadn't been neck high in writing some climacterics for my *Bridge* poem. That simply carried me out of myself and all personal interests from the dot of five until two in the morning sometimes—for several days during which I was extremely happy. Those were also the very days when I wanted most to write you,—paradoxically as it sounds, I *was,* of course, for you and I meet on the same platform in our best and most impersonal moods,—SO, I've been with you very much. The thing which hurts me now that I have the time to write letters, is that I not only have left the creative currents that would have prompted me to better statements than I am usually equal to,—but also that I'm in a low state of reactions towards everything, following an evening with Mr. J——. Malice seems to settle inertly but very positively in some people, and as he is somehow attached to several really fine friends of mine whose company I would hate to forego on such account, I suppose I must learn to face this little clown with better results. So far, I can only say that wine is no ally against such odds. It even turns to vinegar! and that is much less pleasing than pure water. I don't need to say any more to you about this man, his vacant mind, vague eyes and empty hands. We've given that enough attention. I rant here merely because I have been cheated (willy-nilly) of pouring out a clearer cup today, as I had planned. I, in the end, am really the one to blame.

When I say that I welcomed your letter it doesn't mean that I was unconcerned enough with its testament of pain and accident not to think about you and your situation many hours. What the details of those matters were certainly would not help me to realize any the better that you have been going through a very tumultuous period and that it has been very fortunate that you should arrive in the country when you did, not that you escaped them,—but that you were able to *see* them more tranquilly. The city is a place of "brokenness," of drama; but when a certain development in this intensity is reached a new stage is created, or must be, arbitrarily, or there is a foreshortening, a loss and a premature disintegration of experience. You are setting the keynote now for a higher tranquillity than ever. It is an even wider intensity, also. You see, I am writing to you perhaps very egoistically, but you will understand that I am always seeing your life and experience very solidly as a part of my own because I feel our identities so much alike in spiritual direction. When it comes to action we diverge in several ways,—but I'm sure we center in common devotions, in a kind of timeless vision.

In the above sense I feel you as entering very strongly into certain developments in *The Bridge*. May I say it, and not seem absurd, that you are the first, or rather the purest living indice of a new order of consciousness that I have met? We are accomplices in many ways that we don't yet fully understand. "What is now proved was once only imagined," said Blake. I have to combat every day those really sincere people, but limited, who deny the superior logic of metaphor in favor of their perfect sums, divisions and subtractions. They cannot go a foot unless to merely catch up with some predetermined and set boundaries, nor can they realize that they do nothing but walk ably over an old track bedecked with all kinds of signposts and "championship records." Nobody minds their efforts, which frequently amount to a great deal,—but I object to their system of judgment being so regally applied to what I'm interested in doing. Such a cramping cannot be reconciled with the work which you have done, and which I feel myself a little beginning to do. The great energies about us cannot be transformed that way into a higher quality of life, and by perfecting our sensibilities, response and actions, we are always contributing more than we can realize (rationalize) at the time. We answer them a little vaguely, first, because our ends are forever unaccomplished, and because, secondly, our work is self-explanatory enough, if they could "see" it. I nearly go mad with the intense but always misty realization of what *can* be done if potentialities are fully freed, released. I know you to feel the same way about your camera,—despite all that you actually *have* done with it already. In that sense I hope to make it the one memorable thing to you in this letter that I think you should go on with your photographic synthesis of life this summer and fall, gathering together those dangerous interests outside of yourself into that purer projection of yourself. It is really not a projection in any but a loose sense, for I feel more and more that in the absolute sense the artist *identifies* himself with life. Because he has always had so much surrounding indifference and resistance such "action" takes on a more relative and limited term which has been abused and misunderstood by several generations,—this same "projecting." But in the true mystical sense as well as in the sense which Aristotle meant by the "imitation of nature," I feel that I'm right.

I shall go on thinking of you, the apples and the gable, and writing you whenever I can get a moment. So much has to be crammed into my narrow evenings and holidays, that I am becoming a poor correspondent with everyone, I fear. You will realize how much I am with you, I feel sure, by other signs. I am sending you a roughly typed sheet containing some lines from *The Bridge*.[1] They symbolize its main intentions. However, as they are fragmentary and not in entirely finished form, please don't show them around. I only want you to get a better idea of what I'm saying than could be "said" in prose. Some of the lines will be clear enough to give a glimpse of some of my ideas whether or not the Whole can be grasped from such fragments or not. — — — —

149: To Charlotte Rychtarik

[*New York City*]   *July 21st '23*

Dear Charlotte: Your lovely letter came to me this morning . . . I read it on the way to work. And I am full of happiness that you think of me as you do,—both you and Richard. Yes, it is my birthday and I must be a little sentimental,—especially as all my friends have recently left the city for places more cool and green and watery. It has been a frightful day, torrid and frying. And I have just come back from a lonely meal in Prince Street,—the place where Richard ate with me, and where I have been many times since he left. Ah, yes, *there* is wine, but what is wine when you drink it alone! Yet, I am happy here in my room with the Victrola playing Ravel,—the

1. See Weber, *op. cit.*, pp. 426-28.

Faery Garden piece which you and I heard so often together up in
my room in Cleveland. When I think of that room, it is almost
to give way to tears, because I shall never find my way back to it. It
is not necessary, of course, that I should, but just the same it was
the center and beginning of all that I am and ever will be, the center of such pain as would tear me to pieces to tell you about, and
equally the center of great joys! *The Bridge* seems to me so beautiful,
—and it was there that I first thought about it, and it was there that I
wrote "Faustus and Helen," which Waldo Frank says is so good that
I will be remembered by that, whether or not I write more or not.
And all this is, of course, connected very intimately with my Mother,
my beautiful mother whom I am so glad you love and speak about.
Indeed it was fine of you to go over and see her as I asked you to do,
Charlotte and Richard! And may I also say, in the same breath, that
your letter was very painful? It really was,—because I have known all
the things you said about her unhappiness for many, many months.
And there is really nothing that can be done: that is the worst of it.
I am sure if you think a minute about my Grandmother's age you
will realize from that alone that my Mother could not possibly leave
her to come here or anywhere else. And my Grandmother, at her age,
cannot move. My mother has had her full share of suffering and I
have had much, also. I have had enough, anyway, to realize that it
is all very beautiful in the end if you will pierce through to the center
of it and see it in relation to the real emotions and values of Life. Do
not think I am entirely happy here,—or ever will be, for that matter,
except for a few moments at a time when I am perhaps writing or
receiving a return of love. The true idea of God is the only thing
that can give happiness,—and that is the identification of yourself
with *all of life*. It is a fierce and humble happiness, both at the same
time, and I am hoping that my Mother will find that *feeling* (for it
need not be a conscious thought) at some time or other. She must *accept everything* and as it comes (as we all must) before she can come
to such happiness, glorious sorrow, or whatever you want to call it.
You must never think that I am not doing all I can to make my
Mother's life as bright as possible, even though I do not always succeed. I am doing work of a kind which I should not choose to do at
all except that it makes me (or will make me) more money in the
end than the simpler things which would satisfy my own single requirements—and just because I want to provide for my mother's future as much as I can. We shall be together more and more as time
goes on, and this separation at present is only temporary. You don't
know how grateful I am that you have given her your sympathy and

love, and that has been *real* or she would not have confided in you the way she has. −/−/

I hope that I have not put you and Richard to too much trouble about those books. They will be fine here with me in my room. Mother sent me my trunk (that much debated question which you will remember!) this week, and it was full of all kinds of dear familiar things that you have seen and touched in my room. There is that ivory Chinese box, for instance, which is here before me as I write. It looks very charming on the black table next to the jade Buddha that Harry [Candee] brought me from China.

I have not written much this last week,—too hot for one thing,— and then there are always people dropping in in the evening. But I am sending you a copy (to keep) of the last part of *The Bridge* which is all that I have done so far, that is, in a lump.[1] You will remember enough of what I told you a long time ago about my general ideas and the plan of the entire poem to understand it fairly well anyway. It is sheer ecstasy here,—that is, all my friends who have seen it, say that. It was written verse by verse in the most tremendous emotional exaltations I have ever felt. I may change a few words in it here and there before the entire poem is finished, but there will be practically the same arrangement as what you see. If I only had more time away from office work I should have made much faster progress, —but I am perfectly sure that it will be finished within a year,—and as it is to be about four or five times as long as the enclosed fragment when it is complete,—I shall have been working about as fast on it as I have ever worked in the past. I am especially anxious to finish it, however, because than I shall have all my best things brought out in book form, and with a jacket or cover by Richard Rychtarik, I hope. Waldo Frank is anxious to introduce me to his publisher when the right time comes, and so there is no doubt but that the book will come out eventually. In the meantime there is a long essay that I hope to write on the photography of Alfred Stieglitz. I ought to have about two weeks for that *away from everything,* when I could shut myself up somewhere and not have my mind taken away from it for a moment. In it I shall have to go very deep,—into, perhaps, some of the most delicate problems of art in the future. You see, I too, have my moments of despair,—for there is so little time for me to think about such things. I am succeeding in my position with the advertising agency quite well,—but all that means *more* work there, and even *less* time for what I want to do. I am forced to be ambitious in two directions, you see, and in many ways it is like

1. See Weber, *op. cit.,* pp. 428-9.

being put up on a cross and divided. I hope to succeed in them both,
—the reasons you will easily understand. This last week I got pro-
moted to the copy department, and on Tuesday night I shall take
the train for Chicago. Business of the company, of course, which will
keep me out of New York for probably about ten days or two weeks.
Being with the largest advertising agency in the world is giving me
fine experience that will get me higher-paid positions in other places
after awhile. In many ways I have been very lucky to get placed so
well at my age, so I complain about nothing except that I would
like to have the days twice as long as they are—for all I want to do.
—/—/

150: TO ALFRED STIEGLITZ

[*New York City*]   *Aug 11" '23*

Dear Stieglitz: The imagination dwells on frangible boughs! For ten
days now I've been travelling through the middle west on *business*
for the company. Investigating certain sales facts and figures among
hardware and paint dealers on "Barrelled Sunlight," a kind of white
paint! My mind is like dough and *The Bridge* is far away. Your
card was a warm signal to me on the morning of my joyful return.
I never saw the Venus in her sphere before—looking on the world
with the wind from Delphos in her hair! How do you do it? You have
the distinction of being classic and realistic at once. That, of course,
is what *real* classicism means. You don't know how much I think
about my essay on you and your work! Please don't think me faith-
less. I fly in a rage when I think of the sacrifices I pay just to feed
myself in the hope of time—a rightful heritage of all of us—and it
takes time to say and think out the things I feel in your photographs.
I'll try and write you more soon, but don't misunderstand any si-
lences from me. *I am your brother always*—

151: TO HIS MOTHER

[*New York City*]   *Aug 11 '23*

Dear Grace and Grandma: —/—/ I came near a collapse near the
middle of the week—the trip, hot weather, etc., certainly tested me
and worries kept me from much sleep—as things are. N.Y. is bad in
the summer anyway—takes all the vitality you have to give and gives
you back nothing to build with or repair. I hope things are going
better now. I'll write maybe during next week—but worry about
correspondence is a burden sometimes when I have so much new

work to think about. You'll understand me, I hope, in any case. I enjoyed your letter, Grandma, and it wasn't too long. You write extraordinarily well!

152: To Charlotte and Richard Rychtarik

[*New York City*]   *Sunday, Aug. 19th*

Dear Lotte and Richard: Not much has happened since I got back, but it will interest you to know that — — — — came around for lunch one day last week—and we had a talk about the book, *Ulysses!* I didn't openly accuse him of *stealing* it, just "borrowing" it,—but he certainly revealed a very weak position, leaving me to think more than ever that he is dishonest. He denied that he had been up to my room at all until I reminded him that he had told me so himself just a few weeks before, and that, anyway, my Mother had mentioned that he had been up there and had spoken about "borrowing" the book himself. This seemed to throw him into great confusion. He said he would look around among his things in his trunk, then, and "see" if he had taken it and forgotten to mention it to me. Imagine! Anybody who takes a book of such a size and value DOES NOT FORGET ABOUT IT SO EASILY. It seems to me that in admitting a thing like that he has practically admitted all I suspected. I told him to go ahead and look for it,—but he has probably sold it, and he will also probably keep away from me until I go after him in earnest. It would not have been tactful of me to accuse him of stealing right away,—but if he has done that I think he is going to be sorry for it. Isn't it hard to believe!!!!

I also talked to him about the way he acted about your pictures—and told him that I had agreed with you both in your attitude. It seemed to make him furious that you had spoken to me about it, and he said he was going to write you—evidently an angry letter. Maybe you have got it by this time. It is all too bad—it has really shocked me enormously to have discovered such crooked hypocrisy in such a good mind. I was anxious that you should know about my conversation with — — — — because, if he does write you as he said he would, you will know that I have tried to be as honest as I know how to be. —/—/

It is a beautiful day here, but as usual, I am sitting in, reading and writing. Just had breakfast with Gorham Munson and Liza, his wife. You would really like Liza, Charlotte. She teaches dancing and is dark and quiet and beautiful. The Munsons are about the only friends of mine who are now in town—all the rest being away in the country. —/—/

153: TO HIS MOTHER

[New York City]   *Aug. 24th, '23*

Dear Grace: —/—/ But I didn't accuse him of anything further at the time—and haven't since,—hoping that he would possibly be able to get hold of the book and return it to me somehow, if he got frightened enough. However, I have a letter all written to him. It will be sent just as soon as I get time to type it out; probably this week-end. There's nothing doubtful about what I say in it either. I'm only sorry that no action can be taken against him. We are both out of the state where the theft occurred—and the book has been banned by the mails, anyway, so I wouldn't get much favor in the courts on that account. — — — — had the brass to come here the other day (this makes me think him almost nutty) and instead of having himself announced at the outer reception room—comes ranging around among the people in the office, inquiring for me, and then comes up and stands and chats at my desk without the least concern! AND— what do you suppose he wants of me. —/—/ Just think of such an idiotic project—to say nothing of assuming that I would care to risk my standing around here for such a project! Then he keeps asking me out to the — — — — with a kind of desperate insistence, as though he thought I could be recompensed for his defaulting by satisfying some "social aspirations." He certainly is terrible, silly as well.

I feel one hundred per cent better since I got back to copy work. I'm up on the fourteenth floor now with a wonderful view out over the Murray Hill section and the East River right off the edge of my desk. I'm far from being dissatisfied, as you suggested. The plain fact was, and still is—that New York takes such a lot from you that you have to save all you can of yourself or you simply give out. I need a good bed, but it will be a long time before I can get one unless you feel like shipping that little brass bed on the third floor down here to me sometime. That would be fine, and could serve me always here, but you'll probably think it is out of the question to send it. It doesn't make much difference how early you go to bed if you can't get to sleep—you know that. And that has been the state of things with me for some time here. However, I'm really feeling all right. It's just tiredness—and worry that you are very, very unhappy—what to do— etc.

I don't know what is wrong with Charlotte and Richard. They

haven't sent my books to me on the date they said they would, nor have I had a word from them since Cleveland. If they are going to get upset and offended about something that I don't even guess having said to injure them—then, they, like a whole lot of other people who go around just aching to cut their own heads off, will have to do it. Perhaps they've just been very busy, though; it's certainly too early yet to make any definite assumptions. —/—/

154: To Alfred Stieglitz

New York City   *Aug. 25th, '23*

Dear Stieglitz: I am hoping that you have seen Waldo, as you mentioned in your letter, by this time. The idea seemed so sensible to me, knowing as I have, the uneasy frictions that have bothered both of you and having regretted so much the evident misunderstandings all around. It is very important for us all—that is, all who are trying to establish an honest basis for what work we get a chance to do. It isn't, as you say, a matter of politics,—but something akin to our spiritual bread and butter. Not all our manna comes from the skies. And we suffer all-too-much from social malnutrition once we try to live *entirely* with the ghostly past. We must somehow touch the clearest veins of eternity flowing through the crowds around us—or risk being the kind of glorious cripples that have missed some vital part of their inheritance.

It's good to hear that you have been "at the camera" again and that you are recovering, with physical and nervous rest, that extremity of delicate equilibrium that goes into your best activities. I know what it is to be exiled for months at a time. They're the usual things with me, and lately it has been especially hard to be cut up between the necessities of a readjustment at the office (they've put me into a new department and I enjoy writing copy again to some extent) and the more natural propulsion toward such things as *The Bridge*. I've been in such despair about this latter for some time!— not seeing my way to introduce it in the way I want (the end and climax, what you have seen, is all that's done so far) and not getting the needful hours to ripen anything in myself. If I can once get certain obligations disposed of in my family, I shall certainly break loose and do only such simple labor for my room and board as will not come into my consciousness after "working hours." Streams of "copy" and ad layouts course through my head all night sometimes until I feel like a thread singed and twisted in the morning. This has been, very likely, as strenuous [a] year and as wasteful a one as I shall encounter for a long time, although you can never foretell such things as long as you have a family and connections. But I am looking forward to a more equable program when winter comes, when people's windows are shut, cats are quieter and the air more bracing.

Every once in a while I [get] a statement or so noted down in regard to my interpretation of you and your photographs. There are still many things in the lucid explanation of them that simply baffle me. To use a modern simile that occurred to me in that connection— it's like trying to locate "the wires of the Acropolis"; indeed, I may call my essay by that name before I get through. A little recent study of Picasso and his Harlequins has been illuminating on the inner realities and spiritual quantities that both of you possess, and perhaps by the time you get back to town I'll have some other comparisons ready for you to deny or substantiate. I certainly miss seeing you, now, and wish you might send me one or two of those prints that are otherwise committed to the waste basket sometime soon.

155: To His Mother

[New York City]   Sept. 8th, '23

Dear Grace and Grandma: Both of your last letters have been so sweet and gratifying that I am very grateful. I am glad to think of you as located for the winter, putting in coal, and assured of the comforts that I know you ought to have. They have raised the rent on Gorham and Liza,—and they have been trying to locate a new place at a more reasonable figure, but they may not move at all— so discouraging is the search. That's one of the banes of New York —one is on a moving cloud here most of the time, for, either the house you live in is being torn down for an apartment, or else the landlord is gouging you constantly for your last cent. I never want to have any of us without some property of our own—land and building—whether we live in it or not, but just so that "we have it" and are not entirely subject to the whims of fortune. If I ever get any money, I know that I shall attend to that investment before I travel or anything else. You've got to have an anchorage somewhere if you are ever to have any repose of mind.

Of this latter-mentioned article—I can't say I have had much recently. Of all the abominable snakes I ever heard of — — — — is the worst. I got a letter on Wednesday from — — — —. He had evidently feared my exposure of him to them—and to ward it off he took the pains to tell her that I was a venomous person, upset by the heat of the City, and trying to torture him for mere pleasure. She recommended a dose of pills, a swim, etc., as a means of clearing up my head—and otherwise insulted me. The next morn—comes a letter from — — — — himself—in which he denies that his letter constituted a confession at all, said that the money was sent merely out of consideration for my loss, etc., and other kinds of weak trashy statements. I shall not reply to him, but I wrote — — — — that if she had any interest in the truth or cared to alleviate her own responsibilities in imposing such opinions on me—she might come into town someday next week and take lunch with me. I mentioned that I hadn't the time to write out the extensive evidence that I had, but that I should be glad to discuss them with her viva voce. The whole matter made me ill the next day—but the worst now is over, whether I ever get anything out of — — — — or not. I shall not press the claim further than the telling of the story to — — — —; it isn't worth it. There is absolutely no doubt about the confession in the letter, however, and I am keeping it well out of reach in my trunk.

—/—/ By the end of a summer in New York everybody is at the limit of endurance; there is no place to rest, get away from the constant noise and vibrations of trucks, etc., and there's a kind of insidious impurity in the air that seems to seep from sweaty walls and subways. Next year I shall have at least a month in the open country or by the sea—I haven't had a real vacation now for several years, you know. The time spent in idleness when out of a job was always a worse strain than the hardest kind of labor, so that hasn't counted for much with me.

—/—/ I see much of Gorham and Liza—they are restful to me and always kind. I don't think I should care to stay in New York long if they weren't here. —/—/

156: TO CHARLOTTE RYCHTARIK

New York City   *Sept. 23rd, '23*

Dear Charlotte: —/—/ I am planning to move myself, and shall probably share with the Munsons in their [new] apartment. That would enable them to get a better place and I should have hot water and good heat for the winter which the place I am in now does not provide. I am wondering if you and Richard could spare me a loan of fifteen dollars to help me over the expenses of moving my things. I have not yet received a raise in salary at the office, and I have been getting so little that I am kept down to the bare necessities of life all the time. When something extra is demanded I have nothing to fall back upon and the situation is really far from pleasant. If you could do this I shall be able to pay you sometime soon, I think, and I would be a thousand times obliged.

I am getting along very well at the office, but I intend to speak up for an advance in pay very soon. The wages they have been paying me have been much less than my capabilities are worth, and I don't think I shall have much trouble in getting that raise if I speak about it to them. They are putting new responsibilities upon me all the time, and I am learning quite a good deal. But there is something necessary in life besides learning, as we all know. It is quite a stylish and almost snobbish set of educated people at J. Walter Thompson's —they are very lofty and certainly seem to think that the social superiority of the place is enough to make up for low salaries. When they can pay one of their art directors 30,000 a year they can afford to pay some of their copywriters more than they do.

I am working still on *The Bridge,* but it is far from complete yet. In the meantime I am working on some smaller poems that crop out from time to time very naturally. The situation for the artist in America seems to me to be getting harder and harder all the time. Most of my friends are worn out with the struggle here in New York. If you make enough to live decently on, you have no time left for your real work,—and otherwise you are constantly liable to starve. New York offers nothing to anyone but a circle of friendly and understanding brothers,—beyond that it is one of the most stupid places in the world to live in. Of course, one's friends are worth it,—but sometimes, when you see them so upset by the fever and crowded conditions, the expenses and worries—you wonder whether or not there is much use in the whole business. I am, of course, rather tired out when I say these things. I shall probably be in a different and better mood later on when the weather cools, and when there is some life in the air. I have been through the hardest summer in my life—the hardest year, perhaps, when you consider the developments I have been through and the material difficulties that I have encountered. I want to keep saying "YES" to everything and never be beaten a moment, and I shall, of course, never be really beaten.

—/—/ He is in a very strange state of mind now that is dangerous. He and his wife, — — — — have separated. I have heard them each tell their stories, and there is nothing nasty or petty about it at all— they have simply agreed that they have failed in establishing a certain deep relationship which they had felt was a part of the reason for their being together, and they are still very good friends. It is complicated for both of them, however, by the fact of their baby boy, which both are very attached to.

I have been making a number of drawings lately. One of Jean Toomer, one of Waldo, and one of an amusing young lady. They are all very interesting, and even Gaston Lachaise, who was in to see me recently, thought that they were worth while. If I had time I should do more, but it is really only when I am not doing what I want to in my writing that I am very much tempted to draw. So I shall probably not do any more drawings for a year or so. —/—/

157: To His Mother

New York   *Oct. 5th '23*

Grace, dear! I had just got my pajamas on last night when there was a rap on the door. I opened and in walked Waldo Frank—behind him came a most pleasant-looking, twinkling, little man in a black derby—"Let me introduce you to Mr. Charles Chaplin,"—said Waldo, and I was smiling into one of the most beautiful faces I ever expect to see. Well!—I was quickly urged out of my nightclothes and the three of us walked arm in arm over to where Waldo is staying at 77 Irving Place (near Gramercy). All the way we were trailed by enthusiastic youngsters. People seem to spot Charlie in the darkness. He is so very gracious that he never discourages anything but rude advances.

At five o'clock this morning Charlie was letting me out of his taxi before my humble abode. "It's been so nice," he said in that soft crisp voice of his, modulated with an accent that is something like Padraic Colum's in its correctness. Then he, blinking and sleepy, was swung around and was probably soon in his bed up at the Ritz.

I can't begin to tell you what an evening, night and *morning* it was. Just the three of us—and Charlie has known Waldo quite a while—they've been in Paris together and have a few mutual friends.

Among other things Charlie told us his plans (and the story of it) for his next great film. He has a five acre studio all his own now in Berkeley, and is here in New York at present to see that the first film he has produced in it gets over profitably. He doesn't act in it. But he wrote story, directed and produced it entirely himself. It's running now for just a week or so more at the "Lyric" theatre to box prices. Then it will be released all over the country. *A Woman of Paris* it's called. I haven't seen it yet.

Our talk was very intimate—Charlie told us the complete Pola Negri story—which "romance" is now ended. And there were other things about his life, his hopes and spiritual desires which were very fine & interesting. He has been through so much, is very lonely (says Hollywood hasn't a dozen people he enjoys talking to or who understand his work) and yet is so radiant and healthy, wistful, gay and *young*. He is 35, but half his head is already grey. You cannot imagine a more perfect and natural gentleman. But I can't go on more now. Stories (marvelous ones he knows!) told with such subtle mimicry that you rolled on the floor. Such graceful wit, too—O that man has a mind.

We (just Charlie & I) are to have dinner together some night next week. He remembered my poem very well & is very interested in my work.

There's nothing else worth telling you about since my last letter. I am very happy in the intense clarity of spirit that a man like Chaplin gives one if he is honest enough to receive it. I have that spiritual honesty, Grace, and it's what makes me clear to the only people I care about.

158: To His Mother

[*New York City*]   *Oct. 12th,'23*

Dear Grace and Grandma: —/—/ It has been a very busy week. I have not seen Chaplin as I expected to, he has been under the weather up at the Ritz — — — —. But Jean Toomer, Margaret Naumburg and Waldo Frank have been very much in evidence, and to the extent of a very fine home-cooked chicken dinner one evening at Margaret's which almost left me gasping—I ate so much. Toomer and I are great friends. I want to send you a copy soon of his book of short stories and a play which has just come out. It may interest you to read the inscription which he placed in the copy of this book which he recently gave me:— "For Hart, instrument of the highest beauty, whose art, four-conscinal, rich in symbols and ecstasy, is great—whose touch, deep and warm, is a sheer illuminant—with love, Jean.—New York, 24th Sept 23."—/—/

Since the weather cooled I have felt almost a new being. Having had the gas turned on in my radiator and tried it out several times, I am now confident that I shall be able to keep quite warm during the winter. Two friends of mine have offered me the use of their tubs and faucets whenever I want a hot bath, which I shall avail myself of, providing I cannot succeed in persuading the landlady to install a hot water heater here. I do not think I shall have to buy any more clothes before spring what with the suit you are sending and what I have on hand to use. This certainly is fortunate, as my present salary at Thompson's just suffices for rent and food, really nothing more. I am waiting until the end of this month, the sixth month, to inquire about the possibilities of a raise. If I find that I am stalled off, I shall quietly investigate for a position elsewhere. —/—/ I have been working very hard this week on a stiff sort of proposition. So far they have given me only tough little nubbins to handle—jobs that didn't pay them anything and could best be turned over to a cheap man,—these little left-overs are, however, very often the most uninspiring and difficult things to handle.

—/—/ I think of you a great deal, and you must not be lonely. We are all going on in the regular course of things toward a higher consciousness of life and what it means. We have no reason or right to suppose that it should be predominantly happy—seen completely, from end to end, however, I think it is a great happiness. We must keep on over-riding the details of pettiness and small emotions that dwarf it to keep on seeing it that way, and that can't be done without a real conscious effort and vision. We know each other too well to let physical separations mar very much. Christmas is not so far away now, either, and then I shall see you for several days. —/—/

159: To His Mother

New York City   *Oct. 20th, '23*

Dear Grace and Grandma: —/—/ I've been feeling so altogether rotten lately that my energies are about reduced to their minimum. In fact I am seriously considering going to the Isle of Pines this winter for a thorough rest and recuperation from the strain of the last five years. This is no sudden idea in my head,—it is something I have reconsidered many times for several months, and always with the growing conviction that it is the thing to do. I think that in weighing the numerous reasons you will agree with me quite thoroughly.

In the first place—my state of nerves and insomnia here due to the mad rush of things, and the noisy nights around the place I am obliged to live in, makes it imperative that I get away before I have a real breakdown. I feel that this is certain to happen before the winter is over unless I get some relief. And, as there seems to be no prospect of a raise in my salary at the office, I cannot afford necessities here that make life bearable and sufficient to keep me in a state of health.

And then, besides all this, the Island needs some personal attention from someone in this family. You, neither of you, are able to go, and if you were, it would cost you three or four times as much as I will need to live there. (My expenses would be just the boat fare and after that about 5 dollars a week for board with the Simpsons.) I need absolutely no more clothes or equipment in any way than I presently have, so that needn't be bothered about. I would have a chance to breathe in some clear air, swim and use my body a little freely. I could live very simply and constructively—and really make it pay besides by seeing the lay of the land, how things are being cared for, what marketing opportunities are developing in the way of cooperative fruit markets, etc.

I think this and other letters of mine have said enough about living conditions in New York as it has now become—to make it plain that you will never want to settle here. I have never accented these points in any particular relation to you—but I am more and more certain that you will never want to *live* here. Rents are terrific, food very high and unless you have unlimited funds you have to content yourself with trying to keep clean in a dinky stuffy apartment without a porch or any of the outdoor privileges that go with the poorest shanty. I think we have been not fools, but fooling ourselves, to have worried so about selling the island place. That is the best place to live I know of,—the place where you will be far happier than ever tied up in an overcrowded city—paying out every month more money than your food would cost you for a year on the Island. Besides,— that grove is going to pay, and *pay well* sometime. It will pay you well enough to afford a month's change in New York every year. And that's enough! I have learned that from plentiful experience.

After the winter I can come back here to New York and get plenty of jobs that will pay more than what I have now. I can come back with a fund of health and energy that simply couldn't be gained here even if I weren't working at all. I think I deserve this much assistance not only as a son—but as [a] man who has done his best to cope with all situations that have come up, and I have been faced with some hard ones. This isn't a dodge—it's a sane precaution, and if you really care for me in [the] right sort of way you will give it your approval, I'm sure.

Please don't think that I'm flat on my back or anything like that— by what I've said. I have been at the office every day and doing my regular work. It's the steady and growing strain of it all that I feel— without relief or rest, and I don't want to disregard too many red signals—at least with the obvious means we have of checking danger of this seriousness. I don't want you to waste a lot of money by coming down here in the belief that I need bedside attention, I only want you to know the facts as they are. If I went I should certainly spend a week with you beforehand. But, of course, I'll never consider living in Cleveland again permanently—no matter what happens.

Write me soon what you think of my suggestions. I think we should certainly not let that island property slip away. It's a clean home with beautiful surroundings and sunshine with quiet and tranquillity—compared to this metropolitan living with its fret and fever—it's a paradise.

160: TO ALFRED STIEGLITZ

New York City   *Oct. 26th, '23*

Dear Stieglitz: I hardly know how to begin—such confusion reigns at present. It's the usual state, however, with the additional complication that my nerves are a little frazzled. In fact they got so on edge writing that damned advertising under the pseudo-refined atmosphere of the office I was working in that I had to resign the other day to save my mind. I have the prospect of coming back after a six week's vacation if I want to—but I don't want to, and as things stand at present, haven't got the money to carry me through the rest and contemplation that I need. Rather wound up, you see!

Your mention of the "sky" pictures really excited me. The greatest beauty comes out of repose, and I knew that as certain disturbances settled (were fought through) you would recapture the basis (on a higher plane than ever) for new penetrations and syntheses of vision. I had hoped to go down to a plantation that my grandmother and mother own in the West Indies this winter, in fact that was largely the basis of my leaving the job. My intention was to get the unbroken time there to write the essay on your work which I have never had the opportunity of doing here. I was also expecting to finish my *Bridge* poem (which, done, would complete the material for my first book of poems). But these things must evidently wait. It is certain that they cannot be undertaken while my mind is divided between them and an office job. They are both of them too large conceptions to be accomplished under such tour de force conditions. Now, my mother writes me that the place may be sold at any time and that it is out of the question for me to go at all. *If* I can get somebody to lend me the money, however, I may possibly go right ahead, regardless. Both of my parents are interested in money only in connection with my actions, and I have never been persistent enough in the past to really clear that notion away.

Munson said that he had a fine letter from you, and he has probably answered it by this time, telling you a number of things about his present position with regard to *Broom* and *Secession*. He is the noblest young man I know in this country. Experience seems only to sharpen a native integrity and an almost clairvoyant sense of spiritual values. He was obliged to leave the city for his health, and while I miss him a great deal, I hope that he will remain where he is for the rest of the winter. Waldo [Frank], as you know, leaves for Europe tomorrow. I am sorry that he couldn't get time to make you that visit. I have seen him going through a good deal, both in work and experience, and there is no use of trying to write out any details of these things. We shall talk about it some time. Margaret [Naumburg] has also meant a great deal to me lately. Isn't this little handful of us fighting though?!

161: To GORHAM MUNSON

[*New York City*]   *Oct. 28th, '23*

Cheero, Old bird! I have just seen the "last" *Secession!* and I am in no position, I must admit, to quarrel with you about your decision to destroy the garbled pages of "Faustus and Helen." A beautiful bit of business—"blues in your breasts," and the two lines that our hero decided were inessential to the poem! That damned note at the end with its ill-advised quotation from your personal comment is still worse. But never mind, I don't care at all if you will make the necessary clipping. Some few friends of W[heelwright]'s have probably already received copies to treasure as their vision may permit, but I should like to keep as many people in America free from misconceptions about me as possible. Why don't you wire the consulate in Florence to stop W. from any further rape of *S.*—it is a positive elopement that seems to have no prospect of termination. I am thinking of starting abroad with *The Dial,* calling it "The Pile," hemorrhoid, or something like that! My cable, of course, failed.

Waldo left today in a better state of health than he was in when you were here. I don't know whether or not it was due to evasion of certain difficulties. I have no right to make any judgments of that kind, after all, until his writing indicates it. I am always his enthusiastic friend and brother, whatever happens. We had lunch together day before yesterday and he was in thorough approval of my resignation and trip to the Isle of Pines. I have since heard from my mother, however, that the place is liable to be sold at any time, and as that would contribute to a feeling of real unease in going there, I have about decided to come up to Woodstock for awhile for a rest and air, and then come back to town for either free-lancing or a return to advertising. I might get something at Harcourt Brace now, if Smith warms up a little. Certainly I am not at all regretful for what I have done, it being a purely organic necessity. I should have been "flat" if I had tried to keep up that damned hypocrisy of advertising much longer—at least for the time being. I am going to exact some meager contributions from my family—and not be sentimental about it. They want me to come home, but that is, at present, out of the question. The money it would cost for train fare would more than pay for my recuperation at Woodstock. I wish you would ask Brown and Nagle if it would be convenient for them to have me stay with them for awhile, beginning about next Saturday. Underwood expects to come here for a month and asked me to look him up a room. If I can get him to take this at 45 Grove, I shall have my rent free. Jean [Toomer] may arrive any day, also, and he is sure to want it if Wilbur [Underwood] doesn't.

This is a mad letter. I am trying to get it off—along with the transcription of the English equivalents of the Sayn quotations from Frank and the *Fugitive* finales—in time to get a bath at Lisa's and over to the Lights in time for a free dinner. Please don't forget your vote on the *Fugitive* prize, the extra hundred is worth having these days! I'll tell you all that amounts to anything about the *Broom* meeting when I see you. At present Cowley feels that you have broken relations with him by your last letter which he read the night I dined with them. He additionally feels that you may naturally presume that his presence at the Burke farm on the day that B. resigned had a good deal to do with Ken's action—which he says is not the case at all. I didn't say that you had all along been wishing that K. would resign! I wouldn't make any compromises with C. I like many things about him, but he is still in his adolescence when it comes to certain reactions. We really have two groups to the former ONE of *Secession,* and there is no use trying to evade that fact,—as, obviously, you are not trying to do.

162: To His Mother

[*New York City*]   *Nov. 1st, '23*

Dear Grace and Grandma: —/—/ Tomorrow afternoon I leave, stopping off for a couple of days at Ridgefield, Conn., as a guest of Eugene O'Neill (the author of *Anna Christie, Emperor Jones, Beyond the Horizon,* etc.). I met O'Neill at some friends last week end when he was in town. He likes my poetry very much and invited me to come to stay with him. He has a regular estate, I am told,—an establishment that is quite complete, and breakfast for guests is never served out of bed. If everything goes right they are to drive me up to Woodstock on Sunday,—about three hours through beautiful hills and foliage. My address from then on will be *Woodstock, N.Y. care-of Slater Brown.* —/—/

I am depending on you to help me some, as I said in my last letter. I think you will agree that a thoroughly out-of-doors life for a month is not only a sensible thing for me, but really due me after all the time I have denied myself such a natural privilege. If you don't understand such a rightful desire on my part, then I can only say that your vision is warped. It was fine of you to ask me home, but I know you will realize that the atmosphere of Cleveland is anything but conducive to rest *for me.* The amount to which I am asking you to help me will not exceed the carfare to and from Cleveland— at most. Brown is poor and can only offer me the hospitality of the house he has taken,—and extra board he is unable to provide, so I am anxious to do my part and be decent about not stretching his hospitality unreasonably. So please send me fifteen dollars in cash or check at Woodstock sometime next week. Even if you have to pinch a little bit, I think that the things I am trying to do deserve a few sacrifices. I make as many as I can myself, and still keep sound and living,—and I hope you will [be] faithful enough—whether you see my complete ends or not—to lend me some assistance. I hope you are both well and happy. Don't worry about me. I know damned well what I'm doing.

163: TO HIS MOTHER

Woodstock, [New York]   *Nov. 8th,'23*

Dear Mother and Grandmother: Felling trees and piecing them up for warmth is a new sport to me, but I have taken to it with something like a real enthusiasm. This is my fourth day here in the mountains, but already I feel like a new person. My muscles are swelling and blood simply glowing. It is quite cold, even snowed today and the top of the nearest mountain is hooded white.

Slater Brown and Nagle make wonderful people to live with. I told you how fond I was of B. when I was home last summer. I am made to feel not at all a guest, as to a large extent I am not, of course, but they want me to stay all winter here with them now. I may and I may not, depending on how I find I can manage to earn enough money by poems and articles. Certainly I should like to become a giant again in health, as I naturally am. And I have never had an outing like this before in my life.

We do all our own cooking. Brown has developed a surprising faculty for supplying tempting and enormous meals. You have no idea what an appetite is developed with wood chopping, sawing, and much walking in the brisk air. I have a heavy army shirt of wool and corduroy trousers. I got all this along with some woolen socks for surprisingly little in an army and navy store in New York before I came out here. It was a good thing, now, that you sent that heavy underwear of mine in the trunk when you sent it.

The house we are living in is, of course, already furnished by a family that lives here only in the summer. There are four bedrooms, a bath, dining room, large studio with a huge open fireplace where we burn our logs, and kitchen provided with an oil stove. There's just enough furniture and not too much, simple and in pleasant taste. The town is about two miles away. Walking in for our provisions is very pleasant—over rolling land, set in a valley by low mountains on all sides around. We are quite set away from everybody—no people passing to speak of and in a quietness that is a tonic after the endless noise and reverberation of New York which you feel there even in your sleep.

I certainly am hoping that nothing serious has happened to prevent you from writing to me. I have been expecting a letter from you for several days now. — — — —

164: TO ALFRED STIEGLITZ

Woodstock, NY   *December 5th, '23*

Dear Stieglitz: Your fine description of the snow makes me glad that I'm going to stay here until January—by which time I am sure that I may see a few pure flakes myself. So far, we have only had a gentle sleet—once and at nightfall. Today it rains and rains, and our usual wood foraging is broken.

Slater Brown and Ed Nagle are my hosts here in the shadow of the mountains. They were kind enough to ask me up here after I had to give up the trip to the West Indian plantation because I found out that my mother was trying to sell it as soon as possible. We're about a mile and a half from the village and very much by ourselves. My first taste of the country for years—and a month of it has put me in a steadier mood than I remember since childhood. But enough of this god damned autobiography! When I get back to town I may drive trucks, stevedore, steward on a boat or even go back to advertising. I shan't be serious enough about any of 'em to worry now. I'll certainly be glad to see you again and peer at some of your new pictures if you'll let me. We can have some walks in the snow, too, I hope. Winter in New York is stimulating, and most of our talks, so far, have been carried on under the torrid auspices of summer.

There was a great crowd out here from the City for Thanksgiving, and the preparations, celebration and "aftermath" are still rather buzzy in my head. Altogether, it has kept me from writing you much sooner. When your letter came yesterday I felt and still feel very remiss, the most so now that my imagination, sunk in a kind of agreeable vegetable existence, refuses to offer you any real evidence that life in the country has been of personal benefit to me. But it's rather pleasant to be irresponsible and purely bovine once in five years or so. About all I am doing besides the many chores is—grow a mustache (very slight so far!). You will probably see Munson very soon. He left here about ten days ago, and, I think, intends to remain the rest of the winter in Town writing as usual. His honesty IS outstanding and he has a veneration for that fundamental beauty in yourself which is not easily swerved. I'm hoping that you see more of Kenneth Burke, too. He is using my room at 45 Grove St. at present and is perfectly free with his time so far as I know. Burke (between us only) keeps fighting off a true spiritual revelation which is really his birthright, though he can't consciously recognize it. So he falls a prey to Spengler and the cynics of more reasonable tongue —and lives in a rather unhappy and delicate state of scepticism. He sees the surface of your work and admires it intensely, but he simply thinks I'm cucu when I remain unconvinced that he has really SEEN one picture of yours.

Please let me know if you hear of any job—of any sort—that I could begin to "fill" about Jan. 1st. I think I'll write Zigrosser if he knows of anything, too. —/—/

165: To His Grandmother

Woodstock, N. Y.   *December 5th '23*

My dear Grandma: Your interest in my culinary triumphs is certainly very much appreciated. I've been waiting quite a while for the moment to tell you about the Thanksgiving dinner, etc., and have just about got adjusted again, the house in order and our simple program restored although the last guest left on Monday. Altogether, the party and every detail of the festivities was quite a success. Some things were very funny and some were a little aggravating. I think I did most of the cooking when it came right down to the last moment, as both my confreres were so occupied with their lady friends and rather daffy that they went around like dizzy roosters, and keeping the rest of the company entertained and out of the kitchen was some job, too.

The people we bought the turkey from had already cleaned it and plucked it, and had promised to make the stuffing. But at the last moment they went back on the stuffing, and so it was left to me entirely. You should have seen me going at it, sewing it up tight afterward and everything! Everyone said the stuffing was great, and I liked it myself. I rubbed the outside all over with salt and butter, and then the ten pound bird was put into a wonderful roasting machine that Lachaise brought out from New York which he got in the French bazaar. You put the bird on a long spit which had a crank and catches. One side of the cage was entirely open and that was turned toward the fire in the big studio. I never ate more luscious turkey than this process produced. You must have seen one of these roasting devices because similar ones have been used in New England for many many years. It's a large, fat oval shape and looks a little like a big tin pig on its legs. We kept turning the bird around inside until it was a rich brown and thoroughly done. The meal began wth potato and onion soup made by Nagle. Then turkey with mashed potatoes, cranberry sauce, squash and gravy. Celery too. Then I made some fine lettuce salad with onions and peppers and French dressing. Dessert was composed of pumpkin pie and mince pie and the marvelous fruit cake. We had cider in abundance, Marsala wine and red wine as well as some fine cherry cordial. Nuts, raisins, etc. Quite a dinner, you see. And everyone went wild about the cake. We had all the walls hung with candles as well as the table. Sat down at five and didn't get up to dance until eight. I danced fat Mme. Lachaise around until we both felt almost exhausted. Then there was a girl who could match me on my Russian dance and we did that together at a great rate. I forgot to mention that we had a Victrola, of course, which Lachaise bought in Kingston just the day before. Lots of jazz records, etc. Most of the guests had left by the following evening, but we have spent most of the time since in getting things straightened around again and catching up on our supply of wood. −/−/

166: To CHARLOTTE RYCHTARIK

Woodstock, New York   *December 10,'23*

Dear Lotte: I guess you and Richard have deserted me . . . anyway I don't hear from you any more. —/—/

You should not forget me. I am free now—at least more so than ever before in my life, but that doesn't mean that I forget such people as you and Richard who have been so fine to me and whom I shall love always—even though I haven't any way of proving it but to just keep on saying so. I hear that my Mother has taken a job of some kind and is working very hard. I am sorry to hear it, but I also know that she did not need to do it unless she felt like it. Everything is being sold as soon as possible. Only I refuse to sell myself any longer than I absolutely have to. I shall beg and steal when necessary to avoid it.

This letter is very intimate, and I have written it at the risk of a great deal of misunderstanding from you, I well know. Who knows, —perhaps you have some quaint ideas about me by this time. But I do hope that you will write me soon if you feel like it—and tell me all about yourselves, how you are playing and how R is painting. I am sure you are gaining on Time! One must.

167: To GORHAM MUNSON

Woodstock, New York   *Dec. 10th,'23*

Dear Gorham: Both Nagle and B. were enthusiastic about your investigation in obstetrics (needn't voice my own disgust, I trust!). I am still a little blushing about my premature delivery of two poems and a quite personal letter to Miss Gregory as (already) Editor Managing of *The Dial,* asking for reviews, etc., etc. However, I do hope through her gentle accession and the rape of a former — — — — to inveigle my brain children into a little more acceptance thereabouts—in time.

I approve of your going, as announced, to Croton. Do not become as other infectious bugs there—however much on second thought the worst vermin seems to haunt nearer, far nearer precincts adjacent to King Street, Lincoln Highway and the Battery for daily duels. (What you started rolling on your return to NY or what Burke had started just before that I am wild to know about. Cowley wrote the most mystifying hint of volcanic disorders at the end of a letter he wrote to B. anent *Broom* and its publication in Kingston, *which fell through,* by the way). There have been three days of agony around here, just terminated, during which beads of sweat were wrung and sighs heaved perpetually, but B's review of Cummings for *Broom* at last is in the mailbox and I will get a chance to write a few letters, I hope.

Last Friday I climbed the mountain (Overlook) and called on the caretaker who lives in the house beside the ruins of the hotel. He is very anxious to leave, has been there for seven months, etc., and I am seriously thinking of taking the place myself at pay of 40 bucks per month and all expenses gratis. It would be a hard winter, perhaps a terrific experience, but I should like to keep away from the city and its scattered prostitutions for awhile. The man who owns the place lives in Brooklyn and I expect to hear detailed terms from him in a few days. B. is very keen about going with me, but his previous arrangements with Nagle may check that on grounds of honorable understanding. Certainly I should much prefer to have B. with me there, but the whole plan is in embryo now, and nothing may come of it. The prospect so far as money goes is so threatening and hopeless as I see it in New York that I may take this strenuous means of asserting myself against the traditional conflicts of my past. —/—/

Fisher has been over a couple of times for dinner and an evening. I couldn't read the James book at all under present aspirations and interests, but I have been amazed much at the finesse and depth of Pater in his *Plato and Platonism* which Fisher has subsequently loaned me. I think it beats *The Renaissance* all hollow for style and ratiocination. What are you reading—and, more important, writing? I have been very lazy, but am growing more tight and particular— perhaps a favorable change after my somewhat flamboyant period in NY just before I left. I enclose the new version of "Recitative" (which may not be final, but which I think is really better than the original confession).[1] — — — —

168: TO GORHAM MUNSON

Woodstock   *December 20th, '23*

Dear Gorham: I had a kind of dirge all written to send you this morning before the mail came: fortunately I reconsidered sending it before one of us went into town, returning with your good news. I'm not worried about the *Fugitive* prize because I had not been

1. See Weber, *op. cit.,* p. 224. For line 13, word 2, read: alternating.

planning at all on it anyway, and I am enormously pleased at your news about *The Dial's* acceptance of you. IT WAS ABOUT TIME, however. What you have won there, too,—you may be sure—has been gained against a deal of prejudice against you, due mainly, of course, to your liaison with Waldo's work, etc.

The folks at Cleveland have disappointed me much, not only by sending me only half as much money as I asked for and require, but by a great deal of wailing. I guess I told you before you left here that my mother has taken a position, since explained to me as helping a friend of hers in a very de luxe antique and what-not establishment just started. It involves nothing but standing around and talking to people, I'm sure, yet mother is reported to return home every night so exhausted and wrecked that she can hardly speak. She has not personally written me for a month now. All the reports and symptoms come from my grandmother. But would it have been so much different had I been at Thompson's during these two months, I am tempted to ask. They won't stop to think or plan,—either of them,—beyond the next day ahead. And woes continue indefinitely. —/—/

Brown tells me and Nagle so little about *Broom* that I don't know how well founded your report from Burke may be. Brown loves his little secrets (of all sorts) and it's pleasant to leave his surface sobrieties unchallenged. Certainly Matty is not going to let go of his sheet until it is either so dead as to be hopeless or else so loaded with debts that his successor would be crushed under them. But there is much mail every week to B. from *Broom*, and Cowley, Matty and B. seem to have an enviable little love nest all to themselves.

Jean [Toomer] hasn't written me for a long time, and I have the suspicion that he a little resents my not writing to Margaret Naumburg. The fact is—I've often thought of it and delayed because I somehow felt that I wasn't ready to say the sort of things to her which would interest her. I have certainly, as far as that goes, no flattering chart of developments within myself to report to anyone. This sojourn has meant little more to me so far than a purely physical rehabilitation. That is something, but not a very absorbing topic to write about.

Fisher has been over a number of evenings since you left—for tea, too, several times. He has a great fondness for Brown and myself, too, I think. I certainly enjoy him most alone, as the other day when I came over to his place in the afternoon and stayed until nearly midnight. This poet, Greenberg, whom Fisher nursed until he died of consumption at a Jewish hospital in NY, was a Rimbaud in embryo.

Did you ever see some of the hobbling yet really gorgeous attempts that boy made without any education or time except when he became confined to a cot? Fisher has shown me an amazing amount of material, some of which I am copying and will show you when I get back. No grammar, nor spelling, and scarcely any form, but a quality that is unspeakably eerie and the most convincing gusto. One little poem is as good as any of the consciously-conceived "Pierrots" of Laforgue. —/—/

169: To His Mother

Woodstock, NY   *Dec. 21st, '23*

Dear Grace: —/—/ We are, all of us, in something of a strained state this Christmas but I don't think we need to be so much wrought up about it as you and Grandma apparently are. After all, Christmas is only one day in the year—and as a special day, I don't get half so excited about it (and haven't for some years) as I used to. It's too bad that we can't all be together, but that can't be helped. It wouldn't have made any difference so far as I could see, had I remained at Thompson's during all this time—so far as [the] money side [of] it goes. I was just keeping things going as it was, and had nothing left over for travelling expense, and had I remained I might have incurred much more expense by this time by being flat on my back. I think you take my little rest and vacation a bit too strenuously. I'm going back to NY on the second or third of January (if I can get the carfare) and after that I won't ask for any more money. I don't know what I'm going to do, but I can probably wash dishes or work on the docks or something to keep skin and bone together. I shall keep my old room at 45 Grove Street (which is as cheap as any that can be found anywhere) as long as I can bamboozle the landlady. After that I'll have to depend on my good coat, or the kindness of friends. I've been able to store up a sufficient reserve of physical and nervous force while out here in the country to last me quite awhile, I think. I am not at all discouraged about anything, and I think that if you and Grandma will use your natural wits at a little better planning— you'll be able to get along fairly comfortably without working so hard. One can live happily on very little, I have found, if the mind and spirit have some definite objective in view. I expect I'll always have to drudge for my living, and I'm quite willing to always do it, but I am no more fooling myself that the mental bondage and spiritual bondage of the more remunerative sorts of work is worth the sacrifices inevitably involved. If I can't continue to create the sort of poetry that is my intensest and deepest component in life—then it all means very little to me, and then I might as well tie myself up to some smug ambition and "success" (the common idol that every Tom, Dick and Harry is bowing to everywhere). But so far, as you know, I only grow more and more convinced that what I naturally have to give the world in my own terms—is worth giving, and I'll go through a number of ordeals yet to pursue a natural course. I'm telling you all this now, dear, because I don't want you to suffer any more than inevitable from misunderstandings—for once we see a thing clearly, usually nine tenths of our confusion and apprehension is removed. Surely you and I have no quarrels, and I think you understand me well enough to know that I want to save you as much suffering from Life's obstacles as can be done without hypocrisy, silliness or sentimentality. You may have to take me on faith for some things, because I don't know whether it is possible for all people to understand certain ardours that I have, and perhaps there is no special reason why you, as my mother, should understand that side of me any better than most people. As I have said, I am perfectly willing to be misunderstood, but I don't want to put up any subterfuges before *your* understanding of me if I can help it. You have often spoken to me about how you lamented the fact that you didn't follow certain convictions that you had when you were my age because it wasn't easy enough; and I know what strong obstacles were put in your way. I, too, have had to fight a great deal just to *be myself* and *know myself* at all, and I think I have been doing and am doing a great deal in following out certain natural and innate directions in myself. By Jove—I don't know of much else that is worth the having in our lives. Look around you and see the numbers and numbers of so-called "successful" people, successful in the worldly sense of the word. I wonder how many of them are happy in the sense that you and I know what real happiness means! I'm glad we aren't so dumb as all that, even though we do have to suffer a great deal. Suffering is a real purification, and the worst thing I have always had to say against Christian Science is that it wilfully avoided suffering, without a certain measure of which any true happiness cannot be fully realized.

If you will even partially see these facts as I see them it will make me very happy—and we can be much closer and more "together" that way than merely just living in the same house and seeing each other every day would ever bring about alone. I have been thinking much about you and about dear Grandma—and I shall have you with me much on Christmas day. We'll be dancing a little, and are invited around to a couple of celebrations at other houses here, but there will be no such pretentious preparations as for Thanksgiving and no extra guests here. —/—/

1 9 2 4

170: To Charlotte Rychtarik

New York City   *Jan. 6th, '24*

Dear Charlotte: Your lovely gift and long beautiful letter made me feel a little bit ashamed that I had written you such a hasty and doubting letter. Isn't it funny that just about the time one doubts humanity and begins to take some kind of active resentment against it, along comes fresh proof that there are, after all, many noble people that make life worth all kinds of trouble for the reward of having known them, kissed or shaken hands! I have been looking into your eyes—whether you knew it or not; you looked into mine in that letter—and I'm grateful for the confidence that you had in me, even though something made you doubt me a little. I really am just the same old person—just as moody and unreliable as ever I was in Cleveland when we used to exchange our troubles and get rid of them in some music or over a book or a picture.

What I said about "prostituting my mind," etc., I really meant. I *do* resent it—and because so many others as good and better than myself must also do the same in order to live and breathe doesn't help things at all. I shall keep right on talking that way—and probably not practice what I preach at all. I seemed very bitter in my letter because my mother seemed to think that a vacation was an extravagance—while I knew that it was the only thing for me to do in order not to go all to pieces. I feel now like a new man—better than I can ever remember feeling and realize that the country and hard work out in the keen sparkling air are the finest things in the world. Of course I should like to have stayed in the mountains even longer, but I know that I must now get to work again and earn some money. And I don't mind it a bit, either, feeling as I do.

I have two appointments tomorrow and I don't think I shall have such a slow time finding work as before. It is a better season, "business is better" and I have had "experience in N.Y." which counts some. —/—/

171: TO ISABEL AND GASTON LACHAISE

[*New York City*]   *Jan. 9" '24*

Dear Mme. and Gaston! There are no memories stronger than the
spiritual outlines of rock and branch so bare and fine as winter
mountains yielded me while I was with you and two precious others
recently. So, in a moment of enthusiasm for all things great I must
inscribe a greeting and regret (thus floridly!) that we can't presently
walk and talk "all together." And, as a sort of apology, offer the enclosed poem[1] to your appreciation, or extenuation of such in relation to at least one other admiration of yours—reflection to my better
moods. Especially do I send it—because I feel it had its first thought
in the dance of music, flesh and stone wherein you live always—
you two! — — —

172: TO GORHAM MUNSON

[*New York City*]   *Jan 9, '24*

Dear Gorham: Back in the welter again. I've been so pressed with
various desires and necessities that the thought of writing any one
at all has seemed nearly impossible. I've lunched and dined with
Burke and the Cowleys, seen the new Stieglitz clouds, Sunday-break-
fasted with Jean [Toomer] and Lisa [Munson], argued an evening
with Rosenfeld and Margy [Naumburg], chatted with O'Neill, Macgowan & R. Edmond Jones—Wescott, Matty, Light, and been to concerts with Jean—etc., etc. All this besides running around and looking for jobs. As all these contacts have brought so much in my mind
to talk to you about, I began to and still do despair of including
anything but the above catalogue in this letter. It will, after all, be
only about a week longer before I see you and then we can have an
extensive outburst. Meanwhile—I somehow feel about as solitary as
I ever felt in my life. Perhaps it's all in the pressure of economic
exigencies at present—but I also feel an outward chaos around me—
many things happening and much that is good but somehow myself
out of it, between two worlds. Of course none of this would be were
I creating actively myself. It certainly helps things a lot that you are
working on so well and it is very gratifying to see Burke and Cowley
gravitating constantly more parallel to your initial theories and convictions. Cowley's gaucheries in admitting his mistakes and *tactics*
are really funny. But I can't write you more details now.

1. "Interludium."

Along comes a letter from my father this morning offering me a
position with him as travelling salesman! This is unacceptable, of
course, even though I now can't complete the rent on the room for
the rest of this month and simply don't know what is going to happen. If worse comes to worse I can go back to Woodstock and stay
with Fisher who urgently invited me to stay a month or so whenever I liked. Just now I haven't made up my mind about anything.
I have no more illusions about advertising, yet that is the only thing
I can talk about at all. Leffingwell (at Thompson's) is out of town,
so I have not been able to attempt any reinstatement there. The lady
at *Machinery* says she wants to use me there sometime and *may soon,*
but the vacancy so far doesn't exist there. Hal Smith at Harcourt
seems to be neither sufficiently interested in me nor my work to fulfill any of my hopes there. And so it goes. There's no point in going
into more details.

Jean's new hygiene for himself is very interesting to me. He seems
to be able to keep himself solid and undismayed. Certain organic
changes are occurring in us all, I think, but I believe that his is more
steady and direct than I have been permitted. My approach to words
is still in substratum of some new development—the same as it was
when we talked last together—and perhaps merely a chaotic lapse
into confusion for all I dare say yet. I feel Stein and E.E.C.[1] as active
agents in it, whatever it is, and I've a short poem to show you soon
which presents more interesting speculation to myself than it does
to anyone else. Suffice to say that I am very dissatisfied with both
these interesting people and would like to digest their qualities without being too consciously theoretical about it.

Stieglitz liked the drawings I brought back—and you'll like the
one of Brown I think. I'd like to paint and draw half the time, and
write the rest. "Prince Llan" is published and I admire its strenuous
prose. —/—/

173: To His Father

New York City   *January 12th, '24*

My dear Father: Your letter has been on the table for longer than I
had expected. I had wanted to answer it more promptly in view of
your real consideration in offering me such a favorable opportunity
in your business, but I've been so altogether occupied since I came
back from Woodstock in looking around here for a new position, in-

1. E. E. Cummings.

terviewing people and answering advertisements, that there has been only the evenings—when there was either someone in to call, or I was too tired to write you as I wanted.

By all this you will probably have guessed that I don't find it practical to accept your offer, kind as it is, and beyond all that I must also add in justice to us both that it would also not be honest of me to do so, either. I realize that in order to be understood in both the above reasons it is necessary that I at least attempt to explain myself in more detail than I may have gone into with you ever before, and as that is rather an unwieldy process within the limits of a letter I may only touch on a few points about myself and try to make them clear, leaving the rest to some later date when you may care to look me up in New York, provided I am here at your next visit. In what follows, father, I hope that you will take my word for it that there is no defense of my personal pride involved against any of the misunderstandings that we may have had in the past. I have come to desire to talk to you as a son ought to be able to talk to his father, that is, in a pure relationship, without prejudices or worldly issues interfering on either side. That was the basis of my first letter[1] to you in three years—that I wrote a little over two months ago, and I hope it may be the basis of your interpretation of what I am writing you now. I, at least, am doing the most honest thing I know to do in whatever I have said to you and in whatever I may say to you since that time. That's a pledge from the very bottom of my heart.

In your letter you carefully advise me to turn a deaf ear to your offer if I find my advertising work so absorbing, pleasant and profit-

1. Crane had written his father a six-line letter on Oct. 20, 1923 requesting that his father telephone him on the occasion of his next New York visit. Mr. Clarence A. Crane regarded this letter as an aggressive unaffectionate note after three years of silence on Crane's part (Letter, Oct. 27, 1923, C.A.C. to H.C.). Crane replied on Nov. 13th, informing his father of his trip to Woodstock. His father's letter acknowledged that he viewed the Nov. 13th letter as a sign of friendship, and stated that he would be in New York sometime in 1924 (Letter, Dec. 10, 1923, C.A.C. to H.C.). On account of business expansion and relocation problems, it seemed doubtful that Crane's father would be in New York as expected. Accordingly, in a letter of Jan. 7, 1924, he offered his son a travelling salesman's job. After three years of satisfactory performance, his son would assume control of the wholesale portion of the business. This letter of Jan. 12, 1924, is Hart Crane's response to the offer. His father responded sympathetically; he sent his son a check, stated that he would continue to provide financial assistance, recognized the sincerity and wisdom of his son's choice, and attempted to demonstrate a similarity between them by asserting that he (like his son) was primarily interested in "accomplishment" rather than "money" (Letter, Jan. 15, 1924, C.A.C. to H.C.). Hart Crane viewed his father's letter of the 15th as a "sincere and cordial document" (Letter, Jan. 19, 1924, H.C. to his mother).

able that I might in later time regret a transfer into so widely divergent an enterprise as your business. You were perfectly right in presupposing that I had a considerable interest in this sort of work, for in less than three years I had got into the largest agency in the world and was to all outward appearances very much engrossed in carrying myself through to a highly paid and rather distinguished position.

But if there had been any chance to tell you before I should have stated to you I had no interest in advertising beyond the readiest means of earning my bread and butter, and that as such an occupation came nearest to my natural abilities as a writer I chose it as the quickest and easiest makeshift known to me. Perhaps, in view of this, it will be easier for you to see why I left my position at J. Walter Thompson's at the last of October, unwise as such an action would be understood from the usual point of view. I went to the country because I had not had a vacation for several years, was rather worn with the strain of working at high speed as one does in such high geared agencies, and above all because I wanted the precious time to do some real thinking and writing, the most important things to me in my life. The director of the copy department asked me to see him when I came back to New York, but he has not returned yet from out of town and I don't know whether or not I shall return there. I told Grace that they had asked me to return definitely because I didn't want her to worry about me: she has enough worries as it is. But so much for that. . . .

I think, though, from the above, that you will now see why I would not regard it as honest to accept your proposition, offered as it was in such frankness and good will. I don't want to use you as a makeshift when my principal ambition and life lies completely outside of business. I always have given the people I worked for my wages-worth of service, but it would be a very different sort of thing to come to one's father and simply feign an interest in fulfilling a confidence when one's mind and guts aren't driving in that direction at all. I hope you credit me with genuine sincerity as well as the appreciation of your best motives in this statement.

You will perhaps be righteously a little bewildered at all these statements about my enthusiasm about my writing and my devotion to that career in life. It is true that I have to date very little to show as actual accomplishment in this field, but it is true on the other hand that I have had very very little time left over after the day's work to give to it and I may have just as little time in the wide future still to give to it, too. Be all this as it may, I have come to recognize that I am satisfied and spiritually healthy only when I am fulfilling myself in that direction. It is my natural one, and you will possibly admit that if it had been artificial or acquired, or a mere youthful whim it would have been cast off some time ago in favor of more profitable occupations from the standpoint of monetary returns. For I have been through some pretty trying situations, and, indeed, I am in just such a one again at the moment, with less than two dollars in my pocket and not definitely located in any sort of a job.

However, I shall doubtless be able to turn my hand to something very humble and temporary as I have done before. I have many friends, some of whom will lend me small sums until I can repay them—and some sort of job always turns up sooner or later. What pleases me is that so many distinguished people have liked my poems (seen in magazines and mss.) and feel that I am making a real contribution to American literature. There is Eugene O'Neill, dramatist and author of *Anna Christie, Emperor Jones, The Hairy Ape*, etc.; Waldo Frank, probably the most distinguished contemporary novelist; and others like Alfred Stieglitz; Gaston Lachaise, the sculptor who did the famous Rockefeller tomb at Tarrytown and the stone frescoes in the Telephone Building; and Charlie Chaplin, who is a very well-read and cultured man in "real life." I wish you could meet some of my friends, who are not the kind of "Greenwich Villagers" that you may have been thinking they were. If I am able to keep on in my present development, strenuous as it is, you may live to see the name "Crane" stand for something where literature is talked about, not only in New York but in London and abroad.

You are a very busy man these days as I well appreciate from the details in your letter, and I have perhaps bored you with these explanations about myself, your sympathies engaged as they are—so much in other activities, and your mind filled with a thousand and one details and obligations which clamour to be fulfilled. Nevertheless, as I've said before, I couldn't see any other way than to frankly tell you about myself and my interests so as not to leave any accidental afterthought in your mind that I had any "personal" reasons for not working in the Crane Company. And in closing I would like to just ask you to think some time,—try to imagine working for the pure love of simply making something beautiful,—something that maybe can't be sold or used to help sell anything else, but that is simply a communication between man and man, a bond of understanding and human enlightenment—which is what a real work of art *is*. If you do that, then maybe you will see why I am not so foolish after all to have followed what seems sometimes only a faint star. I only ask to leave behind me something that the future may find valuable, and it takes a bit of sacrifice sometimes in order to give the thing that you know is in yourself and worth giving. I shall make every sacrifice toward that end.

P.S. When you next write better address me care of G. B. Munson, 144 West 11th Street. I may not be able to hold on this room longer than the end of Jan.

174: TO HIS MOTHER

[New York City]   *Jan 24–'24*

Dear Grace and Grandma: −/−/ Along came a note from B. W. Huebsch, who evidently had some proposition to talk to me about. It only said to phone him, which I did today, and we're to have lunch together on Saturday just for the personal pleasure. I told you, I guess, that I find him one of the smartest men in New York—and he certainly is the most cultured publisher here. I am thinking of submitting my book to him when it is ready, in preference to Gorham's publisher who is pretty commercial and pettifogging.

To give you many details of my activities and contacts since I got back from the country would take four or five pages. I was pretty blue for awhile and poor, as you know, but that didn't prevent my plunging into a lot of varied company, meeting new people and revisiting the old, dining here and there and enjoying free tickets to modern concerts, plays and exhibitions of modern painters, etc. New York is abristle with its first acceptance of European art and artists this year. It's become fashionable for the high-hatted uptowners now to buy Matisse's paintings, Picasso, and all the other cubists, and there's a great amount of "patronizing" going on. And talk, talk, talk!!! My visiting list has reached its limits. I'll be glad to quietly come home evenings and work when I get into the treadmill again. I know about the most interesting and vital people in New York, but there isn't time to take advantage of all that constantly. Some day when we get together you will be astonished at the flow of anecdotes and amusing trifles that'll just naturally begin to rise out of me, but which can't be written about. −/−/

175: TO HIS MOTHER

[New York City]   *Jan 29th, '24*

Grace dear and Grandma: −/−/ I started in yesterday morning, and have been working like a tiger since then, of course. So far I like boss

and office very much. There is only one other copywriter besides myself, and he is an old friend of Gorham's. The two stenogs and office
boy are the only otherwises. I, personally and alone, occupy the nicest niche I ever sat in—15 stories up, and the corner of the building
with windows, of course, on two angles. Perfect privacy and quiet
and a desk and chair that are quite massive and comfortable. Every
hour or so the office boy comes in, inquiries if I want anything; otherwise I press a neat button on the corner of the desk and service is
immediate.

I always get mixed up in some strange topic. This time it is a book
on cheese, how happy it makes you and how good it is for tissues,
stomach, and bowels, etc. A large importing house wants it, and I've
been having to write it in no time. I hope to finish it tonight. Life
certainly is amusing. I've been quite happy up there the last two
days. —/—/

I don't believe that I told you about my second interview with
B. W. Huebsch, the publisher. It was at his request, and when I got
there and found what he wanted I fairly whooped. His office isn't
ready for it yet, but he said that he had been wishing that in time I
might enter his employ as a kind of personal assistant to him and his
responsibilities. The combination of my advertising and literary
judgment, he said, was rather rarely found, and he thought I would
be able to read manuscripts, attend to certain details of printing, and
superintend the publicity where certain others would be too limited
for that range. I felt considerably complimented, especially after so
brief an acquaintance with him. As you [know], that sort of work is
what I have been looking for for years in New York.

Well, inasmuch as I told him that I was at least temporarily bound
to work at this agency, I would have to postpone his offer at least a
few weeks. But he wants me to take lunch with him a couple of weeks
from now and let him know how I like my present work, and discuss
the prospects with us both as they stand then. Right now, I am only
interested in making as good as I can at this job, and I'm not going
to let that prospect, alluring as it is, absorb me much. However, it's
fine to have it to occasionally ponder, and, of course, something may
develop.

I had loaned my room during the last few days to Elizabeth Smith
and the writer she was working for. Last night when I came in she
was almost in tears,—said he had just paid and fired her, and that he
couldn't stand the room. Well,—Eliza was a little foolish in not finding herself a separate room away from the club sorority, Smith Girls
Home, or whatever it is—so that she could have carried on his work

under pleasanter conditions. I know that in time I should certainly have had to ask [her] to seek other arrangements because—after all, on Sat. afternoons, I would havè felt the lack of a place to go and work. She's out of the Macy book store possibilities, too, now—and running all over town for something else today. It's too bad, but I did my best,—even to the extent of putting down money for a phone installation (which she said was necessary) when I don't have any use for it myself. She'll find something, though, I'm sure. —/—/

176: TO HIS MOTHER

[New York City] *Feb 3rd,'24*

Grace, dear: —/—/ Yesterday afternoon I had a long talk with CA [Crane] up at the Waldorf. He phoned me at my office yesterday morning and asked for that time. He had been here since the morning before, but had been so tied up with engagements, he said, that there had not been time even to phone me before. Frances [Crane] was also along, but I didn't have to see her. They are returning home tonight.

We talked from 3 until five—and in the end it was very satisfactory. He began in the usual arbitrary way of inquisition into my attitude toward business life, etc., just as though there had been no exchange of letters and recent understandings on that subject, and did his best to frighten me into compromises. I parried these thrusts very politely, although it was very hard many times not to jump up and begin declaiming. However, I realized this time that my ordinary language about such topics is simply beyond his comprehension, so I quietly kept on doing my best to explain myself in terms that he would understand and not resent any more than possible. He finally ended by accepting me quite docilely as I am: in fact there was nothing else to do, especially as I did not so much as hint that there was anything I hoped he would do for me—or was ever planning that he would do for me.

Then he talked to me, as usual about his own affairs, and finally came around to asking my advice on a new product of his, its proper naming, and the best way to advertise it. He is going to send me data on the subject, and wants me to write some ads for him about it! You see, from this alone (and I have also other grounds to judge by) that he really respects me. He inquired in detail about you and Grandma and seems to have the right sort of interest in you. He also came around to agree that I was quite exemplary of both sides of my family in not being made of any putty—knowing what I want to do, and sticking it out despite adversities. At parting he spoke of his anticipations of more extended contact with me on his next visit here, urged me to write him often, and thrust a greenback in my pocket. So that's that!

The work at the office goes smoothly enough to reassure me somewhat. My copy on the cheese book went over without any changes whatever, and that makes one write the next job a whole lot faster and imaginatively. Your own dear special has just come, and I'm awfully glad to know that things are alright and that my letters are worth something to you in spite of the haste they always have to be written in.

Tonight is the opening of a new play at the Provincetown Theatre and I am invited to attend with Sue [Jenkins], who is the wife of James Light, the stage director. Through Light and O'Neill I know the whole crowd over there now, and it is very interesting to watch this most progressive theater in America in the details of its productions,—going behind scenes, watching rehearsals, etc. I have changed my opinions, or rather prejudices, about Claire Eames since meeting her there and watching her work in two recent productions. She isn't at all stiff or pompous,—and as an artist she is very flexible and exact. O'Neill, by the way, recently told a mutual friend of ours that he thinks me the most important writer of all in the group of younger men with whom I am generally classed.

Last night I was invited to witness some astonishing dances and psychic feats performed by a group of pupils belonging to the now famous mystic monastery founded by Gurdjieff near Versailles (Paris), that is giving some private demonstrations of their training methods in New York now. You have to receive a written invitation, and after that there is no charge. I can't possibly begin to describe the elaborate theories and plan of this institution, nor go into the details of this single demonstration, but it was very, very interesting—and things were done by amateurs which would stump the Russian ballet, I'm sure. Georgette LeBlanc, former wife of Maeterlinck, was seated right next to me (she brought them over here, or was instrumental in it, I think) with Margaret Anderson, whom I haven't seen since she got back from Paris in November. Georgette had on the gold wig which the enclosed picture will show you, and was certainly the most extraordinary looking person I've ever seen; beautiful, but in a rather hideous way. —/—/

177: To His Mother

[*New York City*]   *Feb 13th, '24*
Dear Grace: There's a pack of troubles to listen to shortly so don't mind too much.

In the first place, I have been sick with the grippe for three days, but am getting better. In the second place I lost my job on Monday last—because, plainly, the man who had employed me had over-estimated the volume of his business. I had heard that he was prone to extravagances of such sort from one of the other men in the firm before I took the job, but I took the chance. He couldn't say a thing against my work or copy as an excuse, but he had to invent some fantastic pretenses that I saw through right away as grounds; it was a dirty deal, and the only hope I have is that Huebsch is still considering me for the position there, which, if it eventuates, will certainly be better than anything I have ever had yet. To make matters worse, just a moment ago I got a letter from the man from whom I have been renting this room and its furniture. He is coming back to take possession again on the first of March! I have only fifty dollars on me in the meantime and my 30 dollars rent for this remaining month on the room has not been paid.

So, you see how matters stand. I am going to try some feature articles for the newspapers while I am looking for another job, but I have not yet got paid for them yet, nor even made connections, nor written them. *I shall do my best.* Right after this letter I am going to write CA [Crane] and ask for a *loan* of a hundred dollars to carry me over. If he can't do that at 6% interest I think he is rather careless, to say the least. Otherwise I shall fare as best I may among my friends. They have been so kind, and they so respect my genius that probably you need not worry about anything serious happening to me. I feel quite indomitable. I shall not return to Cleveland to live permanently, at any rate, until I am such a wreck that I might as well go there as anywhere else. I am so sorry about all this because I had been planning on saving the first sixty dollars possible to save and returning for a week end to see you and dear Grandma. You don't know how I have longed to see you: But we must wait. It may be [a] long or a short time still before that is possible. There are opportunities for quick and plentiful money in the newspaper field if I am lucky. —/—/

178: To Allen Tate

NYC   *March 1st '24*

Dear Allen: Somehow I imagine that you aren't finding it so bad to stand on the platform and dispense judgment and information after all! Whatever your attitude may now be, I must say that I am

damned glad that you got the job,—first, because its remunerations
may bring you to me here in NY, and less selfishly, because I think
that the activity will put you in better spirits, whatever erosions and
disgusts the job may incidentally incur.

I'm dead tired. . . . You will note by the above [address] that I
am finally moved. It has taken more time and consternation than
seems believable,—all for just a few clothes, books, knicknacks and
pictures: but while I'm against my will now in a furnished room, I
must admit that it seems good to get to a comfortable bed that hasn't
ridges in the middle! and to have someone to clean things up for
me (the old room I had was conducive to more dissipation and unease in some ways than any place I have ever been, and I seem to
have had to get away before realizing it!). Forgive all this domestic
bosh, please,—and consider my mind for just what it is at present,—
a melon sort of pulp, recuperating into better shape.

Your comments on my poems were so sharp, yet at the same time
so pleasing to me, that I had to read them to Munson when he came
in yesterday. "Possessions," it gives me much joy to know, hit you
squarely as you say: I cannot help thinking that more of "Recitative"
will get over better at some later date if you happen to re-read it.
It is complex, exceedingly,—and I worked for weeks, off and on, of
course,—trying to simplify the presentation of the ideas in it, the
conception. Imagine the poet, say, on a platform speaking it. The
audience is one half of Humanity, Man (in the sense of Blake) and
the poet the other. ALSO, the poet sees himself in the audience as
in a mirror. ALSO, the audience sees itself, in part, in the poet.
Against this paradoxical DUALITY is posed the UNITY, or the
conception of it (as you got it) in the last verse. In another sense,
the poet is *talking to himself* all the way through the poem, and
there are, as too often in my poems, other reflexes and symbolisms in
the poem, also, which it would be silly to write here—at least for
the present. It's encouraging that people say they get at least some
kind of impact from my poems, even when they are honest in admitting considerable mystification. "Make my dark poem light, and
light," however, is the text I chose from Donne some time ago as
my direction. I have always been working hard for a more perfect
lucidity, and it never pleases me to be taken as wilfully obscure or
esoteric.

Your second version of "Light" was much improved, I think. But
still I don't like it as well as that charming [the rest of this letter is
lost].

179: TO CHARLOTTE AND RICHARD RYCHTARIK

New York City   *March 5th, '24*

Dear Charlotte and Richard: —/—/ This afternoon I went around to an exhibition of sculpture by Maillol (who is an honest workman, but not very creative), and in the same rooms were some large canvasses by Rousseau (le douanier) the first I have ever had the chance of seeing. Next door was a limited but splendid exhibition of Picassos, Braques, and Duchamps. This is a very active year in New York for painting, shows, etc. Modern painting seems to have come into its own here at last. Stieglitz's wonderful new cloud photographs are also on show at the Anderson Galleries this week along with Georgia O'Keeffe's work. And there is the Independents at the Waldorf and an exhibition of Marins which I have not seen yet. What with one's work, one's friends, books, writing, eating and sleeping, things are certainly rushed! It almost makes me long for quiet Cleveland. It really is good to be thoroughly bored once in awhile, don't you think so?

I have seen a great deal of Eugene O'Neill and his wife lately. They have been wonderfully kind to me, invited me out to their house in the country. O'Neill thinks my poetry is better than that of any other American writing today, and in many ways we seem to agree about things. I wish you could both see the charming play called *Fashion* which they are running now at the Provincetown Theater. An old play written seriously in 1840, but the funniest thing in the world to see now. Such costumes and settings by Robert Edmond Jones! You may have seen in the papers what a terrible row is being stirred up all over the country by the prospect of acting O'Neill's new play, *All God's Chillun Got Wings,* in which a white woman marries a Negro. There will be some kind of mobbing or terrors on the first night, and I expect to be there with my cane for cudgeling the unruly! He is frightfully upset about it, and receives terrible threats and insults through the mail from the KU KLUX Klanners. This country is very immature as yet. Such actions prove that thoroughly.

I didn't hear Bloch when he was here, and have been awfully sorry about that. In fact I have been to only three concerts this winter. One was a miserable performance by Hofman of his own feeble compositions. The other two were more stimulating, but rather exhausting. Bartok, Varèse, Arnold Bax, Casella, Szymanowski, Lord Berners, and Schoenberg, the last one named is my preference among them all as being the only one who approached the magnificence of Bloch's work as I still remember it from Cleveland performances.

I have just finished reading a new novel by Waldo Frank in mss. which is very exciting,—a sort of spiritualistic detective story that carries one into abysmal terrors. Frank has been staying with the Arabs in an oasis in the Sahara Desert for several months, and is probably now in Spain. Munson and I have had some fine letters from him, although he is in a broken state of mind and has had much trouble this last year. —/—/ By the way, I think you would both enjoy reading a new book of his, a collection of essays, which has just come out. It is called *Salvos,* and contains his notable essay on Jacques Copeau, and the Theatre de Vieux Columbier.

Munson is very busy writing his new book. . . . It will be a series of criticisms on present-day influences and personalities in American letters. *The Dial* will soon publish one of them,—on the critic, Van Wyck Brooks, who got the *Dial* prize this last year. Did I write you that I met and talked an evening with Paul Rosenfeld a few weeks ago? He had some good things to say, but flopped into a frightful sentimentality before the evening was over. When attacked he becomes like an over-nervous prima donna and is really quite funny. I'm afraid we shall never become intimate although I hear he recently asked Frank's wife if she thought I would like to be asked out to dine with him!?—

I am writing,—a little now and then. About the same speed as always, never as much as I should like but enough to help me keep some faith in myself. In a few days you will get the next number of *Secession* with my "Faustus and Helen" printed complete at last! I think you will also enjoy the essay by Frank. I enclose the last poem I have written, which you may not like at all. I haven't much idea what you will say. I would to God that I could get more done on my poem, to be called *The Bridge,* but it cannot be the least bit hurried, not when one has to spend so much time at the office. —/—/

180: TO HIS MOTHER

[New York City]   *March 8th*

Dear Grace and Grandma: —/—/ It has been like spring here. The weather veering from bright skies into showers. The wind blew a little snow this morning, but not a handful, and now there is brilliant sunlight, the wind continuing in almost a gale. It is always so pleasant to hear you mention spring in your letters: the note is so genuine. And while I like winter, too, and don't respond as entirely to that season as you do, I sympathize with you much. It always makes me hope that we shall have a place in the country some time where I can come and go, and bring friends occasionally that will charm you, while you can have endless days and weeks for quiet reading and gardening. That beats life in the city all to pieces! —/—/

My dear, you know I can't tell you much more about CA's letters than I have been doing without retyping them or forwarding them on for you to return.[1] I am telling you all there is in them that is definite enough to matter, and while I have thought of sending them to you to read successively as they came,—something has made me feel that while there might be no harm in it, no real injustice, at the same time and in the sum of things, I think it a little confusing, somehow not quite right. I can't put it into better words, but perhaps you will feel what I mean, and not misunderstand and think me obtuse or ungrateful, or unfeeling toward you. You see, it's just because this present relationship between himself and myself was started on such an entirely fresh basis, without any more elements of the past entering into it than could be helped. And also, because, really I don't yet have much idea as to how he really feels about me. He is a long time answering my letters, and I now haven't heard from him for over two weeks and don't know when I'm going to. I don't feel that there is anything at present between us but a fragile thread of feeling and communication: perhaps there never will be anything more. At any rate we can speak on the street without getting upset about it. —/—/

181: TO HIS MOTHER

[New York City]   March 23 '24

Dear Grace: —/—/ Before anything else I want to thank you for the fine long letter you wrote, its assistance and thoughtfulness and its

1. "And there have been other complications which may afford you the pleasure of vindictiveness against my ideas and standards. . . ." (Letter, Feb. 14, 1924, H.C. to C.A.C.) Crane's father resented this remark, and denied ever being able to derive pleasure from such an attitude to his son's life and work. He explained his attitude as a failure to understand how his son could ever hope to support himself unless he took his advertising work seriously, and stated that he would be more sympathetic if his son were to regard his writing as an "avocation" rather than a "vocation," a hobby similar to the pastime of "golf." (Letter, Feb. 21, 1924, C.A.C. to H.C.) In the letters which follow Hart Crane's rejection of a place in his father's business, the elder Crane appears bitterly hurt that his son doesn't want to work with him. At the same time, he makes it quite clear that he has a genuine affection for his son, and reiterates that he does not question the devotion to poetry, only its inability to provide financial returns. Later, in a letter of Nov. 25, 1925, he introduces the point that he believes his son to be interested in "pleasure," rather than in following his own example of a man who "worked strenuously."

unwavering confidence in me—the last-named most of all! And the suit came, too—and seems to look better than ever on me.

Your advice about self-reliance, etc., is, of course, quite right. But there are times when everyone I know has had to ask for a little help. This has been one of those times with me:—otherwise you would not have known by this time quite where even to write me. I went over and saw O'Neill, but finally didn't ask him for any loan whatever. Instead, almost right out of the sky the next day came a cash gift from a friend of mine who was managing editor of *The Dial* when my first poem was accepted there, and who simply had heard from others that I was in a predicament. Consequently, my rent is now paid for two weeks more, and I can keep on feeding a few more days. I've been invited out for dinner considerably, and have accepted more generally than I should if I had a job—for the obvious reason that free meals are a considerable help. The Habichts last Sunday evening, Claire and Hal [Smith] on Friday night, and I generally eat with Gorham and Lisa one night a week, if not oftener. Then there are numerous other friends of mine about whom it is useless to mention much as they are too unfamiliar to you. I certainly am developing some interesting and perhaps valuable connections here as time goes on, and my natural manners seem to induce a certain amount of popularity and comment. How strange it seems to me sometimes to be gradually meeting and talking with all the names that I used to wonder over years ago,—and to find how, in most cases, I am valued as an individual—for the attributes most natural to myself! It does give me more confidence than I ever thought I should have.

—/—/ I have a revived confidence in humanity lately, and things are going to come very beautifully for me—and not after so very long, I think. The great thing is to Live and NOT Hate. (Christian Science, in part, I think; and a very important doctrine of belief. Perhaps the most important.)

I hope that CA will realize just a little bit of this truth before it is too late for him to think of anything at all,—even his business! But we are really so far apart, I'm afraid, that I have few ways of knowing whatever he does think about practically anything. I shall keep on doing my best to NOT DENY him anything of myself which he can see as worth realizing (which means *possessing,* also), meanwhile not depending on him either in thought or deed for anything whatever. He has not answered my letter yet. And despite what you say about his probable need for quiet and recuperation, he must be reading his mail all the time. The trouble is that he might much prefer me off the scene anyway,—and it's just possible that such a thought was behind his urging me when he was last here to go to the Isle of Pines (not a bad idea, I think, myself), but I realize your feelings on the subject. His problems are many, and I think he may realize in time that they are more than strictly those concerned with his business, however much and fast they multiply. What I love to think about is the way YOU have come through! And myself! It's a great game. We may realize that we are always losing, but it means a lot to realize that, also, all the while you are losing you are also gaining! And I think we both understand what that means. —/—/

182: To Waldo Frank

Brooklyn, NY   *April 21st, '24*

Dear Waldo: For many days, now, I have gone about quite dumb with something for which "happiness" must be too mild a term. At any rate, my aptitude for communication, such as it ever is!, has been limited to one person alone, and perhaps for the first time in my life (and, I can only think that it is for the last, so far is my imagination from the conception of anything more profound and lovely than this love). I have wanted to write you more than once, but it will take many letters to let you know what I mean (for myself, at least) when I say that I have seen the Word made Flesh. I mean nothing less, and I know now that there is such a thing as indestructibility. In the deepest sense, where flesh became transformed through intensity of response to counter-response, where sex was beaten out, where a purity of joy was reached that included tears. It's true, Waldo, that so much more than my frustrations and multitude of humiliations has been answered in this reality and promise that I feel that whatever event the future holds is justified beforehand. And I have been able to give freedom and life which was acknowledged in the ecstasy of walking hand in hand across the most beautiful bridge of the world, the cables enclosing us and pulling us upward in such a dance as I have never walked and never can walk with another.

Note the above address [110 Columbia Heights], and you will see that I am living in the shadow of that bridge. It is so quiet here; in fact, it's like the moment of the communion with the "religious gun-man" in my "F and H" where the edge of the bridge leaps over the edge of the street. It was in the evening darkness of its shadow that I started the last part of that poem. Imagine my surprise when E—— brought me to this street where, at the very end of it, I saw a scene that was more familiar than a hundred factual previsions could have rendered it! And there is all the glorious dance of the river directly beyond the back window of the room I am to have as soon as E——'s father moves out, which is to be soon. E—— will be back then from S. America where he had to ship for wages as ship's writer. That window is where I would be most remembered of all: the ships, the harbor, and the skyline of Manhattan, midnight, morning or evening, —rain, snow or sun, it is everything from mountains to the walls of Jerusalem and Nineveh, and all related and in actual contact with the changelessness of the many waters that surround it. I think the sea has thrown itself upon me and been answered, at least in part, and I believe I am a little changed—not essentially, but changed and transubstantiated as anyone is who has asked a question and been answered.

Now I can thank you for the wisdom of your last letter to me, and most of all for your confidence in me. (It is strange, but I can feel no place for paragraphs in this letter!) (Yet one goes on making paragraphs.) It came at the very moment of my present understanding, and it is as though it, in some clairvoyant way, included it. Only, I so much wish you were here these days for you are the only one I know who quite encircles my experience. I shall never, of course, be able to give any account of it to anyone in direct terms, but you will be here and not so far from now. Then we shall take a walk across the bridge to Brooklyn (as well as to Estador, for all that!). Just now I feel the flood tide again the way it seemed to me just before I left Cleveland last year, and I feel like slapping you on the back every half-hour.

Malcolm Cowley was very nice in telling me about an opening in the office of Sweet's Catalogues (architectural and engineering), and for the last two weeks I've been up there at five dollars a week the better salary than Thompson's gave me. The work involves no extraneous elements like "human interest" and such bosh, albeit a great deal of care and technical information: but so far I've been able to straddle it, and here's hoping.

If it hadn't been for the delicacy and generosity of people 'like Gorham, Sue Light, Stewart Mitchell, and at the last, E——, I might have been back in Cleveland long ago. My family did, I suppose, what they could, but finally stopped at everything but my carfare back. I'm glad now that I refused that. My father is still silent after over two months since, when I asked him for a slight loan. The past would evidently like to destroy me, at least I can interpret things in no other light.

But you, Cummings and Gorham are good people to talk to, and

I guess I [can] get along without the past entire! And my eyes have been kissed with a speech that is beyond words entirely.

Allons! but I have written few poems during all this rumpus. I enclose what I have,—the "Lachrymae Christi" written two months ago, and a kind of sonnet written last week and, still unfinished.[1]

— — — —

183: TO HIS MOTHER

[*Brooklyn*]   *May 11th, '24*

Dear Grace and Grandma: I am told that this section of Brooklyn around here (Brooklyn Heights) is very much like London. Certainly it is very quiet and charming, with its many old houses and all a little different, and with occasional trees jutting up an early green through the pavements. I have just come back from breakfast and saw some tulips dotting the edge of one of the several beautiful garden patches that edge the embankment that leads down to the river. It certainly is refreshing to live in such a neighborhood, and even though I should not succeed in acquiring a room that actually commands the harbor view I think I shall always want to live in this section anyway. Mr. ————, who has such a back room in this house, has invited me to use his room whenever he is out, and the other evening the view from his window was one never to be forgotten. Everytime one looks at the harbor and the NY skyline across the river it is quite different, and the range of atmospheric effects is endless. But at twilight on a foggy evening, such as it was at this time, it is beyond description. Gradually the lights in the enormously tall buildings begin to flicker through the mist. There was a great cloud enveloping the top of the Woolworth tower, while below, in the river, were streaming reflections of myriad lights, continually being crossed by the twinkling mast and deck lights of little tugs scudding along, freight rafts, and occasional liners starting outward. Look far to your left toward Staten Island and there is the Statue of Liberty, with that remarkable lamp of hers that makes her seen for miles. And up at the right Brooklyn Bridge, the most superb piece of construction in the modern world, I'm sure, with strings of light crossing it like glowing worms as the L's and surface cars pass each other going and coming. It is particularly fine to feel the greatest city in the world from enough distance, as I do here, to see its larger proportions. When you are actually in it you are often too distracted to realize its better and more imposing aspects. Yes, this location is the best one on all counts for me. For the first time in many many weeks I

1. See Weber, *op. cit.*, p. 395.

am beginning to further elaborate my plans for my *Bridge* poem. Since the publication of my "Faustus and Helen" poem I have had considerable satisfaction in the respect accorded me, not yet in print, but verbally from my confrères in writing, etc. Gorham has made the astounding assertion that that poem was the greatest poem written in America since Walt Whitman! Malcolm Cowley has invited me to contribute about a dozen poems to an anthology that he is planning to bring out through a regular publisher, and I am inclined to assent, as the other contributors are quite able writers and it will be some time before my *Bridge* poem is completed and I bring out my efforts in individual book form. —/—/

184: To His Mother

[*Brooklyn*]   *June 19th '24*

Dear Grace: The "wind-up" of your last letter was far from gratifying and I am sorry that anything so common as my usual lack of time for writing should have given you the impression of indifference or ingratitude on my part. Now—lest I get no other seconds before Sunday in which to write you, I'm going to get this off—for tomorrow evening I'll be tied up with a kind of picnic to Coney Island that the office is giving and there won't be a moment before midnight for myself.

—/—/ I wish I could be more interested in politics, but I guess it takes a different kind of mind than mine and a different education. You, however, seem stimulated very much by the spectacle and it makes me almost wish that you would become more active in some work of that sort.

As for myself this last week—I've been most unhappy. My uric acid resulted in urethritis which has been very painful and nerve-wracking. A steady diet of buttermilk has finally relieved me, however, and I am going to continue it for some time yet. I'm looking better now than when you saw me in Cleveland but get neuralgic immediately as soon as I deviate the slightest from my diet. I was in a perfect panic for several days, fearing I had a venereal disease, but a complete examination of my body and urine disproved any trace of that. I know now, however, just how one is paralyzed with fear at any such suspicion. Believe me, it's awful! —/—/

185: To Gorham Munson

[*Brooklyn*]   *July 9th, '24*

Dear Gorham: —/—/ I do want to thank Lisa [Munson] especially —however late—for the last and very pleasant evening at your place.

Allen [Tate] enjoyed it, he told me, more than any evening he had had in NY, and I admit to a gratifying sense of excitement when I left that recalled some of the earlier Munson-Burke-Toomer-etc. engagements that took place before the grand dissolution, birth control, re-swaddling and new-synthesizing, grandma-confusion movement (of which I am probably the most salient example) began. Allen has a very good mind and a kind of scepticism which I respect. I got very few chances to really talk with him, but I suspect that at least we have established an idiom or code for future understandings which may make our correspondence at once a simpler and more comprehensive pursuit. The boy left NY in a frightfully feverish state, however, and I am a little worried about what's happening to him since. He was to have written over a week ago. I shall be pleased to know what he eventually comes to think about this bronco-busting city. I liked his sense of reserved opinion on some matters, and it may well be that a place like NY means less to him than to the usual young literary man.

I have just re-read your Eliot article in *1924*, and hope I may congratulate you again on some very accurate estimates and constructive motives. The little magazine is better than I thought it might be,— really quite sensible looking, and better in its initial contents than several issues of *The Trans-Atlantic Review* that I have seen. (Even Seaver's poetry surprises me!) It certainly is to be hoped that the *Secession-Broom* crowd can supply it to the point of crowding out the ever willing members of the milky way that flutter into every little magazine around the place.

I envy you the long walks and cool evenings. The office and all it means gets rapidly unbearable again with this anvil weather. I feel less querulous today, however, as E. is back with me again—to stay an indefinite brevity but under much more favorable circumstances than before. — — — —

186: TO HIS MOTHER

[*New York City*]   *Aug. 12th '24*

Dear Grace & Grandma: I hope you got the postcard—it was all I could muster up for the time being. Three more hellishly hot days since and at 4 this morning it began to rain. I hope it pours for days —as I have been having queer feelings in my head from lack of sleep, swilling spells and all the nervous tremors that go with such a state of disorder. You may be glad to be in a place where you can have some privacy, go riding in the country and take your time about things. If you were once to pile into a steaming, rushing mob in the subway where the stinks of millions accumulate from day to day—you'd see how I feel about the next day's work after a sleepless night. And when one goes to one's room afterward, believe me, it isn't to write letters! There isn't much you can do in N.Y. in the summer but work & complain. I seem to be doing both, I guess. —/—/

I don't know what CA's doing these days as I never hear from him. And I'm not going to try to keep up a one-legged correspondence. I think of him entirely too much however—as a poisonous and unnatural person—whom it puzzles me to feel any attitude whatever toward, because from all angles he is so baffling. If he would lose all his money and feel himself disgraced I might come to have some feeling for him better than hatred. But now—I can only think of him in profane terms. But enough of this! I'm in a trap that will probably confine me the rest of my life, so I might as well laugh at such a world as my imagination qualifies me for.

When people like Gorham & Waldo Frank ask me why I don't write more, it fairly makes me rage. They—with money supplied them and their time all their own!

But there's no use in my going on like this when I know it will displease you. You *will* have *letters* though!

187: TO HIS MOTHER

[*Brooklyn*]   *Aug 17th—24*

Dear Grace and Grandma: —/—/ The last few days have been cool enough to allow me a slight recuperation from the mood in which I last wrote to you. I also admit feeling better, due to a long talk I had the other evening with Waldo Frank, just back from abroad, on the present situation and hopes for the artist in America, etc. In order to make some money, Frank has signed up for a literary lecture tour beginning next March, which will take him through the middle west and to Cleveland. He is planning on calling on CA for a little persuasive exercise in arousing CA's interest in me. I told him that I certainly wanted him to meet you, whatever else he did while there, and that he is planning on. You, I'm sure, will give him readier welcome than the chocolate maggot.

Frank has been showing some of my work to several of the finest writers in France (most all of whom read English very well) and says there will even be a little audience there for my first book (when it comes out!). But that will be years from now, at my present rate.

Even so it's not so bad. Conrad and Anderson did not begin to write until they were over thirty-five. And Frank seems to think that I have written a few classics already. I can allow my best, and that only, whatever happens; there are too many others writing trash and near-trash these days for me to envy them. —/—/

188: To Waldo Frank

[*Brooklyn*]   9/6/24

Dear Waldo: Your love and thought were so welcome! For I had wanted to see you; and I was afraid that I had proved not very encouraging of (perhaps) your ideas of myself—I refer to my doldrums when we met last. And now—I can't tell you how glad I am that you know and realize me more firmly. And, I know, I can thank you for all this without apologizing for my real despair and torture at the time—and that still tracks me a good share of the time.

The above[1] is an attempt at an approximation to the accompaniment of your own words—an "even so" and "All hail!" to a love that I have known. If it can give you anything like the illumination that the poem by Jimenez has given me—I shall not be sorry I copied it out for you.

189: To His Mother

[*Brooklyn*]   *Sept. 14th, '24*

Dear Grace and Grandma: I have just come back from a breakfast with Sam [Loveman], and he has left to spend the rest of the day with the widow of Edgar Saltus (whom you must have heard him talk about enough to identify). I have been greeted so far mostly by his coat tails, so occupied has Sambo been with numerous friends of his here ever since arriving; Miss Sonia Green and her piping-voiced husband, Howard Lovecraft (the man who visited Sam in Cleveland one summer when Galpin was also there), kept Sam traipsing around the slums and wharf streets until four this morning looking for Colonial specimens of architecture, and until Sam tells me he groaned with fatigue and begged for the subway! Well, Sam may have been improved before he left Cleveland, but skating around here has made him as hectic again as I ever remember him, and I think he is making the usual mistake of people visiting NY, of attempting too much, getting prematurely exhausted, and then railing

1. An early version of "Voyages IV."

against the place and wanting to get back home. This last alternative is really what I am expecting him to do, although he has not yet finally decided. But he does think that NY is too swift for him—and perhaps it is, I don't know. Sam is so often in an unsettled state of mind, however, that it is hard to know in what direction to urge him. —/—/ So far, his most coherent and welcome conversation has been about you, Grace, and several matters that you seemed to think were inadvisable to put on paper to me.

But why you have been so cautious, or sweetly shy, I'm at a loss to understand, because I certainly would never be timorous about writing you any news about myself, however intimate, and feeling quite sure enough that you would not be apt to quote it either far or near—just from the very facts of our relationship. However, I don't want you to think that I in the least minded hearing such delightful news quite orally from dear old Sam: good news is too welcome, however it comes. And now I want you—or rather want to reassure you about something that I have intended to write for some time, and in which you must believe my fullest and most intense sincerity is voiced.

When grandma wrote me awhile ago about Mr. Curtis and his devotion to you—describing as she did, such a human and very lovable person, I was exceedingly happy. But when—later in the course of the letter she mentioned that you felt that no alliance was worth anything that "broke" our relationship—that made me very worried and sad. (I have spoken to you about this attitude of yours before, and you should not persist in assuming [that] what I feel is a somewhat biased and un-natural attitude toward it. I also feel that you are unduly influenced by what Zell [Deming] has to say on such subjects, and you should know that she is a very different type of personality than you and is in a very different relationship to life. The same differences—you should be aware of in whatever opinions you hear from other people on the same subject. And remember that people—sometimes no matter how much they like you—are quite ready to sacrifice your personal happiness to prove or falsely prove their own merely personal theories, etc.) What I want to repeat to you again—and with emphasis—is that I, first, have an incessant desire for your happiness. Second, that I feel you are naturally most happy—or would be, given the proper opportunity—as a married woman. And thirdly, that I have perfect faith in your ability to select a man that loves you enough, and who has spirit and goodness enough to not only make you happy,—but to please *me* by his companionship. And you must remember, that *whoever you chose*

*and no matter what the circumstances might be, no such element
could ever affect our mutual relationship* unless you positively willed
it,—which doesn't seem likely by the undue circumspection you feel
about the matter.

You must remember, dear, that nothing would make me happier
than your marriage—regardless of such matters as money. And for
God's sake don't marry—or at least *seek* to marry a mere moneybag.
It has always hurt me to hear you jest about such matters. A few material limitations are not so much to the heart that is fed and the
mind that is kept glowing happily with a real companionship. That's
what I want to caution you now,—and I must speak plainly before
it is too late, because you have made as many mistakes in your life
as the average, and I don't want you to persist in what is a very sentimental attitude, I fear, regarding my reactions to your natural inclinations. As the years go on I am quite apt to be away for long
periods, for I admit that the freedom of my imagination is the most
precious thing that life holds for me,—and the only reason I can see
for living. That you should be lonely anywhere during those times
is a pain to me everytime I contemplate the future; you have already
had a full share of pain, and you must accept—learn to identify and
accept—the sweet, now, from the bitter. And that you are able to do
that if you follow your trained instincts—I have not the slightest
doubt. I'm not urging you to do anything you don't want to; you,
I hope, will see that clearly enough. I only want you to know that
life seems to be offering you some of its ripeness now, and that if you
will stop trying to reconcile a whole lot of opposing and often very
superficial judgments—and recall some of the uninjured emotions
of your youth which have revived, very purely in your heart, I know
—you will better decide *your happiness* and *mine* than if you allow
a clutter of complex fears and unrelated ideas to determine your
judgment. I shall always love you just the same, whatever you do;
and you know that. I can't help but say that I shall respect you even
more as a woman, however, if you learn to see your relationship to
life in a clear and coherent way; and you are doing that, I must
say, with more grace and rectitude every day. —/—/

190: TO HIS MOTHER

Brooklyn, NY   *9-23-24*

Dear Grace: I allowed myself the luxury of three roses last Sunday,
and I intend to make it as much a habit as my more persistent taste
for "smokes" and wine will allow me—so pleasant have they made

the room these last three days. But you are already aware of how much flowers affect me. And I am feeling better gradually as the cool days increase and the sneezing and nervous fever attending it begin to subside. You ask me about my summer, and I feel like answering that I am glad you feel that you have known little about it for summer in a place like New York (and especially when you are rushed with work as I have been) is provocative of little but groans and sarcasms. Now it's over and "Sweet's Architectural Catalogue" is ready for press. I may be laid off, because of this latter fact, because there is very little to do there for three months following the grand climax of the publication of that monstrous volume; but whatever happens it wouldn't be as bad as the stifling days and nights and the strain of working with your head as raw as beefsteak. Of course I had always some solace from my happy times with friends, and I had a little swimming at Long Beach and one weekend visit to the country, but you know about that already. O'Neill has been at his place in Provincetown, Mass., all summer, so I have not seen him as you thought. My happiest times have been with E——, and I am looking forward to his return again from another South American trip next week. He is so much more to me than anyone I have ever met that I miss him terribly during these eight-week trips he takes for bread and butter. He doesn't know his father has died during his absence, so it will be a considerable shock to him on landing.

———— I can scarcely imagine the old house as a foreign property, perhaps no more standing. It's so deep in my consciousness and so much the frame of the past. When it comes to my things, please chuck what books are in the glass-doored bookcase (never mind the others) in the drawers of my desk, the only article of furniture which I should like to keep. If you can't keep that you might box the books and mss. and send them on to me here. There are photos, clippings, letters, etc., in the desk which I should like to try to hold on to. I have gotten so used to never being sure of next week's rent, however, that I feel like never accumulating an extra sheet of paper because it's painful for me to think of giving up things that have become a sort of part of me. I should rise above such feelings, I know, but I haven't been able to thus far.

Sam [Loveman] is still here, and sleeping in the back room. His catarrh improved. What his present plans are—I don't know, as I have scarcely had a word with him since last Friday night. He doesn't evidently think about spending much time with me. . . . He has really had enough opportunity, and even broken engagements on the spur of the moment. It is all right with me, because I realize that Sam touches life at very few points where I do, and this even comes into our abstract discussions of literature, quite naturally, of course, because I see literature as very closely related to life,—its essence, in fact. But for Sam, all art is a refuge *away* from life,—and as long as he scorns or fears life (as he does) he is witheld from just so much of the deeper content and value of books, pictures and music. He sometimes talks about them in terms as naive as an auctioneer would use. Yet he is instinctively so fine and generous that I will always love and pity him, however much my admiration is curtailed. I don't think he will remain in New York much longer. He is really bound to his family more than we've ever realized, although I have thought of that a good deal. He must have the assurance of his mother's attendance and he fancies that the "quiet" of Cleveland is a more normal environment for him. Well, if he feels that way, it's so. Feeling, his own feeling, is the only scale there is to use in such a matter, and I shall not urge him to stay here against his will—which couldn't be done anyway.

I have only written three short poems all summer, although I have had four previous ones published: two in *The Little Review* and two in *1924*, a magazine published in Woodstock. These have brought me the usual amount of select applause, but no money. I have sent a recent work to *The Dial*, from which I hope to God I get twenty dollars because I'm in bad need of a new suit—and that would help. Becky must have mis-read the *Times* if she saw any reference to me or a book of mine in it. I am being urged frequently to publish a volume, and I think I would have no trouble in finding a friendly publisher, but so far I have been witheld by my own desire to complete a long poem I am working on,—you have heard me speak of the *Bridge* poem—before gathering my things together. I need one good sized slice in the basket, and *The Bridge* I expect to fulfill that part. But a long poem like that needs unbroken time and extensive concentration, and my present routine of life permits me only fragments. (There are days when I simply have to "sit on myself" at my desk to shut out rhythms and melodies that belong to that poem and have never been written because I have succeeded only too well during the course of the day's work in excluding and stifling such a train of thoughts.) And then there are periods again when the whole world couldn't shut out the plans and beauties of that work—and I get a little of it on paper. It has been that way lately. And that makes me happy. —/—/

191: TO HIS MOTHER

[*Brooklyn*]   *Oct. 21st,'24*

Dear Grace and Grandma: The last day of my vacation, and somehow the best! So cold and sharp it is, you might think it time for
turkey. You know how keenly brilliant the atmosphere around these
parts can be—frequently in any season. On such days one gets an even
better edge to this glorious light here by the harbor. The water so
very blue, the foam and steam from the tugs so dazzlingly white! I
like the liners best that are painted white—with red and black funnels
like those United Fruit boats across the river, standing at rest. And
you should see the lovely plumes of steam that issue from the enormous height of the skyscrapers across the way. I've been toasting
my feet at an electric stove, a kind of radio heater that I have in my
room, and glancing first at the bay, then with another kind of satisfaction at my shelves of books and writing table,—for a long time
unable to think of anything but a kind of keen sensual bliss, that
is in itself something like action—it contains so much excitement
and pleasure. —/—/

192: TO HIS MOTHER

[*Brooklyn*]   *Nov. 16th—24*

Dear Grace: Another very active week. Luncheon with someone different every day,—and nearly always someone to take up the evening.
But I have been so interested in several incompleted poems that I've
sat up very late working on them, and so by the advent of Saturday
felt pretty tuckered out. There's no stopping for rest, however, when
one is the "current" of creation, so to speak, and so I've spent all of
today at one or two stubborn lines. My work is becoming known for
its formal perfection and hard glowing polish, but most of these
qualities, I'm afraid, are due to a great deal of labor and patience on
my part. Besides working on parts of my *Bridge,* I'm engaged in
writing a series of six sea poems called "Voyages" (they are also
love poems), and one of these you will soon see published in *1924,* a
magazine published at Woodstock and which I think I told you
about heretofore.

It darkened before five today and the wind's onslaught across the
bay turns up white-caps in the river's mouth. The gulls are chilly-
looking creatures—constantly wheeling around in search of food here
in the river as they do hundreds of miles out at sea in the wakes of

liners. The radiator sizzles in the room here and it is warm enough for anyone's comfort, even yours. I feel as though I were well arranged for a winter of rich work, reading and excitement—there simply isn't half time enough (that's my main complaint) for all that is offered. And the weeks go by so fast! It will soon be sneezing season again before I know it.

—/—/ He [Eugene O'Neill] seems to have Europe in applause more than America. That is true of Waldo Frank's work in France, also, where he has been much translated and more seriously considered, far more so, than here at home. The American public is still strangely unprepared for its men of higher talents, while Europe looks more to America for the renascence of a creative spirit.

Your letter came last night—was tucked under my door when I came in at one o'clock. Its tenderness and affection were welcome adjuncts to a good long sleep. I thought of you, too, just "turning in" —very likely—after the dance you mentioned, and I was very happy to think of your having had a lyric evening, dancing as you so enjoy doing. I'd like to see the A——s and the P——s myself. They were a little unfair to me—but good sports too, in a way, and unusually merry bosses. I still like to think of those five o'clock booze parties we had in the office and how giddily I sometimes came home for dinner. You were very charming and sensible about it all, too, and I thank my stars that while you are naturally an inbred Puritan you also know and appreciate the harmless gambols of an exuberant nature like my own. It all goes to promise that we shall have many merry times together later sometime when we're a little closer geographically.

My—but how the wind is blowing. Rain, too, on the window now! There was a wonderful fog for about 18 hours last week. One couldn't even see the garden close behind the house—to say nothing of the piers. All night long there were distant tinklings, buoy bells and siren warnings from river craft. It was like wakening into a dreamland in the early dawn—one wondered where one was with only a milky light in the window and that vague music from a hidden world. Next morning while I dressed it was clear and glittering as usual. Like champagne, or a cold bath to look [at] it. Such a world!

193: To His Mother

[*Brooklyn*]   *Nov. 26th, '24*

Dear Grace and Grandma: —/—/ Paul Rosenfeld, the critic, of whom, as you know, I am not especially fond, has just called up and invited

me to a sort of reception he is going to give on Sat. evening for Jean
Catel, a French critic formerly on the staff of the *Mercure de France*.
When Rosenfeld gives this sort of party—whatever you may feel
about it—you at least know that everybody (spelled with a capital E)
in modern American painting, letters and art generally—will be
there. Well, I'm not only invited, but am urged to give a reading
before them all from my poems. Alfred Kreymborg and Miss Marianne Moore will also read from their poems. So far I have declined
to read anything—as I am no vocalist, and I certainly fear the stage
fright. But on the other hand, I probably shall essay a poem or so,
if I'm feeling at all assured at the time, as I hate to be known as too
shy a wall flower to speak to even such a "picked" audience as that
will be. While I lack almost no assurance on the value of my poems,
taken generally, I admit that I am considerably flattered at this invitation occurring, as it does, before I have published a single volume. (The other two have been known for years.) And so, pray with
me that the tongue be less stubborn than usual in conveying my
intentions from the written page. —/—/

194: TO HIS MOTHER

[*Brooklyn*]   *Nov. 30th, '24*

Dear Grace: —/—/ On Friday night I am quite certain that I suffered
at least a mild attack of the real ptomaine poisoning from something I ate at dinner. I started to walk home after dinner, and before I got half way I began to swell up and burn like fire. Just the
usual and bad-enough case of the hives, I thought at first. I finally
managed to get to my bed, but was deathly sick besides. My pulse
was pumping so that at the sink, as I was drinking some bicarbonate
of soda, I lost my sight and hearing in a kind of rushing and smoth-
ering of the blood, and would have fainted had I tried to stand up
any longer. Later on, when the case had apparently subsided and I
was lying rigidly still in bed, it began all over again. It was perfectly maddening, and I never slept a wink all night. All this con-
vinces me that my malady was something more than urticaria, and
that I had eaten something positively poisonous. I was able to
evacuate in both directions during the night, however, and somehow
managed to go up to the office yesterday morning, retiring back to
bed again as soon as work was over and not getting up until it was
time to go to Rosenfeld's. In the meantime I had refrained from
practically all food and taken a great deal of Alkalithia and milk of

magnesia, hot bath, etc. I was still very weak when I got to the party, but as whiskey and soda was served I quickly revived, and everyone thought I was a picture of health.

I'm very glad to have made the effort, after all, for I have reason now to feel more assured than ever in regard to my poetry. The crowd was representative as I had expected, delightfully informal, and proved very receptive. I had met at least half of them before,— Stieglitz, Georgia O'Keeffe, Seligmann, Jean Toomer, Paul Strand and his wife, Alfred Kreymborg, Marianne Moore, Van Wyck Brooks, Edmund Wilson and Mary Blair, Lewis Mumford, etc., etc. There was music by Copland, a modern composer, and after that the readings by Miss Moore, myself, Kreymborg and Jean Catel (who read a long poem in French by Paul Valéry) occupied the rest of the time until one-thirty when the crowd broke up. I began by reading three of my shorter poems: "Chaplinesque," "Sunday Morning Apples" (the poem to Bill Sommer which seems to be talked about everywhere since it was printed last summer in *1924*), and thirdly, a new poem which has not been printed, called "Paraphrase." As I was urged to read "Faustus and Helen" I finally did so. Kreymborg came to me afterward and said that it was magnificent and even the conservative Van Wyck Brooks clapped his hands, so Toomer told me. I certainly read more deliberately and distinctly than I ever thought I should be able to, and I find I have already been recognized with the applause of the most discriminating. — — — —

195: TO GORHAM MUNSON

Brooklyn, NY   *Dec. 5th, '24*

Dear Gorham: I'm extremely sorry to have caused you such doubts and misunderstandings by what I said yesterday at lunch, and I'm further glad to say that I do not deserve all of them. In fact before your letter reached me I suddenly remembered my mention of the proposed attack on you and Waldo, and that I had given you a very incomplete account of it.

When this came up at the coffee house a week since yesterday I at once interrupted it by offering to withdraw from any participation in the issue whatever. Allen Tate was there at the time, and as a fairly neutral party I think you can rely on him to check my statement as a fact. At any rate I hope you will ask him about it when you next see him. I have so consistently defended you and Waldo in that particular company that I have so far derived little from the meetings but an unnecessarily aggravated state of nerves and feelings.

From your standpoint, I have long been aware, there is no excuse for my association with people whose activities are so questionable from several angles. And especially since I have been as strong in denunciations of them as anyone. (And let me add that I have taken no pains to conceal these opinions from anyone whatever.) Yet, at the same time, and whether fortunately or otherwise, I have not been so situated that I could possibly maintain the complete isolation which it has been your desired good fortune to maintain. While there is danger, and a good deal of it, I dare say, in my position, I have also felt that in yours, Gorham, lurked the possible blindfolding of certain recognitions, which, attached personalities being removed, you would have naturally found interesting and worthy. I can summon very little that is definite to support my feelings about this at the present time. Issues are not at all clear, and I am disgusted most of the time. You have set yourself to a rigorous program, part of which I subscribe to in action, a larger part of which I applaud you for as a critic, and another part of which I feel is unnecessarily unwieldy, limited and stolid. Perhaps all this assurance-plus is necessary in fighting as stringently as you have done and are doing, but so far I am not crystallized enough, as it were, to accept the whole lock-stock-and-barrel of it. To a certain extent, as Wyndham Lewis says, one must be broken up to live. Which I defend myself by interpreting—the artist must have a certain amount of "confusion" to bring into form. But that's not the whole story, either.

Regardless of these issues you will be assured, I hope, that I have so far found nothing in either your work or Waldo's which I would wish to attack. Your generosity, meanwhile, certainly deserves my thanks for appreciating the sometimes necessary distinctions between a personal friendship with a man and one's opinion of his work.

My rewards or discredit from participation in a magazine issued by your enemies will be bound to be, to a certain extent, somewhat embarrassing, yet, as you recognize, I still feel that I can owe myself that freedom on a clear responsibility. I am growing more and more sick of factions, gossip, jealousies, recriminations, excoriations and the whole literary shee-bang right now. A little more solitude, real solitude, on the part of everyone, would be a good thing, I think.

Let us have lunch together soon. I won't take absolute "vows" before that, for this letter is a very crumb of my feelings.

196: TO GORHAM MUNSON

[Brooklyn?]   *Dec. 8th,'24*

Dear Gorham: Reflecting on our conversation at lunch today I have come to feel bound to suggest that you take whatever decisions or formalities are necessary to "excommunicate" me from your literary circle. How much further you may wish to isolate me depends entirely on your own personal feelings, but I am not prepared to welcome threats from any quarters that I know of—which are based on assumptions of my literary ambitions in relation to one group, faction, "opportunity," or another.

1 9 2 5

197: TO HIS MOTHER

[Brooklyn]   *Jan. 4th,'25*

Dear Grace and Grandma: I might say that this is the first "day of rest" that I've had since I came back,—but fortunately that doesn't mean that I am all fagged out by any means.[1] I've managed to get some regular sleeping hours, have curtailed my liquor rations (since New Year's eve) and am feeling as well as anyone could ever ask. Just came back from a luscious breakfast (I make a practice of a regular meal on Sunday mornings because I sleep so late and also walk a good distance to the restaurant) and have bought some gay marigolds and narcissi from the funny little florist woman nearby who has a regular case on me, or rather has an amusing way of flattering one. She's a sight, alright! Bumpy body, pocked face, mussy hair and a voice that simply barks at you, it is so raucous. I can't be seen passing her place without her glimpsing me, and signaling. When I enter she jumps at me with such phrases as—"Well my handsome Good Looking again! How's my big boy? Ain't he a dandy!," etc., etc., etc. I generally get enough from her to make my room gay on a quarter, and indeed, today, with my Christmas decorations still up and the snow-light coming in from the roofs of the piers below me—it is festive. Allen Tate, Sue [Jenkins] and Brown are coming over for tea this afternoon, so I won't be the only one to look past the little flying swan still dangling in the window.

Tuesday night as I sat alone in my room I pictured you at the

1. Crane had visited Cleveland.

Miracle. You must tell me how you like it, and what you did on New Year's eve. Our party at Squarcialupi's (what a name!) was a delight. I was sent out to get some more Victrola needles about midnight, and before I got back the whistles began to blow. Even though it was in an uncrowded neighborhood—people began throwing their arms around each other, dancing and singing. Whereat I went into such an ecstasy as only that moment of all the year affords me. I hugged my companion and started singing Gregorian chants or something of my own version approaching them, and I hope in good Latin. O New York is the place to celebrate New Year's! There is such spirit in everyone, such cordiality! Your telegram came next morning before I was up (I didn't retire until 6) and I trust you got my answer on my way to breakfast. I am very happy these days and the more so because I trust you are. —/—/

198: To His Mother

[New York City]   *Feb. 10th, '25*

Dear Grace: I suppose you've been reading about the great unprecedented fog here, which still more-or-less continues. Well, it's just been hell for me over at Columbia Heights. I haven't had 6 hours of solid sleep for three nights, what with the bedlam of bells, grunts, whistles, screams and groans of all the river and harbor buoys, which have kept up an incessant grinding program as noisesome as the midnight passing into new year. Just like the mouth of hell, not being able to see six feet from the window and yet hearing all that weird jargon constantly. It does no good to go to bed early under such circumstances, yet I'm forced to do so, just because I'm too tired to do anything else. I hope tonight will be somewhat better. —/—/

I'm hoping to hear from you today or tomorrow. Please give my best to Charles [Curtis] which reminds me that I do not share your trepidations concerning him which you expressed in your last letter. I don't think you ought to let such minor doubts annihilate the affection and devotion that he has proffered you so beautifully. I'm really planning on your marriage this spring, and I think you will be foolish to delay it until later.

199: To His Mother

[Brooklyn]   *Monday*

Dear Grace and Grandma: It being the birthday of our country's father and a legal holiday, I'm not obliged to be at the office. But it doesn't mean that I haven't been mightily busy. In fact, for the last three days I have been working very hard to finish up a series of poems for my book (if the printer ever gets around to take it seriously) and they are about done. There are two more to be finished —and then I'll feel better, even if the book is a year in getting printed. You know one makes up one's mind that certain things go well together—make a book, in fact—and you don't feel satisfied until you have brought all the pieces to a uniform standard of excellence. I have revised a good many poems, and had to complete others that were half finished, and it all takes a great deal of work. This sounds as though there were going to be a great number of poems in the book, which, however, isn't exactly so. But the book will at least afford me some credit in the world, if not at once, at least later on. —/—/

200: TO CHARLOTTE AND RICHARD RYCHTARIK

[Brooklyn]   *Feb. 28th, '25*

Dear Lotte and Ricardo: My grandmother sent me a picture of the artist before the Public Hall garden model, clipped from the paper —and as tonight is the night the beds were announced as being supposed to first bloom, I think of you as walking in a perfect Venusberg of flowers and shrubbery. Alas for me! I have only one white hyacinth in my window and a bad breath from last night and luncheon today. But, for once, I was able to retire to my room— away from friends and "enemies" and spend a quiet and economical Saturday evening. I owe enough answers to letters to keep me in a week, but I know well enough that tomorrow night will find me in a Spanish restaurant near here, recently discovered, which serves the finest ruby-colored and rose-scented wine in N.Y. besides delicious smoky tasting sardines and hidalgoesque chicken. Waldo Frank knows Spanish very well, and was able to convince the management, thereby, that we were not revenue officers. Since then life even in "my" retired neighborhood in Brooklyn has been gay. I know you think me terrible, and given over entirely to pleasure and sin and folly. Certainly I am concerned a great deal with all three of these—and even so, don't get *all* I want. What worries me is that I'm so restricted in other ways besides. Even, yea, on the holiest impulses. For didn't I promise to take Richard's drawings or rather photos around to *The Dial*—and haven't I, so far, completely failed to make a move? Really, I ought to sob in your laps for forgiveness. But to save your patience, I won't even mention excuses. I'll only

mention that the matter has been frequently on my mind and that
I'll try to do something about it very soon. I'll also try to get back
to you somehow without damage the drawings (originals, etc.) which
I've kept so long.

It's fine to know you have a new piano. Sam [Loveman] says that
it's a beauty. If I ever get any money that is one of the first things I
shall put it into. After so many years of negligence, however, I doubt
if I shall be able to perform much on it! Which reminds me that I
almost never get to hear any of the fine concerts here, after all.
Money, lack of time and other things conspire to keep me away.
Only once this winter have I stared at the baton,—and that was
Stravinsky's. But he disappointed both Waldo and myself by not
including the *Sacre du Printemps* on the program. I don't care for
what I heard of his *latest work*. Indeed, the *Petrouchka* was the only
fine thing on his program. I can probably bet on your having heard
him in Cleveland.

My book is indefinitely stalled as the printer has run out of
money, but I've been working hard to get finished with a f !!!?!!?!

18 hours later

Sunday, March 1st:

WELL! It isn't often that one gets an earthquake inside a letter,
but this letter carries the evidence of one to you this time! Thank
God I'm living still to finish the ending of that last sentence. I had,
as you see, started the word "few" meaning to follow it with "poems"
—when the room began swaying frightfully and I had the most
sickening and helpless feeling I hope to ever have. By the time I got
down the stairs people were coming out of other rooms all over the
house, etc. I ended up with making a call and drinking wine, and so
your letter has been waiting almost twenty-four hours for me to re-
cover. The feeling was simply frightful. But you have probably read
all the details in the papers by this time. I understand it was even
noticed in Cleveland.

201: TO HIS MOTHER

[*New York City*]   *March 10th, '25*

Dear Grace: It takes this night work at the office to make me continually sulky, and with two more nights of it again this week in
prospect, don't blame me if I'm not exactly gay. I would have written you on Sunday had I been in a better mood. I certainly resent

going around and around feeling as though my legs as well as nerves would give out at any moment. I dread to think of the summer and all that it means—and it's not so far away. I have pretty definitely made up my mind to take a job on a boat for S. America during that season, at any rate, and avoid the otherwise exhausted state of mind and body that the city, heat and my hay fever always cause. But more of that later. The trip to Norway possibly may not come through at all as there has been some difficulty in settling the estate of E——'s father, and things are at present very much tied up. —/—/

Gorham, of course, I don't see at all, nor hear much about. I understand that he regrets his awkwardness in dealing with me as he did, etc. But his change of personality which had long preceded this particular situation at which I took offense, had already changed my feelings about him considerably, and I strangely enough don't miss seeing him half as much as I had once thought I would under such circumstances. Of course, I'm really his friend, as I know he is mine, but it may do us good to separate a little while. Many of his ways and opinions had begun to bore me a great deal, and that feeling may have been mutual, so far as I know. —/—/

202: To His Mother

[*New York City*]   *3/28/25*

Dear Grace and Grandma: —/—/ I have also been in a state of rush regarding the completion of a few remaining lines and corrections on poems to be included in my book, which the printer is beginning to set in type. This little man, Jacobs, by name, certainly is devoted to the cause of literature in going ahead as he is—paying for the cost of the paper and binding as well as dedicating his time and strength—free of charge—to the details of typography, setting, etc. For he is well enough convinced that he will on no account reap any more remuneration from the book than I will. Poetry of my kind is not popular enough nowadays, you know, to sell.

Nevertheless, I am somewhat stimulated by the fact of the book being actually now in progress. Getting that wad of my past work into permanent collection and out of the way, so to speak, is an hygienic benefit. Then—I shall feel myself all ready to begin the honest-to-goodness efforts on my long *Bridge* poem. —/—/

203: To Charlotte and Richard Rychtarik

Brooklyn   *April 9,'25*

Dear Charlotte and Ricardo: —/—/ It will be amusing to ask Sam [Loveman] about this person when I next see him. We generally

have Sunday morning breakfasts together in a Spanish restaurant
nearby and talk over our troubles as well as pleasant reminiscences.

As you picture matters, the usual bacchanale of life around here
and among my friends still occupies me a good deal. Some of it is
sweet and clarifying—but as time goes on I tire of certain repetitions
that occur in it and seem to be developing certain reactionary
tendencies toward solitude and more austere examinations of myself. Above all, with the regular amount of highly detailed work I
have to do every day at the office,—the "grind" in other words, and
all the tempting other activities outside my real self, I feel worn out
most of the time and so distracted that I lack the reflection and
self-collection necessary to do the work, the *real* work that ultimately
concerns me most. Still, considering the slight time which I have
for any real freedom I think I have done a good bit of work during
the last two years. But I cannot profess to any real ability in measur-
ing it. One struggles along blindly most of the time. —/—/

You both should read *Port of New York,* a book by Rosenfeld
dealing with Stieglitz, Marin, O'Keeffe, Sessions, Hartley, Williams,
etc.—I differ with Rosenfeld on many matters, but the long chapter
on Stieglitz in this book is very fine indeed and [the rest of this letter
is lost].

204: TO THOMAS SELTZER

Brooklyn, N. Y.   *May 4th, '25*

Dear Sir: In the same mail with this letter I am submitting the mss.
of a book of poems, *White Buildings,* for your consideration.

Mr. Samuel Jacobs, already known to you, I believe, by reason of
his composition work on the *Tulips and Chimneys* book by Cummings, had thought of bringing out this book himself, but recently
has become involved in other work to such an extent that he feels it
would be better handled by a "regular" publisher. He has, however,
recommended that I send the mss. to you. And his steady interest in
the matter is, I think, well evinced in the free cooperative services
he says he is glad to offer the publisher of *White Buildings.*

Mr. Jacobs has made me a cost estimate on an edition of five
hundred copies, quoting the prices of all work as done by his press,
The Polytype Press, 39 West 8th Street. In the following quotations,
which are based on an edition that should be admirable in every
detail, Mr. Jacobs has eliminated the cost of composition, which
he says he would like to do free of charge, on account of his personal

interest in the poems and in having them well set up. I quote from his signed estimate:—

500 copies—*White Buildings*—64 pp.

Stock (Warren's Oldstyle)	$ 17.00
Makeup (by Pelley Press)	16.00
Lockup & Presswork	40.00
Casing and Shipping	2.00
Binding (@ 25¢ per copy)	125.00
TOTAL	$200.00

In view of the fact that Mr. Jacobs' reputation as a typographical expert and producer of notably beautiful books is so well established by this time, I feel that the above estimate is surprisingly modest. I have taken the liberty of introducing it in such detail at this time because it represents a considerable economy in proportion to the book's probable production cost through other hands.

As to the selling qualities of *White Buildings,*—I surrender that prophecy to the publisher. That there are admirers of my work to the number of five hundred, I am certain. And I can personally guarantee the sale of at least 150 copies through the various mailing lists to which I have ready access, and through the interest of my friends. Mr. Waldo Frank has admired my poetry considerably, as well as Eugene O'Neill. I have been assured that both of these writers will be glad to be quoted to that effect on a jacket or announcement accompanying the book. And these statements might have an appreciable effect on both sales and reviews. Not to enumerate the reasons here, I have reason to expect that *White Buildings* will receive favorable review from at least six out of ten writers who would be likely to treat with it, anyway.

The bulk of the book has already appeared in the following magazines: *The Little Review, The Dial, Secession, The Double Dealer, 1924, The Fugitive, Broom,* etc. I am hoping that I may hear something from you regarding your decision on this mss. within a month's time, as I may be out of the city for a period after that date.

205: To His Mother

[*New York City*]   *May 7th,* '25

Dear Grace and Grandma: The photos of the cherry tree in bloom were a joy to have and keep. I like especially the one with yourself, Grace, standing underneath. The attitude and expression you took were gracious and lovely. The tree and the entire yard, for all that, have a great place in my memories, and now that the place is liable to be sold at any time I'm especially glad to have the pictures.

By this time I hope and pray that you are both fully recovered from your attacks of grippe and indigestion and nerves. The recent weather has been pretty decent here, and as far as myself is concerned, great improvements have been made. I'm feeling even better than at Christmas when I was in Cleveland, and guess my color shows it. Diet and general caution have put me in fine shape along with some slight medicine the doctor gave me. It certainly makes a big difference in one's mental reactions and attitude, as you said in your letter, Grace.

Last Monday I had luncheon with Bill Freeman, and with the result of some statements that may interest you. We talked about everything else under the sun *but* business during the meal, but before we left the table Freeman abruptly introduced the proposition which I had faintly expected. He asked me if I ever expected to go back to Cleveland to live, and I replied that at present I had no wish to do so, but that such a thing was by no means improbable if, for certain reasons, I should sometime feel obligated to. Then he went on to say that the Corday and Gross Company needed someone of my type in their copy department very badly, and that they would be glad to connect with me in case I cared to go back. He further mentioned that I was the one "brilliant" copywriter they had ever had there, that the company had fully realized, long since, that they made a great mistake in letting me be lured away without raising my salary, etc., etc. Well! I must say it was a satisfaction to be so spoken of. I was glad to know, too, that such an opportunity will always be at least plausibly open to me in case I am ever again located in Cleveland for any length of time. I suggested to Freeman that I might still do some writing for the company on a free-lance basis, here, if they cared to commit some special job to me now and then, and from his answer I judge that the possibilities on that score are not exceedingly remote. I would certainly like to make a little extra cash on the side, as you know how pared down my present salary keeps me.

I went in and made application for a raise again the other day, this time with the expressed desire of knowing definitely within a week, as I said "the decision will affect my future plans." Which is no threat merely, but a fact. I think I will get the raise, but if I don't—it's me for the sea during these summer months, and a change from office routine for awhile. It is going to be hot enough without

working nights at the office here, the way we shall undoubtedly be
forced to, at a bare living sum! If I can't be paid enough with all
the time and effort here at the office to save at least $5.00 a week,
then I might as well, for all I can see, be seeing a bit of the world
while I'm young enough. Two more years of this routine here will
kill my imagination anyway, but I'd rather stay around here awhile
now until my book is published and out of the way. —/—/

On the whole I think it's better that the printer acted as he did,
as it will mean much more recognition from the general public to
have the insignia of a regular and recognized publisher on the
volume than it would to have just a printer's sign. That would suggest to the general public, whether true or not, that I had paid to
have the book brought out myself, which makes a bad impression on
reviewers, and puts me in an unpleasant position. That's one thing
I would never do,—at least with a first book. It's enough to put good
food on the table, without having to rub people's noses in the plate
who don't want to eat! —/—/

206: To His Mother

[Brooklyn]   *Sunday afternoon*

Dear Grace and Grandma: —/—/ I am enjoying a quieter afternoon
than I had expected, due to the happy failure of some people to call
whom I had invited for tea. I have received so many courtesies at
one time and other from Gaston Lachaise and his Madame that I
invited them along with Slater Brown and Sue [Jenkins]. But each
of the parties finally phoned and called it off for various reasons.
The Lachaises are soon to leave for their country place near Bath,
Maine, and have been nice enough to urge me to an extended visit
with them this summer if I can possibly do so. Just a mile from the
ocean—and a wonderful beach set in a cove of rocks topped by pines!
How I would love to go—and I really may decide to. As I have been
mentioning, the summer at the office and the extra night work required looms up before me as almost unthinkable. I have asked for
a raise—but it has not been settled as yet. I think I impressed it upon
the boss, however, that if it isn't forthcoming I have other plans.
I inquired again yesterday, but have been put off until Tuesday.
Well, we'll see. I have got into such a rut of repetitious feeling,
thought and dissatisfaction with myself that it seems the only salvation to break away for awhile into some change of work and environment. I am still considering a trial of ocean. Even if it's not at

all ideal it may jog me up a bit. I really need more air and exercise at my time of life, and after four years or more of this sedentary office routine you can hardly blame me. Sam [Loveman] would take over my room and things while I'm gone. All in all, though, I've repressed my instincts so much that I can't seem to make up my mind with any decision about anything. —/—/

I have not yet heard what Thomas Seltzer, the publisher, thinks about my book, but I ought to before another week. When I told Waldo Frank about submitting there he became somewhat excited, said that he had wanted to bring it to his own publisher, Boni and Liveright, and made me promise to turn over the mss. to him immediately if Seltzer didn't take it. As you perhaps remember, Waldo had originally intended to take the book to Liveright, but told me some weeks ago that Liveright was not in the proper mood to be talked to at the time, etc., etc. Well, I got little satisfaction from waiting around indefinitely—so decided to start the book on its rounds. It takes long enough to find a publisher, as a rule, without depending on the moods of any one of them. Even now, if the book were accepted today, it would probably be next spring before it could actually appear. I'm figuring that publication in book form will give me at least enough prestige to get a little money for my magazine contributions. Besides this, I have begun to feel rather silly, being introduced everywhere as a poet and yet having so little collected evidence of the occupation. There won't be any explosions of praise when the book appears, but it will make me feel a little more solid on my feet. —/—/

207: To His Mother

[*New York City*]   *May 28th, '25*

Dear Grace: —/—/ I gave notice to the boss as soon as I found out definitely that I was not going to get a raise. The time is set for a week from this Saturday. You know my feelings and reasons well enough from former letters, so it's not necessary for me to repeat them now. Later on in the summer I may take a boat job on the South American or West Indian Routes, but at present I have been very lucky in being invited out to a lovely farm near here (Brewster, N.Y.), to spend a month or so. Brown has just bought it, and has urged me to come out and help him plant the garden, etc. And this is just what I have been needing, exercise, open air, and relaxation from the tension of the desk (which had become very threatening to my health and nervous stability, I can assure you). This invitation came subsequent to my resignation at Sweet's—so don't think that I have been seduced by a tempting prospect of any kind. I was ready for ANYTHING after the prolonged tension and confinement here for the last year, and whatever happens I shall not regret having left the office.

E—— has or rather will take my room over at Columbia Heights, and I have reserved it for myself again after October, as it's such a good room I don't want to loose my hold on it if possible. Write me there up to June 6th, when I leave for the country, and I shall write you much more in a few days. You certainly haven't been very generous, yourself, with correspondence lately. I hope you are both very well. C.A. [Crane] looked me up here recently and offered me a job which I was all ready to take. Whereupon he became so pettily dictatorial that I withdrew quickly. In some ways it was all very funny, and I'll write more about it later. We parted on friendly enough terms, I guess. — — — —

208: TO HIS MOTHER

Brooklyn, N.Y.   *June 4th, '25*

Dear Grace and Grandma: Practically everything is packed up. There has been a real turmoil, too, I can tell you. The frightful and sudden heat of the last 3 days brought on a fearful attack of uric acid trouble—headaches, bladder trouble and urethritis. No sleep for three nights and I have been dieting on buttermilk and crackers. Besides trying to complete all arrangements by Saturday and still give some time to the office, I have had 3 engagements with the dentist. I thought one tooth had an abscess and had to have an x-ray taken to find out that it hadn't. There is one more trial with a filling tomorrow and then I'll be through. I'm about done out, however, and a feather could knock me over. Furthermore, all these exigencies have about used up all the money I had saved up, little enough! —/—/

I did enjoy that talk with you over the wires to Cleveland! Your voice is so much better than ink and paper.

Have a good time in Chicago, and, by the way, why don't you explain my case to the Ross's—that is—if any opportunity appears. They give thousands to charities every year—and boast about being patrons of art. Why don't they help some artist who is trying to live—and still get something done? A small allowance for me six

months of the year would mean almost nothing to them—and it
would keep me alive and productive in some cheap place in the
country. You might mention Frank's and O'Neill's and Anderson's
admiration for my work,—and that I have a book about to be published.

They won't be hard to convince on C.A.'s neglect of me, as they
have had their own evidence of that side of him.

Everyone thinks it a crime the way I have been treated. I'd be
glad to work six or eight months of the year if I could have the remaining time for my natural creative activity. Please see what you
can do about this.

I hope Grandma is not too overborne by this torridity.

209: To His Grandmother

Patterson, New York   *June 17th, '25*

Dear Grandma: —/—/ As for myself—things couldn't be better. I
have great quantities of fine Guernsey milk every day from a neighboring farm, the finest butter and eggs and fresh vegetables—and
so much outdoor exercise than I am brown as a nut already with the
sun and all greased up at the joints. Sleep nights like a top and the
uric acid trouble has disappeared completely—at least for the time
being. When you consider that this is only about my tenth day out
here such results seem astonishing, don't they? I should have written you more if there had been a moment, but you have no idea how
busy we have all been. There has been a great deal—tons—of wood to
clear away from the house, rubbish, also, and a lot of old plaster
they threw out in making alterations. Then we have been building
bookcases, shelves and tables for the inside, as well as scrubbing and
rubbing down floors. Getting up every morning at five-thirty. The
air is so fresh and the birds so sweet that you simply can't stay in
bed a moment longer. And how good breakfast tastes! We have
bought a good oil stove, which works on about 10 cents a day. All
our cooking and lamp-oil comes to much less cost than similar
means in the city would cost. Brown has a Ford which he got for
35 dollars! We go marketing about 7 miles away to the nearest town
every three or four days. This place, you know, is quite delightfully
isolated from other houses. It's about 150 years old—and did I tell
you that a lot of wonderful old rope beds and furniture came right
along with it? —/—/

210: TO HIS MOTHER

Patterson, N.Y.   *July 10th, '25*

Dear Grace and Grandma: —/—/ Life has been going along here at Brown's farm as pleasantly as anyone could wish excepting that the last few days I have had a considerable touch of the [rose] fever. I had expected to evade the whole season, but I guess I'm in for a few days of it here, despite the altitude and other favorable circumstances. We have the house painting almost finished. I've already mentioned how I enjoyed doing that. Brown and I have been making screens for the last couple of days and now I defy a mosquito to attack my slumbers or a fly to fall into my soup. Although planted very late in season Brown's garden is about up, peas and beans, and soon will follow a whole menu of delicious vegetables for the table. This is the kind of place I am going to have when I can afford it. Perfect quiet and rolling hills, almost mountains, all around—with apple orchards and lovely groves of trees and rocky glens all about the house. Yesterday afternoon we picked blueberries—about four quarts in an hour—and there's nothing better to eat with cereals for breakfast I can tell you. It's pleasant to pick them, too—great patches of bushes laden to bending with the beautiful milky-blue fruit that looks the freshest thing on earth. The huckleberries will be out later—and there will be simply bushels of them. Brown also has great quantities of raspberries, blackberries, currants and gooseberries— as well as elderberries on his place. Also plenty of sap maples and walnut trees. I haven't yet stopped enthusing about the place, you see, and when you mention buying land in Florida, that dry and tourist-ridden place, I find it hard to agree with you. Brown has even been so nice as to offer me a strip of land as my own and a great pile of cut timber to build me a cabin—if I will stay here with him and Sue [Jenkins]. You can't beat his affectionate generosity in any friend on earth. I wish you could know Sue, also. Well, someday you will, I'm sure, as I'm not likely to lose my enthusiasm for them very soon.

This Florida plan of yours prompts me to worry a little, Grace. You must certainly be cautious about investing your money there the way things are going at present. Of course I have been hearing all that you have about the tremendous sums exchanged there in real estate, and maybe more than you. That information is certainly nothing that one has to be "tipped on" these days. Everyone—even the farmers around here—are scraping their coins together and rush-

ing down to Miami to buy little lots, and I know well enough that
at least *some people* have made and are making fortunes there. But
doesn't such a great campaign of advertising as this now seems to
be—doesn't it arouse your suspicions as to the validity of the proposition to the small investor? Remember, Grace, that the stock market is run on the same plan and with the same tactics—and the daily
crop of suckers can be reaped in other fields and byways than Wall
[Street], and often is. If you had thought of investing in Miami
property a year or so ago it would undoubtedly have meant a considerable profit. But—as I see the situation now—the whole proposition there is like a whirling roulette wheel that with every revolution spins a higher figure—but which has already begun to slow
down. I don't see how the situation can be otherwise when there
has been such a wholesale flux of gamblers to the place as there already has been. For certainly there is a limit to the value of property—and there is a limit to the present national craze of flocking
to Miami. I may be wrong, of course, but it seems to me that most
of the fruit down there has been picked up already. It might net
you something to try and sell for others down there, but I would be
awfully slow about making any investments myself—at least until
after I had been there long enough to ascertain some direct information of my own about matters. In such "gold rushes" watch out
for the boom psychology that animates everyone concerned—even
the losers—into bursting their voices with salutary legends of their
luck and the general prospects of the place. It amounts to as much
a conspiracy as though they had all sat down together at a great mass
meeting and agreed to swear they each saw Jesus bathing on the
beach. Of course I can see your special interest in going to Miami
this winter to make money—but I'm blind to the other advantages
of the plan. Especially when you have as lovely a place—only a day
and a half further away—down on the island [Isle of Pines] to go to,
and where living expenses will be about one third as much. (Miami
is a very expensive place to stay, I understand, especially since this
boom.) Further—it seems to me you ought to take a run down there—
for at least two weeks—regardless of other plans. Or otherwise, after
all this time, who is to know what is becoming of the place? I'd
jump at the chance to go there myself. Please don't resent my advice
about these foregoing matters. My opinions on such matters have
to be got off my chest naturally—as they are inevitable concomitants
to my interest and affection in you both. I certainly have no desire
to stand in the way of anything you wish to do.

My trip to South America is as hazy as it's always been. It may be that line of boats or some other across the Atlantic for me when I get back to New York—I won't be able to wait long for employment anywhere as I have only about the carfare back to town. I may even take some other kind of office job. My chiefest concern while I have been out here is to avoid worries of whatever kind for awhile; doing that, you know, takes a kind of discipline after one has been so constantly precautious and apprehensive as I have been for the last five years. With my health and nerves all ready to snap beneath *that* strain I decided that life wasn't worth it—and the pretense of living under such an attitude of mind year after year was certainly not worth continuing. So I am—at least for awhile longer—content to drift a little, let things take care of themselves, reduce my needs and requirements to a minimum and avail myself of as much time for free breathing and meditation as possible. The boat job would—on the South American line—permit me practically three weeks of time (absolutely to myself) out of every eight. This time would be spent in Buenos Aires at one end of the trip, and at New York at the other. I might get some time to write and read again. I really hope very much to make connections with this line for that reason, even though the first job I could get wouldn't amount to more than 65 dollars a month. At least three-fourths of my living expenses while on the job would be gratis, of course. And I even long to be entirely away from the best of friends at time. It gives you a fresh picture of the world. One trip would decide whether I cared for the job or not—six weeks and 12,000 miles. I could probably get a job as night watchman or as engineer's writer. But you have to take what places are open when the ship comes in.

Exactly how much longer I shall stay here isn't decided yet. But it will probably not be more than two weeks from now. In New York I shall stay with either Allen Tate or E——, —probably with the latter as E—— is still staying in my old room at Columbia Heights. At any rate that will be the place to write me. I'll let you know more details of course, when they are settled. In the meantime I have written to Freeman who is still with the New York office of Corday and Gross if he has any free-lance ad writing which I could do for them while I am out here. That will probably amount to nothing at all, but the idea occurred to me and I thought I ought to try it out at least. If I could pay my share in household expenses here I should like to stay all summer as I have certainly been made to feel extremely welcome. Otherwise I can't go on accepting things as they are. —/—/

Eugene O'Neill wrote me that he was enthusiastic about some re-

cent things I had sent him, and I have enough enthusiasm from
other astute and discriminating people in America to make me feel
that my writings are justified. Publishers shy at it, of course, because they know it won't make them money. Meanwhile the same
flood of mediocrities in verse continues to be printed, bound and
sold year after year.

Your story of the Fourth sounded very jolly indeed. Nothing could
beat the hilarity of this place—with about an omnibus-full of people
here from New York and a case of gin, to say nothing of jugs of
marvellous hard cider from a neighboring farm. You should have
seen the dances I did—one all painted up like an African cannibal.
My makeup was lurid enough. A small keg on my head and a pair
of cerise drawers on my legs! We went swimming at midnight,
climbed trees, played blind man's buff, rode in wheel-barrows and
gratified every caprice for three days until everyone was good an'
tired out. The guests are still recovering, I understand, in their separate abodes in the city. It certainly is infinitely pleasanter drinking
and celebrating on a wide acreage, like this farm, than in the tumult
and commotion of the city. Aside from this one blowout I have not
had a drop since I have been here—and have not felt like drinking,
either. The desire for booze in the city comes from frayed nerves
and repressions of the office, I'm sure. —/—/

211: To Waldo Frank

Patterson, New York   *Friday*

Dear Waldo: I'm awfully sorry about the Jimenez translations: they
are locked in my trunk at Columbia Heights in my letter file. But
I'm going back to New York about a week from tomorrow and I'll
be glad to copy them—and either send them on to you—or directly
to *The New Republic,* as you may direct. That would be—at most—
only a few days later than they would arrive had I sent them along
with this letter. I don't know what you are accenting in your thesis
on the poet, but I think [the] short poem on the Virgin better than
the one called "The Three." I think you sent me only these two.

Along with your letter today comes the news from my mother
that transactions are about completed for the sale of our home in
Cleveland. If this really eventuates I may be called upon to help
them move—which will defer my plans for sea roving at least until
after September. However, I may decide to evade the moving: I
can't at present see my way to make any definite plans without risk-

ing some kind of unpleasant entanglement. I wish that "wile" and "guile" were easier instruments for my imagination to use! There is always some other immediate duty or requirement for me to per-form than creation. I've had only above five hours at the writing table since I came out here, and now it's about time to look for a postage stamp—I mean the wherewithal for it—to post this letter! Of course I've had a good time, find I enjoy painting house, gar-dening, etc. BUT——.

At any rate your sanguine hopes for *White Buildings* warms me. It came back from Harcourt yesterday. They couldn't make any-thing out of most of the poems. My "obscurity" is a mystery to me, and I can't help thinking that publishers and their readers have never heard the mention of Sir Thomas [John?] Davies, Donne, Bau-delaire, Rimbaud, Valéry or even Emily Dickinson. Within a few days, probably, I'll get time to make you a copy of the mss. It has been loutish of me not to have delivered the poems to you long be-fore this, but hurry and general confusion have been mainly re-sponsible. In looking over the selection I hope you will (when the leisurely moment arrives) have the impulse to make what comments and criticisms occur to you. I am dissatisfied with at least half the poems, but I realize that this will possibly always be so with regard to poems written more than two years back. Reason seems to dic-tate, then, a certain amount of necessary indifference, that is, if I'm ever to print any collection of poems before the grave. —/—/

212: To Waldo Frank

New York   *July 23rd*

Dear Waldo: —/—/ After the quiet and freshness of the country the New York or rather Manhattan mid-summer seems more than ever intolerable. Rather ghastly, in fact. But Cleveland won't be much better. Gorham was thoughtful in writing me news of a pos-sible position with Henry [Robert] McBride as publicity man. I am going to see them about it before leaving,—as it might be a decent sort of thing for me.

Dos Passos has just come back from the hospital, after about two months of some influenza complication which has almost finished him. Cummings looks bilious and harried. His connections with *Vanity Fair* are broken and like the rest of us he is looking for pen-nies. Jimmy Light has just sailed past Columbia Hts. for England where he expects to put on some O'Neill plays. He has sole direction of the Provincetown theatre (not Greenwich Village branch) when he comes back in September. Have you thought of sending your play to him? The repertoire that is at present planned doesn't sound any too brilliant to me. Haven't seen Jean or Gorham yet,— but expect to tomorrow. Such is the news in a hasty batch. . . . —/—/

213: TO WALDO FRANK

Cleveland   *Aug. 19th*

Dear Waldo: I have been trying to get time and clarity to write you for the last two weeks—ever since I sent you the mss. of *White Buildings*—but the nightmare hurly-burly and confusion here intercepted me consistently. Three more weeks of it and I shall be able to get back to Brown's place in the country and collect myself. Our old home will be rented by its new owner to a fraternity, my mother and grandmother will be leaving for Miami, and Cleveland will become for me, I hope, more a myth of remembrance than a reality, excepting that my "myth" of a father will still make chocolates here.

There has been one bright afternoon, however—last Sat. when I went out to Brandywine valley (between here and Akron) and re-visited Bill Sommer. The old baldpate was asleep on a sofa when I looked through the screen door and knocked. Arose a great bulk in white undershirt and loose white duck pants—the black eyes revolving in the pallid or rather, dusty-white miller face like a sardonic Pierrot's. The few hours I was there were spent with him out in the old school-house studio, surrounded by a flower garden and filled with plentiful new wonders of line and color. I wish you could have seen several of the oil children's portraits that he has been doing! And there is a line drawing of a head and hand that I am bringing back to New York that you will greatly care for. While we were both chewing, smoking and listening to the crickets I finally found out why Sommer has been so remiss about joining in with me in my several efforts to expose him to fame and "fortune." He hates to let his pictures leave him. Against that impasse, I guess, nobody's efforts will be of much avail. It's just as well, of course, if he has triumphed over certain kinds of hope. I admit that I haven't, at least not entirely. I still feel the need of some kind of audience.

By the way—do you know if O'Neill is at present a resident anywhere on Nantucket? He has promised to write some kind of notice for my book, and I should like to get in touch with him. He wrote me from Bermuda, but where he has settled since returning from there I don't yet know. If he has been near you I hope that you have got together.

I am enclosing an improved version of "Passage,"—the poem I wrote in the country this summer. It should replace the version that is in the mss. you have. To me it is still the most interesting and conjectural thing I have written—being merely the latest, I suppose. I'm particularly anxious to know what you think of its form. On sending it to *The Dial* I recently got this comment from Miss Moore:

"We could not but be moved, as you must know, by the rich imagination and the sensibility in your poem, Passage. Its multiform content accounts I suppose, for what seems to us a lack of simplicity and cumulative force. We are sorry to return it."

It seems almost as though Miss Moore might be rather speaking of her own poems with such terms. . . . Allen Tate is writing a short essay (he intends a longer one later) on my work to appear along with four of the "Voyages" in the next copy of *The Guardian*. You will probably see it. It does hearten me somewhat that you and a few others have been so actively interested in what I'm trying to do. Certainly I have never done anything to personally deserve it, but I think my personal and economic embarrassments and frustrations have curtailed a good many of my intentions. —/—/

214: To Charlotte and Richard Rychtarik

New York *Sept. 15th, '25*

Dear Charlotte! dear Richard! —/—/ I am ready to send you one of the Light masks (from last year's production of *The Ancient Mariner*). Jimmie promised me one of them, and I can think of no one better to send it to than you. I'll get a box tomorrow, pack it and send it along. You can have some great fun playing with it in pantomime around the house. The effect is unearthly—the mask belonged to one of the angels, in fact, that are described as standing on the deck of the ship as it reaches the harbor in Coleridge's poem. —/—/

I am so afraid that the land up there will get away from me before I get there that I can hardly sleep nights. I find that O'Neill is not in town and the other person, the publisher, from whom I had planned to possibly borrow the money is away also. Would it strain your pocketbook at this time to lend me the amount, so that I can at once clinch the bargain? It was so good of you to make the offer in the first place that I feel [I] am possibly taking advantage of your friendship. But if I could just settle the matter there before it is too late, I could later borrow the money from O'Neill, or someone else and return you at once the money borrowed. I will need a little over two hundred dollars as otherwise I shall not have anything to pay the lawyer's fees with for looking up the deed, etc. Would $25.00 extra be too much? You must allow me to pay 6% interest on the loan—and to send you a regular note for the money. I would like the time stipulation about 5 years, but I would repay it as soon as possible before that. I know you trust me, but I also want to assure you of protection in the matter. —/—/

215: TO CHARLOTTE AND RICHARD RYCHTARIK

Patterson, New York   *Sunday*

Dear Charlotte and Richard: I think I have found an even better solution for the "land problem" than the first proposition offered. A friend of Brown's, Miss Bina Flynn, has just bought a lovely place within a half mile from Brown's place, wonderful old Dutch house in good condition and built about the time of the American Revolution and with 160 acres of land around it. She needs money to help pay for it and has offered me 20 acres of the best of her land for $200.00. The piece that I have picked to buy is on the top slopes of a hill that overlooks the valley and it contains several open fields and a great deal of forest land. As it is much more convenient (within better access from the main road), and as it contains no useless swamps or wasteland as the other property included, I think I am getting as much of a bargain, if not more. Twenty acres is plenty to spread out in anyway, and there will be plenty of room on it for whatever place you would want, too.

Miss Flynn is out here today transacting the purchase of her property and I expect to settle with her very soon. More and more I become convinced that this is the only way for me to live, that is, when I can make arrangements to afford it as a permanent way of living, and I am sort of planning to come out here next summer and put up a temporary cabin which will at least do during the warm weather. I shall roll in the grass with prayers and pleasure when I really get this tract of land for my very own. And such beautiful country you will not find in many sections of this vast continent. Enclosed is my note for the $225.00 which I intend to pay *much before* the stipulated time. I shall, in fact, probably take a job in New York or on the sea this winter which will enable me to pay it back before a year is over—at the latest.

Today it is raining, but the ten days before it have been as divine as anyone could wish for. We have had big fires in the evenings, long walks, big meals almost entirely of lettuce, carrots, beets, turnips, squash, etc., just taken from the garden. Sue [Jenkins] seems to be very contented out here and is busy every moment making jellies, jams, pickles, etc. The hills are covered with wild grapes, elderberries and apple orchards. Don't you think the quince is a beautiful fruit? There are about a dozen quince trees on Brown's property —all loaded with their sort of kid glove golden fruit. Yesterday we had a great time making six gallons of ale. It must ripen for about five days in a warm corner of the chimney in a huge crock, and then we can begin to drink it. Brown also has a complete distilling outfit out in the shed. He makes wonderful apple jack from cider. But this is a forbidden drink for me these days!

All my furniture and things arrived in perfect condition. In addition I have been making tables and cupboards from old loose wood that has been lying around for years. They really look like antiques, all right! But I do love the weather stains and silver streaks on the surfaces. Most of the wood is oak and quite strong.

So you see how the days go. . . . In addition I am getting back to enough poise to read a good deal. It's funny! Here I've been for over two weeks, now, and without a cent of money to my name. But I haven't felt uncomfortable by any means. I know I can go back to a job now with a much better feeling of independence than before. —/—/

216: TO SLATER BROWN

[*Brooklyn*]   *Oct. 21st, '25*

Dear Tories: There have been numerous "celebrations" besides the already recounted one (by Bina) on the great transaction, and the Punch Palazzo has had due patronage. The engrossing female [Laura Riding] at most of these has been "Rideshalk-Godding," as I have come to call her, and thus far the earnest ghost of acidosis has been kept well hence. My real regret, however, is that I just missed getting the pick of jobs of the S. Am. line, last steamer—said occupation being deck yeoman at 20 minutes work a day, all freedom of ship, mess with officers or any first class passengers that seemed colloquial, white uniform, brass buttons, cap, meditation on the sun deck all day long, and seventy-five dollars a month clear sailing! The chief officer had already approved me, but before I could get over to the offices for final approbation they had already sent someone else over to the ship. We must have passed under the river. However, I noticed that my questionnaire (filled last June) had won an OK sign in the upper right corner, and I have been told to come around again on the 26th when the next boat arrives. I'm not waiting for that, however, as I need instant cash and there is not one chance in a hundred of a similar vacancy soon. Otherwise I have finished "The Wine Menagerie" and have sent it off, along with "Passage," to *The Criterion.* Since the last (yesterday) *Guardian* has come out *without* the "Voyages" I am thinking of trying to become a literary ex-patriot. It's just as tiresome as ever. This issue contains a lot of tommy-rot by Seaver and an "announcement" in the bargain that reads unforgivably: "Voyages, four remarkable poems by Allen Tate" will appear in the next issue! —/—/

Am on my way to *The Dial* to have lunch with K. B[urke] and shall try to bag a review or briefers from the Rt. Rev. Miss Mountjoy [Moore]. A momentous morning: Frank is going to try to corner Liveright on my vol., also. —/—/

217: TO WALDO FRANK

[Brooklyn]   *Oct. 26th*

Dear Waldo: Your advice and stimulation are still with me. Your solidity and conviction seemed never more firm or luminous than during our last talk.—I was glad to see you looking so well. I wrote this out this morning, thinking it might go well in the book.[1] No other news yet.

218: TO WILLIAM SOMMER

Brooklyn, N. Y.   *Oct. 27th, '25*

Dear Bill: —/—/ I know you'll be glad to know that there is a good chance of my first book of poems, *White Buildings,* being published by next spring. In fact Boni & Liveright (at Waldo Frank's persuasion) have practically agreed to bring it out if Eugene O'Neill will consent to write a short foreword. They have lost so much money on the better kind of poetry (which simply *doesn't* sell these days) that they want to hook the book up with an illustrious name and catch the public that way as much as possible. Gene is a good friend of mine and admires my work—I know that—but whether or not he feels like performing this favor I haven't yet heard. Frank

1. A version of "At Melville's Tomb."

thinks he can engineer the matter anyway—in time, but I don't know. He would glady write the foreword himself if he thought his name would count sufficiently, and at any rate will write a whole page of praise for it in *The New Republic* when it comes out. This and other favorable reviews that I am sure to get from friends of mine ought to make quite a sensation for the book. I'm a little up in the air with the uncertainty and excitement of the present situation. It would be fine for me in so many ways if the thing did go through!

Have been reading Ernest Hemingway's *In Our Time,* a new book that is full of startlingly simple and vivid description. –/–/

219: TO HIS FATHER

[Brooklyn]   [November 21, 1925]

Dear Father: I was very glad to hear from you and it was generous of you to thus come to my aid.[1] The only pity is that artificial theories and principles have to come so much between us in what is, after all, a natural relationship of confidence and affection.

You may not believe it, Father, but in spite of what opinions you may hear that I have against you (and, not knowing what is told you, I still refuse to acknowledge them, either way), I still resent the fate that has seemed to justify them and God knows how much we all are secretly suffering from the alienations that have been somehow forced upon us. If we were all suddenly called to a kind of Universal Judgment, I'm sure that we would see a lot of social defenses and disguises fall from each other, and we would begin from that instant onward to really know and love each other.

I feel rather strange these days. The old house sold in Cleveland; Grandmother ill in Florida; Mother somewhere in Cuba or the Isle of Pines; and I not hearing from either of them for the past month. Altogether, it's enough to make one feel a little foot-loose in the world. But I'll have a job soon, and will probably be reassured in the mail that everything's all right. At such times, though, I realize

1. Crane had asked his father for money in a letter of Nov. 4, 1925. His father responded with a check for $50, accompanied by a letter in which he expressed resentment at his son's contemptuous tone and was himself sarcastic at his son's expense. (Letter, C.A.C. to H.C., Nov. 17, 1925). Replying to this letter of Nov. 21, 1925, C.A.C. denied being uninterested in his son's life, denied that " 'fate' " had caused their estrangement, and put the blame on his son instead. He reiterated his belief in the necessity for earning a living and putting writing on a subsidiary level, and expressed a desire for friendlier relations in the future. (Letter, C.A.C. to H.C., Nov. 25, 1925.)

how few we are and what a pity it is that we don't mean a little more to each other.

Please let me hear from you when the spirit moves you.

220: To Charlotte and Richard Rychtarik

Brooklyn, NY   *Dec. 1st '25*

Dear Charlotte and Richard: —/—/ The facts are hard, but true, I have not yet succeeded in finding myself a job, and even after trying every sort of position, like selling books in stores during the Christmas rush, ship jobs, etc., etc., and I have just been kept going by the charity of my friends. The nervous strain of it all has about floored me, and I feel as though the skin of my knees were quite worn off from bowing to so many people, being sniffed at (to see whether I had "personality" or not), etc. How I shall love it when, some day, I shall have a little hut built on my place in the country to live in— and get out of all this filthy mess!

Even the publication matter of my book of poems has not come through the way I had expected. O'Neill is writing the Foreword, after all, but he took so long to notify Liveright (the publisher) about it that I must now try to place it somewhere else. This may not be so hard, but it probably means that it will not come out until next autumn, and I had so hoped to have it printed before that. . . .

So you see how it's been! I don't mean to wail, but it is hard to keep up and going sometimes. —/—/

—/—/ I have an appointment tomorrow with a possible job. I certainly hope to get it, and begin paying back what you were so kind in lending me. *The Dial* bought my "Wine Menagerie" poem— but insisted (Marianne Moore did it) on changing it around and cutting it up until you would not even recognize it. She even changed the title to "Again." What it all means now I can't make out, and I would never have consented to such an outrageous joke if I had not so desperately needed the twenty dollars. —Just one more reason for getting my book published as soon as possible!

221: To His Father

Brooklyn, N. Y.   *Dec. 3rd, '25*

Dear Father: Your letter was appreciated in many respects and I don't want you to think that I wasn't glad to hear from you. But there were recriminations in it which assumed a basis for apologies and regrets on my part which I don't feel I at all suggested in my last letter and which I certainly cannot acknowledge now or later. In fact, you always seem to assume some dire kind of repentance whenever I write you or call on you, and so far as I know I have nothing in particular to repent. I simply said I was sorry that you could not see me in a clearer light, and it seems I shall have to go on lamenting that to some degree for the rest of my life. If I began to make recriminations on my behalf there wouldn't be any use writing at all, for though I have plenty to mention, I don't see what good it would be to either one of us to embark on a correspondence of that sort. My only complaint right now is that you seem determined to pursue such a course, and I can only say that if you persist I have no answers to offer. You and I could never restore our natural relationship of father and son by continually harping on all the unnatural and painful episodes that life has put between us via not only ourselves but other people during the last ten years, and if you are not willing to bury such hatchets and allow me, also, to do so, then I'll have to give up.

For the last six weeks I've been tramping the streets and being questioned, smelled and refused in various offices. Most places didn't have any work to offer. I've stepped even out of my line as advertising coypwriter, down to jobs as low as twenty-five per week, but to no avail. My shoes are leaky, and my pockets are empty; I have helped to empty several other pockets, also. In fact I am a little discouraged. This afternoon I am stooping to do something that I know plenty of others have done whom I respect, but which I have somehow always edged away from. I am writing a certain internationally known banker who recently gave a friend of mine five thousand dollars to study painting in Paris, and I'm asking him to lend me enough money to spend the winter in the country where it is cheap to live and where I can produce some creative work without grinding my brains through six sausage machines a day beforehand. If he refuses me I shall either ask Eugene O'Neill who is now writing the Foreword to my book and won't refuse me for some help to that end, or I'll take to the sea for awhile—for I'm certainly tired of the desolating mechanics of this office business, and it's only a matter of time, anyway, until I finish with it for good. I can live for ten dollars a week in the country and have decent sleep, sound health and a clear mind. I have already bought ten acres near here in Connecticut and it's just a matter of time until I have a cabin on it and have a garden and chickens. You see I have a plan for my life, after all. You probably don't think it's very ambitious, but I do. As Dr. Lytle

said to me when I was last in Cleveland, "What does it all amount
to if you aren't happy?" And I never yet have spent a happy day
cooped up in an office having to calculate everything I said to please
or flatter people that I seldom respected.

I wish you would write me something about yourself these days.
Let's not argue any more.

222: To Otto H. Kahn

Brooklyn, N.Y.   *December 3, 1925*

Dear Mr. Kahn: Yesterday I telephoned Mr. Sharpp, your secretary,
to request an interview with you regarding some temporary assistance which I felt you might possibly care to render me under the
pressure of my present circumstances. Mr. Sharpp advised that I
write you first, explaining the exigencies of the situation and the
application I wished to make. I shall try to be as definite and as
brief as possible.

My first collected poems are about to be published (probably next
spring) with a Foreword by Eugene O'Neill. Although my poems
have appeared from time to time in various magazines such as *The
Dial* and *The Little Review,* I am not yet well enough known to reap
any substantial benefits from what I have written. I am twenty-six
years of age, and for the last seven years I have been entirely dependent on my efforts as an advertising copywriter for my living. What
real writing I have done has had to be accomplished after office
hours and sometimes at the risk of losing my position. Last June, as
a result of ill health and nervous exhaustion, I had to resign my
position with Sweet's Catalogue, regardless of my dependence on my
salary there, and live in the country until my health recovered.

For the past eight weeks I have been back in New York, endeavor-
ing by every means to secure work again as a copywriter. As I have
been unfortunate in not finding any openings I have recently attempted to get any other kind of work available, but as I find myself now completely without funds, my circumstances seem to be
rather acute. One of my friends has suggested that you might be
sufficiently interested in the creation of an indigenous American
poetry to possibly assist me at this time. As I have never before
asked for such assistance I run the risk of writing you quite pre-
sumptuously, and I certainly wish to beg your pardon if my letter
seems so.

Besides the poems collected into my forthcoming volume I have
partially written a long poem, the conception of which has been in

my mind for some years. I have had to work at it very intermittently, between night and morning, and while shorter efforts can be more successfully completed under such crippling circumstances, a larger conception such as this poem, *The Bridge,* aiming as it does to enunciate a new cultural synthesis of values in terms of our America, requires a more steady application and less interruption than my circumstances have yet granted me to give to it.

If the suggestion seems worthy and feasible to you I should like to borrow the sum of a thousand dollars, at any rate of interest within six percent. With this amount I could live in retirement and cheaply in the country for at least a year and not only complete this poem, but also work on a drama which I have in mind. As security I can only offer an unconditional sum, amounting to five thousand dollars, which by the terms of my deceased grandparent's will, I inherit on the death of his widow. I do not know whether such bequests are open to outside inquiry, but the proper reference, in case you are interested, is Mr. Stockwell, Trust Department, Guardian Savings & Trust Co., Cleveland; estate of C. O. Hart.

As to the estimation my work deserves, I naturally do not feel free to do more than quote a few statements from critics who have seen my poems in print and read my mss. I include these on a separate sheet herewith. Let me say in concluding that I should appreciate an interview with you at your offices, Mr. Kahn, and that I honestly feel that my artistic integrity and present circumstances merit the attention of one like yourself, who is and has been so notably constructive in the contemporary and future art and letters of America.

Statements on my writings—

"It is time that your poetry should appear in a volume. You know what I think of it. I have done my best these years to spread my recognition of your genius not alone here but abroad. But it has been hard, without a volume of your work to go on. WHITE BUILDINGS will be an event in American poetry—a major event. Not the sort of event that journalists make paragraphs about, three times a week. But the sort of event that literary historians make chapters about—years later. You are a real poet.

"I promise you, that when your volume appears, I shall devote a long article to your work, in one of our leading literary magazines." WALDO FRANK

"The publication of WHITE BUILDINGS is one of the five or six events of the first order in the history of American poetry. It is doubtful if any other first volume since Whitman's, in 1855, has so definitely exceeded promise and reached distinction on its own account. Hart Crane's poetry, even in its beginnings, is one of the finest achievements of this age. So one must predict the reviewer's protest—'Incomprehensible!' " ALLEN TATE—Reviewer for *Nation, New Republic,* etc.

"Many thanks for sending me copies of your recent poems. I have taken them with me on my brief vacation and I have greatly enjoyed reading them. They have refreshed my conviction that you are writing the most highly energized and the most picturesquely emotionalized poetry in 'These United States.' 'Voyages' is the finest love suite composed by any living American." GORHAM B. MUNSON—Managing editor of *Psychology,* and critic; contributor to *Dial, New Republic, Criterion, New Age, Europe,* etc.

Other references—Eugene O'Neill, Greenwich Village Theatre, or Ridgefield, Conn.; James Light, Provincetown Theatre; Miss Eleanor Fitzgerald, Provincetown Theatre; Waldo Frank, 150 East 54th St., N.Y.C. Telephone: Plaza 2342; Marianne Moore; Jane Heap; Harrison Smith; Paul Rosenfeld.

223: TO HIS MOTHER

[*Brooklyn*]   *Dec. 9th,'25*

My dear Mother: For almost six weeks, now, I have not heard from you or Grandma. Though Mr. Curtis was thoughtful enough to notify me that you have been taken ill, the circumstances did not seem to describe a situation so severe that you could not have taken pen in hand and at least have written me once yourself during that time—especially, it seems to me, since you knew by my several letters that I was having a difficult time and was without funds entirely. I have put off writing you under these conditions; there was enough reason to so do simply on the basis of your own indifference, or possible disgust with me. And I admit that it was a shock for me to realize that you needed me so little. I have gone through a good many realizations of various sorts during the last six months and they are not without echoes of certain things you said to me last summer, trying as I may have been.

I don't know where you may be at this time, but in case you may for any reason wish to write to me I am writing to say that I shall be probably for the next year at the following address: c/o Mrs. Addie Turner, Patterson, New York, R.F.D. I am unusually well provided for and shall leave for the country next Saturday. Yesterday afternoon I had the pleasure of being rewarded in some measure for some of the work I have been doing. You have probably heard of the banker, Mr. Otto H. Kahn, who has kept the Metropolitan Opera and various other artistic ventures endowed for years. After an interview with Mr. Kahn at his home at 1100 Fifth Ave., I was given the sum of two thousand dollars to expend on my living expenses during the next year, which time is to be spent in writing the most creative message I have to give, regardless of whether it is profitable in dollars & cents or not.

Mr. Kahn was keenly interested in what Waldo Frank and Eugene O'Neill had said about my work, and it makes me very happy indeed to have this recognition from a man who is not only extremely wealthy and renowned on that account, but who is also very astute and intelligent. I am very tired now—with all the strain and effort of the last two months, but I shall probably pick up as never before when I get into the quiet of the country and have the first real opportunity of my life to use my talents unhampered by fear and worry for the morrow.

If you are not too prejudiced about me by this time, you may also be interested in this turn of affairs.

Let me hear from you sometime soon.

I certainly hope you and Grandmother are feeling better.

224: To Charlotte and Richard Rychtarik

[Patterson, New York]   New Year's Eve '26 [25]

Dear Charlotte & Ricardo: Here I am at this date and sixty-six miles from a drink. Isn't it tragic! And there will not be a whistle or a shout to tell me it is a new year. I shall probably be fast asleep, unless I get scared and stay up blinking over a book—for it must be a bad omen to be asleep at the switch of the new twelvemonth. But tomorrow night I shall make up for it. That is, if certain friends come out from New York with all their bottles on them.

Life out here so far has been ideal—even if it has been below zero much of the time. But I came prepared for all kinds of weather and dress every morning in boots, woolens, and furs. I shall have my picture taken and you shall see how very impolite I look.

Imagine paying only ten dollars a month for the rent of a whole house (8 rooms)! I share it with Allen Tate and his wife and have a suite all to myself on the second floor—1 room I do not use at all, a bedroom with a fine old "sleigh bed" and a study, spacious and light, in which the sun streams every morning. My pictures and nick-knacks look wonderfully jolly on the simple kalsomined walls and the books fairly glisten on the shelves. This room is kept well heated by two oil stoves. Downstairs we cook and heat with wood-burning stoves which means enough daily exercise to keep us glowing.

Otherwise all I have to do is wash dishes. Mrs. Tate cooks lunch and dinner and Allen gets breakfast! This routine plan is the only way for all of us to get each his work done—I mean our writing. Mrs. Tate is writing a novel (her second) and Allen is *supposed* to be writing reviews, etc. Nothing much *yet,* however, has been done by any of us. There have been food supplies, appliances and sundries of all sorts to order—and then came Christmas with flocks of people visiting Brown's place (about ½ mile away) and drinking and talking day and night. Allen also has dissipated terribly with a gun he bought (called *"The White Powder Wonder")!* and has so far spent most of his time ranging over the hills shooting at sparrows. He did get a squirrel one day, however, and we had an exclamatory time over the stew it made. — — — — There are all kinds of game around here, even deer, and it's a temptation to hunt, of course.

Well, the expected results have already been noticed on my family! Long and arderous letters from uncles, aunts, etc. (not Zell [Hart Deming], but she's in Europe anyway), and a fat check from my father for Christmas. They all want me to come out and visit again—which I see no reason for doing at this time. I want to get into my work. My God, it's the first time anyone paid me to do it or even encouraged it in any substantial way! Of course—to them the $2,000 seems like some kind of shower bath without any connection with any conceivable responsibilities. You can have responsibilities toward your time clock, your cow or your maiden aunt, but you can't mean to say that poems or pictures demand anything but aimless dreaming! No. I'm not coming until spring—unless there is serious need of me.

Mother, it seems, has been terribly ill in Miami, and did not even go to the Isle of Pines. As she was scheduled to leave for there on a certain day and, failing to, did not inform me I went on writing her there and as I got no word of her from *anywhere* I finally gave up writing at all. Finally I got word through Mr. Curtis that he had been called to Miami to take care of them both—but I still didn't understand her not writing me in all that time, and thought she must be angry about something.

Everything was all mixed up. And I finally had a long letter from her rejoicing in my good luck and full of the harrowing details of how very ill she had been with all sorts of complications. Miami turned out to be more terrible than even I had predicted—and what this folly has cost those women in pain and in expense God only knows. Both in bed for weeks. Six doctors, nurses, compartments on trains, etc., etc., Grandma got back about 2 weeks before Grace was able to leave. The latter joined her finally and they are living at the Manor—where they should have been all the time, of course. I'm sure they would love to see you both, and believe me, there were no complications, as I had thought, between us.

I'm expecting you both to visit me here next summer. Plenty of room for you—and you'll be sure to relax. I bought some wonderful snow shoes with some of Otto's money and so I pray for heavy storms. —/—/

PART THREE

West Indies-Europe

(1926–1930)

1 9 2 6

225: To Malcolm Cowley

[*Patterson*] *Jan 3rd*

Dear Malcolm: The poem[1] has been read with approval—is flatteringly apocalyptic and has the proper nautical slant. . . . Seriously, though, it seems to stand on its own feet as a poem and I appreciate a very great deal the tonality and direction of it in its more intimate aspects. You and Peggy [Baird] have been more than good in remembering me—thanks for the photo, too. —/—/

Are you reviewing *Doc. Transit* anywhere? Schneider finally sent me out a copy. It intrigued me more than any such tour de force since Poe, though it has its obvious weaknesses. Some chapters, however, of great imagination. I didn't anticipate half so much from the earlier things I've read by Schneider.

I'm coming in town probably about two weeks from now, and should like to know what day or days about that period you'll be there also. You know what the Governor of North Carolina said to the Governor of S. Carolina—! I'm such a rum-scallion that I never even planned to stay put anywhere very long in the woods. Let me hear from you soon. —/—/

226: To His Grandmother

Patterson *Jan. 5th '26*

Dear Grandma: I was sorry to hear from Grace yesterday that you have been undergoing more pain and illness—and I only hope that this finds you MUCH improved. I wish I could be near you—and have a long talk. We certainly will manage that when I come out to Cleveland next spring.

Yesterday I finally got started into my *Bridge* poem—really the first full day I have [had] for the work since arriving. And from now on I hope to have the necessary inspiration to keep steadily at it. One really has to keep one's self in such a keyed-up mood for

1. "The Flower in the Sea," by Malcolm Cowley, dedicated to Crane.

the thing that no predictions can be made ahead as to whether one is going to have the wit to work on it steadily or not.

It is fine to get somewhere where I can sleep soundly again. I'm beginning to feel very much rested. I'm so glad that you both are located in a place where there is nothing more to do than to care for your personal comfort. —/—/

227: TO HIS MOTHER

Patterson   *Jan. 7th*

Dear Grace & Grandma: —/—/ There isn't much news—only the good news (to me!) that I've been at work in almost ecstatic mood for the last two days on my *Bridge*. I never felt such range and symphonic power before—and I'm so happy to have this first burst of substantiation since I had the good luck to be set free to build this structure of my dreams.

I sent New Year's greetings to Kahn and in the mail today comes the most cordial answer—wishing as he puts it, "that you will prove yourself a master builder in constructing *The Bridge* of your dreams, thoughts and emotions." —/—/

228: TO WALDO FRANK

Patterson, N. York   *Jan. 18th '26*

Dear Waldo: I am not through working on it yet, but I thought you might care to see this last part of *The Bridge,* oddly enough emergent first.[1] It is symphonic in including the convergence of all the strands separately detailed in antecedent sections of the poem— Columbus, conquests of water, land, etc., Pokahantus, subways, offices, etc., etc. I dare congratulate myself a little, I think, in having found some liberation for my condensed metaphorical habit in a form as symphonic (at least so attempted) as this.

The bridge in becoming a ship, a world, a woman, a tremendous harp (as it does finally) seems to really have a career. I have attempted to induce the same feelings of elation, etc.—like being carried forward and upward simultaneously—both in imagery, rhythm and repetition, that one experiences in walking across my beloved Brooklyn Bridge. I'm now busy on the Niña, Santa Maria, Pinta episode—Cathay being an attitude of spirit, rather than material conquest throughout, of course.

1. See Weber, *op. cit.,* pp. 430-432.

I know I can depend on you to mention the flaws and shortcomings. This section seems a little transcendental in tendency at present,—but I think that the pediments of the other sections will show it not to have been. —/—/

229: TO HIS MOTHER

Patterson   *Jan. 26*

Dear Grace: It *is* a good thing I got your letter yesterday—or I *should* have been sore. I was so tired last night I simply fell into bed at 10. We had spent most of the day shopping in town and I later built me some bookshelves which are very simple but extend to the ceiling—the kind I have always wanted. My study now is a picture to enjoy. When I was in New York I bought some beautiful and rare Congo wood carvings—and added to my Sommer paintings and your photograph they make a marvelous room.

My hands are so stiff from wood-cutting that my writing looks funny. It is very, very cold today, was yesterday and promises to continue. We all go about shivering most of the time and I'm sorry to say get too little freedom for our writing. Certainly the spring warmth will be unusually welcome to all of us.

—/—/ We do not correspond—except at considerable intervals as I hesitate to presume much on his [Otto Kahn] attention. There are so many others whom he is always helping that his time is largely taken up anyway. What with two personal secretaries and a whole corps of personal office help—*besides* his huge financial machine (his interests occupy a building of about 22 stories) he must be a busy man. He wants to hear from "time to time" as he puts it—about how my poem is progressing. But, since writing him New Year's I shan't presume again until next March or so. My second thousand is not payable until along in May. At which time I shall probably personally talk to him again. Beyond this money I have no expectations of more assistance, but if my poem when completed seems good enough to him, it may be, of course, that he will be further interested. I'm thankful enough for what I already have, however!

Your news about Grandma is rather heartrending. I do hope she won't have to suffer much longer—and if she does that she will be given enough sedatives to keep the pain dulled, no matter what the consequences. It would be best if she really gives up more—for the remainder of her existence—under any conditions—promises her only misery. —/—/

230: TO HIS GRANDMOTHER

Patterson, New York   *January 27th*

Dear Grandma: —/—/ I am hoping to hear from Grace tomorrow all
about how you are. Much better, I hope.

We had a brief flurry of snow again today, but not enough yet to
permit me to use my scrumptious snow shoes. I have been reading
the *Journal of Christopher Columbus* lately—of his first voyage to
America, which is concerned mostly with his cruisings around the
West Indies. It has reminded me many times of the few weeks I spent
on the Island to hear him expatiate on the gorgeous palms, unexpected pines, balmy breezes, etc., which we associate with Cuba.
— — — —

231: TO GASTON LACHAISE

Patterson, New York   *Feb. 10th, 26*

Dear Lachaise: Constantly your seagull has floated in my mind—ever
since I saw it, and it will mean much to me to have it. I can't thank
you enough. I am enclosing an amount which I hope will to some
extent defray the cost of materials, and you must let me know if
more is needed.

I envy you your occupation out here in the extreme cold of the
last two weeks—wiggling a pen or tapping a typewriter is hardly as
conducive to good circulation or warmth while every breath one
takes comes out like a steaming snort from a dragon! At present the
snow is so deep that we are obliged to use snow shoes or skis to get
anywhere. Fortunately we are well supplied with wood and oil and
provisions.

When I get to New York—probably not for six weeks or so—I hope
to find you in. If the white bird is done before then you can express
it out to Patterson, or I'll be glad to carry it back when I come in.
— — — —

232: TO CHARLOTTE AND RICHARD RYCHTARIK

Patterson, New York   *March 2nd*

Dear Charlotte et Ricardo: —/—/ In spite of many inconveniences,
however, I am glad of coming out here. Temperate living, good sleep
and considerable outdoor exercise have had their usual effects. The
cold has kept us hopping, though, and I'll be glad to greet the first
warm days that come. Then there will be both more time and more

comfort for reading and *The Bridge*. The finale of which is just about completed—but the antecedent sections will take me at least a year yet. At times the project seems hopeless, horribly so; and then suddenly something happens inside one, and the theme and the substance of the conception seem brilliantly real, more so than ever! At least, *at worst,* the poem will be a *huge* failure! If you get what I mean. When I am a little better satisfied with certain details of the part already finished I'll send it on to you, although I really shouldn't—as isolated from the rest of the poem it would probably not be interesting.

Mother wrote me that you called on her. She was extremely pleased, and remarked how beautiful and youthfully radiant my Charlotte was! —/—/

233: TO GORHAM MUNSON

Patterson, N.Y.   *March 5th*

Dear Gorham: The long siege of snow—the mail delivery has been discontinued for six weeks, and isn't resumed yet—despite occasional sportiveness with snow shoes and skis, has been a burden. Especially as I was swindled on a fifty-gal. drum of kerosene I bought for the stoves in my study, and have had to risk chapping hands every time I came near the typewriter to say nothing of tumbling through many a chilly night with chilblains from cold floors, damp, etc. It really would have been alright had I had pure kerosene, though. Nothing but the swindler is to blame.

None-the-less, I've read considerably—Aeschylus (especially the *Oresteia*) was a revelation of my ideal in the dynamics of metaphor —even through the rather prosy translations[1] one gleans the essential density of image, impact of substance matter so verbally quickened and delivered with such soul-shivering economy that one realizes there is none in the English language to compare him with.— Then Prescott's *Ferdinand & Isabella, Journal of Columbus,* a book on Magellan by Hildebrand (this was rather inexcusable), Melville's delightful *White Jacket* as well as a marvelously illustrated book[2] on whaling and whaling ships, published by the Marine Research Society, Salem, Mass. . . . In the midst of my readings of *Science & the Modern World,* Whitehead,—along comes *Virgin Spain.* I'm about half way through this at present and feel like telegraphing

1. *The Oresteia of Aeschylus,* trans. George Warr (Longman's Green: 1910).
2. George Francis Dow, *Whale Ships and Whaling* (1925).

Waldo my immediate uncontrolled and unstinted enthusiasm! As prose it certainly is his climax of excellence—and as a document of the spirit one of the most lively testaments ever written. I had been dwelling with a good deal of surprise in a pleasant conviction that Lawrence's *Plumed Serpent* was a masterpiece of racial description. It certainly is vividly beautiful, its landscapes, theatrical vistas, etc. —but Waldo's work is a world of true reality—his ritual is not a mere invention. Only my interest in Maya and Toltec archaeology led me to order Lawrence's book. It was poor in this—at least regarding the details I had hoped for, but I was rather astonished at the calibre of much of the prose.

As Waldo may have mentioned, the finale of *The Bridge* is written, the other five or six parts are in feverish embryo. They will require at least a year more for completion; however bad this work may be, it ought to be hugely and unforgivably, distinguishedly bad. In a way it's a test of materials as much as a test of one's imagination. *Is* the last statement sentimentally made by Eliot,

> "This is the way the world ends,
> This is the way the world ends,—
> Not with a bang but a whimper."

is this acceptable or not as the poetic determinism of our age?! I, of course, can say no, to myself, and believe it. But in the face of such a stern conviction of death on the part of the only group of people whose verbal sophistication is likely to take on interest in a style such as mine—what can I expect? However, I know my way by now, regardless. I shall at least continue to grip with the problem without relaxing into the easy acceptance (in the name of "elegance, nostalgia, wit, splenetic splendor") of death which I see most of my friends doing. O the admired beauty of a casuistical mentality! It is finally content with twelve hours sleep a day and archaeology.

I am glad that you have switched over to the more profitable and leisurely programme which you describe. And that you've gone back to writing again with such vim. The social distractions of NY are so terrific that I hope to never live there again beyond six months at a period. I'm really just getting around to a working basis, the first real platform of my life—here. In many ways it proves to be a revelation of certain potentialities.

Do send me your comments on Crane. And may I be frank— without seeming to reflect on any personal relationships of the past— in stating my reactions? Not that I shall desire to exert any changes, but that there may possibly arise (between ourselves) certain questions of direction, aims, intentions, which I may feel are erroneously ascribed to me. At least my agreements or objections may interest you. — — — —

234: TO GORHAM MUNSON

Patterson, New York   *March 17, '26*

Dear Gorham: My rummy conversation last Monday offered, I fear, but a poor explanation of my several theoretical differences of opinion with you on the function of poetry, its particular province of activity, etc. Neither was I able to express to you my considerable appreciation of many accurate distinctions made in your essay which certainly prompt my gratitudes as well as applause. It would probably be uninteresting as well as a bit excessive for me to enumerate and dwell on these felicitations, however gratifying to myself I may feel them to be. Your essay is roughly divided in two, the second half including our present disagreement, and inasmuch as I have never really attempted to fulfill the functions therein attributed to the poet, your theories on that subject can be discussed from a relatively impersonal angle so far as I am concerned. Furthermore, it is *one* aspect of a contemporary problem which has already enlisted the most detailed and intense speculation from a number of fields, science, philosophy, etc., as you, of course, know. I'm not saying that my few hasty notes which follow are conclusive evidence, but the logic of them (added to the organic convictions incident to the memorized experience of the creative "act," let us say) is not yet sufficiently disproved for me by such arguments, at least, as you have used in your essay.

Poetry, in so far as the metaphysics of any absolute knowledge extends, is simply the concrete *evidence* of the *experience* of a recognition (*knowledge* if you like). It can give you a *ratio* of fact and experience, and in this sense it is both perception and thing perceived, according as it approaches a significant articulation or not. This is its reality, its fact, *being*. When you attempt to ask more of poetry,—the fact of man's relationship to a hypothetical god, be it Osiris, Zeus or Indra, you will get as variant terms even from the abstract terminology of philosophy as you will from poetry; whereas poetry, without attempting to logically enunciate such a problem or its solution, may well give you the real connective experience, the very "sign manifest" on which rests the assumption of a godhead.

I'm perfectly aware of my wholesale lack of knowledge. But as Allen said, what exactly do you mean by "knowledge"? When you

ask for exact factual data (a graphic map of eternity?), ethical moral-
ity or moral classifications, etc., from poetry—you not only limit
its goal, you ask its subordination to science, philosophy. Is it not
equally logical to expect Stravinsky to bring his fiddles into dissent
with the gravitation theories of Sir Isaac Newton? They *are* in
dissent with this scientist, as a matter of fact, and organically so; for
the group mind that Stravinsky appeals to has already been freed
from certain of the limitations of experience and consciousness that
dominated both the time and the mind of Newton. Science (ergo all
exact knowledge and its instruments of operation) is in perfect an-
tithesis to poetry. (Painting, architecture, music, as well). It operates
from an exactly opposite polarity, and it may equate with poetry,
but when it does so its statement of such is in an entirely different
terminology. I hope you get this difference between *inimical* and
antithetical, intended here. It is not my interest to discredit science,
it has been as inspired as poetry,—and if you could but recognize it,
much more hypothetically motivated.

What you admire in Plato as "divine sanity" is the architecture
of his logic. Plato doesn't live today because of the intrinsic "truth"
of his statements: their only living truth today consists in the "fact"
of their harmonious relationship to each other in the context of his
organization of them. This grace partakes of poetry. But Plato was
primarily a philosopher, and you must admit that grace is a secondary motive in philosophical statement, at least until the hypothetical basis of an initial "truth" has been accepted—not in the
name of beauty, form or experience, but in the name of rationality.
No wonder Plato considered the banishment of poets;—their re-
organizations of chaos on basis perhaps divergent from his own
threatened the logic of *his* system, itself founded on assumptions
that demanded the very defense of poetic construction which he was
fortunately able to provide.

The tragic quandary (or *agon*) of the modern world derives from
the paradoxes that an inadequate system of rationality forces on
the living consciousness. I am not opposing any new synthesis of
reasonable laws which might provide a consistent philosophical
and moral program for our epoch. Neither, on the other hand, am
I attempting through poetry to delineate any such system. If this
"knowledge," as you call it, were so sufficiently organized as to
dominate the limitations of my personal experience (consciousness)
then I would probably find myself automatically writing under its
"classic" power of dictation, and under that circumstance might be
incidentally as philosophically "contained" as you might wish me

to be. That would mean "serenity" to you because the abstract basis of my work would have been familiarized to you before you read a word of the poetry. But my poetry, even then,—in so far as it was truly poetic,—would avoid the employment of abstract tags, formulations of experience in factual terms, etc.,—it would necessarily express its concepts in the more direct terms of physical-psychic experience. If not, it must by so much lose its impact and become simply categorical.

I think it must be due to some such misapprehensions of my poetic purpose in writing that leads you to several rather contradictory judgments which in one sentence are laudatory and in other contexts which you give them,—put me to blush for mental attitudes implied on my part. For instance, after having granted me all the praise you do earlier in your essay for "storming heaven" as it were, how can you later refer to that same faculty of verbal synchronization as to picture me as "waiting for another ecstasy"—and then "slumping"—rather as a baker would refer to a loaf in his oven. Granted your admiration for the "yeastiness" of some of my effusions, you should (in simple justice to your reader and your argument) here also afford the physical evidence (actual quotation or logical proof) of the "slump," the unleavened failure. There really are plenty of lines in this respect which could be used for illustration. What I'm objecting to is contained in my suspicion that you have allowed too many extra-literary impressions of me to enter your essay, sometimes for better, sometimes for worse. The same is true of your reference to the "psychological *gaming*" (Verlaine) which puts the slur of superficiality and vulgarity on the very aspects of my work which you have previously been at pains to praise.—And all because you arbitrarily propose a goal for me which I have no idea of nor interest in following. Either you find my work poetic or not, but if you propose for it such ends as poetry organically escapes, it seems to me, as Allen said, that you as a critic of literature are working into a confusion of categories. Certainly this charge of alternate "gutter sniping" and "angel kissing" is no longer anything more than a meretricious substitute for psychological sincerity in defining the range of an artist's subject matter and psychic explorations. Still less should it be brought forward unless there is enough physical evidence in the artist's work to warrant curiosity in this respect on the part of the reader.

Your difficulties are extra, I realize, in writing about me at all. They are bound to be thus extra because of the (so far as the reader goes) "impurities" of our previous literary arguments, intimacies of statement, semi-statements, etc., which are not always reflected in a man's work, after all. But your preoccupations on the one hand with a terminology which I have not attempted and your praise on the other hand of my actual (physical) representation of the incarnate *evidence* of the very knowledge, the very *wisdom* which you feel me to be only conjecturally sure of—makes me guilty of really wronging you, perhaps, but drives me to the platitude that "truth has no name." Her latest one, of course, is "relativity."

Apropos of all this the letter by Nichols in *The New Criterion* will interest you when you read it; there are interesting quotations from Goethe, Santayana, Russell, etc. And I am enclosing a hasty bundle of notes written at O'Neill's request for what angles they might suggest to him in writing a foreword for my book. (This, I hope, may be returned.)

Allen tells me that he has just mailed his note on me—for possible use in *The New Masses*. I told him to do this, not remembering definitely what you had told me about it before. It can do no harm anyway. I'm enclosing copies of the poems which Potamkin had intended using. It certainly was very kind of you to have suggested these matters to the *Masses* editor. Do let me hear from you soon.

PS—Needless to say, the notes for O'Neill contain repetitious matter for you, and certain accents were especially made against biases and critical deficiencies which I felt [might] lead to unwarranted assumptions, misplaced praises, etc., on his part. But the definitions of the "logic of metaphor," "dynamics of inferential mention," etc., I think are quite exact.[1]

235: To Otto H. Kahn

Patterson, New York   *March 18, 1926*

Dear Mr. Kahn: You were so kind as to express a desire to know from time to time how *The Bridge* was progressing, so I'm flashing in a signal from the foremast, as it were. Right now I'm supposed to be Don Cristobal Colon returning from "Cathay," first voyage. For mid-ocean is where the poem begins.

It concludes at midnight—at the center of Brooklyn Bridge. Strangely enough that final section of the poem has been the first to be completed,—yet there's a logic to it, after all; it is the mystic consummation toward which all the other sections of the poem converge. Their contents are implicit in its summary.

1. See Philip Horton, *Hart Crane* (New York: W. W. Norton & Co., 1937), pp. 323-28.

Naturally I am encountering many unexpected formal difficulties in satisfying my conception, especially as one's original idea has a way of enlarging steadily under the spur of daily concentration on minute details of execution. I don't wish to express my confidence too blatantly—but I am certain that, granted I'm able to find the suitable form for all details as I presently conceive them, *The Bridge* will be a dynamic and eloquent document.

As I said, I have thus far completed only the final section,—about one hundred lines. I am now going straight through from the beginning. There has been much incidental reading to do, and more study is necessary as I go on. As I cannot think of my work in terms of time I cannot gauge when it will be completed, probably by next December, however.

There are so many interlocking elements and symbols at work throughout *The Bridge* that it is next to impossible to describe it without resorting to the actual metaphors of the poem. Roughly, however, it is based on the conquest of space and knowledge. The theme of "Cathay" (its riches, etc.) ultimately is transmuted into a symbol of consciousness, knowledge, spiritual unity. A rather religious motivation, albeit not Presbyterian. The following notation is a very rough abbreviation of the subject matter of the several sections:

I   Columbus—Conquest of space, chaos
II   Pokahantus—The natural body of America-fertility, etc.
III   Whitman—The Spiritual body of America
      (A dialogue between Whitman and a dying soldier in a
      Washington hospital; the infraction of physical death,
      disunity, on the concept of immortality)
IV   John Brown
      (Negro porter on Calgary Express making up berths and
      singing to himself (a jazz form for this) of his sweetheart
      and the death of John Brown, alternately)
V   Subway—The encroachment of machinery on humanity; a kind
      of purgatory in relation to the open sky of last section
VI   The Bridge—A sweeping dithyramb in which the Bridge be-
      comes the symbol of consciousness spanning time and space

The first and last sections are composed of blank verse with occasional rhyme for accentuation. The verbal dynamics used and the spacious periodicity of the rhythm result in an unusually symphonic form. What forms I shall use for the other sections will have to be determined when I come to grips with their respective themes.

I would gladly send you the completed section for present reading, but unless you especially wish to see it now I should prefer your judgment on it later when a more synthetic reading will be possible.

I hope that this extended amount of particulars,—evidence, perhaps, of an excessive enthusiasm on my part, has not been tedious reading. Your interest and confidence have proved to be so great a spur to me that I must mention my gratitude again.

236: To Waldo Frank

Mid-channel [Patterson]   *March 20th, '26*

Dear Waldo: Just a word to say I have finished my first reading of your *Spain*. It is a book I shall go back to many times. Its magnificence and integrity are so rare that they constitute an embarrassment to our times in some ways. "The Port of Columbus" is truly something of a prelude to my intentions for *The Bridge*—which I seem to have got back to today after a hideous experience in New York and in spite of a very bad cold I seem to have caught from overheated city buildings.

I can't resist sending you the first verse[1] at this early time, along with the revised version of the finale. Your discipline and your confidence are so dear to me that in moods like this today (adrift a music that is almost a burden) I have to be a little uncontained and remind you of my love. Will send the Kahn article next week when a fresh copy arrives. . . . Temporarily—Don Cristobal—

237: To Malcolm Cowley

[Patterson]   *March 28*

Dear Malcolm: The news of your plans for the summer is good to hear! We're all anticipating the first of May—though you *will* be a little distant. Five miles walking says Mrs. Turner, coming out of her aunt's part with the tea.

After a perfect spasm of sentiment and "inspection" I was released from the fond embrace of my relatives in Cleveland—only to fare into rather more than less spasmodic embraces in N.Y.—a one night spree—on my way back. Since which I have been reading the philosophies of the East until I actually dream in terms of the Vedanta scriptures. Also am finding Marco Polo pleasant to incorporate in the subconscious.

1. Early version of lines for "Ave Maria."

I've often wondered how you got home that night. After you left I was roused from my stupor by an amazing scandal at the next table. Benét, Wylie and some others discussing ——— who, it seems, doesn't write at all. Her father does the trick—works off "suppressed desires" that way, etc., etc. I was very good after that and stormed over to the Albert, lectured the clerk for not admitting my friends, and went to bed, tout seul.

The next morning after the next I was discovering that my mother knows how to mix the best cocktails I ever drank.

Are you going ahead with the Boyd proposal? I think you should —a fine weapon against further attacks from that gent. again—and not, however, implying any concession whatever on your part. —/—/

238: To His Mother

Patterson   [*March 29, 1926*]

Dearest Grace: Your letter came yesterday. And I was *immensely* glad to hear from you. Altogether, the news seemed good, too, and I'm *so* glad you and Charles [Curtis] have made a definite decision! By *all* means make The Little Church the scene. Then I can be there and we can all take a bus ride afterward. Of *course* you'll be acceptable—who ever heard of such distinctions being made in any Protestant church against widows and widowers, grass or otherwise! Then maybe you could make my humble domicile one of the stops on your celebration.

I, too, think I made my visit at just the proper time. I'll never forget how really eloquently Grandma looked, how intelligent and fresh. And *you* looked so good to me, too. Remember, that suffering does, if borne without rancour, it does build something that only grows lovelier with time—and it is a kind of kingdom among those *initiated*, a kingdom that has the widest kind of communion. You and I can share our understanding of things more and more as time goes on. I loved you *so much* for many of the things you said when I was with you.

Yes, I hope you never will turn your back on me, as you say. And this is not to say that there may come occasions for it—but there may, after all, be times of temporary misunderstandings as there have been before. I can be awfully proud of *you*, however less occasion I may [have] to feel similarly about myself. I do some awfully silly things sometimes—most of which you don't know about, but which I sometimes (not always) regret. Don't let this stir your apprehensions, any, however. I'm in no particular pickle at present.

We have had another snow and I'm just disgusted. I had counted on a modified weather on my return and instead it's been just one snow flurry after another. Sore throat is some better, but I'm still threatened with tonsilitis. No chance to start gardens yet. —————

239: TO GORHAM MUNSON

Patterson   *April 5*

Dear Gorham: It seems evident that I somewhat too egoistically argued what I intended as simply a defense of the position and province of poetry, as an art form, rather than any claims my work might or might not have to critical praise. This has been my attitude throughout our discussion, and though certain contentions are still unresolved, it doesn't in the least conflict with what you say in your last letter. Indeed, I should say that your essay rather over-estimates my achievements in some particulars. Please don't think me ungrateful or disgruntled, anyway.

Rorty was so swift in returning Allen's NOTE that I have been wondering if he had actually taken some interest in the "Voyages" I sent you. I should have sent them direct to him had I known that he was subsequently to write me a request for something. Sheer inadvertency on my part not to have mentioned my intentions in sending them to you. Allen gave Untermeyer and Kreymborg such digs that it's not surprising that Rorty summarily returned the mss. I shall be surprised if he fancies my work.

The Cowleys move up here May first. I hope to have a few "animations" with Malcolm before I, the climate, the solitude, or whatever it is, drives him into the kind of shell that Brown and Tate seem to have retired into lately. My mood being pre-eminently N. Labrador these days—I should like a little good company immensely. A life of perfect virtue, redundant health, etc., doesn't seem in any way to encourage the Muse, after all. I almost feel like coming to town and seeking a job, at least that would make me part-time useful, meantime there wouldn't be the suspense of weeks going by without a written line. I'm afraid I've so systematically objectivized my theme and its details that the necessary "subjective lymph and sinew" is frozen. Meanwhile I drone about, reading, eating and sleeping. It's really quite agonizing. For in so many ways I know what I WANT to do. . . . The actual fleshing of a concept is so complex and difficult, however, as to be quite beyond the immediate avail of will or intellect. A fusion with other factors not so easily named is the condition of fulfilment. It is alright to call this "possession," if you will, only it should not be insisted that its operation denies the simultaneous functioning of a strong critical faculty. It is simply a stronger focus than can be arbitrarily willed into operation by the ordinarily-employed perceptions. Do you find anything in my rough notes that's interesting?

240: To His Mother

Patterson, New York   *April 18th*

Dear Grace: It would be a relief to be able to talk with you an hour or so today. I'm in such an uncertain position in regard to a number of things that I feel as though it would be a fitting end to settle it with powder and bullet. The whole benefit of my patronage from Kahn, my year of leisure, my long fight with the winter, etc., out here is about to be sacrificed — — — —. I refer to Mrs. Tate, and Allen. But primarily it has been Mrs. Tate who has influenced matters until they came to a head the other day, since which time I have had a note from each of them, respectively — — — —.

I am accused of having victimized their time and their quarters by intruding without regard to their wishes, etc. This is in part justified,—justified, I say because the contingency of such a matter was bound to exist between two families which had agreed on sharing a common water pump. I had to have access to it as much as they did, and had to pass through their kitchen occasionally on my way. When Mrs. Tate—this occurred last week—instead of simply telling me that she wished I would avoid such passage in the future —when she began putting bolts on her doors, and all that—I could take the *hint* without having to be knocked down by a hammer, and so removed my shaving utensils, etc., which had been beside the pump, into Mrs. Turner's kitchen. Why this should make them mad, I don't know, and why it should make them mad because I immediately began avoiding their parts of the house *completely* (not being invited to do otherwise) I can't see, either.

Of course when I encountered them outside, and saw how sulky they behaved, etc., I began to lose all respect for such behavior— made up my mind to ignore them as much as decency permitted, although I realized that with such an atmosphere about the place it would be very difficult to proceed with any creative work. Matters came to a climax day before yesterday, shortly after breakfast. I had been talking to Mrs. Turner around on "our" side of the house about some plans for cleaning up some rubbish, etc., when suddenly a door opens from the Tates' kitchen and Allen shouts out,

"If you've got a criticism of my work to make, I'd appreciate it if you would speak to me about it first!" Then the door savagely banged, and Mrs. Turner and I (who hadn't mentioned him or anything that concerned him) were left staring at each other in perfect amazement. I can't easily describe how angry I was. I felt myself losing all control—but I managed to address the Tates without breaking anything. Mrs. Turner came in with me and corroborated the facts of the matter, and it turned out that the Tates hadn't heard actually a thing I was saying—their imaginations, they evidently felt, were perfectly justified in building up a perfect tower of Babel out of nothing.

Nothing was touched on at that fiery moment, but the immediate circumstances of what I had said and what I hadn't, Tate finally admitting that he was all wrong. My feelings remained little cooled, however. The rest of the time since then has been simply hideous. The next morning (I, not sleeping, had heard the Tates getting out of bed during the night and pounding out something on the typewriter), I found a couple of the nastiest notes under my bedroom door that I ever hope to get from anyone. Mrs. Tate began by saying that they had arrived in the house first; that they had invited me to share quarters with them in the first place because I was penniless in New York at that time, and that as soon as they found out that I had been fortunate in acquiring funds they immediately had begun to doubt the advisability of inviting me out, but *of course* hadn't felt privileged to say anything about such matters before this. I'm not quoting *insinuations* in any of this, I'm using practically their own words. Then she went on to say that they had allotted me one room only (this is an absolute lie; they assumed that I was to have a bedroom and my study besides) and that I had from the moment of arrival proceeded to spread myself and possessions all over the house, invading every corner; and so on,—finally ending up with the assertion that I had been busy ever since I arrived in trying to make them menial servants of my personal wants! The contents of Mr. Tate's letter were about the same, a little more gracefully phrased, that's all.

As a matter of fact, I have never, so long as I've been here, requested a single favor from either of them. You know the story about the cooking arrangements already—how I changed over to Mrs. Turner —/—/. Since then—even though I derived no benefit from the wood stove that the Tates use in their kitchen—I've been careful to go out and help Allen cut and saw, etc. And made it a point to mention—that while I couldn't constantly keep after him

with questions as to when he wanted to saw and when he didn't—
if he'd let me know about such occasions I'd be glad to join him
whenever possible.

It's all simply disgusting. I don't know how much money they
owe me exactly—but I have told them that I was always glad to advance them funds whenever needed, and while they haven't been
extravagant—they have nevertheless been momentarily relieved from
sudden circumstances by frequent access to my funds. On top of all
this I have practically given Allen the fare for two trips to New
York (on one occasion I was so anxious for him to have the chance
to hear a certain opera that I gave him ten dollars to get a good
seat), I've had them in to dinner with Mrs. Turner and myself
frequently, I gave Carolyn my old typewriter to work on her novel
— — — —. She didn't have one herself and would otherwise have had
to depend on such moments as her husband wasn't using his to write
at all, while I on the other hand, should certainly have been able to
make a good discount on my new machine by turning in the old
had I not purposely wished to be amiable about the matter. There
have been lots of other amenities which I enjoyed extending. And
you know me not to obviously hold such things over people's heads.
Doesn't it all look as though, *as Mr. Tate says,* I valued their friendship only for the purpose of exploiting their services to me.

Mrs. Turner has cried for two days and nights about the matter
—she hates to have me leave so. She says there is another room in
the upstairs which I can use and not be obliged to have anything to
do with the Tates' part of the house, their rent or their arrangements. I must say I'm stumped. How can I, on one hand, persist in
staying here after such an insulting statement from the Tates to
the effect that I was originally their guest and that I was invited on
the grounds of charity rather from any other motives? This is one
of the hardest matters I have ever had to decide. For I feel that I
owe some sense of economy to Mr. Kahn, who didn't give me money
to keep moving about — — — —. My money is very low now. The first
thousand is gone—it cost me more than I ever would have guessed
to have just got settled here with all my books and materials at
hand as they are. I wrote Kahn recently that I needed more money,
and he very speedily and kindly replied with a check for five hundred. At the same time the Rychtariks wrote from Cleveland that
they needed the money they had loaned me for my land—that they
required it for the summer trip to Europe, etc. And so two hundred
will have to be taken out of the Kahn money at once.

It really is tragic. The whole fruit of the first opportunity of my

life to write an extended poem is apparently about to be blighted
— — — —. As I say I don't at this moment know which way to turn.
If I remain here (spring is just coming on—and the best time for
work, so long waited for, has come!) if I remain here under such
unpleasant relations it is very doubtful whether or not I can overcome the hypnosis of evil and jealousy in the air enough to get back
into my poem, really just started. But if I move away it means that
so much of my slight funds will be wasted in just the cost of travel,
etc., that in less than a month I'll be back looking for a job again—
and in the middle of the summer, the most devilish and exhausting
time to work in the city. I don't feel that I ought to let my indigna-
tion and pride affect me so far as the hasty and ill-founded remarks
of the Tates are concerned. I would sacrifice all that to my work and
remain here if I felt enough assurance of being *able* to work under
such circumstances.

If you feel at all sympathetic to this situation of mine I wish you
this time be generous enough to let me go to the Island and finish
my poem there. At least I should not have to fear being put off the
little land that is still ours in the world. I have ample money to get
there and to live economically for some time. It may reasonably be
expected that Mr. Kahn will come forward with the other five hundred which he promised within a certain time, meanwhile I can't
ask him for more before six months without risking the charge of
extravagance. I think that I can re-sell the land I bought to Miss
Flynn from whom I purchased it. Summer in the tropics isn't of
course the paradise of the winter months, but it is a thousand times
better than a hall bedroom in New York without light or air, to
say nothing of the fact that it might cost me a hundred or so of
what I have left just spent in *looking* for work. You know how long
it is sometimes.

If I can't somehow succeed in taking advantage of this one opportunity given me by Mr. Kahn, I don't know how I'll feel about
life or any future efforts to live—and if you can't see how it is reasonable for me to request under the circumstances some privileges
from my family I shall be amazed. You've already said that you
didn't think I'd like Mrs. Simpson, etc. Well, do you think *that* is
half so important to me or to anyone else after all. I'm not able to
reason why this issue should hang on the whimsical temper of an
old woman. If I went to the island I should do my best to preserve
the most pleasant relations with Mrs. Simpson, and I haven't much
doubt but what I should succeed. I ought to be able to live a few

months in the house my grandfather built without being put off by a hired keeper of the place—especially when I am much better fitted naturally, by simply being a male, for keeping up the place than she is.

I'm asking you for this refuge. I've always been refused before. If you deny it now I'm not sure how much farther away I'll go to accomplish my purposes. Perhaps to the orient, even if I have just enough to get there and no more.

I shall go into New York early in the week, perhaps tomorrow. Perhaps several days later. I'll let you know where I settle and what plans are finally adopted. Meanwhile please write me here, as before; Mrs. Turner will be sure to send my mail to whatever address I have at the time.

I'm sorry to have such melancholy news, especially after such lovely letters as recently came from you and Grandma, but it can't be helped. It all may be very much for the best in the end. I do hope you'll be generous enough to give me your sanction on the Island matter—that's all I'm requesting. I can always get money enough to get back (from at least 5 people) and go into an office again. But that isn't the issue now. I'm writing a poem that is bound to be a magnificent thing *if* I can escape the — — — — long enough to build it. Won't you help?

241: To Charlotte and Richard Rychtarik

Patterson, New York   *April 25th, 1926*

Dear Charlotte and Richard: I hope you won't think me insincere anywhere in this letter. A complete picture of my feelings and present circumstances would be hard to give, simply impossible. I'm relying on you for more than friendship in asking such considerations. I'm asking your love. And, of course I realize that I'm in immediate danger of losing both. But the story has got to be sold somehow for you to understand why I'm asking what I do. The thing is—in my state of mind (and after three weeks of such torments) it is hard to know where to begin. But let me say that the picture is somewhat different than it was when I was so happy with you in Cleveland. And I must ask you to let me off for the time being on paying you the full sum I borrowed. I can only send you a hundred dollars now. I can send the rest within seven months. Or at least I don't think you would want me to give up the entire *Bridge* and go into

an office at once. You see, I'm assuming a great deal of interest on
your part which may not be there. I wanted to state this request first,
before telling you why and wherefore. Otherwise my story would
seem featured too theatrically. —/—/

Well, I got so morbid about the matter that I finally decided to go
into New York for a few days and think as clearly as possible. What
to do! I have finally decided to go to my grandmother's place on
the Isle of Pines in the West Indies. Getting there will be almost as
cheap as moving my things anywhere else—and living will be very
cheap for [me] there. I must tell you that Mr. Kahn sent me only
$500 instead of the entire second $1,000. It is to be presumed that
I'll get the other half later on. But I can't ask for more at present,
and you can see that there is just about enough to keep me there
(my transportation also has to come out of this) until more comes.
Out of this I can send you the hundred I mentioned. Won't it be
just as easy for you to wait just a little longer for the rest? I never
hated to ask a question so much in my life—but I am simply crushed
if I can't go on a little longer with my effort on *The Bridge*.

It's the one opportunity I may ever have, and I feel I owe something to the faith that Mr. Kahn has put in me. I am not seeking
any thrills or pleasure by going to the West Indies in the middle
of the summer—I'm sure you can understand how it would be much
pleasanter for me to go to the seashore. But *that* would eat up my
little remaining money in two or three months. I need longer to
work on *The Bridge,* and I'm willing to go into a furnace for awhile
if I can only feel sure about the ground under my feet. On my
parents' property I won't need to feel that I'll be insulted again, or
forced away. I can *at least* be sure of that. And that means a lot
when you are trying to keep your imagination free and creative.
Also, I can live very cheaply there. I may not have enough money
to get back when I want to, but I'm not worrying about that—or
other hardships.

My mother has made a terrible fuss against my going, but is
finally reconciled. I realize it's hard for her to think of me as so far
away—but I'll be still farther away, I think, if my *Bridge* breaks
down entirely. I can't allow it all to be the victim of malice, envy,
jealousy and petty-mindedness.

I won't indulge in any more raving and fury now. But I do hope
that you believe me sincere. You very possibly have a right to be
angry with me (certainly I have never done anything half so kind
to you) but I'll prove to you in the end that I am sincere in my
regard for you. I don't think I'm a dishonest person.

I am sailing for Havana next Saturday. When I get back to New York on Wednesday I'll send you the hundred dollars. Will you write me a word or so before I go? Send it care of Gorham Munson — — — —.

242: To — — AND — —

Isle of Pines [*Cuba*]   *May 7*

Dear — — and — —: It is still one day less than a week since we sailed, our second on the Island. Frank got Ward Line accommodations, which cut a day off the sea; and we were rather sorry. Still, passing Pam Bitch, My ammy and other Coney islands at midnight wasn't especially thrilling: that part of the trip was too close shore. But Havana was more and better than I had imagined. Architecture rather like Chirico—some Spanish plateresque and physically metaphysically suggestive. But mostly on the surface, there isn't other evidence.

F.'s Spanish brought us off all beaten paths. We didn't visit an American haunt except the steamship office. The rest was mostly bars, cafes and theatres—filled with blacks, reds, browns, greys and every permutation and combinations of southern bloods that you can imagine. Coronas-Coronas, of course, for 15¢, marvelous sherry, cognac, vermouth and "Tropical" (the beer that I was talking about). Am. boats seem to be easy, by the way: we had St. Julian and Sauterne all the way down at table. Then we went to the Alhambra, a kind of Cuban National Winter Garden Burlesque. Latin "broadness" was somewhat veiled from me as far as the dialogue went, but actions went farther than apparently even the East Side can stand.

Gratings and balconies and narrow streets with plenty of whores nodding. The day of our departure a great fleet of American destroyers landed. Streets immediately became torrents of uniforms— one sailor had exactly the chinese mustache effect that I aspire to. But no J— — F— —: his boat must have passed to Brooklyn—passed in the night. Taxis anywhere in town for only 20¢, but that's about the only cheap feature. Great black-bushed buxom Jamaican senoritas roared laughter at us, old women hobbled up offering lottery tickets (I finally got one on a hunch). The whole town is hypersensual and mad—i.e. has no apparent direction, destiny, or purpose: Cummings' paradise. I shall have to go up for a real spree sometime when cash is plentiful, meanwhile this isle is enough Eden.

Poor Mrs. Simpson hadn't expected us for at least three days

more—and F. of course, the extra party, almost bowled her over at
first sight. She had a violent coughing fit, at which I thought the
fragile frame of her would break and during which a parrot
screamed from a corner somewhere, "Damned poor dinner!" She has
recovered, and is really lovable and quite the contrary of all I had
expected. I've had one pleasant shock after another. The house is
much more spacious than I had remembered, the island much more
beautiful. . . . The approach from the sea is like the Azores, F.
says. To me, the mountains, strange greens, native thatched huts,
perfume, etc. brought me straight to Melville. The heat *is* different
from northern summer heat and the parroty phrase does hold—"it's
always cool in the shade." It was cool enough for F. to put a coat on
at sundown today, "breezes prevail." Oleanders and mimosas in full
bloom now make the air almost too heavy with perfume, it's another world—and a little like Rimbaud. I'm surprised that I didn't
carry away more definite impressions from my first visit 11 years ago.

We discovered a beach yesterday, very near our house. We bathed
late in the day and the water was almost too warm. The rest of the
time we've wandered over the grove, bought fish, played with a baby
owl that suddenly appeared, drunk punch, picked coconuts (which
are a meal by themselves). You ought to see that owlet (Pythagoras)
make away with a chameleon! No bigger than a fat sparrow, it
blinked and swallowed a lizard whole. I've nearly died laughing at
the creature. We brought it to table and it turded in F.'s salad, it
sits on your finger and squeaks like P—— does when she gets tipsy.
I'll probably be taking it to bed with me, like B——, when I first get
tipsy (No I haven't been tipsy since I left NY).

I spose Bina [Flynn] has already told you the details of the
parental wedding in NY. Those last three days in town were mad
ones for me. —— sister, gnawed at my hand for quite a while
at the dinner with the Cowleys. I don't remember what it was all
about, but I think we fell in love with each other. I finally brought
the bridal pair [Crane's mother & her husband] to lunch with
Lachaise and Mme. A good time was had by all. I insisted on my
bringing the famous bird with me. All my fears about the trunks
were wrong, they brought everything in fine shape, even china unbroken.

I feel like a gastric museum at present, a cross cut of Tahitian
stomach coast—but not in especial distress—at least so far. Uric acid
won't have a whispering chance in a few days what with all the
strange fruits and vegetables I'm trying. Casavas, guavas, bread fruit,
limes, cumquats, kashew apples, coconuts, wild oranges, bananas,

God I can't remember any more of the damned names. O yes, mulberries and avacadas and papayas! And mangos! Maybe I don't get enough of it yet! Tamarinds . . . pomegranates . . . grabanas . . . O sacre Nom de. . . . —/—/

243: To His Mother

[*Isle of Pines*]   *May 14th*

Dear Grace and Grandma: We haven't had altogether more than 3 hours of rainfall since arriving. Rather less than usual, Mrs. Simpson says, for the rainy season. Today the sky is overcast, making it much cooler than usual, and the rain of last night promises repetition at any moment. When there is a good wind, like today's, it sweeps the bugs away somewhat—but otherwise they are terrific,—especially around Casas Villa [the Crane house], which so far as I have been able to judge by contrast with other places is become the buggiest place on the island. This is mostly due to the thick growth of trees and shrubbery surrounding the house—which hardly lets a zephyr through and which harbor and incubate millions of insects. It is, of course, a great mistake to have planted so many fruit trees so close to the house. They give practically no shade—and simply stifle every breeze that approaches.

Yesterday we rented a car from Herrin and I drove Mrs. S. and Waldo over to the Jones's Jungle. Mrs. S. had prepared a wonderful picnic lunch which we finally shared with the Jones's in their bungalow. Both Waldo and myself went quite wild about the beauties of the place, the marvelous work they have accomplished there is equalled, I'm sure, by nothing else in the West Indies or N. America. Waldo says he remembers visiting a place in the Azores, owned by a wealthy Portuguese prince, which was something like it, but I have never seen anything so amazing before.

The Jones's are by far the pleasantest and most cultured people I have met on the island. The tragedy of their life here is pitiable to the point of tears. After twenty-three years of unremitting toil on their place, to have it all brought to naught—as it is now, since the treaty matter, makes them the saddest kind of jests of fate. Jones says that the Cuban bureaucrats may seize his place at any moment without offering more than five dollars an acre, and he can have no recourse whatever. Furtherfore, they are both quite penniless, and live entirely on what he can gather as a taxi-driver and the little fee they charge for visiting the jungle. But Jones is no worse off than others—in many ways. He is only too old to ever hope to take hold anywhere else again. —/—/

244: TO WALDO FRANK

[*Isle of Pines*]   *May 22nd*

Camerado: In the middle of the terrible little performance we left you to attend and below the crash of floods on the roof—I was astonished to hear the whistle of your boat, whooping, I hope, a really final salute: I had supposed the Cristobal Colon long since departed. After so long a wait I hope you at least had a private and quiet rest in your stateroom, or rather, cabin.

Today frequent downpours and your card from Havana. Also a letter from O'Neill—more mysterious than ever. I'll quote exactly and all the words pertaining to the Liveright matter:

"There seems to be a misunderstanding about this Liveright matter somewhere. He isn't waiting for any foreword from me *yet* —at least not according to what he said when I saw him last before I wrote you the last time. He was waiting for more stuff from you apparently. And he spoke of having talked about you with Otto Kahn and so forth.

"However, I expect to be back in New York within a month and I will see him then and get this matter straightened out."

You will remember my descriptions of the situation up to this point with sufficient accuracy without further repetitions; I can only say with regard to it all that Gene has either misinformed me in his previous letters or else is suffering from a lapse of memory. At any event, I hope that the conversation with Kahn alluded to, hasn't twitched Liveright into the decision to hold up my book until *The Bridge* shall be completed. If he doesn't really want the book of course nobody can force him to take it,—in which case I hope it won't be too much trouble for you to return the mss. to the Boni Bros. There seem no end to the complications with L. The mysterious "yet" in Gene's statement (my underlining) is simply inexplicable.

Mrs. Simpson is having some duplicates made for you of the beach pictures and wishes to be remembered to you. Attaboy frequently calls out "Waldo!" Mrs. Durham (whose name I remember always just in time by thinking of the Bull) has come to stay at least for the week-end. And I have just written a little unconscious calligramme on the mango tree which I enclose.[1] —/—/

1. An early version of "The Mango Tree."

245: To — —

Dear — —: The post-Crane period in Patterson seems to have been full of excitements. Your letter, with its news about the incomparable J—— was corroborated in the same mail by no less than a letter from the noble tar himself. Poor J—— spent no little time and trouble, coming clear up from Norfolk. Mrs. Turner had been forwarding warnings of the impending disaster, first a letter from Norfolk on the date of landing, then a letter on the Potomac boat bound for Washington; I began to feel as though the wireless would be necessary to save my honor. His people live at P—— and it was there, after his excursion north, that he finally got a card I had mailed from Havana explaining things. He's back on the job now, but quits June 6th. I commend your control under the penetrating gazes of Mrs. T. J——'s letter contained a closing greeting from "me, J——'s sister, M——" written in a very elegant hand, so I guess I'm well introduced when I come to P——. Anyway, he bane good company and I'm awfully sorry to have missed him.

Yesterday I got tight for the first time, on Bacardi. Cuban Independence day. Falling in with a flock of goats on my way home (I was trembling at what Mme. Sampsohn would say) I stubbed my toes and skinned my knee. Arrived home in a somewhat obvious condition, there was nothing to be done but have it out with Mme. . . . Waldo having left Tuesday night, we had it fair and square. It is now established that I can drink as much as I damned please. A couple of murdering desperadoes got loose from the penitentiary here recently—and I think she's glad to have my company. But she's been so damned pleasant and considerate that I haven't any reason to think she doesn't like me on less fearful grounds. I'm rather jealous of Mrs. T's old love, the weather, however.

Yes, Marianne [Moore] took the little specialty I wrote for her, and even proof has been corrected and sent back. This time she didn't even suggest running the last line backward. "Again" is in the May issue; I spose you've seen the happy mixture. I enclose an accidental calligramme committed this morning accidentally on my way to *The Bridge*. I'm convinced that the Mango tree was the original Eden apple tree, being the first fruit tree mentioned in history with any accuracy of denomination. I've been having a great time reading *Atlantis in America,* the last book out on the subject, and full of exciting suggestions. Putting it back for 40 or 50 thousand years, it's easy to believe that a continent existed in mid-Atlantic waters and that the Antilles and West Indies are but salient peaks of its surface. Impossible forever to prove, however.

I'm glad that Malcolm [Cowley] has had such luck. It's likely he's made for life—once he enters the Lorimer field; and the articles ought to be interesting, certainly the material is. Because Poole's book, *The Harbour,* was said to have been written while looking from the windows of 110 Col. Hts., I had the idea that it might contain something—and have just finished reading it, a thin-chested little affair if there ever was one! I wonder if McFee's books are quite so ordinary. — — — —

246: To His Mother

[*Isle of Pines*]   *June 1, 1926*

Dear Grace: —/—/ Mine own true self has been chewing its cud, mostly, i.e., trying to imagine itself on the waters with Cristobal Colon and trying to mend the sails so beautifully slit by the Patterson typhoon. The Island grows more attractive to me as I get more acclimated and we have had constant breezes and cool weather ever since Waldo left, just two weeks ago today. There are many things that need to be done about the place, but I am attacking them with some deliberation—one has to respect the ferocity of the sun and the insects not a little. I have succeeded in eradicating the carcasses of several dead and dying orange trees in the front yard, putting young royal palms in their places. How I wish you had thought of planting some of these perfect delights when the place was being built; they are the one perfect sort of tree to have round a house, their ornamentation, stateliness and open-airiness can't be surpassed.

Mrs. Simpson is going to help me put up some new gate posts of rocks and cement. The entire fencing directly in front of the house is ready to collapse and there are so many breaches in the line down by the grove which we need repair at once (pigs can't be kept out, but some of the cattle can be) that something should be done about it as soon as possible. Of course I'm constantly at a loss to know what attitude to take about these and other highly necessary repairs, —not knowing what you really intend doing about the place. Most important of all, of course, is an entirely new roof for the house. I don't think you'll ever get pin money for the sale of the place until this, at least, is done, for it's the first and outstanding fault to be noticed even from the road.

Moreover, the inside of the house—its whole structure, in fact—will soon begin to deteriorate so rapidly for the want of dry sheltering that whatever value the place has now will be sacrificed. If I were you, and relished the tropics during the winter as much as you do, I'd economize in some way or other so as to afford a new roof as soon as possible. The house is really so comfortable and so very well built that it's a shame to let it run down. A few shingles and patches here and there won't meet the situation at all. The whole roof is rotted, loosely assembled and full of perforations. And, as I said, it looks it. Patches would only make it look a little worse.

Mrs. S. and I think that tile roofing, while costing a little more than the cheap shingles that we put on first, is the proper thing for the climate, exigencies of grass fires, etc. Asbestos shingling would be good, but not so permanent— and although I don't know for certain as yet, I think it would be about as expensive as tile. Tile would also look better. Now we are going to ask Mr. Jones, whose honesty and disinterestedness is unquestionable, to make an estimate on what tile roofing would cost, also what he would charge for his services in undertaking the job. As soon as possible I'll write you about the figures, or Mrs. S. will. It can do no harm to go this far, anyway. And as the Island is so infinitely superior to Florida, California or any other place you might go for the winters—*and so much cheaper a place to live when you get here*—I think you will agree with me that investments in repairs on the place here are ultimately cheaper than hotel rooms at ten to fifteen dollars a day with nothing to keep when you leave. A new roof, some new screening and a fresh coat of paint are all this house needs for years to come if someone like Mrs. Simpson or myself stays here. I don't forget the water tank, but that isn't so crucial; water can, after all, be pumped by hand. Let me know a little more of your present attitude about the property here, then I can better judge whether or not you want my reports, advice, etc.

Thursday (June 3rd) I'm sailing on the schooner for Grand Cayman. There are two days on the water each way, and I may spend a week on the island if the boat stays that long. I'm looking forward with great glee to my first real sail—and they tell me that Cayman is lovelier than anything around. Bread, cheese and cookies are to be packed by Mrs. Simpson and I'm hoping not to feed the fishes. If I do,—well then I'll have at least found out that I'm a good-for-nothing landlubber. The trip will be worth while from any standpoint.

247: TO WALDO FRANK

[*Isle of Pines*]   *June 19th '26*

Dear Waldo: Late amends for your last three letters, the first of which I got just as I was taking the schooner for Cayman! the last two yesterday when I returned. The trip was strenuous, four days instead of the expected two—each way, on account of head winds and calms. And let me tell you that to be "as idle as a painted," etc., under this tropical sun with thirty-five cackling, puking, farting Negroes (women and children first) for a whole day or so (the water like a blinding glassy gridiron) is a novel experience. The first moral of the sea with the white man is clean decks; it's the last considered with the Indian black. Vile water to drink, etc., etc., there's no use recommending the facts further. And the much bruited Grand Cayman was some torment, I can survive to tell you. Flat and steaming under black clouds of mosquitoes, and not a square inch of screening on the island. I had to keep smudge fires burning incessantly in my room while I lunged back and forth, smiting myself all over like one in rigor mortis and smoke gouging salt penance from my eyes. The insects were enormous; Isle of Pines species can't compare in size or number. After nine days and nights of that I staggered onto the schooner—and here I am—with a sunburn positively Ethiopian.

I have pleasantly proved to myself, however, that under more sociably agreeable circumstances there is nothing to compare with a sail boat. The motion made me anything but sea-sick, with a good wind the rhythm is incomparable. More gorgeous skies than even you saw, acres of man-sized leaping porpoises (the "Huzza Porpoises" so aptly named in *Moby Dick*) that greet you in tandems (much like M. & Mme. Lachaise if you have ever seen them out walking together) and truly "arch and bend the horizons." One enormous shark, a White Fin, lounged alongside for awhile. Had there been a place to sit or stand a few moments in the shade and fewer basins and chamber pots under the nose the trips would have been far from onerous.

In spite of all, I find myself rather toughened and well. The exasperations and torments of such a siege make one grateful for modest amenities. Mrs. Simpson yesterday for the first time appeared to me as the Goddess of Liberty.

I am not writing to O'Neill about *White Buildings*—and do not expect to write him until I hear directly from him. He is supposed to be back in NY by this time, and in his last letter he said that he expected to see Liveright on his return and talk things over. He knows that I have prepared in mss. all the poems which are to be included in the book and that all that can now hold it back is the lack of his foreword. It was hard for me to ask him to write such a thing for my book, and it has been harder and more embarrassing still for me to have kept trailing him with letters of urgence. . . . It's impossible for me [to] address him again on the subject. I'm sorry that what-ever-it-was made him feel constrained to promise the favor initially. It will be just as well for me to forget publishers for awhile, I think, though I can't forget how steadfastly you have persevered in helping me—whatever the results have amounted to. And don't think too much about me; my judgments are too un-settled these days to make me feel that I deserve much attention, much less the faith that you assure me of. The situation is really unique with me; it is absurd to say that one is battling indifference; but neither does one build out of an emptied vision. Mere word-painting and juggling, however fastidious,—a prospect of this doesn't excite one very much. At times it seems demonstrable that Spengler is quite right. At present—I'm writing nothing—would that I were an efficient factory of some kind! It was unfortunate in a way to have been helped by our friend, the banker,—with my nose to the grind-stone of the office I could still fancy that freedom would yield me a more sustained vision; now I know that much has been lacking all along. This is less personal than it sounds. I think that the artist more and more licks his own vomit, mistaking it for the common diet. He amuses himself that way in a culture without faith and convictions—but he might as well be in elfin land with a hop pipe in his mouth. . . . No, *The Bridge* isn't very flamboyant these days.

I'm glad that the Mango poem meant something to you. I'm cook-ing up a couple of other short poems to go with it ("Kidd's Cove," & "The Tampa Schooner") under the common title of "Grand Cay-man." Maybe I can sell them to Marianne M[oore]. Word was just forwarded from Patterson that Edgell Rickword, who edits *The Calendar* (London), has taken three poems I sent him about eight weeks ago, "At Melville's Tomb," "Passage" and "Praise for an Urn." *The Calendar* is a very decent quarterly, and I'm glad to get the "Melville" in print—not one magazine in America would take it. You ought to send them something of yours—(1 Featherstone Buildings, London, W.C.1.)

So far no zonite, but gratitude none the less. The only people who can get records to me securely are the Victor headquarters, I'll order direct from them. There's a duty of about 90% on all records!

But I do wish you would have *The New Republic* send me the Gide article. . . . As much of your work as is printed there and elsewhere. I read *Moby Dick* between gasps down in Cayman—my third time— and found it more superb than ever. How much that man makes you love him! —/—/

248: TO WALDO FRANK

[*Isle of Pines*]   *June 20th*

Dear Waldo: Recollection of certain statements made in yesterday's letter to you prompt me to a little better account of myself—not that I committed any insincerities (though the letter might seem to solicit sympathy or encouragement) but that I feel guilty of an injustice to you in some sort of way. You certainly do not deserve to have such fare set before you. . . .

So I apologize for my crudity, with the foreknowledge of your understanding that there are times when it is a torture to write anyone sincerely—as I must always write to you. My statements may appear in a less insane light after you have read what has principally spurred them—the Spengler thesis. This man is certainly fallible in plenty of ways but much of his evidence is convincing—and is there any good evidence forthcoming from the world in general that the artist isn't completely out of a job? Well, I may not care about such considerations 2 hours from now, but at present and for the last two months I have been confronted with a ghostliness that is new.

The validity of a work of art is situated in contemporary reality to the extent that the artist must honestly anticipate the realization of his vision in "action" (as an actively operating principle of communal works and faith), and I don't mean by this that his procedure requires any bona fide evidences directly and personally signalled, nor even any physical signs or portents. The darkness is part of his business. It has always been taken for granted, however, that his intuitions were salutary and that his vision either sowed or epitomized "experience" (in the Blakeian sense). Even the rapturous and explosive destructivism of Rimbaud presupposes this, even his lonely hauteur demands it for any estimation or appreciation. (The romantic attitude must at least have the background of an age of faith, whether approved or disproved no matter).

All this is inconsecutive and indeterminate because I am trying to write shorthand about an endless subject—and moreover am unresolved as to any ultimate conviction. I am not fancying I am "enlightening" you about anything,—nor, if I thought I were merely exposing personal sores, would I continue to be so monotonous. Emotionally I should like to write *The Bridge;* intellectually judged the whole theme and project seems more and more absurd. A fear of personal impotence in this matter wouldn't affect me half so much as the convictions that arise from other sources. . . . I had what I thought were authentic materials that would have been a pleasurable-agony of wrestling, eventuating or not in perfection— at least being worthy of the most supreme efforts I could muster.

These "materials" were valid to me to the extent that I presumed them to be (articulate or not) at least organic and active factors in the experience and perceptions of our common race, time and belief. The very idea of a bridge, of course, is a form peculiarly dependent on such spiritual convictions. It is an act of faith besides being a communication. The symbols of reality necessary to articulate the span—may not exist where you expected them, however. By which I mean that however great their subjective significance to me is concerned—these forms, materials, dynamics are simply non-existent in the world. I may amuse and delight and flatter myself as much as I please—but I am only evading a recognition and playing Don Quixote in an immorally conscious way.

The form of my poem rises out of a past that so overwhelms the present with its worth and vision that I'm at a loss to explain my delusion that there exist any real links between that past and a future destiny worthy of it. The "destiny" is long since completed, perhaps the little last section of my poem is a hangover echo of it— but it hangs suspended somewhere in ether like an Absalom by his hair. The bridge as a symbol today has no significance beyond an economical approach to shorter hours, quicker lunches, behaviorism and toothpicks. And inasmuch as the bridge is a symbol of all such poetry as I am interested in writing it is my present fancy that a year from now I'll be more contented working in an office than before. Rimbaud was the last great poet that our civilization will see—he let off all the great cannon crackers in Valhalla's parapets, the sun has set theatrically several times since while Laforgue, Eliot and others of that kidney have whimpered fastidiously. *Everybody* writes poetry now—and "poets" for the first time are about to receive official social and economic recognition in America. It's really all the fashion, but a dead bore to anticipate. If only America were half as worthy today to be spoken of as Whitman spoke of it fifty years ago there might be something for me to say—not that Whitman received or required any tangible proof of his intimations, but that time has shown how increasingly lonely and ineffectual his confidence stands.

There always remains the cult of "words," elegancies, elaborations, to exhibit with a certain amount of pride to an "inner circle" of literary initiates. But this is, to me, rivalled by numerous other forms of social accomplishment which might, if attained, provide as mild and seductive recognitions. You probably think me completely insane, talking as obvious hysterics as [a] drunken chorus-girl. Well, perhaps I need a little more skepticism to put me right on *The Bridge* again. . . . I am certainly in a totally undignified mind and undress—and I hope to appear more solidly determined soon.

Please don't think that the O'Neill foreword has precipitated anything, nor that I [am] burning manuscripts or plotting oriental travels. . . . Desolately I confess that I *may* be writing stanzas again tomorrow. That's the worst of it. Mrs. S asks to be remembered to you.

—All this does not mean that I have resigned myself to inactivity. . . . A bridge will be written in some kind of style and form, at worst it will be something as good as advertising copy. After which I will have at least done my best to discharge my debt to Kahn's kindness.

249: TO WALDO FRANK

[*Isle of Pines*]   *July 3rd, '26*

Dear Waldo: I must thank you immediately for your wireless. The news is most welcome—and your affectionate haste in notifying me is not without results in piercing the miasmas of these tropics.

Also comes a letter from Sue [Jenkins]. It seems the news has reached Patterson via Jimmy Light. I copy Sue's account of the circumstances given her by Jimmy, as having been so active an agent in the matter you probably will be interested. "The way it came about is not without interest. About a month ago Liveright, Jimmy and others were at Otto Kahn's for a week-end. L. had the mss. with him at that time and on the boat coming back he said he had decided not to publish it—that he didn't care for the poems and so far as he could see, nobody understood them. Then, a little over a week ago, Jimmy and O'Neill were in L.'s office on business and your mss. was on the table. Jimmy asked him if he had stuck to his decision and he said 'Yes.' Then Jimmy and Gene both told him they thought he would eventually be 'proud' of having published your first volume, so that even if he himself did not care for the poems, as a publisher he was failing to take advantage of an opportunity. So finally L. came around to his old position of saying that he would publish them if Gene would write a preface. (Previously L. had said that he did not want to publish the poems at all—preface or no preface.) Gene protested some, saying that while he liked the poems he wasn't at all sure he could tell why he liked them, that he was by no means a critic of poetry, and that L. was preparing a fine opportunity for him (O'Neill) to make a fool of himself. But finally it was decided that the preface would be written, L. phoned immediately to the printer and dictated the announcement. And I understand that the preface is already written and in L.'s hands."

Probably I'll hear something direct from Liveright within the next week; nothing so far has reached me. If the book is really scheduled for fall it will relieve me of numerous embarrassments, especially with the family, who, I think have already ceased to believe any statements from me about my work, publications, etc.

Last Sunday I was obliged to go to Havana to consult with a doctor. For the last two weeks I have been suffering intensely from two abscesses, one in each ear, added to which apparently alarming symptoms of fever, and lung trouble had seemed to develop. Of these latter the doctor says there is no need to worry, but the abscesses have not healed yet, and are distracting to say the least. I shall be glad sometime to get a good night's sleep. Doctor says they were caused by sun-exposure on my boat trip.

I have been reading *Quixote* and *Swann's Way*. My money is practically exhausted, but I think I can get a hundred by writing to Patterson and having my property there sold. The final 500 from Kahn can't be solicited until August or later—if at all, for I shan't ask for it unless I am writing again by that time. Mrs. Simpson has been so kind and altogether gracious that I couldn't ask for better care.

When I'm feeling better I hope to write you a decent letter—the last two have been so haphazard, violent and vulgar. I hope these days of sea and sunshine and breezes are resting you and improving Tom.[1] In Havana I bought a *New Yorker* and read your van Loon snapshot—marvelling again at your flexibility and dash. Otherwise I was sipping the glorious limonades most of the time! couldn't get my mouth open wide enough to receive much other nourishment! Took long walks around the harbour and along the Malacon. A lovely city, albeit insipid; full of white and gold and azure buildings. Even plaster has something to say.

1. Thomas Frank.

250: TO — —

Isle of Pines, Cuba   [*July ?*]

Dear — —: —/—/ I have not been able to write one line since I came
here—the mind is completely befogged by the heat and besides there
is a strange challenge and combat in the air—offered by "Nature" so
monstrously alive in the tropics which drains the psychic energies.
—And my poem was progressing so beautifully until — — — — took it
into her head to be so destructive! How silly all this sounds! Howso-
ever—it's a cruel jest of Fate—and I doubt if I shall continue to write
for another year. For I've lost all faith in my material—"human nature" or what you will—and any true expression must rest on some
faith in something.

It has been so disgusting to note the sudden turns and antics of
my "friends" since I had the one little bit help I ever had toward my
work in the money from Kahn. Everytime I came into N.Y. from
the country I'd hear new monstrosities of fables going about town as
to how I was squandering money on pate de foi gras, etc. And worse
whisperings. It's all been very tiresome—and I'd rather lose such
elite for the old society of vagabonds and sailors—who don't enjoy
chit-chat.

Two of the latter, by the way, are keeping up a regular flow of
letters and cards to me here. One, F——, came clear up to Patterson
to see me during May—but found me gone, of course.

I was very touched to hear that he had journeyed all the way from
Norfolk—in memory of two evenings in Brooklyn last January. Im-
mortally choice and funny and pathetic are some of my recollections
in such connection. I treasure them—I always can—against many
disillusionments made bitter by the fact that faith was given and
expected—whereas, with the sailor no faith or such is properly *expected* and how jolly and cordial and warm the tonsiling *is* sometimes, after all. Let my lusts be my ruin, then, since all else is a fake
and mockery. —/—/

251: TO HIS MOTHER

[*Isle of Pines*]   *July 8th, 1926*

Dear Grace: Well,—after two months of absolute silence I'm glad to
hear from you—and sorry to know that you are so disturbed and
worried as you are, and sick in bed. —/—/

The trip to Cayman I'm still trying to get over. Everyone (I don't know why native Americans here should tell such stories) had been telling me how charming the little island was. More than that, the sea-sailing to and fro had interested me. Being in a very dull mood (the intense and sudden heat here had made me torpid and inactive) I thought the trip would spur me, stimulate me a little toward continuing my writing on the *Bridge* poem, not a line of which I had been able to add since I came down here.

Instead of a two days trip over, it took four. Headwinds all the way. It was not until the island was cleared that I realized how many were on that sixty-foot schooner. Thirty-five! and all of them niggers who proved to have no idea of ordinary decent cleanliness, and the crowd made it almost impossible to find a place to stand, lie or sit for ten minutes at a time—not to mention the fact that there was no shade from the intense blaze of the sun unless one could brave the stinks and fumes of a dozen odd sick and wailing nigger females below decks. Most of these never emerged from their hole there during the entire voyage, but pots, bowls, basins, fruit peelings and a thousand shrieks and wails were raised up every hour of the day and night to be emptied on the deck, my nose and ears being kept busy, I can tell you!

When we at last were in sight of the island we were greeted (even three miles out) with such droves of savage mosquitoes as I had never imagined outside of Bon Echo, Canada. And when I was landed I found them to be far, far worse. There was only one place on the island (no hotel) where I could be accommodated. A sort of boarding house kept by a woman who used to cook over at Santa Fe. Whether they were hers or not, I don't know, but the house was packed with infants and children who kept up a constant racket and screaming. All the Negroes on the island were very pious, and about the time the children would quiet down a whole band of them in the house next door would raise their voices to God in hymns that would scrape the varnish off the woodwork. Worst of all, there was not an inch of screening on the house. I spent literally dollars buying insect powders and keeping a constant smudge going in my room so that my eyes were in a constant stream of tears from the smoke and my lungs nearly burst with suffocation.

Even then, one side of my face and neck were so badly poisoned from the constant bites that they were quite swollen. The beautiful beaches that I had heard about on the island I never saw. To walk more than half a mile from your doorstep was almost to court madness, St. Vitus dance, or death. The very arm with which you were attempting to beat off the regiments of insects would become so covered with them (even while in violent action) that you gave up any hope of relieving yourself of their company.

You can picture me, then, pacing back and forth in my room, very much in the mood of old Mrs. Johnson, in our kitchen at 1709 [Cleveland home of Crane family]—with a hand pressed on the top of my head, whispering to myself that I would soon be quite insane and relieved of my torments.

Someday I'll tell you more about this famous "vacation" and "holiday" in the picturesque West Indies. I had *ten* days and long nights of it before the boat captain finally pulled anchor and started back to Gerona again. The load this time was as heavy as before and equally dirty. The trip was equally long. We lay for two whole days in midocean and a dead calm, the water so still that you could see yourself in it like a mirror. The sun was terrific and the decks scorched your feet. Not a bit of shade, and I couldn't go below decks without nausea. Our island seemed like Paradise and Mrs. Simpson like the goddess of Liberty when I finally got home. Two days later I was taken with abscesses in both ears, and I am still suffering night and day, though they seem to be on the mend.

Added to this, during the first week home, I had such difficulty in breathing, especially at night—with pains in the chest and terrific sweats—that I became seriously alarmed. Mrs. S. and I both agreed that I had better go at once to Havana and consult with an able physician. Which I finally did. Doctor A. Agramonte, Velado—a grad. of Columbia University, etc.

He pronounced me alright except [for] a slight infection of the throat, which may have been contracted from the common water supply on the boat, so musty and contaminated that at the time I almost parched my system by attempting to avoid all drinking. The ear trouble he said was probably due to sun exposure. I was given some prescriptions and returned on the next boat. Mrs. Simpson has been goodness itself in douching my ears and in giving me whatever other attentions I have needed. The last three days it has almost disappeared and then come again, by turns. I am hoping that nothing chronic ensues. The pain has been nerve wracking and my whole system is at present functioning "below par". . . . So much for the Cayman trip. —/—/

252: TO WILLIAM WRIGHT

Isle of Pines   *July 16, 1926*

Dear Bill: —/—/ I liked the poem from *The Bookman*—even, if as you say, you don't attempt more than a play of words. Convictions of any sort are hard to maintain these days—and maybe Spengler is right. Have you read his *Untergang des Abendlandes*—now translated (Knopf)? I envy people like Wheeler Lovell—who have intensive work to do without having to wrestle with either angels or devils to continue with it. I get awfully exhausted sometimes, trying to achieve some kind of consistent vision of things. But I don't seem to be able to relax—and knowing quite well all the time that most of my energy is wasted in a kind of inward combustion that is sheer nonsense. All else seems boresome, however,—so I must continue to kill myself in my own way. —/—/

253: To Waldo Frank

[*Isle of Pines*]   *July 24, 1926*

Hail Brother! I feel an absolute music in the air again, and some tremendous rondure floating somewhere—perhaps my little dedication ["To Brooklyn Bridge"] is going to swing me back to San Cristobal again. . . . That little prelude, by the way, I think to be almost the best thing I've ever written, something steady and uncompromising about it. Do you notice how its construction parallels the peculiar technique of *space and detail division* used by El Greco in several canvasses—notably the *Christus am Olberg?* I've just been struck by that while casually returning to my little monograph as I often do.

> And obscure as that heaven of the Jews
> Thy guerdon . . . Accolade thou dost bestow
> Of anonymity time cannot raise;
> Vibrant reprieve and pardon thou dost show.

Read the above between the 6th & 7th stanzas of the last I sent—and you have the poem complete. It's done, and I won't bother you with any more scraps. . . .

The news of Allen Tate's generosity refreshed me a great deal; truly beautiful of him. You must know by now, how little I credited the Light gossip; I simply thought you'd be interested in hearing the sort of thing that goes around. I don't mean to say I sensed the ultimate facts as your enclosure establish them—but I have always known that your efforts were the *sine qua non* in this situation . . . your devotion and courage the sustaining factor.

I shall not write Kahn for awhile, or if I do it will be in a different mood than you need to fear of. I sent Spengler to you registered, two weeks ago. Don't know any exact date for the appearance of *White B's*, the contract specifies only in "the fall of 1926"; November, perhaps. —/—/

254: TO WALDO FRANK

[Isle of Pines]   *July 26th, '26*

Dear Waldo: Dear repository of my faith, will you also serve as sanctum of some [of] my "works"? By which I mean that, though I shouldn't bother you now while you are busy with inner work of your own, I still must ask you to keep the enclosed somewhere.[1] One never knows what may happen, fires burn the house here, etc., and mss. be burnt or otherwise lost—and in the case of this *Bridge* I feel enough honor-bound to desire preserved whatever evidence of my industry and effort is forthcoming.

I don't presume to ask you for comments. Read it if you like and fold it away somewhere. You have the last section ("Atlantis," as I have decided to call it) haven't you? I have discovered that it IS the real Atlantis, even of geology!

My plans are soaring again, the conception swells. Furthermore, this Columbus is REAL. In case you read it—(I *can't* be serious)— observe the water-swell rhythm that persists until the Palos reference. Then the more absolute and marked intimation of the great *Te Deum* of the court, later held,—here in the terms of C.'s own cosmography.

Mrs. S. is the god's own gift. This were a perfect place for work but for the prostrating heat. I think of next winter! Last night a wonderful breeze came up—and you can walk singing through the grove with a great moon simply bending down.

255: TO MALCOLM COWLEY AND PEGGY BAIRD

Isle of Pines, Cuba   *July 29th*

Dear Malcolm and Peggy: I've been wanting to tell you how glad I've been to know about your good luck with the *Post* business, etc. —but you probably know by this time what I've been going through with. . . . There's really no news except that I'm better and have begun to write—for a period until prostrated by the heat—like mad. Columbus has been cleared up—and a lot of other things started within ten days.

In the middle of *The Bridge* the old man of the sea (page Herr Freud) suddenly comes up. I enclose this section,[2] hoping you'll like it. Please mention or display it to no one but Allen and les Browns

1. "Ave Maria" (*The Bridge*).
2. "Cutty Sark" (*The Bridge*).

for the time: it makes me nervous to have parts of an unfinished drama going about much before the curtain goes up.

It happens that all the clippers mentioned were real beings had extensive histories in the Tea trade—and the last two mentioned were life-long rivals. Rather touching. . . .

256: To His Mother

[Isle of Pines]   *July 30th*

Dearest Grace: —/—/ Everything new sent down here now incurs terrific customs duty, so don't send me any luxuries—or necessities either until I ask for them. Waldo sent me some ointment for bug bites after he went north—and the duty came to over the original price in NY; I was so angry I threw it back into the post office and refused to have anything more to do with it (by which please understand I *didn't* pay the duty).

You already have most of the news from Grandma's letter, and Mrs. Simpson's letter also must have arrived explaining the cable matter. I wasn't worried about it because I was certain that you had received my letter almost immediately afterward—couldn't have *before* or else how could my *whereabouts* have been questioned in the cable. I'm feeling quite well now—all but sleep, and whether that's due to the heat, chronic insomnia or my present ferment of creative work, I don't quite know. Certainly the hayhennies and crowing roosters (at all times of nights) and the breathlessness of the "air" don't encourage one to slumbers. In a number of ways, however, I'm better acclimated, and I don't need to memorize your advice to know enough to keep out of the sun and physical work! My spasm of hay fever seems to have gone—at about the same time it leaves in the north, that is, the spring session.

In all other ways this is the most ideal place and "situation" I've ever had for work. Mrs. S— lets me completely alone when I'm busy; let's me drum on the piano interminably if I want to—says she likes it—and has assumed a tremendous interest in my poem. . . . She reads and sews a great deal and just talks enough to keep on splendid and equable terms with me. She's a perfect peach, in other words. The result is—that now that my health's better I'm simply immersed in work to my neck, eating, "sleeping," and breathing it. In the last ten days I've written over ten pages of *The Bridge*—highly concentrated stuff, as you know it is with me—and more than I ever crammed into that period of time before. I can foresee that everything will be brightly finished by next May when I come north, and I can make a magnificent bow to that magnificent structure, The Brooklyn Bridge, when I steam (almost under it) into dock! For the poem will be magnificent.

Meanwhile my other book, *White Buildings,* will have been published. It comes out sometime this fall. I have my contract and the $100. advance royalties mentioned in Grandma's letter. O'Neill finally backed out on the foreword, as I thought he would. He's enthusiastic about my work, I've never doubted that, but he didn't have the necessary nerve to write what his honesty demanded—a thorough and accurate appraisal of my work. He can't write criticism, never has tried even, and I foresaw the panic that this proposal on the part of our mutual publisher would precipitate in his bosom. . . . None other than Allen Tate!, it seems, is to write the foreword. I was informed by my publisher of all this—along with the acceptance. Has written it, in fact. . . . And (mum's the word on this!) I was very much touched to hear from Waldo, who knows all the inner workings on this, that Allen offered his foreword under O'Neill's signature when he heard that O'Neill had backed out. Of course I wouldn't think of anything like that—so the foreword goes back to its own name. I'm very glad things have turned out this way. My umbrage toward Allen is erased by the fidelity of his action, and I'm glad to have so discriminating an estimate as he will write of me. —/—/

257: TO WALDO FRANK

[Isle of Pines]   *Aug 3*

Dear Waldo: Enclosed is "Atlantis";[1] there have been variances since your copy whether you have it now or not.—So will you kindly humor my present little neurosis, and take care of this. I feel as though I were dancing on dynamite these days—so absolute and elaborated has become the conception. All sections moving forward now at once! I didn't realize that a bridge is begun from the two ends at once. . . . Don't bother to read what I send you; ye Gods I hope to preserve at least the credit of not presuming on you to the point of total vulgarity. It's all right to be elegant—if you are rebellious like Rimbaud; however, I have to admit grosser preoccupations; so I'm sloppy.

Gorham sent me Allen's Preface, which I also enclose (you're

1. See Weber, *op. cit.,* pp. 437-40.

quite sure to want to read this, if you haven't already). I think it clever, valiant, concise and beautiful. I'm more fortunate than I might have been had things gone as they were supposed to have gone. Gorham said he'd been up to see you. I'm trying to let down completely for awhile and "recuperate." "Powhatan's Daughter" must be that basic center and antecedent of all motion—"power in repose."

Mrs. S— has been following me in some of my recent reading,— with the result that she has named one of her roosters "Ferdinand, Count Fathom"! It's a good thing you aren't near to hear our piano going it these days!

I've just sent Kahn the Dedication and "Ave Maria." Please return me A.'s preface. Don't know whether I'll use the enclosed "Notes" or not. A reaction to Eliot's *Waste Land* notes put them in my head. However, the angle chart from *The Scientific Am[erican]* embodies a complete symbolism of both Bridge and Star, even including the motif of the "holy tooth." And I should like to use it on the cover. If the notes amuse you at the moment—as I wrote them—

Have you read how handy our *Orizaba* recently proved in the cyclone off Florida—when Cutty Sark was bobbing up?

258: To Isabel and Gaston Lachaise
(Postcard)

[Isle of Pines]   *[ca. August]*

This quarry is in the mountains, near our place. There's plenty to work on anytime you come! Your bird (the gull) is divine, produces sea music, even winks at times!

259: To Waldo Frank

[Isle of Pines]   *August 12th*

Dear Waldo: Your *Menorah [Journal]* scolding is good and proper. . . . When all America, not only the Jew, takes that to heart it will be well for all of us. I know a number of prosperous Jew families in Cleveland, among my best friends there, but they're mostly alike, sadly similar to your categorical disposals. . . . And, has the Gide essay appeared yet? Remember your promise.

I want to meet Ornstein someday. But I never seem to hear or read of any of these concert tours he is supposed to have to make for bread, etc. Mrs. Simpson was enormously pleased at your postcard; and I with your praise of the Dedication. You generally do pick the weakest link; that verse has bothered me, and will undoubtedly be somewhat amended before the book. I've sent it to *The Dial* and *The Criterion* (London); the little money may help, IF they take it. Probably won't let anything else out of the bag on this side of the water, though, for sometime yet. It keeps too many question marks in my head, albeit a little change in the purse. I play the lottery, though, and like it. I'm going to win a thousand before spring; you see. *"I knew I'd see a WHALE!"*

I'm reading [Sandburg's] *The Prairie Years* now. More of "Powhatan's Daughter" later. It ends up with the prodigal son from the '49. There's to be a grand Indian pow-wow before that. Two of three songs have just popped out (enclosed) which come after "Cutty Sark" and before "The Mango Tree." The last, "Virginia" (virgin in process of "being built") may come along any time. I skip from one section to another now like a sky-gack or girder-jack. Even the subway and "Calgary Express" are largely finished. Though novel experiments in form and metre here will demand much ardor later on.

I'm happy, quite well, and living as never before. The accumulation of impressions and concepts gathered the last several years and constantly repressed by immediate circumstances are having a chance to function, I believe. And nothing but this large form would hold them without the violences that mar so much of my previous, more casual work. *The Bridge* is already longer than *The Wasteland,*—and it's only about half done.

But enough of this shop talk. I'll exhaust your patience with it someday. You know I don't expect comments of any sort, except when they're easy and spontaneous. —/—/

260: TO WALDO FRANK

[Isle of Pines]   *August 19th '26*

Dear Waldo: Here, too, is that bird with a note that Rimbaud speaks of as "making you blush." We are in the midst of the equatorial storm season; everyday, often at night, torrents engulf us, and the thunder rods jab and prospect in the caverns deep below that chain of mountains across. You can hear the very snakes rejoice,—the long, shaken-out convulsions of rock and roots.

It is very pleasant to lie awake—just half awake—and listen. I have the most speechless and glorious dreams meanwhile. Sometimes words come and go, presented like a rose that yields only its light, never its composite form. Then the cocks begin to crow. I hear Mrs. S— begin to stir. She is the very elf of music, little wrinkled burnous wisp that can do anything and remembers so much! She reads Dante and falls to sleep, her cough has become so admirably imitated by the parrot that I often think her [in] two places at once.

I have made up a kind of friendship with that idiot boy, who is always on the road when I come into town for mail. He has gone so far as to answer my saluations. I was unexpected witness one day of the most astonishing spectacle; not that I was surprised.—A group of screaming children were shrieking about in a circle. I looked toward the house and saw the boy standing mostly hid behind the wooden shutters behind the grating; his huge limp phallus waved out at them from some opening; the only other part visible was his head, in a most gleeful grin, swaying above the lower division of the blinds.

When I saw him next he was talking to a blue little kite high in the afternoon. He is rendingly beautiful at times: I have encountered him in the road, talking again tout seul and examining pebbles and cinders and marble chips through the telescope of a twice-opened tomato can. He is very shy, hilarious,—and undoubtedly idiot. I have been surprised to notice how much the other children like him. —/—/

I'm glad to know that *The Bridge* is fulfilling your utmost intuitions; for an intuition it undoubtedly was. You didn't need to tell me that [you] had "seen" something that memorable evening, although I was never so sure just what it was you saw, until now. But I have always carried that peculiar look that was in your eyes for a moment there in your room, it has often recurred in my thoughts. What I should have done without your love and most distinguished understanding is hard to say, but there is no earthly benefit for which I would exchange it. It is a harmony always with the absolute direction [I] always seek, often miss, but sometimes gain.

Your answer to G[orham Munson] on his essay was much more adept than any of my critical armament. It was complete. My greatest complaint against G- is (apparently) an incorrigible streak of vulgarity, arising no doubt from some distrust in experience. Sometimes it makes him personally dangerous when he doesn't intend such. Not especially par example, BUT: when I last dined with G- much happened to be said about my "extravagances"—how I spent K[ahn]'s money, etc. Snowshoes, African sculpture, etc. I happened to mention how useful the snowshoes had been during the storms at Patterson, etc. G- recently visited the Tates and went up to my room, accompanied by Mrs. Turner, who writes me, most unwittingly of the circumstances, that the main thing G- quizzed her about was whether I used my snow shoes or not! Really, it [is] all so ridiculously small. You may think I'm wasting paper on such a silly story. But in any kind of friendship I like to have my honesty sometimes granted on my oath of it, and this is only one of many such little evidences of a real lack of perspective and innate taste on G.'s part. It does leak into his work, the vision of his world. He'd better memorize the last stanza of Baudelaire's famous Epilogue to the *Petits Poèmes en Prose;* as, indeed, I may sometimes tell him to do. His definition of "knowledge" in that essay incorporates the savour of just such a mind as is preoccupied with such details as I've mentioned.

Yes, I read the whole of Spengler's book. It is stupendous,—and it was perhaps a very good experience for ripening some of *The Bridge,* after all. I can laugh now; but you know, alas, how little I could at the time. That book seems to have been just one more of many "things" and circumstances that seem to have uniformly conspired in a strangely symbolical way toward the present speed of my work. Isn't it true—hasn't it been true in your experience, that beyond the acceptance of fate as a tragic action—immediately every circumstance and incident in one's life flocks toward a positive center of action, control and beauty? I need not ask this, since there is the metaphor of the "rotted seed of personal will," or some such phrase, in your *Spain.*

I have never been able to live *completely* in my work before. Now it is to learn a great deal. To handle the beautiful skeins of this myth of America—to realize suddenly, as I seem to, how much of the past is living under only slightly altered forms, even in machinery and such-like, is extremely exciting. So I'm having the time of my life, just now, anyway.

261: TO WALDO FRANK

[*Isle of Pines*]   *Aug 23*

Dear Waldo: I feel rather apologetic about sending you so many photographs—but the last seemed to be more what I wanted you to think of me—than any others heretofore.

Work continues. "The Tunnel" now. I shall have it done very shortly. It's rather ghastly, almost surgery—and, oddly almost all from the notes and stitches I have written while swinging on the strap at late midnights going home.

Are you noticing how throughout the poem motives and situations recur—under modifications of environment, etc? The organic substances of the poem are holding a great many surprises for me. . . . Greatest joys of creation.

Forgive me for telling that anecdote about G—. I don't want to seem stubborn or prejudiced, but you, on the other hand, are one who ought to know more or less *why* it is hard for me to maintain a steady sort of whole-hearted confidence and enthusiasm with such constantly recurring "obscurations," if you will. I'm not saying that these ultimately or "aesthetically" matter, but they enter the moral picture of the personality.

Did I tell you that M. Moore has taken the Dedication?—needless to say, without alterations.

262: TO WALDO FRANK

[Havana, Cuba]   *Sept. 3 '26*

Dear Waldo: I'm having my last bottle of "Diamante" before leaving for la Isla tonight. A pestulant[1] Abbe is gulping olives at the next table, and my waiter is all out of patience with him. But I cannot conceal my mirth—cheeks bulge and eyes strain at suppressions. "F—— la Cubana!" says the waiter who is Spanish. Well I never had such a fiesta of perfect food and nectar in my life. Furthermore, if you were St. Valentine—well, maybe you are! So here goes—even if you call my little story stale.

Perhaps you have also experienced the singular charm of long conversations with senoritas with only about 12 words in common understanding between you. I allude to A——, a young Cuban sailor (most of them are terrible but A—— is Spanish parentage, and maybe that explains it) whom I met one evening after the Alhambra in Park Central. Immaculate, ardent and delicately restrained—I have learned much about love which I did not think existed. What delicate revelations may bloom from the humble—it is hard to exaggerate.

So there have been three long and devoted evenings—long walks, drives on the Malacon, dos copas mas—and a change from my original American hotel to La Isle de Cuba, sine commotion, however.

1. If not a simple error, Crane has coined a combination of "petulant" and "pestilent."

I'm going back much relaxed. I got on a terrible tension—not a tennis court on the island! Just day after day in the heat and the house. Now I shall get a fresh view of what I have written and have still to write—and with an internal glow which is hard to describe. Silly of me to say so—but life can be gorgeously kindly at times.
— — — —

263: TO WALDO FRANK

[Isle of Pines]   *Sept. 5th*

Caro Hermano: Estoy en casa ayer de madrugada. No dormaba la noche a bordo mar. Mucha calor, y pensaba en el carinoso A—— y los calles blancas Habaneros, de consigniente dulces con Mi Bien. Encontreremos de nuevo en Deciembre. . . . Busco en diccionario y gramatica, sudo, raspo pelo de suerte que el tierno Cubano-Canario (Parentela los Canarios) mi carta apprendera.

Tell me if any of it is sensible. I am now, more than ever anxious to learn the most beautiful language in the world. And I suddenly conceive it as a necessary preparation for my next piece of work just apprehended in the form of a blank verse tragedy of Aztec mythology —for which I shall have to study the obscure calendars of dead kings. If I have the leisure for this study I shall certainly go to Spain some-time in the next five years. . . . In fact I must manage this anyhow.

Your letter, awaiting my return, conveyed much goodness, the sense of "wholiness"—of a complete return to yourself, from which I hope much; in fact, I'm *sure* of much therefrom. I am so glad that my progress has meant so much to you. —/—/

264: TO CHARLOTTE RYCHTARIK

New York   *Nov. 1*

Dear Charlotte: —/—/ I have no idea of just what the situation is at present with my mother, but I have been terribly worried about it for many, many weeks. The result has been that there was only about four weeks on the Isle of Pines that I managed to accomplish any work at all; my mother's unrestrained letters, the terrific heat and bugs, etc., nearly killed me.

But I've managed to come through, at least with my skin. What has been done of *The Bridge* is superb, according to what those few who have seen it say. The rest I hope to finish up here or in the country. I haven't decided exactly where I am going to stay as yet.

I don't want to do anything to hurt *anyone's* feelings, but I think that unless I isolate myself somewhat (and pretty soon) from the avalanche of bitterness and wailing that has flooded me ever since I was seven years old, there won't be enough left of me to even breathe, not to mention writing. If I could really do anything to help the situation it would be different. But it's a personal problem, after all. I'm doing my best—and I'm grateful to you for appreciating it. I'll write you more later.

I've wondered why I didn't hear from you, but I discover that I've only got about half my letters in Cuba; the Havana post office is in the dirty habit of opening American mail to extract money, when it thinks there is any currency inside. Maybe you didn't get what I sent you. *White Buildings* will be out in Dec. I'm having Laukhuff send you a copy.

265: TO WALDO FRANK

Patterson   *Nov. 21st*

Caro hermano: I am hoping that your country retreat is as pleasant to you as mine is to me. . . . It seems marvelous to sleep again, buried under the sound of an autumn wind—and to wake with the sense of the faculties being on the mend. Now I can look back and enjoy "every moment" of the summer Carib days,—so gracious is the memory in preserving most carefully the record of our pleasures, *their* real savor, *only*.

When are you coming back to town? Will you for a moment consider coming out here for a week-end (or longer) sometime before you leave for Europe? It would be pleasant and quiet, and the country is still interesting if one doesn't demand too much tropical splendor. We could have the good deliberate talk that we couldn't get in NY, of course.

Haven't got my book yet, but expect it next week. Nor am I at work yet on *The Bridge* again. . . . But I'm not worried. I know too well what I want to do now, even if it doesn't spill over for months and months. It must "spill," you know. The little thing above I did yesterday.[1] Write me when you have time. Aunt Sally sends you her best (sometimes "love"!) in her every letter.

Williams' *American Grain* is an achievement that I'd be proud of. A most important and *sincere* book. I'm very enthusiastic—I put off reading it, you know, until I felt my own way cleared beyond

1. An early version of "To Emily Dickinson."

chance of confusions incident to reading a book so intimate to my theme. I was so interested to note that he puts Poe and his "character" in the same position as I had *symbolized* for him in "The Tunnel" section.

266: TO MRS. T. W. SIMPSON

Patterson, N.Y.   *December 5th, 1926*

Dear Aunt Sally: From hurricane to Blizzards—all in six weeks! The fates sure do give me immoderate changes. It's "two below naught" outside, as they say in Hicksville; snowdrifts on the hills and windows, and my room isn't so warm but what tickling the typewriter keys is a stiff proposition. My nose got so cold last night it kept me awake, besides I could hear the congealing water click into ice in the pitcher on the washstand, ticking, ticking—every few moments. But my kerosene stoves are doing better than last winter—better oil, and I think with considerable economy I'll be able to finish the winter here, if I'm not called back to Cleveland.

Utter silence, by the way, from that quarter. It will make it a month since I heard from mother, who evidently is displeased. It certainly is too bad that she doesn't write you; I guess she is in a pretty disorganized state of mind.

I should have known when they said that my book would be out "in two weeks" that it meant a month; but it's promised for certain late this week. I'll be glad when it's over—for though it, or rather the prospect of its appearance doesn't give me such a thrill after all, yet it does keep me a little distracted. I'm sure I shall be better able to work on the new stuff once this first book is really launched and off my mind. Work is going very slowly on *The Bridge,* but I'm not worried. Eventually it's going to be done, and in the style that my conception of it demands. Winters continues to write me most stimulating criticism; his wide scholarship not only in English literature but in Latin, Greek, French and Spanish and Portugese— gives his statements a gratifying weight. I have heard nothing whatever from Waldo since I reached Patterson (a month now), but he was going away to some country retreat himself for awhile. Is very busy writing a play of some kind.

Got a letter from A — — (you remember the Havanese sailor?) yesterday. The second since I got back. I have a great time translating his Spanish—without a dictionary of any size. Once he got his niece to write me a letter in (broken) English. One of the statements ran, "Maximo Gomez, my ship—him sink in ciclon. All my clothes drowned." When I was going through Havana I asked another "Gomez" mariner if he knew anything about the fate of A — — in the storm. I gathered from his signs and contortions that A — — was badly laid up with a broken arm and a smashed shoulder. But later learn that he escaped at least as whole as the Adonis Crane referred to in your last letter. I'm still bent on learning Spanish as soon as my fortune or inheritance permits. With enough Spanish and enough reputation as a poet,—someday I might be appointed to sell tires or toothpaste in Rio de Janeiro!

I was amused to hear about the drunken outbreak of the very red, butter-faced hurricane friend of "ours"—who was looking for an Isle of Pines retreat for his mother—among the ruins. Certain of the actors in the melodramatic episode of wind, rain, lightnin', plaster, shingles, curses, desperation and sailors—never will leave my mind. Especially our little one-step together the morning after, to the tune of "Valencia"! And pillows wobbling on our heads!

I'm glad you have got under a good roof again. You're such a good brick, you ought to get dried before some of the rest. I hope you got my letters, especially the one *containing* the check. The other was self-explanatory, of course, in case anything circumvented the registered letter. I mailed it a day later on purpose. One has to be sly with the Havana post office.

I'm eating like a horse, losing my becoming tan, and getting fat, I fear. How I would like—at the present moment—to step into a grove of royal palms, doff these woolens—and have a good glass of Cerveza with you! The storm is increasing, howling loudly. It looks as though we were to be snowed in for the rest of the winter. Really! —And I may be a good time getting this letter to the PO if mail delivery is delayed, as usual under such circumstances. Don't work too hard! —/—/

267: To — —

Patterson, N.Y.   *Dec. 16 [1926]*

Dear — —: I'm laid up with tonsilitis—but must somehow thank you for your pleasant N.Y. letter and wish you as amusing a New Year as possible. As for myself—I don't expect much.

Nothing but illness and mental disorder in my family—and I am expected by all the middle-class ethics and dogmas to rush myself to Cleveland and devote myself interminably to nursing, sympathizing with woes which I have no sympathy for because they are all unnecessary, and bolstering up the faith in others toward concepts which I long ago discarded as crass and cheap.

Whether I can do it or not is the question. It means tortures and immolations which are hard to conceive, impossible to describe. There seems to be no place left in the world for love or the innocence of a single spontaneous act. Write me here.

P.S.—have you read Norman Douglas' *South Wind?* It almost makes one jolly —

268: To His Mother

Patterson, N.Y.   *Dec. 22 '26*

Dear Grace: — — — — Yes—it is a very melancholy Christmas for all of us. . . . I am certainly anything but joyful.

Insomnia seems now to have settled on me permanently—and when I do "sleep" my mind is plagued by an endless reel of pictures, startling and unhappy—like some endless cinematograph.

Am making as much effort as possible to free my imagination and work the little time that is now left me on my *Bridge* poem. So much is expected of me via that poem—that if I fail on it I shall become a laughing stock and my career closed.

I take it that you would not wish this to happen. Yet it may be too late, already, for me to complete the conception. My mind is about as clear as dirty dishwater—and such a state of things is scarcely conducive to successful creative endeavor. If it were like adding up columns of figures—or more usual labors—it would be different. . . . Well, I'm trying my best—both to feel the proper sentiments to your situation and keep on with my task. *The Bridge* is an important task—and nobody else can ever do it.

My *White Buildings* is out. A beautiful book. Laukhuff has been instructed to send you out a copy as soon as he receives his order. —/—/

I'm glad you have taken up C[hristian] S[cience] again. You never should have dropped it. But it seems to me you will have to make a real effort this time—with no half-way measures. It isn't anything you can play with. It's either true—or totally false. And for heaven's sake—don't go to it merely as a *cure*. If it isn't a complete philosophy of life for you it isn't anything at all. It is sheer hypocrisy to take it up when you get scared and then forsake it as soon as you feel angry about something. Anger is a costly luxury to you—and resentment and constant self-pity. I have to fight these demons my-self. I know they are demons—they never do me anything but harm. Why look at yourself as a martyr all the time! It simply drives people away from you. The only real martyrs the world ever worships are those devoted exclusively to the worship of God, poverty and suffer-ing—you have, as yet, never been in exactly that position. Not that I want you to be a martyr. I see no reason for it—and am out of sym-pathy with anyone who thinks he is—for the *real* ones don't think about themselves that way—they are too happy in their faith to ever want to be otherwise. —/—/

1 9 2 7

269: To Allen Tate

Patterson   *Friday [ca. January 7]*

Dear Allen: I'm tremendously obliged to you for all this British business. . . . I really hope it will go through. I've written Rick-word today immediately on receipt of your letter. I also wrote Liveright yesterday, where to write and who; he forgets things said in conversations very quickly sometimes. Let me know the cost of the cable and I'll send you a check at once.

The company that R. is lined up with [is] called Wishart & Co., address same as *Calendar,* which is continuing, by the way, as a quarterly. A new publisher just starting business in the Spring. You ought to send them something. Garman has gone to Russia for a period, but Wishart is bringing out a book of his poems. As for the preface—your foreword is entirely good enough both here *and* there. Besides, it would destroy all the economic advantage in buying sheets from L. if they had much extra printing to add over there. I therefore made no mention of the idea in my letter. Hope to God, though, that Schneider had sent the copy of *W[hite] B[uildings]* to them that I put on my review list. As I understood from you all review copies were sent out some time ago. A detention of the book much longer is going to ruin all chance of sales from Waldo's article. Lord! is there anything else that can happen to that book! How long *will* it take them to put in those new title pages, I wonder. All of my friends have got tired of asking for the book in Cleveland and I ex-pect there will be a record of less than the famous Stevens-35 to my credit.

Your comments on Gorham's shrine and gland-totemism convince me that Orage talked as vaguely and arbitrarily in your presence as he did in mine on a similar occasion. Some great boob ought to be hired as a kind of heckler and suddenly burst out in one of those meetings held each year to attract converts,—"Come on now, do your stuff—there's millions waiting!" Or some such democratic phrase.

As I seem to be going through an extremely distrustful mood in regard to most of my own work lately, perhaps some of my present temper may unduly limit my perspective in regard to your *Ode*.[1] I have a kind of perpetual dull cold in the head, however, which may better account for my reaction. But if you can bear to listen awhile to Aunt Harriet then here goes. . . .

The obscurities bother me. Stanza I, OK; and I get along very well until I come to "ambitious" Novembers in II. Why this special epithet—this particular designation for the whole season in relation to the headstones, in fact? As it is stressed so much one chafes against the stubborn dullness that blocks one's apprehension of your precise intention. The last 6 lines are particularly fine and The *last*—!

There is no doubt that you make the theme of the poem a living continuity with the exception of the several places where, I admit, I find it difficult to follow you. The theme of chivalry—a tradition of excess (not literally excess, rather, active faith) which cannot be perpetuated in the fragmentary cosmos of today—"those desires which *should* be yours tomorrow" but which, you know, will not persist nor find way into action. . . . Your statement of this is beautiful, and the poem is a POEM with splendidly controlled rhythms and eloquence. But when you come to such lines as "From the orient of the sublime economy/Remember the setting sun" I suddenly feel the thread cut. *Sublime economy* misses its aim with me, I suddenly seem to see a little of Laforgue's mannerism too wittily on the scene. What *is* meant here?

I fancy that you could go much better directly from Bull Run to "You hear the shout," etc. The next verse is superb. The last 7 lines are the climax of the poem. The intensity of this "meditation" gives the lie, of course, to all previous factual statements regarding the impermanency of your grief. . . . But you are, of course, speaking throughout less from a personal angle than a social viewpoint. Or are you? Both, of course. It was fatuous to have raised this point. . . .

Then you go back to speculation in the next stanza. You go *too*

1. "Ode to the Confederate Dead."

far in the succeeding, I think. And it, again, is rather obscure—
exactly what you mean. The capitalization of sentiment, I take it.
A good dig at certain people, but I think the sarcasm is over-bitter,
marring the beauty of the poem as a whole. The fierce resignation
at the last is beautiful, that irony *will* sell, if you get what I mean.

Carolyn [Gordon] said you sent it to *The Nation*. I hope they
have sense enough to reward you; on the other hand, though, how
can they take such a chance with their average reader? Hang crepe
on your door and wait. . . . The sonnet makes me merry, though
it's the lovely last four lines that I like best. They're almost too
good for the rest. The rest is too complicated. I'd chop it apart and
put the lovely windows in another room. —/—/

Further readings may reveal to me the folly of some of my objections. . . . Take issue with me meanwhile wherever you feel justified.

270: To EDGELL RICKWORD

Patterson, New York   *January 7th, 1927*

Dear Mr. Rickword: —/—/ I enclose three poems: "O Carib Isle,"
"Cutty Sark" and "The Harbor Dawn." There is a general emphasis
on the *marine* in all of them, and if you should care to use them all
I suggest that the sequence in which I have named them above
would chart an interesting curve of the underlying element. I must
risk a presumption on your interest in the poems in order to em-
phasize the necessity of printing "Cutty Sark" as closely as possible
to the form as typed herewith, especially in regard to the third page,
which is a "cartogram," if one may so designate a special use of the
calligramme. The "ships" should meet and pass in line and type—
as well as in wind and memory, if you get my rather unique formal
intentions in this phantom regatta seen from Brooklyn Bridge.

Probably no one should be "thanked" for taking an interest in
poetry, but your kindness and interest in what little I've so far
accomplished are much appreciated. It is re-assuring to me—especially from the fact that a couple of years ago I found so much in
your Rimbaud volume which was sympathetic and critically stimulating. — — — —

271: To HIS MOTHER

Patterson, NY   *Jan. 23, '27*

Dear Grace: —/—/ I had heard nothing about the death of Frances
[Crane] until Grandmother's letter reached me, last Friday, I think.

CA [Crane] did not trouble to answer the letter I wrote him in November, and though I shall probably not hear from him, even now, until God knows when—I wrote him a short note of condolence as soon as I heard.

I liked the pictures, especially the one with the hat, and the frame is beautiful. I shall take them with me into NY when I get the job (whatever it shall turn out to be) that I'm at present fishing for. I am trying to get a line on something before going in, as I have scarcely any money left, and I would like to avoid any charities from my friends on this occasion if possible.

Meanwhile I am doing what writing I can, and studying Spanish.

I'm very much amused at what you say about the interest in my book among relatives and friends out there in Cleveland. Wait until they see it, and try to read it! I may be wrong, but I think they will eventually express considerable consternation; for the poetry I write, as you have noticed already, is farther from their grasp than the farthest planets. But I don't care how mad they get—*after* they have bought the book! —/—/

Yvor Winters, who is a professor of French and Spanish at the Moscow University, Idaho, writes me the following: "Your book arrived this evening, and I have read it through a couple of times. It will need many more readings, but so far I am simply dumbfounded. Most of it is new to me, and what I had seen is clarified by its setting. I withdraw all minor objections I have ever made to your work—I have never read anything greater and have read very little as great." Etc. So you see what kind of a review he is apt to write.

Waldo Frank ends his article in *The New Republic* by saying: "At present Hart Crane is engaged in a long poem that provides him with a subject adequate for his method: the subject indeed which Mr. Tate prophesies in his introduction. Yet already *White Buildings* gives us enough to justify the assertion, that not since Whitman has so original, so profound and—above all, so important a poetic promise come to the American scene."

In a way it's a pity that none of the Crane family are readers of anything more important than such magazines as *The Saturday Evening Post* and *Success.* —/—/

The delay in the divorce proceedings may mean that Charles [Curtis] is reconsidering—and it might be just as well all around if he did. I have the idea that you both care for each other more than you thought you did. Such thoughts are neither here nor there,

however, and I'm in no position to form judgments or advise. I've
never been able to figure out what the quarrel was "all about"—i.e.,
the issue involved. I think you had probably better keep your mind
off the subject as much as possible, assuming the issue as closed. But
you must get something to do as soon as you are physically able. . . .
I mean—that without some kind of activity you'll remain in a morbid condition—and your viewpoint will become more warped all
the time. People just have to have some kind of activity to remain
healthy-minded.

But you seem to [be] already much better; and I'm enormously
glad. Don't think I don't care for you,—I can't help it, no matter
how I feel about some things.—/—/

272: TO WALDO FRANK

Patterson, NY   *January 28th*

Querido hermano Waldo: Just a little note to say hello. It's six-
teen below and the sun brightly shining. I'm living in practically one
room—the kitchen—with the old lady these days—to keep warm.
Writing a little again on *The Bridge* and studying Spanish.

Thank you so much for having *The Menorah* [*Journal*] people
send me out your review of Spengler. It's a magnificent rebuttal of
the man's psychology. I don't need to know your philosophical
references well enough to check up on them to feel that. I've sent
the paper on to Tate who was somewhat bowled over by Spengler—as
wasn't I?—thinking it will prick him a bit.

WB's is getting—or is going to get—wonderful reviews. Not to mention yours, there's a great explosion coming from Yvor Winters in
The Dial; another from Mark Van Doren (of all the unexpected!) in
The Nation this week. Seligmann has written a sincere and just
estimate in the *Sun;* Josephson in the *Herald-Tribune;* MacLeish
in *Poetry;* etc. I don't know any further, but there may be other surprises. I certainly feel myself very fortunate, considering the type of
stuff in *WB.*

—/—/ But I'll be glad when all reviews and arrangements are
over—so I can put the book definitely behind me. Present preoccupations tend to "exteriorize" one entirely too much. Winters has a
lovely book of poems coming out this spring, by the way,— and Ford
Madox Ford has recommended Allen's poems highly to Duckworth,
his London publishers. I hope they take it; Allen needs some encouragement very much.

Remember me in your mugs—though I guess you never get in far
enough to become as sentimental as I do. Mrs. Simpson isn't very
well, has overworked since the hurricane. Will you drop her a postcard from some hofbrau? It would tickle her to death. I've an amusing story to tell you sometime about one instance of the "mysticism
of money"—it refers to Kahn and the "gift." It seems I have to pay
$60 odd the rest of my mortal term on life insurance to the Kahn
estate, which, of course I was dumb bell enough not to understand
when he proposed it. Not that I especially mind nor that I'm at all
embittered, but I think I have discovered a new way to avoid income taxes and become heroic—both at once, if you get what I
mean. — — — —

273: To — — AND — —

Patterson,   *Feb. 16th*

Dear — and —: I left town last Sunday—so there was no time to
see you again—and (already) scarce enough cash left to tip the con-
ductor. The last two nights in town were mainly spent on the Hoboken waterfront, where you want to go (though it's for men only)
if you want the good old beer, the old free-lunch counter and
everything thrown in—for 15¢ a glass. Whiskey and gin are also
much superior to the other side of the River and cheaper. Take the
Christopher St. ferry. Walk up *past* Front St. There are three in a
row. Begin with McKelly's—or some such name.

The last night went flying back to Brooklyn with a wild Irish
red-headed sailor of the Coast Guard, who introduced me to a lot of
coffee dens and cousys on Sand Street, and then took me to some
kind of opium den way off, God knows where. Whereat I got angry
and left him, or rather Mike Drayton did. Returning here to the
home roost I found six cards from J—— the Incomparable with much
more than the usual brief greetings, so Caramba!

Mrs. Turner was laid up all day Monday from an excess of oat-
meal eaten at breakfast in celebration of my return. Went up to
Tory Hill yesterday and found everything just as I left it. Encountered Mrs. Powitzki at the Jennings and think she is marvelous.
Did you ever talk to her? I never heard such locutions. I should
love to tickle her. Since which I've been reading the Cock also Rises
(sent me by a Cleveland friend) and have developed a perfect case
of acidosis. No wonder the book sold; there isn't a sentence without
a highball or a martini in it to satisfy all the suppressed desires of

the public. It's a brilliant and a terrible book. The fiesta and bull-fight best. No warmth, no charm in it whatever, but of course Hemingway doesn't want such.

274: To Isidor Schneider

Patterson, NY   *Feb 19th, '27*

Dear Isidor: I like your *Anthony* very much. The theme is as basic as the best of Anderson, by which I don't mean that it's derivative in any sense whatever,—only that Anderson has thrusts toward a similar hygiene of the local soul, though never with such control and comprehensiveness. Forgive me too, for bringing in Jeffers, whom it seems to me you've got beat on a number of counts. He has poignance, but little of the sustained intensity and still less of the metrical ingenuity that I marvel at—the way you interweave action and emotion with precepts and generalities, and manage to make what is, after all, a simple plot,—a glowing canvas alive with irony and illumination.

The rugged-smooth drive of your lines is quite novel. I venture to say that your previous struggles with prose in *Dr. Transit* have helped you here, for many of the best passages have all the weight and definition of fine prose with the additional sharp, leaping movement of the liveliest hexameters in Chapman's *Homer*.

Here and there I think you are too didactic. Your "saint" is sometimes a little *too* consistent—though this latter reaction is so personal merely to me, probably, that it's valueless as comment. The beautifully measured opening lines create a fine abstraction of time and space: out of the clouds the sudden and dramatic introduction of the theme, the earthly conflict. Will you forgive me for echoing something you recently wrote me? I think this beats any and all of what previous verse of yours I've seen. I suppose that it's a case— with all of us—of having to find the right theme. Much of your earlier poetry (and please don't unconsciously include *Doc Transit* here) seemed diffuse to me, and sometimes obscure. This long poem has the amplitude and self-contained movement that I can't seem to find in any recent narrative poetry. I wish I had the facility for mingling fact and inference so neatly—into so organic a rhythm. I'm so hugged and restricted by a single-track, iambic metronometer these days!

Somebody sent me Hemingway's *Sun Also Rises* to read. It certainly does what he evidently intends it doing—I've had a case of acidosis just reading the list of drinks that clutter every page. He certainly knows what dry-throated Americans want; no wonder the book sells. To me it seems brilliant enough (the fiesta and the bull-fight are splendid) but horribly cold. A novel to read if you want a slant at one aspect of the age, but without any of the engraciating qualities that makes *Ulysses,* even that bitter book, a thing to keep and enjoy many times.

I'm still on the watch for a job, so let me know if you hear of anything. — — — —

275: TO ALLEN TATE

Patterson   *Thursday Feb 24*

Dear Allen: I wish I could keep up with Winters. I already owe him several letters, besides comment on the ms. of his "Fire Sequence," which awaited me when I returned from town. All his work is so genuine that it takes close attention, meditation and blood and bone to answer. . . . At present it's too much for me, so I've sent the manifesto on with a brief note to the effect that I agree with most of your marginalia, i.e., where I differ with him. Though I go further than you do in qualification of the Loeb-physics-etc. recipe. . . . Pure hocus-pocus for the poet. Just one out [of] a five-thousand other scientific similes, equally good to go by (regardless of their veracity)—and I venture to say that Winters' work suffers already from such arbitrary torturings—all for the sake of a neat little point of reference. What good will it do him to go on repeating in the background of every poem, that "life is some slight disturbance of the balance," etc., etc?! But we all must have some kind of in-cantation, I suppose. Though I'd rather adopt some of Blake's aphorisms. They're abstract enough. And a lot truer than the latest combination of scientific terms.

Glad you liked the Joyce lyrics. I make the following choice from my own work. If they seem to fit your requirements let me know, and I'll send you copies:

> "Passage"
> "The Springs of Guilty Song" (F & H, II)
> "Voyages (V)"
> "Powhatan's Daughter: The Dance"
> "To Emily Dickinson"
> "Repose of Rivers"

"The Dance" has been expanded to 104 lines, and is now the

best thing I've done. I shall send it soon to you—regardless of the Anthology, as I want you to see and adjudge it. I've had to submit it to Marianne Moore recently, as my only present hope of a little cash. But she probably will object to the word "breasts," or some other such detail. It's really ghastly. I wonder how much longer our market will be in the grip of two such hysterical virgins as *The Dial* and *Poetry!*

We have been without mail service all week. They may get the roads cleared out before Easter, I don't know. To have the sun again and a little warmth again! My present quandaries, that extend to every detail of my life, personal and artistic, have brought me near lunacy. I couldn't go on much longer on such a strain as the last year. Can you send me a few stamps? About a dozen—to last until Andy [the mail carrier] gets back on the road.

276: TO ALLEN TATE

Patterson *March 10th*

Dear Allen: I abducted a copy of your *Sewanee Review* essay from the envelope before sending it on; I hope you don't mind. As you had already promised me one I thought it would save you the trouble of mailing it back. Winters is sure to be interested, and I'm glad you're sending him one.

I'm too addled these days to have any ideas. And I may have a better perspective later—on Ransom. Just now, though, he doesn't impress me very much, at least this last book. But I haven't read nearly so much of him as you have. He, oddly, partakes somewhat of both Hardy and Wallace Stevens. Not that he imitates. . . . but that in my "reading" he seems to share certain aspects of both. And though I grant him a distinct personality I can't feel that either his technique or his attitude come half way up to the importance of either of them. He exploits his "manners" a great deal. But his viewpoints don't seem to me very profound, nor does he possess any overwhelming graces. He never has succeeded—and probably never will— in writing anything that compares with your "Idiot" in respect to these qualities. He can satirize well at times, very well.

Hardy is a marvel in skill. If it weren't for my indifference to his never-absent "message" I think I'd regard him as next to Shakespeare in sheer dexterity. I've been reading him rather thoroughly lately, instigated by Winters' frequent mention of him, I suppose.

Hope Torrence treats us well. . . . I haven't heard anything yet.

Nor from Marianne. What strange people these — — — — are. Always
in a flutter for fear bowels will be mentioned, forever carrying on a
tradition that both Poe and Whitman spent half their lives railing
against—and calling themselves "liberals." —/—/

277: TO ALLEN TATE

Patterson   *14th March '27*

Dear Allen: Miss — — — — won't even take tea, you know, because
she finds it too "stimulating." I've been to her house, so I know.
AND so, what can we expect! I got my verses ["Van Winkle" and
"The Harbor Dawn"] back also. They seemed to be too spacious for
The New Republic. . . . Your letter was of course a piece of folly,
but justified. It won't do Miss T. any good, but it's an admirable relief to me, and probably to you. I envy buckandwing dancers and
the Al Jolsons of the world sometimes. They don't have to encounter
all these milksops . . . and they do *please.* They're able to do some
"good" to somebody and when they laugh people don't think they
are crying. Out here one reads the paper—one sees evidence mounting all the time—that there is no place left for *our* kinds of minds or
emotions. Unless we can pursue our futilities with some sort of constant pleasure there is little use in going on—and we must apprehend
some element of truth in our mock ceremonies or even our follies
aren't amusing. I'm looking around for some new sort of "avocation," but having gone half-blind with conjunctivitis (better known
as "pink-eye") I [am] waiting for the cornea to clear before taking
any leap.

Phallus-es have been known to slyly leap out of some of Mr. Gilmore's poems published in *The Little Review,* so — — — — had better watch out. But she probably doesn't know one when she does encounter it! His poems, about as long as a cicada's whir, might make
an amusing booklet. His plays are even briefer, I'm told.

Thanks for the *NR* copies. Miss T. had informed me of the matter, saying "you must look out for it" (sic), so that I felt I might be
standing in the middle of Seventh Avenue with a huge truck bearing down suddenly. Having bothered you so much lately I tho[ugh]t
I'd worry Bill [Brown] for awhile, so I asked him to send me copies.
I'll certainly have plentEE now! I note that the one quotable paragraph (from the publisher's standpoint) has been lopped off: the
last, with the allusion to Whitman. The rest will be a sufficient
warning to most readers not to read the book, for it's one long dis-
sertation on the subject of OBSCURITY.

The genial tactics of the editorial proofreader have even helped Frank on a little by falsifying his ms.—at least the copy I hold. For instance, "the obscure poet he is likely *for long* to remain" has been changed to read *"ever* to remain." This not only alters the time-limit before my possible admission to the panting bosom of the generous reader, but changes the emphasis of the context in such a way that the reader infers the reviewer's prophecy to be that I shall probably *never* write anything that is comprehensible! With the world all flying into trillions of tabloids I probably shall not!

Your review of Laura [Riding] was just according to my estimates. If I'm as obscure to others as she is to me—then I won't even rail any more at Miss T ——.

GOLDEN TEXT:
  Wondrous the gods, more wondrous are the men,
  More wondrous, wondrous still, the cock and hen! —BLAKE

278: To His Mother

Patterson, NY   *19th March 1927*

Dear Grace: My eyes are so much better today that I'm able to type a little without straining. I had to order a pair of glasses—and that seems to have done more good than medicine. I lost my old pair down on the Island, but really have not worn them for more than a few days at a time for years. Nervous crises always affect my eyes, however, and it may be that this present case of conjunctivitis was caused as much by that as by wind and sunglare on snow. At any rate there's no snow left around here now, and the air is as balmy as you could wish. I do hope that the season has definitely arrived—and no more snow! My spirits react entirely too much to the endless gloomy days we've had for so long.

—/—/ I am so glad that you enjoyed the Columbus part. It is coming out next September in *The American Caravan*, a yearbook of American letters, just started by Paul Rosenfeld, Alfred Kreymborg and Van Wyck Brooks, and published by the Macauley Co. When I was last in NY the owners of the Macauley Co. gave a large party to all the contributors up in a huge but unbelievably vulgarly furnished and expensive apartment on West End Avenue. There seemed to be everybody there I'd ever heard of. Enormous quantities of wine, cocktails and highballs were served. I had just landed in town after three months with the bossy cows—and I had my share. It would take me ages to tell all the amusing things that happen at

such parties. But to come back to the poem: Rosenfeld was so excited about it that he called me up long distance and urged me to
let them have it. I had thought to have to deny it to them on account of some complications on the copyright, conflicting possibly
with my terms with Liveright (he has first option on my next two
books), but after some concessions were made I was glad to have
them take it.

The Dial has just informed me today that they have taken the
main section of Part II, "Powhatan's Daughter." This is an Indian
"Dance"—and will run about 4 Dial pages. I'll be glad to have the
cash to pay my arrears with Mrs. Turner and the doctor. . . . I
have for some strange reason, heard nothing yet from London regarding the projected British edition of White Buildings. What you
say about the reactions to it on Cornell Road are both amusing and
touching. And when I read about Mrs. Jackson taking a copy to read
to the Garrettsville Federated Women's Clubs I rocked with laughter! The poor dears will never, NEVER know what in hell to make
of it all! —/—/

I took enough veronal powders on the Island during those mad
last days to convince me that there's nothing worse. And they didn't
even give me sound sleep! The feelings next day were weird in the
extreme. I hope that CA won't keep them up very long. His attitude
and emotions toward life would probably make one gasp if one
could get a cross section of them. For a long time he has seemed
to me as thorough a specimen of abnormality as I have ever heard
of. I've given up even trying to imagine how he sees or thinks. I
probably shall continue to not write him until he answers some of
my former letters—or gives me some sign that he wants to hear from
me. I sent him a copy of the recent New Republic, but without any
note or comment. He probably likes to build up the picture that
he's creeping around in utter disgrace on account of the public
"disgrace" his son has made of himself. Well, the thirty thousand
people that read The New Republic probably wouldn't give him
much sympathy—regardless of their estimate of my particular value.

That was a happy thought—sending me the picture of the Kins-
man house. It is particularly beautiful. — — — — Every once in awhile
I have a dream with Warren scenes in it. Hall Kirkham, Donald
Clarke, Katherine Miller, Leonard Bullus, Mrs. P——with her great
heart-shaped bosom—and Mrs. G — — gasping with her goitre—what
has become of them all? I wonder. I once wrote a poem with Mrs.
P — — as the subject—but it didn't turn out to be much of anything
but a sentimentality, and I guess I threw it away. You are right; I

should write some prose. But to date I've never been able to think of things with plots to them. Somehow just can't. When I do, there won't be any particular difficulty in expressing myself. We'll see what happens when I get through with this long *Bridge* poem. Right now I'm too occupied with *it* to think of other themes. —/—/

The enclosed letter may interest you. I am also enclosing the poem referred to—"O Carib Isle!"—which is one of three of mine which Jolas has translated into French to appear in a French anthology of American poems coming out this Fall. "O Carib Isle!" was written one hellish hot day on the Island—but the *scene* of the poem and its inspiration was *Cayman!* It is coming out soon in *Poetry* in this country. It's not a bad poem. I'm crazy about those Caribbean waters and skies—even if they *are* hot! There's a lot of the feeling they give you in the Columbus poem—don't you think? *Please return the letter.*

279: To Allen Tate

Patterson   *March 21, 1927*

Dear Allen: —/—/ The B — — casques are 150 gallons full of successful and highly combustible nectar.—I celebrated to the full—returning to my boudoir late Saturday night—and knocking Senora Turner down besides hurling my Corona from the window in a high dudgeon because it wouldn't write to President Calles automatically in Spanish and express my "untold" admiration for his platform. Bill has taken it to the hospital for long and I fear expensive treatment. —/—/

280: To Allen Tate

Patterson   *March 26*

Dear Allen: I hope my letter of yesterday hasn't involved you in any great efforts so far! Written (and suddenly conceived) in the mood of waiting for the post—it reflected a too sudden flare of enthusiasm. There probably is no chance left to write Roebling's life—but I would like the initials of the *right* Furman to address at Macauley's— and sometime when you are up at the Library you might look in the file index and see if any life of Roebling has yet been written. The man was a genius—and his accomplishment stupendous at "that time." There might be only slight public interest in his work. Nevertheless, he was a true Spenglerian hero—and his efforts brought tremendous wealth to his family. *They* might be interested—anyway tho they'd probably want some engineer friend of the family to do it. My "ideas" always have some unlikely catch to them! —/—/

281: TO ALLEN TATE

[*Patterson*]   *Sunday, March 27*

Dear Allen: —/—/ As to the *briefer*,[1] I think that you give good reasons for assuming that Aiken wrote it. It might be more satisfying to ascertain this more definitely—but I do not feel that beyond that there is any particular justification for attacking him. He has a perfect right to claim that many of the poems are specious, and call them intellectual fakes, etc. He may quite well believe that he is right on the score. For years, remember, perfectly honest people have seen nothing but insanity in such things as [Blake's] "The Tiger"—The only pity is what can be done about it. You have Aiken's sentimentality beautifully defined. Personally the man is rather likeable, but I think he is full of poison. Let people like Hemingway have every convert they want. When he writes something vulnerable and signs it—we can backfire—and publicly—and that's the only worthwhile way to spend—"we have so little breath to lose." Thanks for the Davidson review. I certainly appreciate its tone of honesty and sincerity. A copy of *transition* #1 has reached me—and I'm enthusiastic about it. By all means send Jolas some poems—and why not your article on Marianne Moore? It doesn't spoil re-sale of ms. over here, you know. *transition* has some weak contribs, of course, but the majority is respectable. Joyce, Gertrude Stein, Williams, Winters, Laura [Riding], Larbaud, Gide, MacLeish, Soupault, etc. It's a wedge that ought to be used. Malcolm [Cowley] also ought to send things—and it seems to have a proof-reader!

Aunt Harriet [Monroe] has taken "Cutty Sark"—of all things—and I feel more cheerful. Have you sent her anything recently? Now seems to be the time. —/—/

282: TO ALLEN TATE

Patterson   *March 30,*

Dear Allen: Thanks for the *Times* review. I am looking for *Poetry* review today—and by the way, Carolyn [Gordon] forgot to enclose

1. Review of *White Buildings* in *The Dial* (Feb. 1927).

the Fletcher letter to *The New Rep.* I'm anxious to know what it was about.

It's damned interesting to notice how evident it is that your Foreword set the key—at least to a large extent—for most of Gorman's comments on all six poets reviewed. I consider his comments on *W.B.* quite unexpectedly favorable. What they would have been without your preface is hard to imagine. . . . I see we have come to the same conclusions about the Aiken debate—and shall leave him in his achin' void! I enclose a remarkable little surprise from the *London Times* [Feb. 24, 1927]. Altogether it's the most satisfying newspaper mention we have had. One wonders who wrote the notice. As for space—they seldom give more to foreign *editions.* Please don't lose this, as I may want it for quotations—Liveright, I mean.

Altogether, I think this is the last time in our lives to be badly discouraged. The ice is breaking—for both of us, as near as I can see—in several different quarters—and I'm beginning to detect many salutary signals. Apparently our ideas and idiom evokes some response—however slow. And what we do win in the way of intellectual territory is *solid*—it can't be knocked over by every wave that comes along—as could Masters, Bodenheim, Lindsay, etc. We wouldn't believe the developments of the next five years if they could be detailed now!

I'm *so* unhappy without a machine [typewriter]. Hope I get my new one soon. Let us know as much beforehand as possible if (and when) you intend coming. We're down to the last crust in the pantry —and no conveyance in sight to get any marketing done. —/—/

283: TO HIS FATHER

Patterson, NY   *May 7th, 1927*

Dear Father: Your good letter of the third came yesterday, and I have been thinking over your kindness in offering me so pleasant a domicile in the Ohio hills as the tavern plan would seem to present. There is one big bugbear, in my case a permanent one, which you probably didn't think of; and this in addition to a rather temporary but nevertheless important consideration makes me feel that it would be inadvisable to adopt the role of Ohio innkeeper, especially now.

I am referring to such divers matters as hay fever and "bridges." I'm sure I've mentioned more than once that this particular valley out here—for God knows what reason—does, however, as a proven fact furnish me almost complete immunity from that nightmare affliction. It has so happened that for a number of years you haven't seen me under the benign influence of Ohioan pollens during the months of June, July, Sept. & October,—so you probably don't so sharply recollect what a miserable looking critter I become during those twelve or so weeks every year. Cleveland is severe enough, but what those months would mean out in the hayfields—I dread to contemplate. And, wouldn't those be the most active months of all the year for a hostelry? I'm sure you will see my point and realize as well that I wouldn't be much good to you, either, at such periods. I used to be asked to remain away from the office—often for several days— during my hayfever period with Corday & Gross. The fact is that I'm unusually susceptible. The altitude and extreme woodedness of these parts are probably what make the difference here.

The other drawback is the urgency of getting my *Bridge* poem completed by next fall. It will take all the concentration I can give it to accomplish this. And if I came out behind-hand on it I would disappoint Boni & Liveright, my publisher, very much: he wants it to appear by next spring. So you see how things stand. . . . It would be folly for me to add complications, however fine it would be to live in such a lovely place as you describe and be with you. Get the farm though, I think it's a fine idea, and you will get a great deal of pleasure and relaxation out of it. One doesn't lose money often on that kind of real estate, and as for someone good to run it— the range of your acquaintance will probably suggest a number of capable people. —/—/

—/—/ I looked for the May check in today's letter. Hope you won't forget it before plunging into the Canadian wilds as I have obligated myself somewhat for oil and other supplies on the pleasant prospect of being solvent. The Tates are definitely decided against coming out here this summer, so that makes it possible for you to comfortably visit me here whenever you feel like it. I wish you would consider it and come!

284: To His Mother

Patterson   *May 27th 1927*

Dear Grace: We've had four days of continued downpour with such disastrous effects on my garden, newly planted, that I guess I'll have to put new seeds in. There are several brooks and lakes floating around over the bean and corn rows, and I can almost swear there's a geyser or so! —/—/

I'm in a considerable stew about money myself. CA's fine promises have already shown their vacancy. The worst was—that on the strength of his word (I certainly thought he wouldn't fail the very first month!) I went ahead and put in a wholesale supply of a number of commodities necessary here, and have been worrying ever since how I was going to pay for them. Meanwhile he has kept me so busy writing him successive excuses first for not going with him here, or managing some new tavern of his there, or what-not—ever since, that I've had no time to settle down to work or anything! DAMN it all!

This next month *must* see something accomplished on *The Bridge* or I shall be completely discouraged. I have done nothing but insignificant parts since last July, no *major* work has been done since then. And I must have it ready to hand over to my publisher this fall. I've got to clear my head of a lot of things, pleasant and unpleasant, and dig.

I don't know what to tell you about your leg or work or anything. For so much depends on your alimony. If there were something you could work at for awhile, like library work, where you would not have to remain standing for long I should recommend it. But you said you didn't care for that. I want you to come here and visit me later on in the summer when it gets hot and when there are some nice green things to be had from the garden. Meanwhile, can't you make ends meet? While you are here your expenses won't amount to more than ten dollars a week. Please understand me right; you are certainly welcome here at any time. I have the whole house to myself and shall continue to have it—there is a bedroom for you, etc. And the country around here is simply gorgeous. I never saw such profusion of wildflowers. And it is cool here at night throughout the whole year. The best thing in the world for you would be to spend long days of comparative solitude here—away from all the hubbub of life in the city, and in a totally new environment. I think that your nervous feelings are mainly responsible for your swelled leg—disordered nerves generate all kinds of poisons—and you must plan to come here awhile at least some time during the summer. —/—/

If this letter sounds kinda crabby please don't mind. I'm feeling in fine shape—all too well—but you can't blame me for having a conscience and getting a little upset at times at the slow progress my work seems to be making! And if I don't always answer as promptly as you like, you'll realize, I know, that a letter generally means losing a whole day's work—I don't care how slight it is, or to whom, it demands a completely different adjustment and takes one completely out of one's creative subject matter. —/—/

285: TO YVOR WINTERS

Patterson, New York   *May 29th, 1927*

Dear Winters: You need a good drubbing for all your recent easy talk about "the complete man," the poet and his ethical place in society, etc. I'm afraid I lack the time right now to attempt what I might call a relatively complete excuse for committing myself to the above sentiments—and I am also encumbered by a good deal of sympathy with your viewpoint in general. Wilson's article was just half-baked enough to make one warm around the collar. It is so damned easy for such as he, born into easy means, graduated from a fashionable university into a critical chair overlooking Washington Square, etc., to sit tight and hatch little squibs of advice to poets not to be so "professional" as he claims they are, as though all the names he has just mentioned had been as suavely nourished as he—as though 4 out of 5 of them hadn't been damned well forced the major part of their lives to grub at *any* kind of work they could manage by hook or crook and the fear of hell to secure! Yes, why not step into the State Dept. and join the diplomatic corps for a change! indeed, or some other courtly occupation which would bring you into wide and active contact with world affairs! As a matter of fact I'm all too ready to concede that there are several other careers more engaging to follow than that of poetry. But the circumstances of one's birth, the conduct of one's parents, the current economic structure of society and a thousand other local factors have as much or more to say about successions to such occupations, the naive volitions of the poet to the contrary. I agree with you, of course, that the poet should in as large a measure as possible adjust himself to society. But the question always will remain as to how far the conscience is justified in compromising with the age's demands.

The image of "the complete man" is a good idealistic antidote for the hysteria for specialization that inhabits the modern world. And I strongly second your wish for some definite ethical order. Munson, however, and a number of my other friends, not so long ago, being stricken with the same urge, and feeling that something must be done about it—rushed into the portals of the famous Gurdjieff Institute and have since put themselves through all sorts of Hindu antics, songs, dances, incantations, psychic sessions, etc., so that now, presumably the left lobes of their brains and their right lobes respectively function (M's favorite word) in perfect unison. I spent hours at the typewriter trying to explain to certain of these urgent people why I could not enthuse about their methods; it was all to no avail, as I was told that the "complete man" had a different logic than mine, and further that there was no way of gaining or understanding this logic without first submitting yourself to the necessary training. I was finally left to roll in the gutter of my ancient predispositions, and suffered to receive a good deal of unnecessary pity for my obstinacy. Some of them, having found a good substitute for their former interest in writing by means of more complete formulas of expression have ceased writing altogether, which is probably just as well. At any rate they have become hermetically sealed souls to my eyesight, and I am really not able to offer judgment.

I am not identifying your advice in any particular way with theirs, for you are certainly logical, so much so that I am inclined to doubt the success of your program even with yourself. Neither do you propose such paradoxical inducements as tea-dansants on Mt. Everest! I am only begging the question, after all, and asking you not to judge me too summarily by the shorthand statements that one has to use as the makeshift for the necessary chapters required for more explicit and final explanations. I am suspect, I fear, for equivocating. But I cannot flatter myself into quite as definite recipes for efficiency as you seem to, one reason being, I suppose, that I'm not so ardent an aspirant toward the rather classical characteristics that you cite as desirable. This is not to say that I don't "envy" the man who attains them, but rather that I have long since abandoned *that* field—and I doubt if I was born to achieve (with the particular vision) those richer syntheses of consciousness which we both agree in classing as supreme, at least the attitude of a Shakespeare or a Chaucer is not mine by organic rights, and why try to fool myself that I possess that type of vision when I obviously do not!

I have a certain code of ethics. I have not as yet attempted to reduce it to any exact formula, and if I did I should probably embark on an endless tome with monthly additions and digressions every year. It seems obvious that a certain decent carriage and action is a paramount requirement in any poet, deacon or carpenter. And though I reserve myself the pleasant right to define these standards in a somewhat individual way, and to shout and complain when circumstances against me seem to warrant it, on the other hand I believe myself to be speaking honestly when I say that I have never been able to regret—for long—whatever has happened to me, more especially those decisions which at times have been permitted a free will. (Don't blame me entirely for bringing down all this simplicity on your head—your letter almost solicits it!) And I am as completely out of sympathy with the familiar whimpering caricature of the artist and his "divine rights" as you seem to be. I am not a Stoic, though I think I could lean more in that direction if I came to (as I may sometime) appreciate more highly the imaginative profits of such a course.

You put me in altogether too good company, you compliment me much too highly for me to offer the least resistance to your judgments on the structure of my work. I think I am quite unworthy of such associates as Marlowe or Valéry—except in some degree, perhaps, "by kind." If I can avoid the pearly gates long enough I may do better. Your fumigation of the Leonardo legend is a healthy enough reaction, but I don't think your reasons for doubting his intelligence and scope very potent. I've never closely studied the man's attainments or biography, but your argument is certainly weakly enough sustained on the sole prop of his sex—or lack of such. One doesn't have to turn to homosexuals to find instances of missing sensibilities. Of course I'm sick of all this talk about b——s and c——s in criticism. It's obvious that b——s are needed, and that Leonardo had 'em—at least the records of the Florentine prisons, I'm told, say so. You don't seem to realize that the whole topic is something of a myth anyway, and is consequently modified in the characteristics of the image by each age in each civilization. Tom Jones, a character for whom I have the utmost affection, represented the model in 18th Century England, at least so far as the stated requirements in your letter would suggest, and for an Anglo-Saxon model he is still pretty good aside from calculus, the Darwinian theory, and a few other mental additions. Incidentally I think Tom Jones (Fielding himself, of course) represents a much more "balanced" attitude toward society and life in general than our friend, Thomas Hardy. Hardy's profundity is real, but it is voiced in pretty much one monotonous key. I think him perhaps the greatest technician in English verse since Shakespeare. He's a great poet and a mighty man. But you must be fanatic to feel that he fulfills the necessary "balanced ration" for modern consumption. Not one of his characters is for one moment allowed to express a single joyous passion without a forenote of Hardian doom entering the immediate description. Could Hardy create anything like Falstaff? I think that Yeats would be just as likely—more so.

That's what I'm getting at. . . . I don't care to be credited with too wholesale ambitions, for as I said, I realize my limitations, and have already partially furled my flag. The structural weaknesses which you find in my work are probably quite real, for I could not ask for a more meticulous and sensitive reader. It is my hope, of course, not only to improve my statement but to extend scope and viewpoint as much as possible. But I cannot trust to so methodical and predetermined a method of development, not by any means, as you recommend. Nor can I willingly permit you to preserve the assumption that I am seeking any "shortcuts across the circle," nor wilfully excluding any experience that seems to me significant. You seem to think that experience is some commodity—that can be sought! One can respond only to certain circumstances; just what the barriers are, and where the boundaries cross can never be completely known. And the surest way to frustrate the possibility of any free realization is, it seems to me, to wilfully direct it. I can't help it if you think me aimless and irresponsible. But try and see if you get such logical answers always from Nature as you seem to think you will! My "alert blindness" was a stupid ambiguity to use in any definition—but it seems to me you go in for just about as much "blind alertness" with some of your expectations.

If you knew how little of a metaphysician I am in the scholastic sense of the term, you would scarcely attribute such a conscious method to my poems (with regard to that element) as you do. I am an utter ignoramus in that whole subject, have never read Kant, Descartes or other doctors. It's all an accident so far as my style goes. It happens that the first poem I ever wrote was too dense to be understood, and I now find that I can trust most critics to tell me that all my subsequent efforts have been equally futile. Having heard that one writes in a metaphysical vein the usual critic will immediately close his eyes or stare with utter complacency at the page—assuming that black is black no more and that the poet means anything but what he says. It's as plain as day that I'm talking about war and aeroplanes in the passage from "F & H" ("corymbulous formations of mechanics," etc.) quoted by Wilson in *The New Republic,* yet by isolating these lines from the context and combining them suddenly with lines from a totally different poem he has the chance (and uses it) to make me sound like a perfect ninny. If I'd said that they were Fokker planes then maybe the critic would have had to notice the vitality of the metaphor and its pertinence. All this ranting seems somehow necessary. . . . If I am metaphysical I'm content to continue so. Since I have been "located" in this category by a number of people, I may as well go on alluding to certain (what are also called) metaphysical passages in Donne, Blake, Vaughan, etc., as being of particular appeal to me on a basis of common characteristics with what I like to do in my own poems, however little scientific knowledge of the subject I may have.

I write damned little because I am interested in recording certain

sensations, very rigidly chosen, with an eye for what according to my
taste and sum of prejudices seems suitable to—or intense enough—
for verse. If I were writing in prose, as I sometime shall probably do,
I should probably include a much thicker slice of myself—and
though it is the height of conceit for me to suggest it, I venture to
say that you may have received a somewhat limited idea of my interests and responses by judging me from my poems alone. I suppose that in regard to this limitation of poetic focus one should consult the current position of poetry in relation to other intellectual
and political characteristics of the time, including a host of psychological factors which may or may not promote the fullest flowering
of a particular medium such as verse. I am not apologizing. Nor am
I trying to penetrate beyond a certain point into such labyrinths of
conjecture and analysis. It seems unprofitable. One should be somewhat satisfied if one's work comes to approximate a true record of
such moments of "illumination" as are occasionally possible. A
sharpening of reality accessible to the poet, to no such degree possible through other mediums. That is one reason above all others—
why I shall never expect (or indeed desire) *complete* sympathy from
any writer of such originality as yourself. I may have neglected to say
that I admire your general attitude, including your distrust of metaphysical or other patent methods. Watch out, though, that you don't
strangulate yourself with some countermethod of your own!

286: TO HIS FATHER

Patterson, New York   *June 9th, 1927*

Dear Father: Your good letter with check came yesterday. I'm certainly relieved to know that I can now meet my obligations and continue *The Bridge* with a free mind and imagination. You certainly
have my enthusiastic gratitude for your loyalty and the general attitude you have toward my work. I venture to predict that you will
not be disappointed in the final results. —/—/

287: TO MRS. T. W. SIMPSON

Patterson, N.Y.   *July 4th, 1927*

Dear Aunt Sally: Sunshine and a certain amount of heat seem to
stimulate me to writing, that is, judging by the intensive work I did
on the Island with you last summer, and by the returned activity I've
been having lately. We haven't had any particularly hot weather,

but it's been warm enough to sweat a little, and that seems to be good for me. As a little evidence of my activities I'm enclosing a new section of *The Bridge* called "The River." It comes between "Van Winkle" which I sent you in the last letter and the Indian "Dance" which you are familiar with.

I'm trying in this part of the poem to chart the pioneer experience of our forefathers—and to tell the story backwards, as it were, on the "backs" of hobos. These hobos are simply "psychological ponies" to carry the reader across the country and back to the Mississippi, which you will notice is described as a great River of Time. I also unlatch the door to the pure Indian world which opens out in "The Dance" section, so the reader is gradually led back in time to the pure savage world, while existing at the same time in the present. It has been a very complicated thing to do, and I think I have worked harder and longer on this section of *The Bridge* than any other.

You'll find your name in it. I kind of wanted you in this section of the book, and if you don't have any objections, you'll stay in the book. For you are my idea of the salt of all pioneers, and our little talks about New Orleans, etc., led me to think of you with the smile of Louisiana. I continue in a kind of "heat"—and I may have another section or so finished up before August. I sure want to get it *all* done by December.

Well, here it is the Fourth again. I keep thinking of last year at this time. I guess my ears were about healed by that time, but I was still in a blue funk, and I remember how I went to town and after four or five Tropicals came home again and read. We aren't having much of any celebration up here this year. The Browns are rather broke, and so am I—neither of us able to indulge in either fire-crackers or firewater to any extent. Eleanor Fitzgerald is going to give a little levee down at her place, however, and maybe there will be some cider.

I got a card from NY the other day saying that my old jack tar friend, J—— F——, was back from his long trip in European waters, so I just piked in and saw him! He was standing up on the forward deck when I saw him from the pier head, and after taking me all over the ship (a destroyer) we had a very pleasant evening, taking in a movie on hunting in a jungle, full of marvelous tiger close-ups and elephant stampedes. —/—/

I get very little news from Cleveland. But from all I have heard mother and grandma are both fairly well. They have moved into a new apartment, but I guess I mentioned that change as well as the address in my last. I have stopped writing anything whatever to mother about the Island and the Island property, because I don't get any more return comment from her on that subject than you seem to get. She doesn't seem to be able to get her mind settled on any matters relating to that problem. I don't understand why, but I'm sure of this, and I hope you will believe me—she hasn't anything but gratitude to you for all you have done, and certainly entertains the most friendly sort of sentiments toward you constantly. −/−/

I can't get over thinking how sweet it was of you to sell the four copies of *White Bldgs.* Did they arrive alright from the publisher? If they didn't I will see to it that they do. I somehow think of you as being out on the Golfo de Batabano today in a sailboat. Am I right? How I should like to be on the water! The sea's the only place for me, with my *nose.* I'm just getting a little over my spring attack of hayfever now. And the next session begins before September. −/−/

Wish I could read "The River" out loud to you as I used to do last summer! Too damned bad the hurricane came—I liked my little study room there so much, with the mango tree to look at through the back window . . . I achieved some triumphs in that little room.

288: To His Father

Patterson, N.Y.   *August 12th, 1927*

Dear Father: −/−/ Life goes on here pretty evenly and monotonously. I have managed to do a good deal of writing, but not as much of it is on *The Bridge* as I would have liked to have finished by this time. Difficult is no word to describe the sort of things I'm trying to "put across" in that poem, and I've been rather too much on a tension of worry lately about a number of things to give it the requisite concentration. Grace and her present pathetic circumstances is one cause and my own arrangements for the coming fall and winter is another. It's obvious that I must get a job in town, and I'm casting out lines now even—for it generally takes ages to get anything definite worked up. I'm not asking for reassurances, but I do hope that I can count on your assistance to the extent of the monthly amount until I can get something on my hook—for otherwise I may not have the necessary carfare to ride in when the time comes for the preliminary interview! −/−/

289: To Otto H. Kahn

Patterson, New York   *September 12th 1927*

Dear Mr. Kahn: I am taking for granted your continued interest in the progress of *The Bridge,* in which I am still absorbed, and which has reached a stage where its general outline is clearly evident. The Dedication (recently published in *The Dial*) and Part I (now in *The American Caravan*) you have already seen, but as you may not have them presently at hand I am including them in a ms. of the whole, to date, which I am sending you under separate cover.

At the risk of complicating your appreciation of Part II ("Powhatan's Daughter"), I nevertheless feel impelled to mention a few of my deliberate intentions in this part of the poem, and to give some description of my general method of construction. Powhatan's daughter, or Pocahontas, is the mythological nature-symbol chosen to represent the physical body of the continent, or the soil. She here takes on much the same role as the traditional Hertha of ancient Teutonic mythology. The five sub-sections of Part II are mainly concerned with a gradual exploration of this "body" whose first possessor was the Indian. It seemed altogether ineffective from the poetic standpoint to approach this material from the purely chronological angle—beginning with, say, the landing of "The Mayflower," continuing with a résumé of the Revolution through the conquest of the West, etc. One can get that viewpoint in any history primer. What I am after is an assimilation of this experience, a more organic panorama, showing the continuous and living evidence of the past in the inmost vital substance of the present.

Consequently I jump from the monologue of Columbus in "Ave Maria"—right across the four intervening centuries—into the harbor of 20th-century Manhattan. And from that point in time and place I begin to work backward through the pioneer period, always in terms of the present—finally to the very core of the nature-world of the Indian. What I am really handling, you see, is the Myth of America. Thousands of strands have had to be searched for, sorted and interwoven. In a sense I have had to do a great deal of pioneering myself. It has taken a great deal of energy—which has not been so difficult to summon as the necessary patience to wait, simply wait much of the time—until my instincts assured me that I had assembled my materials in proper order for a final welding into their natural form. For each section of the entire poem has presented its own unique problem of form, not alone in relation to the materials embodied within its separate confines, but also in relation to the other parts, *in series,* of the major design of the entire poem. Each is a separate canvas, as it were, yet none yields its entire significance when seen apart from the others. One might take the Sistine Chapel as an analogy. It might be better to read the following notes *after* rather than *before* your reading of the ms. They are not necessary for an understanding of the poem, but I think they may prove interesting to you as a commentary on my architectural method.

1. "The Harbor Dawn":

Here the movement of the verse is in considerable contrast to that of the "Ave Maria," with its sea-swell crescendo and the climacteric vision of Columbus. This legato, in which images blur as objects only half apprehended on the border of sleep and consciousness, makes an admirable transition between the intervening centuries.

The love-motif (in italics) carries along a symbolism of the life and ages of man (here the sowing of the seed) which is further developed in each of the subsequent sections of "Powhatan's Daughter," though it is never particularly stressed. In 2 ("Van Winkle") it is Childhood; in 3 it is Youth; in 4, Manhood; in 5 it is Age. This motif is interwoven and tends to be implicit in the imagery rather than anywhere stressed.

2. "Van Winkle":

The protagonist has left the room with its harbor sounds, and is walking to the subway. The rhythm is quickened; it is a transition between sleep and the immanent tasks of the day. Space is filled with the music of a hand organ and fresh sunlight, and one has the impression of the whole continent—from Atlantic to Pacific—freshly arisen and moving. The walk to the subway arouses reminiscences of childhood, also the "childhood" of the continental conquest, viz., the conquistadores, Priscilla, Capt. John Smith, etc. These parallelisms unite in the figure of Rip Van Winkle who finally becomes identified with the protagonist, as you will notice, and who really boards the subway with the reader. He becomes the "guardian angel" of the journey into the past.

3. "The River":

The subway is simply a figurative, psychological "vehicle" for transporting the reader to the Middle West. He lands on the railroad tracks in the company of several tramps in the twilight. The extravagance of the first twenty-three lines of this section is an intentional burlesque on the cultural confusion of the present—a great conglomeration of noises analogous to the strident impression of a fast express rushing by. The rhythm is jazz.

Thenceforward the rhythm settles down to a steady pedestrian gait, like that of wanderers plodding along. My tramps are psychological vehicles, also. Their wanderings as you will notice, carry the reader into interior after interior, finally to the great River. They are the left-overs of the pioneers in at least this respect—that their wanderings carry the reader through an experience parallel to that of Boone and others. I think [I] have caught some of the essential spirit of the Great Valley here, and in the process have approached the primal world of the Indian, which emerges with a full orchestra in the succeeding dance.

5.[4] "The Dance":

Here one is on the pure mythical and smoky soil at last! Not only do I describe the conflict between the two races in this dance—I also become identified with the Indian and his world before it is over, which is the only method possible of every really possessing the Indian and his world as a cultural factor. I think I really succeed in getting under the skin of this glorious and dying animal, in terms of expression, in symbols, which he himself would comprehend. Pocahontas (the continent) is the common basis of our meeting, she survives the extinction of the Indian, who finally, after being assumed into the elements of nature (as he understood them), persists only as a kind of "eye" in the sky, or as a star that hangs between day and night—"the twilight's dim perpetual throne."

6.[5] "Indiana":

I regret that this section is not completed as yet. It will be the monologue of an Indiana farmer; time, about 1860. He has failed in the gold-rush and is returned to till the soil. His monologue is a farewell to his son, who is leaving for a life on the sea. It is a lyrical summary of the period of conquest, and his wife, the mother who died on the way back from the gold-rush, is alluded to in a way which implies her succession to the nature-symbolism of Pocahontas. I have this section well-nigh done, but there is no use including [it] in the present ms. without the final words.

The next section, "Cutty Sark," is a phantasy on the period of the whalers and clipper ships. It also starts in the present and "progresses backwards." The form of the poem may seem erratic, but it is meant to present the hallucinations incident to rum-drinking in a South Street dive, as well as the lurch of a boat in heavy seas, etc. So I allow myself something of the same freedom which E. E. Cummings often uses.

"Cutty Sark" is built on the plan of a *fugue*. Two "voices"—that of the world of Time, and that of the world of Eternity—are interwoven in the action. The Atlantis theme (that of Eternity) is the transmuted voice of the nickel-slot pianola, and this voice alternates with that of the derelict sailor and the description of the action. The airy regatta of phantom clipper ships seen from Brooklyn Bridge on

the way home is quite effective, I think. It was a pleasure to use
historical names for these lovely ghosts. Music still haunts their
names long after the wind has left their sails.

"Cape Hatteras," which follows, is unfinished. It will be a kind of
ode to Whitman. I am working as much as possible on it now. It
presents very formidable problems, as, indeed, all the sections have.
I am really writing an epic of the modern consciousness, and inde-
scribably complicated factors have to be resolved and blended. . . .
I don't wish to tire you [with] too extended an analysis of my work,
and so shall leave the other completed sections to explain themselves. In the ms., where the remaining incomplete sections occur,
I am including a rough synopsis of their respective themes, however.
The range of *The Bridge* has been called colossal by more than one
critic who has seen the ms. And though I have found the subject to
be vaster than I had at first realized, I am still highly confident of
its final articulation into a continuous and eloquent span. Already
there are evident signs of recognition: the following magazines have
taken various sections:

"Dedication: To Brooklyn Bridge"	*The Dial*
"Ave Maria"	*The American Caravan*
"The Harbor Dawn"	*transition* (Paris)
"Van Winkle"	"
"The River"	*The Virginia Quarterly*
"The Dance"	*The Dial*
"Cutty Sark"	*Poetry* (Chicago)
"Three Songs"	*The Calendar* (London)
"The Tunnel"	*The Criterion* (London)

(I have been especially gratified by the reception accorded me by
The Criterion, whose director, Mr. T. S. Eliot, is representative of
the most exacting literary standards of our times.)

For some time past I have been seeking employment in New York,
but without success so far. It's the usual problem of mechanical
prejudices that I've already grown grey in trying to deal with. But
all the more difficult now, since the only references I can give for the
last two years are my own typewriter and a collection of poems. I
am, as you will probably recall, at least avowedly—a perfectly good
advertising writer. I am wondering if you would possibly give me
some recommendation to the publicity department of The Metropolitan Opera Company, where I am certain of making myself useful. I was in New York two days last week, trying to secure employment as a waiter on one of the American lines. I found that I needed

something like a diploma from Annapolis before hoping for an interview. A few years ago I registered with the Munson Line with reference to my qualifications for a particular position which every ship includes—that of "ship's writer," or "deck yeoman"; but I always found that such jobs were dispensed to acquaintances of the captain or to office workers, and that my references were never taken from the file. I am not particular what I do, however, so long as there is reasonable chance of my doing it well, and any recommendation you might care to offer in any practical direction whatever will be most welcome. My present worried state of mind practically forbids any progress on *The Bridge,* the chances for which are considerably better under even greatly limited time conditions.

I am still assured of a definite inheritance, previously mentioned in my first letter to you; and if you care to consider advancing me, say 800 or 1,000 dollars, on the same basis of insurance security as your previous assistance I should be glad to come into New York and talk it over. There is no monetary standard of evaluation for works of art, I know, but I cannot help feeling that a great poem may well be worth at least the expenditure necessary for merely the scenery and costumes of many a flashy and ephemeral play, or for a motor car. *The Aeneid* was not written in two years—nor in four, and in more than one sense I feel justified in comparing the historic and cultural scope of *The Bridge* to this great work. It is at least a symphony with an epic theme, and a work of considerable profundity and inspiration. Even with the torturing heat of my sojourn in Cuba I was able to work faster than before or since then, in America. The "foreign-ness" of my surroundings stimulated me to the realization of natively American materials and viewpoints in myself not hitherto suspected, and in one month I was able to do more work than I had done in the three previous years. If I could work in Mexico or Mallorca this winter I could have *The Bridge* finished by next spring. But that is a speculation which depends entirely on your interest.

Please pardon the inordinate length of this letter. I shall, of course, hope to hear from you regarding your impressions of the poem as it now stands. Along with the ms., I am enclosing three critical articles which may interest you somewhat.

290: To Samuel Loveman

Patterson, N.Y.   *Sept. 18th, '27*

Dear Sam: I was glad to hear from you. I had been totally at a loss to explain the basis of your resentment, and still am not quite clear on the subject—but as you say that it is now removed perhaps nothing is gained by probing old wounds and asking you what exactly it was all about. Certainly, if I borrowed some money from you and have forgotten to return it I shall have deserved the full measure of disapproval. Memory plays tricks with all of us at times, and mine is no more faithful to me than it ought to be. —/—/

291: TO HIS FATHER

Brooklyn, N.Y.   *October 11th, 1927*

Dear Father: I have just had an interview with Otto Kahn, following his reading of the manuscript of *The Bridge*. Kahn is very enthusiastic about what I have accomplished and is most anxious that I keep on with the composition without interruption until it is finished. I told him about your willingness to extend me the assistance of the monthly allowance of $50 and he has come forward with an additional $300 which will provide me with necessary boat fare to Martinique for the winter. That is a much pleasanter island than the Isle of Pines and I will also be able to learn French and Spanish there, which will make it possible for me to earn my living up here later by translation work.

I know enough about Martinique from people who have recently been there to be sure that the allowance you have been giving me will cover my living costs there. The winter season will insure me against any of the excessive heat that I experienced on the Isle of Pines and I shall be able to get much more accomplished.

I shall probably sail on the 20th (Furness-Bermuda Line) and arrive about 8 days later. Am busy now seeing about my passport. Please let me hear from you soon.

292: TO — — AND — —

[Brooklyn]   *Nov. 16, 27*

Dear — — and —: Traintime approaches, but I hope life does not continue to grow accordingly more hectic, as has been the rule so far! Several times I have all but lost my ticket, presented several days ago. Notably Tues. night in jail. . . .

After a riotous competition with Cummings and Anne [Cummings] in which (I don't *know* but I'm sure) I won the cocktail contest I found myself in the Clark St. station along about 3 o'clock playing with somebody's lost airedale. The cop who rushed at me, asking me what I was doing is reported to have been answered by "why the hell do you want to know?!!!" in a loud tone of voice, whereat I was yanked into a taxi and was sped to the station (slyly and en route tossing all evidence such as billets doux, dangerous addresses, etc., out the window) and the next I knew the door crashed shut and I found myself behind the bars. I imitated Chaliapin fairly well until dawn leaked in, or rather such limited evidences of same as six o'clock whistles and the postulated press of dirty feet to early coffee stands.

I was good and mad. Made an impassioned speech to a crowded court room, and was released at 10 o'clock without even a fine. Beer with Cummings in the afternoon which was almost better than evening before, as C's hyperbole is even more amusing than one's conduct, especially when he undertakes a description of what you don't remember. Anyhow, I never had so much fun jounced into 24 hours before, and if I had my way would take both C'gs and Anne along with me to heaven when I go. —/—/

293: To Charlotte and Richard Rychtarik

Altadena, Cal[ifornia]   *Nov. 29th, '27*

Dear Charlotte & Ricardo: —/—/ I have just been here a week and a day, having left NY on the 17th in company with my new "boss," his valet, chauffeur and 3 dogs. I am more-or-less his secretary and companion, but I'm treated more as a guest and have practically all of my time to myself. Boss is a semi-invalid, a wealthy Wall Street broker who travels most of the time, and who has been sent out here for six months rest by his doctors. Lord! I never lived in *this* style before! It's almost oppressive! But maybe I'll get used to it in time. . . .

As I said, about all I have to do is to be agreeable, talk about Aristotle, Einstein, T. S. Eliot, Gertrude Stein, etc., etc., (in other words, my boss is really a very cultured man and didn't want to take too much of a chance on running into a vacuum as regards companionship out here). He is also interested in my writing, and it is with some regard to helping me with my work that he has taken me out here. We're living in an amazing house, rented for the season from the president of the American Express Company. It is all bath rooms and bad furniture—but such bath rooms! And there is a huge patio in the center, on which all the rooms open—very much the Spanish style of course.

It all came about as a sudden surprise to me. I was in Patterson only about two weeks after I left Cleveland. Came into New York and found a job in a little book shop almost immediately. I thought I was lucky until the bad lighting of the store (it was a black little hole!) got to working on my eyes. But I'd been there less than two weeks when Miss Fitzgerald of the Provincetown Theatre told me about this opportunity. As she is a very good friend of my boss her recommendation was seriously considered, and after a few preliminary "try-outs" dining, riding in the park, etc., I was formally invited. So here I am! —/—/

My boss has a curiosity about meeting some of the movie people—and later on, when he gets to feeling better, expects to do some entertaining. I'm hoping that Charlie Chaplin will remember my evening with him and Frank in NY and possibly be friendly. Then there's an old "flame" of mine from Cleveland, Alice Calhoun, who has since become a movie queen who lives out here. My boss is only 34, a bachelor, and has a furious love of excitement, so there may be some amusing developments. But at present, it's part of my "task" to keep him quiet on a more-or-less intellectual and sedentary diet. Well, well—not at all! Where will I be next? Tahiti? It's not so far from here! — — — —

294: TO SLATER BROWN

Santa Monica, California   *Monday—Dec. 19*

Dear Bill: Yes, one can hear the sea seven flights below—and I've been walking on the beach most of the day. The boss, finding that I didn't get along too well with some of his Hollywood week-end guests, advised my taking a vacation, and with means happily provided here I am until tomorrow night. Wall Street seems to carry a slight oppression and madness with it wherever it "extends." It has been good to come over here where places are rather deserted of crowds and hear the gulls cry overhead and watch the solemn pelicans eye you awhile—and then haul up their legs and sprawl into the air.

Viennese cooking with caviar and port every night for dinner is playing hell with my waistline—and I sleep as never before, excepting the cradle. One can't seem to wake up out here without the spur of scotch or gin. There has been plenty of that—in fact last Saturday night I danced the "Gotzottski" right on Main St. Los Angeles, while —— ——, an aviator from Riverside and a Kentuckian—

danced the Highland Fling—or as good an imitation of it as he
could manage. This after having invaded the Biltmore ballroom and
dancing with fair ladies of the haute mondaine. Albeit—and having
got our waiter drunk and having left in high dudgeon—I don't
think I'll dare attend that[?] supper club again.

After a good deal of fair "sailing" since arriving here—I am now
convinced that "flying" is even better. Right now however—and
until next weekend—I am "all fives" on the ground and life can
run as high as it wants to over in our villa without my batting an
eye. −/−/

God! you never know who you're meeting out here. . . . First
there was a snappy collegiate hanging around the studios, who
turned out to know Allen [Tate]—and then today on the beach a
mile below here, at Venice, I found myself talking literature, Spengler, Kant, Descartes and Aquinas—to say nothing of Charles Maurras
and Henri Massis—to a Bostonian of French descent who knows
Stewart Mitchell, and especially his Aunt, very well! He turned out
to be one of the best scholars I've ever met—a great reactionary toward the same kind classicism that Eliot and Lewis are fostering in
England. I had him spotted as a Romanist in less than five minutes—
but he wouldn't admit until we parted. The dialectic we had was
more rousing than the aforesaid tonic combustions of alcohol, I
admit. . . .

Winters and wife will be here visiting relatives during Christmas
week—and I look forward to that as a real event. Really, it's terribly
dulling having so many servants around, so much food, so much
tiptoeing, and ceremony. −/−/ The present "star" was once "Ariel"
in *The Tempest*—and though she still makes the welkin ring I fear
her voice will never do it again. She has adopted the pronoun "we"
to signalize her slightest thought, whim or act—and her conceit was
so wounded on spying my "Chaplinesque" during the course of her
drunken and exclamatory rampage through *Edificios Blancos*—
that she nearly passed out—and insisted on the spot that I make
instant amends by composing a sonnet to her superb P.A. (Hollywood shorthand for physical attraction) as displayed in her erstwhile success in *Peter Pan*. Hence here I am by the sea—and mightily
pleased—until the storm subsides. . . .

My Spanish quotation from Slater Brown reminds me that I now
have Joyce's *Arista Adoloscente*—a translation sent me by Marichalar who wrote a very interesting introduction.[1] He was greatly in-

1. Marichalar had written on Crane in *Revista de Occidente* (Madrid), February 1927.

terested in *The [American] Caravan* and is going to review it in the
Revista de Occidente. I must get started at my Spanish again.
Richards' *Principles of Literary Criticism* is a *great* book. One of
the few—perhaps the only one in English excepting stray remarks
by Coleridge—that get to bed rock. Weston's book, *From Ritual to
Romance*, was quite fascinating—but Winters claims that scholars
regard half her data and deductions as imaginative bunk. Did I
rave[?] to you about Elizabeth Madox Roberts' new book—*My
Heart and Flesh*—before! Anyway, I hope you'll read it. I think it
a great performance. —/—/

I'm glad you liked the Breughel book. Its humor really belonged
to you, if you get what I mean, and you therefore were more capable
of "owning" it than anyone I ever knew. If you were dead and gone
I think it would have been a better commemoration than flowers—
so take good care of it—and hand it on to your grandchildren—for
you never can tell—you may have them, you know!

1 9 2 8

295: To Peggy Baird and Malcolm Cowley

[*California*]   *Jan. 31, '28*

Dear Peggy & Mal: Writing is next to impossible—what with the
purling of fountains, the drawling of mockingbirds, the roaring of
surf, the blazing of movie stars, the barking of dogs, the midnight
shakings of geraniums, the cruising of warships, etc., etc., not to
mention the dictates of the Censor, whose absence will be welcome
sometime, I hope, when we get together again at the Dutchman's
or some rehabilitated Punch Palace where I'll at least be able to
offer some new words to the (albeit) ancient tunes! My philosophic
moments are few, but when they do occur it is almost always possible
to turn on the radio and immediately expose my soul to the rasp-
ing persuasions of Aimee McPherson, eternally ranting and evangel-
izing to packed houses at the great palm-flanked arena of Angelus
Temple. She broadcasts the news that people are frequently carried
out in pieces, arms broken, heads smashed in the stampede for salvation which she almost nightly stages, thereby emphasizing the
need of arriving early (so as to save one's body as well) and there-
upon lifts her voice into a perfectly convulsing chant, coaxing and
cuddlingly coy about "Come, all ye—" (You can catch her in it on the

Victor) the chorus of which would make a deacon's bishopric leap crimson and triumphant from the grave. . . . I haven't seen her, but they say she has beautiful long, red, wavy tresses. . . .

The peculiar mixtures of piety and utter abandon in this welter of cults, ages, occupations, etc., out here make it a good deal like Bedlam. Retired schoolmarms from Iowa, Kansas and all the corn-and-wheat belt along with millions of hobbling Methuselahs, alfalfa-fringed and querulous, side by side with crowds of ambitious but none-too-successful strumpets of moviedom, quite good to look at, and then hordes of rather nondescript people who seem just bound from nowhere into nothing—one can't explain either the motives nor means of their existence. One can generally "place" people to some extent; but out here it's mostly nix. One begins to feel a little unreal as a consequence of this—and so much more, like the perfect labyrinth of "villas"—some pseudo-Spanish, some a la Maya (the colour of stale mayonnaise), others Egyptian with a simply irresisti-ble amphora perched on the terrace, and some vaguely Chink. Our house, a large *U* with patio and fountain, rambles all over the place, and is almost vertical to the observatory on Mt. Wilson. Plenty of roses, camellias, oleanders, acacias, etc., as well as a good wine-cellar. I've just been interrupted by the butler bringing in a makeshift for champagne, composed of cardbonated apple-juice with a sling of gin; so all attempts at epistolary consecutivety are hereby and hence-forth abandoned! No, I'd better give up—I was just about to say something about the pool rooms down at San Pedro where the battle fleet rides close at anchor. Gradually I'm becoming acquainted with all the brands of bootleg that the Westcoast offers. I haven't been blinded by anything yet but beauty and sunshine, however; but I did have to get glasses to shield me from the violet rays, which are terri-bly strong out here. I'd better stop, I guess.

296: To Waldo Frank

Altadena, Cal.   *February 1, 1928*

Dear Waldo: I thought the enclosed poems might interest you as souvenirs of our tropical sojourn together. The quarry and the road leading to it, the idiot boy, etc., and the "Overheard"[1] which mocks the manner of the typical American settler's comments on the natives. . . . There is another poem, "The Air Plant," properly belonging to this series, which ought to be out soon in *The Dial*.

1. "Bacardi Spreads the Eagle's Wings."

And there was another, "O Carib Isle!," published earlier in *transition*, which also belongs. In "The Hour"[1] I attempted to secure the ground-rhythm of the hurricane.

You have been silent for so long that I cannot but doubt your interest in hearing from me. Yet I so often think of you that I have risked an intrusion regardless. —/—/

297: TO SAMUEL LOVEMAN

Altadena, Cal.   *5th Feb., 28*

Dear Sam: —/—/ First of all: my "boss" has never once failed to play the admirable host, and what is more, I continue to find him at all times most agreeable and entertaining. —/—/

I see my mother on the average of twice a week. She is located so far away that it takes a good two hours to reach her, so it nearly always means devoting practically a whole day to the occasion. My grandmother is better off than at any time for the last three years— the climate has done wonders. They have a small cottage and would be quite comfortable were they more satisfied with the general temper of the woman they brought out here to live with them. I'm not capable of judging the situation very accurately, but there's been a good deal of fretting and umbrage, very discouraging indeed to me at times. Wise has practically asked me to accompany him to Europe in the Spring, but their situation may deny me that opportunity. Mother asked immediately about you. She would rejoice at any word from you whatever.

We have met some movie actors, attended some studio screenings, etc. And I have had a fair amount of swimming and tennis. (The beaches—Long Beach, Venice, Santa Monica—are really a delight, and I have spent whole days watching the gulls, sandpipers, pelicans in their manoeuvres). But I am especially enjoying the wealth of reading and music around the house. Wise is buying all the albums of symphonies, quintettes, concertos and what-not on the Victor list. So I'm living on intimate terms for the first time with Brahms and Beethoven—the two most exciting of all to me.

The Grandmothers, I agree with you, is damned fine, although I think it weakens towards the last; Wescott seems to lose his grip. Then I've immensely enjoyed the trans. of Proust's *Sodome et Gomorrhe*, as well as Gide's *The Counterfeiters*. I also am now introduced to Heathcliff (whom I have put beside Ahab) thanks to your

1. "The Hurricane."

mention of *Wuthering Hts.* And by the way, I'm terribly excited about the poems of Gerard Manley Hopkins. Winters loaned me his copy recently (I had never read any of Hopkins before) and I have discovered that I am not as original in some of my stylisms as I had thought I was. Winters tells me that the book (Oxford edition, edited by Robert Bridges) is now out of print. I'm simply wild to secure a copy—and am wondering if you could locate me anything around New York. I'm willing to pay anything up to $10.00. Failing this, I think I shall go to work and type out the whole volume, for I've never been quite so enthusiastic about any modern before. —/—/

298: TO SLATER BROWN

[California]   *2/22/28*

Dear Bill: —/—/ A paean from Venusberg! Oy-oy-oy! I have just had my ninth snifter of Scotch. O shades of Bert Savoy! They say he had a glass eye as the result of some midnight with a mariner. But I have had no such dire results as yet. Oh BOY! Try to imagine the streets constantly as they were during that famous aggregation last May in Manhattan! And more, for they are at home here, these western argosies, at roadstead far and near—and such a throng of pulchritude and friendliness as would make your "hair" stand on end. That's been the way of all flesh with me. . . . And wine and music and such nights—WHOOPS!!!!!!!

Besides which I have met the Circe of them all—a movie actor who has them dancing naked, twenty at a time, around the banquet table. O André Gide! no Paris ever yielded such as this—away with all your counterfeiters! Just walk down Hollywood Boulevard some-day—if you must have something *out* of uniform. Here are little fairies who can quote Rimbaud before they are 18—and here are women who must have the tiniest fay to tickle them the one and only way! You ought to see B—— C—— shake her tits—and cry *apples* for a bite!

What can I write about? Yes, I am reading Wyndham Lewis' *Time and Western Man,* Fernandez' insufferable *Messages* and all the other stuff. But I would rather do as I did yesterday—after a night of wine—wake up at dawn and dip into *The Tempest,* that crown of all the Western World. What have I to say after that event. I wonder. ??? —/—/ [Act V, scene I, lines 64-68] Maybe with me someday, as good Prospero says. Perhaps—as Ceres says in the same play——/—/ [Act IV, scene I, lines 114-17] But you will tear this up—and keep me true, Bill. And if I come back to you and to the dear hills of Connecticut again, as I hope to, I shall have a cargo for your ears. —/—/

299: To WALDO FRANK

Hollywood, Calif.   *4th March 1928*

Dear Waldo: The date on your generous and welcome letter is an accusation. It is true that I haven't lacked time to answer it, long since,—but the desire to give you something more than a muddled confusion of cross purposes—and my confidence in your preference for reason and order—have detained me, though I am still by no means settled in my present environment nor do I seem any too happily disposed. But at least I have decided on a few details, for better or worse. . . .

My association with Mr. Wise, who brought me out here as private secretary, terminated about two weeks ago. Although it was unsatisfactory (my duties were extremely vague and I was neither servant nor guest) I might have stuck it out until May (when Wise returns to NY) had I felt justified in leaving my mother and grandmother alone out here in their present predicament. However, the experience of the last two years has taught me the futility of any retreat from what I, after all, must regard as my immediate responsibilities. The further I might go from the actual "scene" of operations the more obsessed I tend to become by the inert idea. So I am remaining here with the hope of securing some "literary" connection with the movies which will net me enough to be of some substantial help. When all this is over—someday—I may be able to regain the indispensable detachment from immediate concerns that such a work as my *Bridge* demands. Needless to say, I find Hollywood far from tempting in any way—but my people had moved here before I arrived, and as my grandmother is unable to move more than a few steps from her bed she is hardly in the tourist class.

Your letter was as usual—bracing! You probably don't realize it, but it had been a year since I had heard anything from you excepting a postcard. I was beginning to fear that something spurious had been repeated to you as an emanation of mine, for NY is so full of fabrications of all kinds—so, to know better was a welcome relief, also! I can well appreciate the many preoccupations which beset and hindered you. The marvel to me is the glamor and precision of your new work; I refer to the installments of it in *The N.R.* Some of my copies were lost when I was moving—and my readings were frequently interrupted and only partially realized—but the luminous impulse and essential direction I think I have apprehended. It is something more than mere analysis. Like most of your work it postulates a "Way." I have tried reading Fernandez' *Messages* and Lewis' *Time and Western Man* without being able to wholly approve a single page of either, though Fernandez is more profound. But his style (or the translator's) is abominable as compared to L.'s direct though misdirected thrusts. But L. just goes round in a desolate circle of elaborations—I can't see anything creative in his offering. Beginning with Spengler and Wells, this age seems too typically encyclopaedic. This may assist the artist in time—by erecting some kind of logos, or system of contact between the insulated departments of highly specialized knowledge and enquiry which characterize the times—God knows, some kind of substantial synthesis of opinion is needed before I can feel confident in writing about anything but my shoestrings. . . . These Godless days! I wonder if you suffer as much as I do. At least you have the education and training to hold the scalpel.

If I can't send you a new poem of my own I can at least send you a better new-old one ["Pied Beauty"] (for I don't think you have yet read him) by Gerard Manley Hopkins (Oxford) now out of print—a Victorian, posthumously printed, whose work has been a revelation to me. —/—/

300: To — — AND — —

Hollywood, Calif   *March 27th '28*

Dear — and ——: As I don't seem to get anything more out of you by means of postcards, telegrams, and such-like shorthand signals I guess it's up to me to get busy on the typewriter and pay you your due torture—though I'll try and not inflict such piercing shrieks on you again, such as my last epistle! When I get to feeling like that again I'll begin on Pres. Calles first—and that will probably save you a good deal of amazement and conjecture.

This time the news is more diverse. . . . Life is nothing if not exciting wherever ———— happens to land, if only for a few hours. It took him (or his presence) to arrange the most harrowing weekend yet, and I'm only praying that he's still alive, for when I left him in his berth in the "glory-hole" of the "California" last Sat. night he looked as though he were nearing the Pearly Gates. We were held up and beaten by a gang in San Pedro. . . . The story

is complicated and lengthy—and ———— will probably give you the
full version or as much as he can remember when he sees you.

I left Wise's ménage a week ago today. However, as —— somehow
failed to get my ship letter announcing same and the hour at which
I would meet him—he flew right up to Altadena, leaving me to wait
a *full 8 hours* by the gangway before I saw my dear "Goldy-locks."
By that time I had about finished a half pint of alcohol which I had
brought for our mutual edification, and he had completely emptied
a quart of Bacardi, also originally intended as a mutual benison.

Scene Two. Speakeasy joint with booths. Many bottles of dubious
gin and whiskey—with much "skoling"—and ———— flashing a fat pay
roll—and treating three or four still more dubious "merry andrews"
who had invited themselves to our noisy nook. It being midnight, all
ordered out.

Scene Three. A street, or rather, several streets. Our "guests" very
insistent on taking a hotel room in which to finish the fire water.
———— & I both reeling but refractory. I finally noticed ———— being
spirited away by three of them, while it was evident that I, who had
been more emphatic in my wishes, was being guarded by two others. I
broke away—and had just caught up to ———— who was being put
around a dark corner—when all five started slugging us. I put up
quite a fight, but neither of us were in much condition. They all
beat it as a car turned on a nearby corner. Both of us robbed of
everything, and ———— practically unconscious. After reporting at
police headquarters I don't know how I would have got ———— back
to his ship without the help of a sailor friend of mine whom I had
run into earlier in the evening while waiting for ————. We roused
several of his shipmates—and I'm only hoping that his bumps and
bruises haven't been any more fatal than mine. I finally had to
finish the night in a ward of the Salvation Army Hotel, and it was
five o'clock Sunday before I got enough money to get back to Hollywood. On his way back from Frisco I'm hoping to see ———— again—
but not in Pedro! Probably nothing of this had better be mentioned
to the ————'s. . . . I don't mind my losses, but I feel terribly about
————'s luck. He always seems to get the hardest end of things.

As you can see, we didn't get much time for any gossip. But he did
say that you had the most beautiful baby in the world! Wish I could
see him! Besides which I get terribly homesick out here, but might
as well not indulge myself in that emotion. My resignation from the
Wise entourage was encouraged by a number of dissatisfactions, but
as much as anything by the recognition of the fact that I must settle
here for a while at least, and do whatever I can to help my mother

during her attendance on grandmother. The two of them being completely alone out here, and none too well provided for, I couldn't get a good night's sleep in Conn. So I might as well relinquish my own wishes for awhile and try and earn some cash. Maybe scenario writing eventually. Meanwhile there are mechanical jobs such as title-writing, gag-writing, "continuity" writing, etc. I just had an interview with "Papa" Kahn this morning who is out here for a couple of weeks. He promises to help me connect with Lasky, Paramount, Wm. Fox, etc. At least I have "broken in" the movies in one way, for Pathe Newsreel or some such torture swooped down on us while we were talking in the patio of The Ambassador, and for all I know we may be thrown upon the screen together all the way from Danbury to Hong-Kong and Mozambique! I'm wearing horn-rims now—so don't be shocked.

As for my late employer—the situation became too strained to be continued. —/—/ Such circumstances don't promote a very lively morale—and it's probably better for me to lose a little of the attendant avoirdupois in favor of a more exhilarating outlook. But we are still friends so far as I know.

Every week I scour the pages of *The New Rep., Nation,* and *Herald-Tribune* for the names of our "rising generation." Have seen nothing by Malcolm for some time. Does this corroborate the news I got from Mrs. T[urner] some weeks ago that Malcolm has been laid up? Much by Robert Penn Warren, but little by his friend Tate, excepting a recent review of Winters which I thought excellent. Slater Brown, I long since neglected to mention, scored keenly in tussle with the milksop critic of Estlin C'gs in the Canby Crap Can. "The point was well taken," as my grandmother would say. And how is C'gs? for I think you told me he was pretty hard up. Mitchell seems to be bursting with new energy by the evidence in recent numbers of *The Dial.* And last, but not least in this litry column, how goes it with your translations—and how is ————? No, you're not the last, either! I must say that I haven't yet been able to decipher that defense of me by Laura [Riding], published in *Transition* along with Kay Boyle's explosive boil. I wrote her promptly, thanking her for her sentiments, but questioning her style. Her latest book announced by Jonathan Cape, is *Anarchy Is Not Enough*—and so she seems to be maintaining her consistency. Judging by the time she has already taken before answering me, I judge that I'm off her correspondence list. I shouldn't have been so rude had I thought her tender-hearted. But I can't believe that anarchy is enough—or Gertrude Stein, either. —/—/

301: TO ISIDOR SCHNEIDER

Hollywood, Calif   *March 28th, 1928*

Dear Isidor: —/—/ I often wish I had the scientific and metaphysical
training to appreciate and judge all these Whiteheads, Bradleys,
Fernandez, Wyndham Lewis-es, etc., who keep drumming up new
encyclopedias of the Future, Fate, etc. And now Waldo has written
another, especially devoted to America. I read them, puzzle and
ponder as best I'm able, but Spengler was about the only one who
flattered my capacities to the least extent. They are all so formidable,
bristling with allusions, statistics, threats and tremors, trumpets and
outcries on the least splitting of a hair which I can't locate through
the labyrinth of abstractions. I'm afraid I'd better give up trying to
make any headway in their directions—or else relinquish all attempts
to do any writing myself. For about all they really net me is a constant paralysis and distraction. I think that this unmitigated concern with the Future is one of the most discouraging symptoms of
the chaos of our age, however worthy the ethical concerns may be.
It seems as though the imagination had ceased all attempts at any
creative activity—and had become simply a great bulging eye ogling
the foetus of the next century. . . . I find nothing in Blake that
seems outdated, and for him the present was always eternity. This
is putting it crudely; but when I get some of these points a little
more definitely arranged then maybe I'll have more nerve to continue my efforts on *The Bridge*. The struggle on paper is hard
enough, but certain recent antecedent deliberations are proving
even more stubborn.

I enjoyed your historical notes and orientalia. You ought to hear
Aimee [McPherson] carry on over the radio to get the full blast of
her personality. D. Parker's review of her autobiography (*N. Yorker*)
was amusing I thought. She's a great pious Dame Quickly—and they
almost caught her with her shoes off in that "kidnapping" episode.
Coming from the ridiculous to the sublime—let me thank you for
the Isadora! That book has a certain dignity, despite many lapses,
which I expected from her; a very sad but beautiful book. Her
career would be impossible now since the War. Other reading has
included the cold glitter of Gide's *Counterfeiters* and the tremendous mosaic of Proust's *Cities of the Plain*. I never got one-third
through all the books that Wise continually ordered. But then, I'm
always taking two steps backward to Queen Bess's alleys for every
one step ahead. —/—/

302: TO GORHAM MUNSON

Hollywood, Calif.   *April 17th '28*

Dear Gorham: I certainly feel guilty—and the evidence of your cordiality in sending me your *Destinations* has not made me feel any more exemplary—for not having written you before. However you *are* exacting in the level of response which you expect from your friends, and in as much as I have been involved in a general state of doldrums so far as any creative progress has been concerned for well nigh every moment since I left NY, I haven't felt like burdening you with the mere minutiae of personal trifles in lieu of more "decisive developments" if I could help it. But here goes—anyway— if only to signal to you my pleasure in receiving your opus and to assure you that at any rate my affections are not defunct.

With the general exhortation of your book (as a whole) towards more definite spiritual knowledge and direction I find myself in close sympathy. The spiritual disintegration of our period becomes more painful to me every day, so much so that I now find myself baulked by doubt at the validity of practically every metaphor I coin. In every quarter (Lewis, Eliot, Fernandez, etc.) a thousand issues are raised for one that is settled and where this method is reversed—as with the neo-Thomists—one has nothing as substitute but an arbitrary dogmatism which seems to be too artificial [to] have any permanence or hold on the future. This "future" is, of course, the name for the entire disease, but I doubt if any remedy will be forthcoming from so nostalgic an attitude as the Thomists betray, and moreover a strictly European system of values, at that. Waldo's acute analyses now running in *The NR* strike me as wonderfully promising. He hasn't come to the constructive part of his program yet—but his ideas are promising; in a way they come to closer grips with American bogeys and vampires than any European is probably capable of seeing.

I think that *Destinations* is a transitional book with you. It contains a lot of splendid analysis, especially your discussions of technical procedures and the historical positions and relationships of various writers. Above and beyond (or enclosing) these considerations I think your demand for more order, clearer direction, etc., well justified, but on the other hand, too vaguely articulated to offer any definite system in contrast to the distraction, indifference to major issues, mere intuitiveness, etc., which you complain of in a number of writers whose work you otherwise admire. This was almost inevitable, I am forced to acknowledge, especially as I have already admitted my own quandaries in the face of such problems—but the challenge still rings for all of us. You have certainly done this much: if you have not definitely (or even begun to) articulate the concrete values of the ideal *100* per cent you have at least done some wiping on the slate and postulated *000*, or the position of the questionable ciphers. Skepticism may stop there and still claim gratitude and respect, but I am not exactly satisfied by that, and I doubt if you are. I still stake some claims on the pertinence of the intuitions; indeed some of Blake's poems and Emily Dickinson's seem more incontrovertible than ever since Relativity and a host of other ideologies, since evolved, have come into recognition.

As close and accurate scrutinies I like the Moore and Williams studies best. I don't know Dreiser well enough to judge your opinions. As for Hart Crane, I know him too well to disagree on as many points as I once did, two years ago when I first read the essay. I am certainly grateful for such expert attention, and especially on the technical side I think you express my intentions with a very persuasive gusto that has recently revived in me some conviction of "reality" here and there in my scrap heap. —/—/

303: To Slater Brown

[*California*]   *April 27*

Dear Bill: Your salute to the comments of the ny critics cracks at *him* displayed more life than I have seen around here since I arrived. Although I am still holding my sides, I'm a little sad; for I would like to have been there. Especially with Anne [Cummings] drinking gin and ——— sporting his shiners and shirt front and all the tumult and guzzling there must have been afterward! As for the critics— C'gs can be envied, in the same manner that even I can be envied, whereby I refer to the "clever" handling I recently got from Benét in the Canby crap can. At least we both have managed to evade the proverbial faint praise! Your clipping was the only one I've seen excepting a letter from Dos [Passos] in the last *Sunday Times,* and a laudatory review in the *Wall Street Journal* which Wise had noticed. I hope you and others will make as much of a controversy about it as possible. That's one thing good about Frank—he never hesitates a moment and never tires.

Since the Fleet with its twenty-five thousand gobs has left for Hawaii I have had a chance to face and recognize the full inconsequence of this Pollyanna greasepaint pinkpoodle paradise with its

everlasting stereotyped sunlight and its millions of mechanical ac-
cessories and sylphlike robots of the age of celluloid. Efforts for a
foothold in this sandstorm are still avid, but I have had little yet in
encounter. "Crashing the gate" is a familiar expression out here, and
it seems to be exclusively applied to the movie industry. To cap the
climax I have to endure my mother's apparently quenchless desire
that I become an actor! But if I can hold on until the middle of May
I'm due for an interview with Jesse Lasky (HIMSELF) and maybe
through that entree I can creep into some modest dustpan in the
reading dept. of Paramount. Your friend Dietz, by the way, draws a
cool $750.00 a week as their ad. mgr.

It's good to think of you as back near Patterson. I had a good letter from Malcolm. It all makes me homesick. Things like that cro-
quet game in the rain, the afternoon at the cider mill, the skeleton
surry ride and the tumble down the hill! I haven't a thing to send
for the *transition* Am. issue. I can't imagine ever having anything to
say out here except in vituperation of the scene itself. If I could "afford" to go to work on some ranch it might be otherwise, but that,
under present circumstances, doesn't seem advisable.

Have just discovered the presence here of Mrs. Alice Barney, the
world-famous grande dame and mother of Nathalie Clifford Barney
of Paris, friend of Valéry, translator, — — — —. As she is a great friend
of Underwood of Washington I have been invited to her next weekly
"evening." She ought to be a little different than the typical Hollywood hostess—perhaps mildly Proustian. God knows I need some
sort of diversion besides bus rides and the rigor mortis of the local
hooch. — — —

304: TO WALDO FRANK

Patterson,   *June 12th '28*

Dear goodhearted Brother: Your loan has been a godsend and I am
only afraid I have appeared insensitive in not writing my thanks before. But you've been very busy getting settled, I know, and probably haven't had any such extra thoughts. It's nice, damned fine, of
you to ask me up—maybe I'll be able to make it along in August. But
it's a slim chance. I want above all things to get *The Bridge* completed this summer, and aside from the necessity of taking any work
which may come along I'll need to keep my head or rather my nose
away from too tempting horizons. But at least I *trust* we'll have a
reunion and a long visit in the Fall.

I meant long ago to tell you my rather disappointing experience with Charlie.[1] During my first month on the Coast I happened to meet him sitting in his favorite restaurant one evening. I had a friend with me and he was also engaged, but I stopped for a moment in passing to say hello—identifying myself with you (whose address he wanted immediately). I later sent him an inscribed copy of *White Buildings* along with a letter, but never got any response further than a formal letter from his secretary acknowledging receipt of same, etc. As I had already urged him to dine with me (my boss, Mr. Wise, was simply wild to meet him and entertain him) I couldn't press matters much further. He was simply too busy otherwheres to be interested—that was obviously it—and all the stars have built walls of mystery about themselves as impregnable as Carcassonne! Just try to get them on the phone sometime! But Charlie surely was never so radiant and handsome as when I saw him. . . . Hair snow-white, which means almost as white as the smiling flash of his teeth, and those same eyes of genius.

I'm hardly qualified to give you any fair report on my reactions to your *NR* series. I've missed several and those I did get a chance to read (out west) were read under disturbing circumstances. I remember such chapters as "Let's be Comfortable," "News as a Toy," and the recent chapter on "The Arts" as especially keen analysis. The first two or three chapters seemed to hint at a little strain or rush; this more from their almost painful condensation of material and opinion than from other cause. But I ought to re-read them before barking. I can't think of any living American with greater integrity or courage, you prove it on every page. The completed book will come out in the late fall, I take it. — — — —

305: To Isidor & Helen Schneider

Patterson, N. Y.   *July 16th, 1928*

Dear Isidor & Helen: Your good Parisian letter reached me here on about the third week after my return from the Coast. Leaving about the middle of May, I took the southern route across Texas to New Orleans, then down the Mississippi and up to NY by boat. The old French quarter of New Orleans with its absinthe speakeasies and wonderful cooking seemed unspeakably mellow and gracious after all the crass mechanical perfection of Hollywood, and the six hours New York harbor looked both stridently busy and enormously

1. Charlie Chaplin.

friendly in the early morning light. I was mightily glad to get back among friends; I could find no work in California and excessively hysterical conditions arose between me and my family there. Altogether it was intolerable. I feel more like myself again, back in my familiar room at Mrs. Turner's. Besides, we have located a marvellous bootlegger on a neighboring hill, who makes better beer than I've had north of Cuba! —/—/

306: To His Father

New York City   *August 14th, 1928*

Dear Father: Your letter, forwarded from Patterson, reached me yesterday, I have been offered the use of the flat of a friend of mine [Cowley] who is spending the summer in the country, and I'm fortunate enough to have it for several weeks. I've been cooking my own meals and doing my best without the help of a flatiron to keep myself looking spruce, but my shoes are giving out as well as the several small loans that friends have given me—and so far I haven't been able to make any connection with ad. work. I guess I'll have to give that up.

I agree with you completely in what you say about learning a trade; in fact I have wanted to learn some regular trade like typesetting, linotyping, etc., for a long time back. However, connections that pay anything whatever while learning these trades are hard to find out about. And, of course, I need something more than air to live on in the meantime. I'm going to do my best during the next few days to find a job as a plumber's or mechanic's helper. The work is physically heavier than I have been used to for a long time, but I fancy I can make the adjustment in due time. The way things are now I'll consider myself lucky to get anything. —/—/

307: To His Father

New York City   *August 19, 1928*

Dear Father: I hope you won't blame me for utilizing the check enclosed in your letter for some immediate necessities, without which my first pay day would seem even longer away! I can refund the money to you later. Meanwhile it will seem good to have something definite to do—as well as something definite to eat.

As I wired you, I start in tomorrow. The job isn't much, but it can tide me over to something better. A former Cleveland acquaintance of mine has opened a book store here. He needs to be out a good deal collecting stock, rare editions, etc., and I'm coming in as clerk, besides which I shall have some work to do on his catalogues, make-up, etc. The offer wasn't made until last Friday, else I should have let you know sooner.

This may strike you as a rather poor alternative to your invitation to return to Cleveland, but as there are two or three real possibilities hanging fire here—and of considerable ultimate importance,—I feel that I am justified in staying on the ground. One in particular, the editorship of a magazine, I should hate to risk missing. Thank you a lot though, Father, for your interest and help. —/—/

308: TO CHARLOTTE AND RICHARD RYCHTARIK

Brooklyn, New York   *Sept 16th, 1928*

Dear Charlotte and Richard: It has hurt me to think that you thought me indifferent about returning the remainder of the money that you so kindly loaned me. I confess my guilt: it *could* have been done before. But nevertheless at *no* time since you wrote me asking for it. Owing to the recent death of my Grandmother Hart (in Hollywood) I shall, however, be able to discharge the obligation fairly soon, as I come into a slight inheritance which will take care of several debts. I have been struggling without any money for weeks, but have finally secured a decent job with an advertising agency here.

This is perhaps a futile letter to write, since our friendship seems to have been already sacrificed. But I owe it to myself perhaps as much as to you to give you rightful evidence of my continued intention of honest behavior, no matter what you may have thought of me. You don't know how often I have thought of you and regretted the circumstances of your recent loss of interest in me. You don't know the extent to which I feel gratefully indebted to you both for many things outside the realm of money or anything that money could ever buy. But there is no use in trying to make apologies. As long as I believe in myself I shall insist on my good intentions and with the ultimate faith of putting them into practice. I can never, of course, ask others as much as that.

If you will be friendly enough to answer *this* letter some time in the next three months I shall be glad to know that at least I may be sure of your present address. Otherwise, I'll have to ask someone in

Cleveland to look you up in the directory or telephone book to ascertain your present whereabouts at the time I'm able to write a check out.

309: TO CHARLOTTE RYCHTARIK

Brooklyn, NY   *Oct. 23rd, 1928*

Dear Charlotte: —/—/ Your letter made me feel a lot better. It lifted a load from my spirit that I had felt for many months. I really need to *see* you, *talk* with you to explain what a hell the last two years have been. Perhaps you'd then see how it has been almost impossible for me to write anyone. For who wants to hear nothing but troubles? I've waited, putting off writing again and again, hoping to have something interesting to offer—for that is what such as you and Richard deserve.

I can realize how deeply you have felt the loss of your mother. You seem to have been having your share of tribulations. . . . O, I know. . . . How I wish I could have seen you on your way through New York when you came back from Europe! Now it may be some time before we get together again. There is much to say, but little to tell —if you get what I mean. I haven't had a creative thought for so long that I feel quite lost and *spurlos versenkt*. My present job lasts another week, and then I must tramp around again to find another. Moving around, grabbing onto this and that, stupid landladies— never enough sense of security to relax and have a fresh thought— that's about all the years bring besides new and worse manifestations of family hysteria. It's a great big bore! I feel like saying what the Englishman did: "Too many buttons to button and unbutton. I'm through!" — — — —

310: TO MALCOLM COWLEY

[Brooklyn]   *the 20th of the 28th at the A.M. 7-thirtieth*

Dear Malcolm: After the passionate pulchritude of the usual recent maritime houreths—before embarking for the 20th story of the Henry L Doherty Co's 60 on Wall Street story—I salute your mss which arrived yesterday morning—as well as the really cordial apologies accompanying them for the really unhappy hours inaugurated last week by the hysteria of S. God damn the female temperament! I've had thirty years of it—lacking six months—and know something myself.

It's me for the navy or Mallorca damned quick. Meanwhile sort-
ing securities of cancelled legions ten years back—for filing—pax
vobiscum—With Wall Street at 30 per—and chewing gum for lunch—

But here I am—full of Renault Wine Tonics—after an evening
with the Danish millionaire on Riverside—and better, thank God, a
night with a bluejacket from the Arkansas—raving like a 'mad. And
it's time to go to work. So long. . . . I'll be careful with the mss.[1]
And your book'll be out within 7 months. . . . About time! God
bless you and give my love to Peggy! And as W. J. Turner says: "O
hear the swan song's traffic's cry!"

311: To MALCOLM COWLEY

Brooklyn, NY   *Dec. 1, 1928*

Dear Malcolm: It has been a pleasure for me to spend part of the
last two days in typing the mss. of your book. Certainly I have been
on more intimate terms with the poems than ever, and my enthusiasm has been heightened thereby rather than in any way diminished.

I now have two copies, one to turn over to the "secret" arbiter[2]
here and one to take with me to England. Whatever may or may not
happen over there I'll at least be sure of having you along with me—
which is much. By the way, if the mss. is returned to you, refused, be
sure to send it at once to Coward-McCann, who, I understand, are
calling for new poets and planning some kind of series of them.
Hanna [Josephson] spoke to me about this yesterday.

Although I hope to get off next Saturday (probably on the *Tuscania*) I'm not at all certain. The bank behaves too strangely—now
ignores my letters not to mention telegram. The meddlesome old
nanny that is handling the matter there will soon hear from me
through a lawyer if things don't take a new turn by Monday. That's
the only way to handle it, I guess. I'm to see Art Hays Monday and
talk it over. At any rate, I think it would be foolish to bring my
troubles over to London with me and have them poison my first impressions of the place.

To get back to the poems: I omitted practically nothing but the
Decorations. The arrangement you made is ideal. As to the places
for the following, I think you'll agree that they are ideal:

"Tumbling Mustard" just before "Memphis Johnny"

1. Cowley's *Blue Juniata*.
2. Gorham Munson, at this time an editorial adviser for Doubleday, Doran.

"Still Life" just before "Seaport" (it doesn't fit in the Grand Manner section particularly)

"Two Winter Sonnets" just after "St. Bartholomew" (they come in eloquently there)

Really the book as we now have it has astonishing structural sequence. Most of the more doubtfully important poems come in the central section. There is the fine indigenous soil sense to begin with in the Juniata, and the eloquent and more abstract matter mounting to a kind of climax toward the end. Hope you don't mind my enthusiasm!

See *Show Boat* when you come to town. Wise took me last night; the beautiful new Ziegfield Theatre has them all beat—and the settings, songs, costumes and glistening lithe girlies! Like greased lightning—the suave mechanical perfection of the thing.

You may not hear from me again if I leave next Saturday, but Mrs. Turner will be informed when I leave anyway. I'll see that your mss. (the original) is remailed to you registered, early next week. ——— and I went on the best bat ever last night—Sam's [Loveman] old place —finally two cops came in and joined the party at three o'clock— asked ——— to marry me and live with me in Spain—but she's got to wait for her divorce from the Danish gaucho now on the pampas.

312: TO SAMUEL LOVEMAN

[R.M.S.] Tuscania off Newfoundland   *Dec. 9 '28*

Ahoy Sam! The ship is rearing like a high-strung broncho—and I'm out walking the quarter-deck much of the time—enjoying the rhythmical lift and plunge of it. We've had high seas running and sleet and rain since Sandy Hook but I've been down for every meal. O it's great! The bad gin pains are leaving my head and—taking only the bad memories with them—*not* the pleasant thoughts of you and Mony [Grunberg] and others.

This is a pleasant boat—not at all crowded—and such nice people. English servants know how to be pleasant as well as efficient. And of course I *would* be given the one nearly handsome English waiter in the salon! Rather tough food—but I'm getting used to it. The whiskey—which is all I've tried thus far—is like balm of Gilead—or whatever Poe said. A little goes a long ways—and really doesn't sadden one.

P.S. Melville makes fine reading on this trip.

313: TO SAMUEL LOVEMAN
(Postcard)

Off Cornwall [England]   *[December 13]*

Gorgeous weather all the way. Today is like the "Tristram" verse of
Swinburne. Millions of sea gulls following us and soaring overhead
with such a flood of golden light as seems tropical. The coast of
Cornwall in sight, and Plymouth by tea time.

314: TO CHARMION WIEGAND

R.M.S. Rumrunia off the Coast of Ireland   *near Christmas '28*

Dear Charmion: My performance given at the Anderson party last
summer was but a slight forecast to the splendors of my behavior
night before last—when at a bal masque, dressed in a red coat of a
sergeant-major, sailor hat, shark swagger stick, etc.—I essayed a der-
vish whirl. But I seem to have made no enemies and rum has become the favorite drink throughout the cabin.

If anything, I've had almost too good a time! I have been the only
native American in the whole tourist cabin. The rest being British-
ers, Canadians, Australians visiting relatives abroad, etc.—and all of
them the pleasantest crowd I ever met. Think I'm going to like London entirely too well for an early take-off to Spain. One old squire
took me for a Cambridge man—and I admit that after a day or two
in conflab with some of these natives one does tend to lose one's
"middle-western accent."

You must excuse my exuberance momentarily at least. I can't stop
being tremendously pleased at the wonderful ale, the pleasant manners of practically everybody (and one gets such graceful and attentive service everywhere), the balmy spring air, and the prospect of
meeting more of such people soon on foreign shores. I feel really
rested now, despite a hectic round of pleasures.

It was so nice of you to come to the little beer party. When I think
of the mad rush of that last day I'm moved to wonder how I ever
kept on my feet. But I enjoyed the evening after all. Hope you met
some people that you liked. I'm always a little vain about my
friends. —/—/

315: TO WALDO FRANK

[London, England]   *December 28 '28*

Dear Waldo: Landed here with incipient flu but have managed
to stave it off with good Jamaica rum and quinine. The city is

soberly impressive—full of courtesy and deep character. I feel now as
though I'd like to settle here—and even might—later on. But it's too
expensive to linger long now—and I'm apt to be off to Paris next
week. Shall not stay there very long, either, as I want to get settled
and at work.

Am expecting to meet Edgell Rickword soon but not many others.
Laura Riding and Robert Graves (friend of Col. Lawrence and the
one who introduced Cummings here) have been delightfully hospitable. I had a most luscious plum pudding with them Christmas
— — — — on the Thames at Hammersmith in front of Wm. Morris'
old headquarters.

No snow here at all—and the grass as green as summer in the
parks. I've already seen a great deal—tramping about by myself,
drinking Australian wine with old charwomen in Bedford Street—
talking with ex-soldiers, and then the National Gallery with the
marvelous "Agony in the Garden" of El Greco. The beautiful black
and white streaked stone facades of the buildings make me quite
sentimental. London is negative (as Laura says) but one gets a
chance to breathe and deliberate. And there is something genuine
about nearly every Englishman one meets. I feel almost too much
at home.

Your pipe grows mellower every day. It's a little like Paul Robeson's voice—and I've been enjoying him by the way. He and Essie
have taken a sumptuous home of an ex-ambassador to Turkey for
the rest of his engagement. But he's anxious to get to Paris to earn
some astonishing laurels offered him there. —/—/

1 9 2 9

316: To Samuel Loveman
(Postcard)

[Paris, France]   *[January 23, 1929]*

Dinners, soirées, poets, erratic millionaires, painters, translations,
lobsters, absinthe, music, promenades, oysters, sherry, aspirin, pictures, Sapphic heiresses, editors, books, sailors. *And How!*

317: To Joseph Stella

Paris   *January 24th, 1929*

Dear Mr. Stella: Sometime before leaving America Charmion

Habicht [Wiegand] showed me a copy of your privately issued monograph called "New York," containing your essay on Brooklyn Bridge
and the marvelous paintings you made not only of the Bridge but
other New York subjects. This has been the admiration of everyone
to whom I have shown it. And now I am writing you to ask if you will
give permission to an editor friend of mine to reproduce the three
pictures—"The Bridge," "The Port," and the one called "The Skyscrapers." He would also like to reprint your essay.

I am referring to Mr. Eugene Jolas who is an editor of *transition*
—a magazine which you have probably heard of. He would like to
use this material in the next number if you will be so kind as to
give us permission. *transition* is able to pay little or nothing now
for contributions, but, since our friend Varèse has told me that your
essay has never been printed in any journal, we feel that so splendid
and sincere a document should have wider circulation than private
printing has allowed it.

I have also a private favor of my own to ask of you. I should like
permission to use your painting of the Bridge as a frontispiece to a
long poem I have been busy on for the last three years—called *The
Bridge*. It is a remarkable coincidence that I should, years later, have
discovered that another person, by whom I mean you, should have
had the same sentiments regarding Brooklyn Bridge which inspired
the main theme and pattern of my poem. —/—/

318: To Gertrude Stein

[*Paris*]   *Jan. 31, '29*

Dear Miss Stein: May I introduce myself as a friend of your friend,
Laura Riding?

And on that presumption may I ask to see you some hour early
next week—whenever it may suit your convenience to have me
call—?

I am going away for the weekend, but shall probably be back by
Monday evening. I hope I may hear from you.

319: To Malcolm Cowley

[*Paris*]   *Feb. 4 '29*

Dear Malcolm: Time here flies faster than I can count. And now
along comes the good news from you about the book of poems. Of
course I'm all the happier that you got better terms from Hal

[Smith]—it's all to the good. But I do hope that you have seen Munson by this time, and at least thanked him for his interest. For the very fact that you were able to make such an announcement to Hal may well have influenced his interest to a great extent. Such matters are rather officious for me to mention I fear, but I do think Munson deserves some real credit. —/—/

I'm dizzy, also, with meeting people. "Teas" are cocktails here—and then that's just the start of the evening. And as lions come these days, I'm known already, I fear, as the best "roarer" in Paris.

Have just returned from a weekend at Ermenonville (near Chantilly) on the estate of the Duc du Rochefoucauld where an amazing millionaire by the name of Harry Crosby has fixed up an old mill (with stables and a stockade all about) and such a crowd as attended *is* remarkable. I'm invited to return at any time for any period to finish *The Bridge,* but I've an idea that I shall soon wear off my novelty. Anyway, Crosby, who inherited the famous Walter Berry (London) library, has such things as first editions of Hakklyt [Hakluyt] (I can't spell today) and is going to bring out a private edition of *The Bridge* with such details as a reproduction of Stella's picture in actual color as frontispiece.

He's also doing Lawrence, Cummings and Kay Boyle. It takes a book to describe the Crosbys—but it has (I mean the connection) already led me to new atrocities—such as getting drunk yesterday and making violent love to nobility. As — — — — was just about to marry, I couldn't do better, though all agree (including Kay Boyle and Lawrence Vail) that I did my best. —/—/

320: To Waldo Frank

[*Paris*]   *February 7th, 1929*

Dear Waldo: It would take volumes to tell you all that's happened—mainly the people I've met, I fear, and just that sort of thing. For I haven't got down to work yet, and probably won't do so until I get off to some quieter place in the country. This City, as you know, is the most interesting madhouse in the world. But I intend getting away as soon as possible. Not to Spain, though, for a while. I want to learn French—and as you know, Mallorca won't teach me Spanish either. So the above bank address is good for some time. And please don't forget to send me your *Re-discovery of America* now, as soon as possible. I need it as a balance against the seductions of Europe, for I'm afraid I *am* being seduced by the astonishing ease of life hereabouts. Paris really is a test for an American, I'm beginning to feel. And I'm so far from certain that I'm equal to it in my present mood that I'm quite uneasy. However, things don't look so bad. —/—/ I had thought of going to Villefranche, but after last week-end at Ermenonville I changed my mind. The beautiful grounds of the Chateau, donkeys and bikes to ride, a whole tower to myself and all the service that millionaires are used to having—all that is very alluring, and I would be quite alone except for the gatherings on weekends. But Harry is highly erratic and nothing may come of it. I may go out to Jolas's place in Haute-Marne instead. At any rate I won't be far from Paris.

I can't tell you how deeply I appreciate your generous pains in sending me the letters of introduction. Gide, I heard, left for Africa a few days before your letter reached me. I haven't looked up Larbaud yet, but intend to. I trust that I can use those for Spain at any time in the future, for I do intend going to Spain, you know, perhaps before the end of this year. Jolas took me around to meet Soupault and his wife who entertain a good deal and who have been very generous with me. I haven't had a good talk yet with Aragon but have met him several times along with others. An amazingly handsome fellow, I think, who possesses an elegance that is rare. I went to see Gertrude Stein despite my indifference to most of her work. One is supposed to inevitably change one's mind about her work after meeting her. I haven't, but must say that I've seldom met so delightful a personality. *And* the woman is beautiful! AND the Picassos!

Margy [Naumburg] has been here but I haven't yet seen her. Everyone has been having colds and flu and she didn't escape. There is no point, I'm sure, in listing more names, as it might well bore you. Certainly I'm a bit tired with all the talking and chattering, however interesting it is at times. I feel a great need to get into myself again, and into my work. When I consider that it has been over a year since I have written anything longer than scratch notes for *The Bridge* I'm almost overwhelmed. What a year it has been, too! It has been the most decisive year of my life in a number of ways. But I also find that I now need more strength than ever. —/—/

321: TO CHARLOTTE AND RICHARD RYCHTARIK

[*Paris*]   *Feb. 26th, 1929*

Dear Charlotte & Richard: First of all—before you read another word of this—you must swear to me not to repeat to anyone that you have even heard from me, not even that you know where I am. I hate to begin my letter so seriously, but in time you will know more about *why* I don't want my family to find my whereabouts right now. I am very serious about this request, and I'm sure that you have enough interest in my work to abstain from any action which would cripple me.

It was fine to hear from you—two good long letters—and to know that all is going along so well in every way. I'm especially glad that you, Richard, have received such good notice and representation in the theatre literature which you mentioned. And from the other matters mentioned, I judge that Cleveland has been far from a cemetery—part of the credit for which is due to you both, *I know.* The Christmas card was a beauty, but then, so are all of them that you have ever made!

I scarcely know how to begin to tell you all that's been happening to me during the last year. But here's a brief summary, omitting thousands of details, all of which, however, are really important. . . . During my sojourn with the millionaire in California last winter my mother made life so miserable for me with incessant hysterical fits and interminable nagging that I had to steal off east again, like a thief in the night, in order to save my sanity or health from a complete breakdown. I went back to Patterson and tried to pull myself together, without money or prospects of any kind. Then in September, after I had secured a good job with an advertising agency, my Grandmother died, leaving me the inheritance which my grandfather bequeathed me over fifteen years ago.

Of course there had been a coolness between my mother and me ever since I left California. The net result of this was that (being co-executor of the estate with the Guardian Trust Co.) she held back her signature to the papers for weeks, pretending to be too ill to sign her name. And finally she threatened to do all sorts of things if I did not come at once to California and spend it with her—among which she said she would write to my father and try to get him to intercede with the bank against paying me! This could have no effect whatever, but you may gather a little bit from what I have said about just how considerate and honorable she was! I can't begin to tell you about all the underground and harrowing tactics she employed. Got people who were practically strangers to write me threatening and scolding letters, so that I never came home from work without wonder—and trembling about what next I should find awaiting me. She had, through abuse, destroyed all the affection I had for her before I left the west; but now she made me actually hate her. I finally had to consult a lawyer, who directed his guns on the bank. This finally brought results. In the meantime I had given up all my plans about buying a little country place in Connecticut, for her ultimate home as much as mine. There was literally no other sensible plan but to take my money and get out of communication as soon as possible.

After having received written promise from the bank (as well as an advance) that the money would be in my hands by a certain day, I went ahead and engaged steamer passage to London. But the bank did not even keep its word, and I did not actually get the money until a few hours before the boat sailed. You can imagine my state of mind. I got on the boat more dead than alive. And I have not since had the least desire to know what is going on in California, and doubt if I ever *shall* care. Since my mother has made it impossible for me to live in my own country I feel perfectly justified in my indifference. I have had no particular quarrel with my father, and shall write him sometime after *The Bridge* is done and I don't fear mental complications. Meanwhile I'm so sure that she has carried out her threat and written him certain things that I'd rather keep out of it all. Twenty-five years of such exhausting quibbling is enough, and I feel I owe myself a good long vacation from it all. Neither one of them really cares a rap for me anyway. I have much more to tell you sometime, but this is enough for now. . . .

—/—/ Went to the famous dangerous and tough Limehouse section expecting some exciting adventures, but found that most of the young toughs drank only lemonade—and after I had had several swigs of Scotch they all seemed to be afraid of me! O life is funny! I'd like to go back to England sometime in the summer of the year. The damp, raw cold was like a knife in my throat—and the hotels like cellars. I left there on the 7th of January, and life has been like a carnival ever since—here in Paris.

I've never been in such a social whirl—all sorts of amusing people, scandalous scenes, cafe encounters, etc. Writers, painters, heiresses, counts and countesses, Hispano-Suizas, exhibitions, concerts, fights, and—well, you know Paris, probably better than I do. I had originally intended to stop here only two or three weeks on the way to a permanent location at Mallorca, one of the Balearic Islands (Spain). But I've fallen so much in love with the French and French ways that I've decided to stay here until summer anyway, and try to learn the language before leaving.

All sorts of things have happened. Through Eugene Jolas, editor of *transition*, I met Harry Crosby who is heir to all the Morgan-

Harjes millions and who is the owner of a marvelous de luxe publishing establishment here. —/—/ He has renovated an old mill
(16th century) out on the ground of the chateau of the Comte du
Rochefoucauld at Ermenonville where I have spent several wild weekends. Polo with golf sticks on donkeys! Old stagecoaches! Skating on
the beautiful grounds of the chateau! Oysters, absinthe, even
opium, which I've tried, but don't enjoy. I had the pleasure, last
week, of spending five days out there working all by myself, with
just the gardener and his wife bringing me food and wine beside a
jolly hearth-fire. And the beautiful forests all around—like the setting for *Pelléas et Mélisande!* I'm going out again soon. Meanwhile
I dream of how fine they've promised to publish *The Bridge*—on
sheets as large as a piano score, so none of the lines will be broken—
and they have already sent to the Brooklyn Art Museum to have
the Stella picture of the Bridge copied in color for reproduction as a
frontispiece! —/—/

322: TO SAMUEL LOVEMAN

(Postcard)

[Collioure, France]   *April 23 '29*

Nightingales all night and the sound of surf all day! I don't know
what could rival this spot for form and color. Hope you are alright
—you certainly haven't wasted much ink telling me!

323: TO SLATER BROWN

Collioure, Pyrénées-Orientales   *25 Avril '29*

Bill: Why the hell don't you write to me? You used to. And here I
am, sitting by the shore of the most shockingly beautiful fishing
village—with towers, baronial, on the peaks of the Pyrenees all
about, wishing more than anything else that you were on the other
side of the table.

This begins to look as good as the West Indies. Maybe—if I could
talk Catalan it would be better. I began to feel as you predicted
about Paris. Wish you were with me! I don't know whether you want
to hear from me or not—since you have never written—but here's
my love anyway, Bill—

324: TO GERTRUDE STEIN
(Postcard)

[Collioure]   *[ca. April 29]*

There has been too much wind to notice odors. I like it so far, and
expect to stay awhile. Feel quite indigenous since spending last
night out on a sardine schooner. The dialect isn't so easily assimi-
lated.

325: TO ISIDOR SCHNEIDER

Collioure, Pyr.-Orientales   *May 1st, 1929*

Dear Isidor: —/—/ As regards creative writing—I can't say that
I'm finding Europe extremely stimulating. I left home in a bad
state of nerves and spirit and haven't exactly recovered yet, so perhaps my reactions are not as fresh as they might be. Perhaps a few
weeks of the quiet of places like this ancient fishing port may change
my mind—but at any rate I haven't so far completed so much as one
additional section to *The Bridge*. It's coming out this fall in Paris,
regardless. — — — — If it eventuates that I have the wit or inspiration
to add to it later—such additions can be incorporated in some later
edition. I've alternated between embarrassment and indifference for
so long that when the Crosbys urged me to let them have it, de-
claring that it reads well enough as it already is, I gave in. Malcolm
advised as much before I left America, so I feel there may be some
justification. The poems, arranged as you may remember, do have
I think, a certain progression. And maybe the gaps are more evident
to me than to others . . . indeed, they must be. —/—/ I recently
have been informed that the 1st edition of *White Bldgs.* is sold out.
There won't be another for awhile, I guess. There were only 500
printed, just half the number that I, until recently, had supposed.
But that's the usual number, I'm told.

   I do hope you prevail on L[iveright] to bring out Hopkins' verse.
But I doubt it. I think he's a bit thick-skinned to sympathize. Recently a friend of Laura Riding and Graves, Geoffrey Phibbs, whom
I've never met, sent me a copy right out of a clear sky. I was dumb-
foundered—for it certainly is rare when such wealthy bibliophiles
as Harry Crosby are unable through all their London agents to
locate a copy. So when I come back, we'll have at least one copy "in
the family" as it were! whatever Liveright decides.

London, I can still believe, might be delightful under proper circumstances. I had incipient flu before I landed, then the raw cold of the particular season, the bad hotel accommodations, the indigestible food AND Laura's [Riding] hysterical temper at the time —all combined to send me off with no particular regrets. It's certainly the most expensive place I can imagine—more than even New York unless you're really settled down. I loved its solid, ponderous masonry —and the gaunt black-and-white streakings and shadings. It's a city for the etcher. I must tell you about my excursion to Limehouse sometime—where, expecting to be blackjacked, etc., I drank so many scotch-and-sodas during a game of darts in one of the pubs, that I frightened people, actually scared some of the toughs about—all of whom struck me as being very pleasant people. I'd like to go there again and stay longer sometime—but not during the winter!

As for Paris,, I'll have to wait until I see you to touch the subject. Phillipe Soupault and his wife were about the most hospitable French people I met, and Gertrude Stein about the most impressive personality of all. The marvellous room of hers, the Picasso's, Juan Gris and others (including some very interesting youngsters) on the walls! Then there were Ford Madox Ford, Wescott, Bernadine Szold (just back from the Orient), Richard Aldington, Walter Lowenfels (who has an interesting book of verse coming out in England—(Heinemann), Emma Goldman, Klaus Mann, Eugene MacCown, Jolas (whom I like very much), Edgar Varèse, Rene Crevel, Kay Boyle, (who has decided she likes me) and a hundred others just as interesting, or more so, who aren't particularly known. The Tates are living in Ford's apartment while he is away, and declare they never want to leave Paris. I like it all too well, myself, but would have to live there a long while before I could settle down to accomplish any work, I fear. And lately—all cities get on my nerves after a few weeks. I'd never want to settle down for good over here like many do, however,—town *or* country. For even here by the blue inland sea, with ancient citadels and fortifications crowning the heights of a lovely white-walled, village—I can't help thinking of my room out there in Patterson. Silly, I know . . . but what can one do about it?

My plans are vague. May stay here two months more or only two weeks. Spain is very near, but also, I hear, very expensive. I'm crossing over to a nearby town to see a bull fight in a couple of days. But I may not explore it much further at the time, regardless of my intense interest. There are other small ports between here and

Marseille which are very intriguing. I can't regret not seeing everything this trip—or even never. You see I like France pretty well!
— — — —

326: To Allen Tate

Marseille,   *11 June '29*

Dear Allen: —/—/ I didn't stay more than three weeks at Collioure.
Since then I've been in and about Marseille, a city which has a great
deal of interest to me, although there's nothing whatever here to interest the usual type of tourist. Have just come back from two weeks
visiting Roy Campbell and family out at Martigues, a sort of Venice
and Gloucester combined, being built on three islands made by
canals joining the Etang de Berre with the sea.

I have come to love Provence, the wonderful Cezannesque light
(you see him everywhere here) and the latinity of the people. Arabs,
Negros, Greeks, and Italian and Spanish mixtures. The Campbells
rent a house and have a maid for almost nothing, but swimming
isn't good there and there are other features which might not appeal
to you as much as the country east of here where you are planning
to go. Marsden Hartley whom I encountered here knows the whole
coast, both sides of the Rhone, and prefers it here. I'm coming back
to Paris within a couple of weeks but may take a swift excursion
over to Nice and environs beforehand, just to see what I've missed
by hanging around here so long. Then maybe my advice will be
worth more than at present.

I'm planning on returning to N.Y. before very long. How soon
depends largely on what I hear from the Crosbys on my return to
Paris regarding their edition of *The Bridge.* I'm anticipating a good
visit with you and Carolyn [Gordon] before many days. Thanks a
lot for the money order, exactly correct in amount, and quite provi-
dential at the moment as the bank has been slow in forwarding me
funds. — — — —

327: To Waldo Frank
(Postcard)

[Marseille]   *June 17, 1929*

Can't get around to that long and grateful letter to you that you
so much deserve. Why?—don't ask me yet! But it isn't because I don't
often long to see you. I have been in an undecided state since before
we last met. I pray for relief.

328: To Malcolm Cowley

[Paris]   *July 3rd, 1929*

Dear Malcolm: Since reading the proofs I'm certain that the book is even better than before. And the notes!—When you first mentioned them to me I admit having trembled slightly at the idea. But since seeing them I haven't a doubt. The maturity of your viewpoint is evident in every word. Humor and sincerity blend into some of the cleverest and adroit writing I know of, leaving the book a much more solidified unit than it was before. I haven't had the original mss. with me for comparison, but wherever I have noted changes they seem to be for the better. Nor do I regret any of the additions. I like the added bulk of the book. Really, Malcolm—if you will excuse me for the egoism—I'm just a little proud at the outcome of my agitations last summer. *Blue Juniata* will have a considerable sale for a long period to come, for the bulk of it has a classical quality—both as regards material and treatment—that won't suffer rejection by anyone who cares or who will later care for American letters.

I would particularize more copiously except that I'm expecting to see you within relatively so short a time. . . . I'll be back in NY by the first of September at the latest, and I may be back a month before. Perhaps it's just as well that a good part of my money is tied up in a savings account in New York and inaccessible to me here. As it is, I haven't any great regrets about coming back at this time. When I come to France again I'll sail direct for Marseille—and it's certainly my intention to come again! I'm looking forward to talking it all over with you—so get a little cider ready for the occasion! —/—/

329: To Caresse Crosby

Patterson, New York   *August 8th, 1929*

Dear Caresse: Herewith are the gloss notes that I showed you, now corrected and ready to include with the composition of the first two sections of *The Bridge*. You will see where each block of them falls by the *key lines* typed at the left. I have kept them narrow as that seems to be the custom—and we don't want to crowd our margins. (See MacLeish's *Hamlet* and the version of "The Ancient Mariner" as printed in the *Oxford Anthology*.) I can't help thinking them a great help in binding together the general theme of "Powhatan's Daughter." As for the Columbus note, it simply silhouettes the scenery before the colors arrive to inflame it. . . .

I'm working on the other remaining sections indicated in the index of the ms. as you have it, and hope to get a couple of them off to you within ten days. I haven't had a chance to see Mr. Fox, director of the Brooklyn Museum, yet, as he has been away on his vacation, but have an appointment made with his secretary for early next week. I'm hoping to see Harry Marks as soon as he returns in order to ask his advice about having a copy made of the picture, the amount to pay, etc. Meanwhile, from what Harry [Crosby] said, I judge that you are going ahead with setting certain sections. Don't rush along too fast, though—please! If we get it out by the last of November it will be soon enough. Meanwhile I'm not negotiating with Liveright or anyone else. I don't think there will be any difficulty whatever in disposing of the 250 which you are printing. I don't know how many people have already bespoken copies, and I'll send you a list of names later on which will be pretty sure-fire.

New York seems better than ever to me. The beaches are wonderful—and packed with pulchritude. Where are you these days? I somehow can't picture you as still in Paris.

P.S. Please ask Harry if he can think of any job for that nice Danish boy I introduced him to the morning I sailed. He's without work or funds—and starving. He's an expert trainer and keeper of horses (Danish Royal Artillery) and speaks English fairly well. — — — — Honest, industrious, and will do anything that's honorable.

330: TO HARRY AND CARESSE CROSBY

Brooklyn, N.Y.   *August 30th, 1929*

Dear Harry and Caresse: I had my first visit with Harry Marks today and am glad to hear that he has nothing as yet to report about any work of yours on *The Bridge*. For, as you know, I am anxious to add more—the "Cape Hatteras" section, at least—before you bring it out. This is now being worked out rapidly, and the aeronautical sections which you so much admired have been improved and augmented considerably. However, the line-lengths are longer than in any other section—so long, in fact, that to preserve them unbroken across the page I think we ought to change our plan regarding page size and use, instead of the previously-agreed-on Perse book for a model, your Mad Queen volume—even better looking in other respects, too, I think. I hope I can ask you for this change without appearing too presumptuous!

How did you like the "gloss" I sent you recently? I'm passionately anxious to hear from you as soon as possible. —/—/

I'm settled at last in a comfortable furnished apartment—not far from the navy yard. There have been great house-warmings, especially since I can buy corn whiskey from my janitor for only $6. per gallon! No more querulous, farty old landladies for me for awhile. Write me from now on directly at the above address instead of Patterson. Liveright is issuing a second edition of *White Buildings*—*Vanity Fair* bestows laurels in the Sept. issue—Eliot urges me to contribute as well as old Mamby Canby of *The Sat[urday] Review,* the old enemy camp. So I'm feeling optimistic to a large extent.

331: To Caresse Crosby

Brooklyn, N.Y. *6th September 1929*

Dear Caresse: Just received the first specimen proofs a little late, unfortunately, as my old landlady out at Patterson had thought they were "printed matter" and had failed to forward them as soon as certain other mail. But you'll be writing me direct to the above address in the future anyway.

Please go ahead and set up what sections you already have in the large sized type. I like it much better than the smaller sized Caslon. Only—don't you think that page (I'm using it as a model) would look better balanced, and certainly not crowded, with about four more lines of verse on it? I think that the extreme depth of the bottom margin looks awkward rather than luxurious.

I have more to send—and it's very important. I am working like mad since I've found this apartment where I can keep my own hours, etc. I'm too rushed to type you out a final copy of this finale to the "Cape Hatteras" section yet, but you can get some idea of what I'm accomplishing by the muddled copy I'm including herewith. You'll have the final version—including what you read in Paris—within a few days, aeronautics and all. It looks pretty good to me, and at least according to *my* ideas of *The Bridge* this edition wouldn't be complete or even representative without it.

Then the "Quaker Hill" section—and "Indiana," the final subsection to "Powhatan's Daughter" (which won't require any gloss, I think) will come in quick succession. I know what to plan on fairly well when I get into one of these fevers of work. So please be patient. The book must have these sections and I can promise to have them in your hands by the second week in October! Then clear steaming ahead! I'm very happy about the paper, format and all which you have selected. I'll try to get you the fresh photo of Stella's picture within a few days.

I hope you and Harry are still planning on a visit here next winter. Then maybe I can make up for the kiss I missed when sailing!
Do you really like that little necklace that much?!! My gifts seldom
have so fortunate a reception!

332: TO CARESSE CROSBY

[Brooklyn]   *Sept. 6th '29*

Dear Caresse: I forgot to include this new version of "Cutty Sark"
in the earlier letter sent today. I have changed very little—what
little has been only to promote clarity—which includes a more generous sprinkling of punctuation. So please use this instead of the
version you've had.

The same quotation as before is used on the introductory sheet:

> O, the navies old and oaken
>   O, the *Temeraire* no more!
>   —*Melville*

Hope this doesn't put you out!

333: TO CARESSE CROSBY

Patterson, N. Y.   *Sept. 17, 1929*

Dear Caresse: I sent you, registered, the "Cape Hatteras" last version.
But retyping it for a magazine, I couldn't help glimpsing some necessary improvements. So please use this *second* version, as enclosed.
I vow that you'll be troubled by no further emendations—excepting
perhaps a comma or so on the proofs.

Since I'm writing I can't help saying that I'm highly pleased with
the way I've been able to marshal the notes and agonies of the last
two years' effort into a rather arresting synthesis. . . .

Gosh, how I'd like a bottle of Cutty Sark tonight to soothe my excited nerves! The countryside is the dryest here in years—and nothing to hope for next year, as frost and this later drowth have ruined
the apple crop! I had to flee the heat in the city for a week's work up
here in my old farmhouse room. It's lovely, too. Another week of it—
by which time I expect to have finished the two remaining sections,
—and I'll be back in city quarters (130 Columbia Hts). . . .

334: TO LORNA DIETZ

Patterson   *Wednesday* [*ca. October 23, 1929*]

Dearest Lorna: I've been *weltschmerzing* a little bit all by myself
here since last Saturday afternoon, when I suddenly picked up and
left town. I've never seen such color as this year's autumnal shades,
but the storm that began this morning after three wonderful days of
sunshine probably won't leave so much on the boughs to be gazed at.
. . . Nevertheless I'm staying on at least until next Monday—and
maybe somewhat longer. I feel quite rested already, but I know that
I need a little "reserve" after the way I've been acting. I'm *hoping*
also, to complete the last two sections [*The Bridge*], God 'elp me!
And then to come back to town and see you again in your sweet,
new, cheerful, rosy little nest! — — — —

335: TO CARESSE CROSBY

Brooklyn, N.Y.   *December 26th, 1929*

Dearest Caresse: I am hastily enclosing the final version of "Quaker
Hill," which ends my writing on *The Bridge*. You can now go ahead
and finish it all. I've been slow, Heaven knows, but I know that you
will forgive me. I haven't added as many verses to what you took
with you as I had expected. I had several more, roughly, in notes, but
think that my present condensation is preferable. "Quaker Hill" is
not, after all, one of the major sections of the poem; it is rather by
way of an "accent mark" that it is valuable at all.

By the way, will you see that the middle photograph (the one of
the barges and tug) goes between the "Cutty Sark" Section and the
"Hatteras" Section. That is the "center" of the book, both physically
and symbolically. Evans is very anxious, as am I, that no ruling or
printing appear on the pages devoted to the reproductions—which is
probably your intention anyway.

I have an idea for a change in one line of the dedication "To B.
Bridge." If you don't like it, don't change it. But I feel that it is
more logical, even if no more suggestive. Instead of:

"—And elevators heave us to our day"

I suggest

"—Till elevators drop us from our day"

I'll leave the choice to you.

I think of you a great deal. This letter doesn't represent *me* really,
at all. But I must get it off for the *Mauretania* or else risk the delays
of one of the slower steamers, and I fear that you are already impatient. I shall write you more very soon, meanwhile I hope that you
have recovered somewhat from the exhaustion that must have
followed on your brave and marvelous endurance at the time of
your departure. —/—/

P.S. Please send a review copy to Yvor Winters—RFD1, Palo Alto,
California. — — — —

1 9 3 0

336: TO CHARLOTTE RYCHTARIK

Brooklyn, N.Y.   *February 11th, 1930*

Dear Charlotte: I shoulda, kinda, gotta, really write you before . . .
but how time does fly! No, I'm not in Africa chasing lions and
monkeys, but right here in Babylon hunting jobs. Sometimes I am
sure, very sure indeed, that my days of romance are thoroughly dead
and passed. I happen to be in that mood now—and if money has anything to do with the matter perhaps I'm right. Friends make a big
difference however, and I hope I may always be expecting another
letter from you and Richard.

I almost shed tears when I think of how little I saw of you during
my last visit. My melodramatic departure and the attending circumstances sent me to bed with a backache for three weeks after I got
home. Then, as you guessed, the terrible shock of Harry Crosby's
suicide threw me flat again for another week. I had just given a big
party for him and his wife a few days before that happened, and I
was with his wife and mother on the evening when the disaster occurred. In fact it was I who had to bring the terrible news to those
two lovely women. Mrs. Crosby left for France a couple of days later,
just as she had planned to do anyway. I think she has been a very
brave woman to go right ahead and bring out the Paris edition of
The Bridge on regular schedule. I heard from her yesterday—and by
now the edition is ready to be shipped to the agent here, Harry F.
Marks, — — — —. As I told you, it's a beautiful job of printing. The
type used is a new French type, very much like the face which Richard recommended, Garamond. The Liveright edition (ready April

1st) is in Garamond and will be quite handsome also. Great interest
has been aroused in advance and I am sure to get some very laudatory reviews. I really don't want to write any poetry for awhile now,
but just the same feel somehow depressed that I haven't some ambitious project on hand to take the place of *The Bridge*. I haven't seen
the dancers that you spoke of, but hear that they are very good. If
you ever get a chance to see the pantomime of Angna Enters in
Cleveland be sure not to miss her. She is wonderful! Humor, pathos,
tragedy—the whole gamut of the emotions. And there have been
some wonderful art shows here this winter, better than any I saw in
Europe. The Museum of Modern Art right now has a marvelous
collection of modern French painters, etc. Georgia O'Keeffe, Marin
shows—and I wish you could see the show of a friend of mine, Peter
Blume! —/—/

337: To Waldo Frank

[*Brooklyn*]   *March 16th*

Dear Waldo: It was *so* kind of you to have replied so quickly and
generously! I feel quite guilty for not having thanked you sooner.
I've really never known so discouraging a time job-hunting. Insomnia has got me on the rack—and I really can't envisage just what
is in store, but perhaps after the reviews of *The Bridge* come out
(Liveright's edition is due out next week) I'll possibly be able to
rally my confidence and make a better impression in "the business
world."

Meanwhile the disintegrating forces of N.Y. strike me as pretty
severe!

It was reassuring to know that you got your copy of *The Bridge*.
Cummings and one or two others didn't—quite inexplicably. There's
much in it new to your eyes, and I am quite tremulous of your
opinion, though perfectly content to wait for the time when you can
afford to give it a good reading.

I'll try to find you a first edition of *White Buildings*—but I haven't
much hope of locating one. Among your books somewhere you'll
find the copy I gave you, inscribed too, for I'm awfully certain I
didn't fail in that essential courtesy due long ago. Or you may have
lost it. I'll send you a copy of the second edition anyhow, and if my
memory has served me wrong you'll forgive me I'm sure. —/—/

338: TO PAUL ROSENFELD

Patterson, N.Y.   *April 21st,*

Dear Paul: I'm sorry not to have the "Letter"[1] in your hands by this time. I'm hoping that a week's delay won't afflict your schedule too seriously.

As usual, when I attempt any sort of technical disquisitions I'm struggling against the chronic habit I seem to have—of trying to cram everything into one paragraph! I got clogged up, then paralyzed,—at least momentarily thrown off. But my intentions are honest and good. And I'm hoping to make my promise good by next Saturday.

There's no liquor out here, at any rate.

339: TO HERBERT WEINSTOCK

Patterson, New York   *April 22nd, 1930*

Dear Herbert Weinstock: You have my sincerest gratitude for your enthusiastic review of *The Bridge*. Van Vuren had already sent me a copy, and I was just on the point of writing you my thanks when along came your good letter.

I hope I am deserving of such lofty companions as you group me with. I am almost tempted to believe your claims on the strength of your amazing insight into my objectives in writing, my particular symbolism, the intentional condensation and "density" of structure that I occasionally achieve, and the essential religious motive throughout my work. This last-mentioned feature commits me to self-consciousness on a score that makes me belie myself a little. For I have never consciously approached any subject in a religious mood; it is only afterward that I, or someone else generally, have noticed a prevalent piety. God save me from a Messianic predisposition!

It is pertinent to suggest, I think, that with more time and familiarity with *The Bridge* you will come to envisage it more as one poem with a clearer and more integrated unity and development than was at first evident. At least if my own experience in reading and rereading Eliot's *Wasteland* has any relation to the circumstances this *may* be found to be the case. It took me nearly five years, with innumerable readings to convince myself of the essential unity of that poem. And *The Bridge* is at least as complicated in its structure and inferences as *The Wasteland*—perhaps more so.

1. See letter 340, April 23, 1930.

I shall remember to write you my exact whereabouts in time to reach you before you leave for the East and Europe, and we shall meet somewhere in New York. At present the unemployment situation has me balked for any definite location beyond the next day or so.

340: TO EDA LOU WALTON

Patterson, New York   *April 23rd, 1930*

Dear Eda Lou: I am enclosing an extract from a letter written to Otto Kahn some time ago explaining my intentions in certain sections of *The Bridge*. I submit it to you more or less as I did to him, not as a justification for the poem but as a fairly accurate chart of certain purposes in the poem which I may or may not have succeeded in accomplishing. It may interest you. And since you have been kind enough to include the poem in your course at N.Y.U., it may prove even helpful in elucidating certain aspects of the poem.

Please keep this paper to yourself, however. I am at present busy with an elaboration of it into a more or less formalized essay for *The New American Caravan*. I'd like to have it back within two weeks if it won't trouble you too much.

341: TO SELDEN RODMAN

Brooklyn, N.Y.   *May 22nd, 1930*

Dear Mr. Rodman: Your criticism of *The Bridge* was very much to the point, and I am grateful for your enthusiasm. I also share your admiration for the poetry of Archibald MacLeish, though I feel that at times he betrays too evidently a bias toward the fashionable pessimism of the hour so well established by T. S. Eliot.

I tried to break loose from that particular strait-jacket, without however committing myself to any oppositional form of didacticism. Your diffidence in ascribing any absolute conclusions in the poem is therefore correct, at least according to my intentions. The poem, as a whole, is, I think, an affirmation of experience, and to that extent is "positive" rather than "negative" in the sense that *The Waste Land* is negative.

In a few days I am leaving town for the summer, but I should like to meet you next autumn if you are in this vicnity then.

342: TO ISIDOR SCHNEIDER

Patterson, N.Y.   *June 8, '30*

Dear Isidor: —/—/ That makes me all the more grateful for the evident care which you took in your review of *The Bridge*. Certainly I don't see what more I could ask for—than your generous credit to and recognition of practically all the aspirations implicit in the poem. I hope the actual poem is deserving of it all. If you have read Winters' attack in the June issue of *Poetry* you cannot have been more astonished than I was to note the many reversals of opinion he has undergone since reading my acknowledgment to Whitman in the later "Cape Hatteras" section.

Had it not been for our previous extended correspondence I would not, of course, have written him about it. But as things stood I could hardly let silence infer an acceptance on my part of all the wilful distortions of meaning, misappropriations of opinion, pedantry and pretentious classification—besides illogic—which his review presents par excellence. I must read what prejudices he defends, I understand, against writing about subways, in the anti-humanist symposium. Poets should defer alluding to the sea, also, I presume, until Mr. Winters has got an invitation for a cruise!

I haven't any work whatever in mind. I guess I can trust my father's promise of a small allowance to carry me along out here until fall, when the gates of employment may prove a little better oiled than they have for some time past. If you hear of anything, Isidor, please let me know. I'm aching to get busy at almost anything. —/—/

343: TO ALLEN TATE

Gaylordsville, Conn.   *July 13th, 1930*

Dear Allen: Your last good letter and the admirable review of *The Bridge* in *The Hound & Horn* deserved an earlier response, but time has somehow just been drifting by without my being very conscious of it. For one thing, I have been intending to get hold of a copy of *The Hound & Horn* and give your review a better reading, before replying, than I could achieve at the tables in Brentano's when I was in town about two weeks ago. I still haven't a copy and consequently may wrong you in making any comments whatever. But as I don't want to delay longer I hope you'll pardon any discrepancies.

The fact that you posit *The Bridge* at the end of a tradition of romanticism may prove to have been an accurate prophecy, but I don't yet feel that such a statement can be taken as a foregone conclusion. A great deal of romanticism may persist—of the sort to deserve serious consideration, I mean.

But granting your accuracy—I shall be humbly grateful if *The Bridge* can fulfil simply the metaphorical inferences of its title. . . . You will admit our age (at least our predicament) to be one of transition. If *The Bridge,* embodying as many anomalies as you find in it, yet contains as much authentic poetry here and there as even Winters grants,—then perhaps it can serve as at least the function of a link connecting certain chains of the past to certain chains and tendencies of the future. In other words, a diagram or "process" in the sense that Genevieve Taggard refers to all my work in estimating Kunitz's achievement in the enclosed review. This gives it no more interest than as a point of chronological reference, but "nothing ventured, nothing gained"—and I can't help thinking that my mistakes may warn others who may later be tempted to an interest in similar subject matter.

Personally I think that Taggard is a little too peremptory in dispensing with Kunitz's "predecessors." We're all unconscious evolutionists, I suppose, but she apparently belongs to the more rabid ranks. I can't help wishing I had read more of Kunitz before seeing her review. He is evidently an excellent poet. I should like to have approached him, not as one bowing before Confucius, nor as one buying a new nostrum for lame joints. Taggard, like Winters, isn't looking for poetry any more. Like Munson, they are both in pursuit of some cure-all. Poetry as poetry (and I don't mean merely decorative verse) isn't worth a second reading any more. Therefore—away with Kubla Khan, out with Marlowe, and to hell with Keats! It's a pity, I think. So many true things have a way of coming out all the better without the strain to sum up the universe in one impressive little pellet. I admit that I don't answer the requirements. My vision of poetry *is* too personal to "answer the call." And if I ever write any more verse it will probably be at least as personal as the idiom of *White Buildings* whether anyone cares to look at it or not.

This personal note is doubtless responsible for what you term as sentimentality in my attitude toward Whitman.[1] It's true that my rhapsodic address to him in *The Bridge* exceeds any exact evaluation of the man. I realized that in the midst of the composition. But since you and I hold such divergent prejudices regarding the value

1. In a letter to Crane, June 10, 1930.

of the materials and events that W. responded to, and especially as you, like so many others, never seem to have read his *Democratic Vistas* and other of his statements sharply decrying the materialism, industrialism, etc., of which you name him the guilty and hysterical spokesman, there isn't much use in my tabulating the qualified, yet persistent reasons I have for my admiration of him, and my allegiance to the positive and universal tendencies implicit in nearly all his best work. You've heard me roar at too many of his lines to doubt that I can spot his worst, I'm sure.

It amuses me to see how Taggard takes up some of Winters' claims against me (I expected this and look for more) in his article in the Anti-Humanist volume, especially as that borrowing doesn't seem to have obviated his own eclipse according to her estimate of the new constellation. I have the feeling that Miss Taggard is not only conducting her own education in public (as someone once said of George Moore) but also the education of her subjects. . . . At least she seems now to have attained that acumen which is a confusion to all.

I'm leaving this week-end for a visit to Cummings in New Hampshire. After a final row with Addie M. Turner (who is about to sell her place anyway) I have moved my things down the road to Fitzi's [Fitzgerald]. Occasionally I am appalled at my apparently chronic inability to relinquish some hold or connection that has long since ceased to yield me anything but annoyance—until some violence of fates forces my release. That's one of many ways I seem to keep of wasting time. —/—/

344: TO GUGGENHEIM MEMORIAL FOUNDATION[1]

[*Gaylordsville*]   [*August 29, 1930*]

My application for a fellowship is prompted by a desire for European study and creative leisure for the composition of poetry. I am interested in characteristics of European culture, classical and romantic, with especial reference to contrasting elements implicit in the emergent features of a distinctive American poetic consciousness.

My one previous visit to Europe, though brief, proved creatively stimulating in this regard, as certain aspects of my long poem, *The Bridge,* may suggest. Modern and medieval French literature and philosophy interest me particularly. I should like the opportunity

1. Crane's "Plans for Work" in his application for a Guggenheim Fellowship for 1931-32.

for a methodical pursuit of these studies in conjunction with my creative projects.

My next volume of poetry will probably be issued by Horace Liveright, Inc., who has already issued my two previous books, *White Buildings* and *The Bridge*.

345: To ALLEN TATE

Gaylordsville, Conn. *Sept. 7th, 1930*

Dear Allen: Have you ever had boils? I got my first specimen during my visit to the Cummingses six weeks ago, brought it home along with several up-and-coming progeny, and "the loyal and royal succession of the Plantagenets" (as E.E. referred to them) has not left me yet. Since the throne room is in my right arm pit, not to mention the chamber and royal nursery, I've scarcely been able to manipulate my right arm to the meek extent of writing a letter much of the time. I think that I have now established at least my better intentions!

The pictures of your homestead were much appreciated and widely circulated hereabouts. It's my opinion that you now have about all one could ask for in the way of rural comfort not to mention dignity. Certainly it surpasses anything owned and directed by any of our mutuals in this valley. I should enjoy the visit you suggested (many thanks!) but, boils or no boils, I've got to get located in some office as soon now as possible—or at least be on the scene of interrogation, prison, palace, and supplication. —/—/

I was glad to get your *Three Poems*. The distinguished diction throughout reminds me of the little advance I have ever made in essential flexibility and the finer intonations. These qualities seem most evident to me in the "Message from Abroad," which, though it is largely inferential to me in its substance, is in a way, all the more welcome as a poem to be re-read for a multiple suggestiveness that may very well take on clearer perspective with time. "The Cross" keeps me guessing a little too strenuously. I can't help thinking it perhaps too condensed, and, as Bill [Brown] suggested, a not entirely fused mélange of ecclesiastical and highly-personalized imagery. In which case you sin no more than Eliot in the recent "Ash-Wednesday." The "Ode to the Confederate Dead" is as excellent as ever, I don't think essentially improved except as regards rhythm: the wind-and-leaf interpolations adding a certain subjective continuity.

My summer seems like a blank to me right now. Perhaps my study

of Dante—the *Commedia* which I had never touched before—will
have been seen to have given it some significance, but that isn't much
to boast of. —/—/

346: TO SOLOMON GRUNBERG

N.Y.C.   *Sept. 30th '30*

Dear Mony: —/—/ Now that I am back in town again, looking for
the needles in haystacks and jobs in limbo,—now that the most
monotonous and familiar situation of *all* engrosses, nay inundates
me, I'm taking "time off" to answer in the hope that you'll write
me more news and also be sure to look me up on your next visit to
these parts.

I'm most grateful for your continued interest in *The Bridge*.
After so much grandiose talk as I indulged myself in during its
interrupted progress it's a wonder if most of my friends aren't appalled at its ultimate shortcomings. Some of them are. It's gone into
a second printing, however, which means a sale exceeding the first
thousand. If last spring hadn't ushered in such a calamitous slump
in all books I imagine I might have been more fortunate; at any
rate I can't complain about most of the reviews

My summer was a kind of steady doldrums, enlivened only by a
sudden insight into the values and beauty of Dante's *Commedia*.
Not that I've learned Italian, but that I found a decent translation
(Temple Classics Edition) thanks to Eliot's inspiring essay on
Dante. My recent struggles with a poem of large proportions and
intricate framework, I think, gave me a maturer appreciation of the
Commedia than I could have mustered ten years ago. Sometimes one
feels that one's neglect or "indifference" to a great masterpiece is
almost justified, pending the proper development of one's own
powers of perception proportionate to the opportunity postponed.
(I didn't realize that alliteration was so "on the job" this morning!)
Of course I now realize how much more than ever I have to work to
accomplish anything whatever.

Some conversations with you again would be very welcome inter-
ludes in my present job-obsession. Aren't you planning on New York
before long? — — — —

347: TO SELDEN RODMAN

[New York City]   *October 27th, 1930*

Dear Mr. Rodman: Thank you for sending me a copy of *The [Hark-
ness] Hoot*. The copy that you had previously sent to *The New Re-*

public (via the hands of Slater Brown) had already afforded me considerable pleasure. Despite the unfortunate sentimentality of Hale's
oration the issue is amply justified by your essay on MacLeish, if I
may say so,—the most penetrating estimate that he has so far received.

As for Hale, I recommend his perusal of the recent rape of *The
Woman of Andros* conducted by Mike Gold in the columns of *The
N. R.*—if he wants to see himself outdone on his own ground. Not
that I care for Wilder. Never having read a word he wrote I cannot
be expected to nurse sighs or curses. But I *have* read something of
Spengler—and would just as soon he showed an American visa, for
once, before predicting any more details of "our" future. —/—/

348: To William Wright

Brooklyn, New York   *November 21, 1930*

Dear Bill: —/—/ The details of your summer program and the description of your winter quarters reflect an enviable settled state of
affairs. New York is full of the unemployed, more every day, and
the tension evident in thousands of faces isn't cheerful to contemplate. It is a little strange to see the city so "grim about the mouth,"
as Melville might say. Yours truly has been having his grim moments,
too; in fact I'm pretty well convinced that unmitigated anxiety has
a highly corrosive effect on the resilience of the imagination. I am
trying to write a couple of articles for *Fortune*—that deluxe business-
industrial monthly published by Time, Inc.—and I am appalled at
the degree of paralysis that worry can impose on the functioning of
one's natural faculties. One assignment is a "profile" of Walter
Teagle, president of Standard Oil (N.J.). I managed to keep the oil
king talking far beyond the time allotted, but when I come to write
it up in typical *Fortune* style the jams gather by the hundred.

I am so pleased that you continue to enjoy *The Bridge*. I admit
having felt considerably jolted at the charge of sentimentality continually leveled at the "Indiana" fragment, particularly when such
charges came from people who acknowledged a violent admiration
for Hardy's poetry. For many of his lyrics have seemed to me at least
as "sentimental" as this "mawkish" performance of my own. But I
approve of a certain amount of sentiment anyway. Right now it is
more fashionable to speak otherwise, but the subject (or emotion)
of "race" has always had as much of sentiment behind it—as it has
had of prejudice, also. Since "race" is the principal motivation of
"Indiana," I can't help thinking that, observed in the proper perspective, and judged in relation to the argument or theme of the

Pocahontas section as a whole, the pioneer woman's maternalism isn't excessive.

Did I mention my pleasure in reading a very skillful poem of yours about various types of fur. It came out in *Poetry*, I think. Certainly Baudelaire would have been charmed by its adept blending of beautiful names with a world of tactile sensations. The geographical evocations implicit in the list of animals mentioned were delightful. I see a great many reasons for you to continue writing, especially since it brings you none of the pangs that accompany a more professional concern with the muses. I haven't written a line for over nine months, and nine months is not so promising a period in the seven arts as it may be in the physical sciences.

I'll try not to be so remiss in writing again. Would I be deemed insensitive in requesting a temporary loan to help carry me over till a check from *Fortune* can be expected. Please be very frank. Money is "hard" everywhere these days, and if you can't spare 25 or 50 dollars, or if you have any scruples against such transactions, I shall remain as affectionate and as spontaneous a partner to our friendship as ever. In fact I would prefer to shoulder double my present quandary before exposing you to any stringencies.

I have applied for a Guggenheim Scholarship (which would give me a year's study and creative freedom abroad) and hope to God that I'll gain approval. Announcements are made early in March. Meanwhile I'm praying that I can write well enough on industrial subjects to keep on with *Fortune*. My room here is surprisingly cheap—a weekly rate that barely exceeds rooming house costs—and with these articles I've had to be located where messages could be taken in my absence. The requirement of advance payment is none too comforting, however. —/—/

349: To WILLIAM WRIGHT

Brooklyn, N.Y.   *November 29th, 1930*

Dear Bill: Your imagination is evidently as magnanimous as your hand is. . . . By ascribing my almost chronic indigence to so Nietzschean a program as the attitude of "living life dangerously" infers, you make me blink a little. For my exposures to rawness and to risk have been far too inadvertent, I fear, to deserve any such honorable connotations;—and my disorderly adventures and peregrinations I regard with anything but complacency. However, it isn't everyone who can lend help with such graceful tolerance of evident shortcomings; and your euphemisms make me doubly grateful.

The Teagle article is now awaiting approval. I hope to know more about my immediate fate early next week. If that doesn't eventuate in a check and another assignment, then my best bet lies in the direction of book-selling in one of the many Doubleday-Doran shops in the metrooplitan area. I know someone who may succeed in insinuating me there. In normal times, of course, I should have been located with an advertising agency months since. No, teaching isn't a solution for me, Bill. I haven't any academic education whatsoever. You may have forgotten that I left East High without even a diploma—in my junior year. Mirabile dictu! . . . Noblesse oblige! . . . Pax vobiscum! . . . Nunc dimittis est . . . so who am I, therefore, to rule a class!

I'm hoping that I won't need to cash your second check, a contingency which I'll do my best to avoid. You'll hear from me again very soon. Meanwhile I can't tell you how much I appreciate your kindness.

350: TO ISIDOR SCHNEIDER

Brooklyn, N.Y.   *December 2nd, 1930*

Dear Isidor: —/—/ As for the "Hymn Against Violence," I'm all for it! It is beautifully sustained, amazingly compact; its imagery is often as startling as Rimbaud's:
> "—then overhear
> reiteration's tremor drum
> upon your brain the changeless diaries of fear."
> and "Harder curds
> the cloud. Waking in us no ease,
> night comes of terror darkened infinite, of dying herds."

A strange and sombre metre. Biblical as it is, and owing something perhaps to Hopkins' exclamatory use of violent internal stresses, it is still highly original and by all odds the best poem of yours that I have yet seen. It's a poem that I imagine Eliot would be very glad to have for *The Criterion*. But you probably got much better remuneration from *The Menorah*; besides, Eliot is apt to deliberate a year or so before informing one of his decision. —/—/

351: TO SAMUEL LOVEMAN

[Chagrin Falls, Ohio]   *December 29th, 1930*

Dear Sam: To make partial amends for my neglect of you, I am, as you see, giving you the full, blazing benefit of the official stationery!

Of course, had I been consulted, I should never have permitted so harmless a slogan as "The place to *bring* your guest." The fourth word would still have begun with "b," but there would have been more action implied in the order of the other letters substituted, or I'm no befriender of monks and monkery.

However, that might belie the nights hereabouts. As I have just written to B—— A——, *la vie sportif* continues its reckless pace hereabouts without any too great abundance of absinthe, gobs, applevendors or breadlines. It's too bad that all this drouth and quietude should have produced, so far at least, nothing better than a maidenly complexion and a bulging waist line. Gone is that glittering eye of Sands St. midnights, erstwhile so compelling; and the ancient mariner is facing the new year with all the approved trepidations of the middle west business man, approved panic model of 1931. So much for resignation. It brings me at least a little more sleep than I was getting in New York.

For about ten days I was busy at my father's store on Euclid, near Higbee's [Cleveland]. Driving in from the Falls here, wrapping Xmas parcelpost bundles, and driving back at night, I lived in a veritable whirl of excitement. Now that the Xmas "rush" is a memory only, I am casting about for some connection or other with what remains of the direct mail advertising business here. So far it doesn't look promising. But unless I manage to turn a few honest pennies I mayn't get back to your skyline for many months. Of course I knew that when I came out here, but I had borrowed all I felt justified in borrowing and the situation in NY looked, and still looks, hopeless. As you had no doubt observed, it had gotten considerably under my skin. —/—/

PART FOUR

Mexico

(1931–1932)

1 9 3 1

352: To Solomon Grunberg

Chagrin Falls, Ohio   *Jan. 10*

Dear Mony: —/—/ I got terribly run down with the worry of it all—
and since my father had expected me out here for the holidays anyway I felt I owed him the courtesy of complying, especially since he
had been so generous with me for some time past. Since the Teagle
(Standard Oil) article proved to be a flop there wasn't much use in
persisting longer—in the face of the bread lines.

This humiliation, severe for awhile, doesn't seem to have ruined
me, however, and in view of certain recoveries and gains in poise, I
don't seriously regret my move. My father, of course, expects me to
remain in this locality permanently. I of course keep all contrary
plans very much to myself, including the secret of a bank balance
sufficient at least to my carfare east again, whenever my return seems
advisable. But enough of such explanatory details!

I'm anxious to hear from you—and what your plans are, etc. This
is dull enough around here to encourage a good deal of reading—
which I am enjoying. Spinoza (Einstein's grandpop) furnishes plenty
of discipline. Cleveland has one of [the] best libraries in the country,
admirably conducted and with shelves practically wide open.

No writing is being done yet—or even in prospect. Can't fool
myself that way, as you know. An old thing of mine from my West
Indian days in a forthcoming issue of *The New Republic* which you
may like, however. — — — —

353: To Samuel Loveman

[Chagrin Falls]   *January 16th, 1931*

Dear Sam: The Bridge photos were a joyous surprise! I can't have it
from too many angles! And the roof portrait of yourself with all
the chimney pots! You are as generous and thoughtful a friend as
ever.

Nothing much happens hereabouts. I haven't even seen Bill

[Sommer] yet, but I have a line out. Did I tell you that I called on D—— B. one morning? That was almost three weeks ago. He looked haggard, his complexion splotched, and thoroughly miserable; though he made an effort to be as suave as possible, I'm sure, it was evident that he *was* making an effort. I made no further than a general allusion to his illness and as no details were proffered I left him as ignorant in such respects as I had come. There seemed to be no way of arousing his interests to any extent. He's evidently in a hell of a state, physically and mentally—a combination of both interacting, I suppose.

You'll be interested in the story of the enclosed card, I'm sure. I chanced upon it just the other day in one of the local news stores. Then someone told me a few anecdotes concerning the local blacksmith, named Church, who died not so very long ago and was regarded as a most "peculiar" individual by most of the townspeople. What struck me in the first place was the obvious coincidence of a parallel use of symbols, the serpent and the eagle, with my lines on Pocahontas in *The Bridge*.

"Time, like a serpent, down her shoulder, dark,
And space, an eaglet's wing laid on her hair."

The serpent isn't hard to locate, and you'll see the rather dim outlines of the fore part of an eagle just below where I have indicated in the margin. This blacksmith aroused considerable conjecture by his midnight absences, until someone followed his lantern down to this rock where he was busy night after night on this frieze. I think it has a real aesthetic value, like other primitive sculpture—and I'm planning an expedition to the rock as soon as the snow melts a little.

The blacksmith's character must have been rather Blakeian, for he also carved his own tombstone—a lion couchant beside a lamb and a figure of a man walking. And imagine the surprise of his survivors when on the occasion of his obsequies his own voice pronounced his own funeral sermon from the disk of a phonograph! Well, I guess Sherwood Anderson didn't quite scoop up *all* the characters of Winesburg!

My father and his wife have just left for a vacation in Havana, with extensive notes in their pocket from me as to what French wines to order, where to go, etc. Mrs. Crane #3 has never seen palms and sparkling waters and was deservedly rife with expectations. It's the first real vacation either of them have had for several years and they will forget business for the time being, I certainly hope, and have a splendid time. They certainly have my affectionate wishes.

I'm going into town this afternoon for dinner with the Rychtariks, with a Bloch quartet this evening. Altogether I'm feeling much better, Sam, despite certain restrictions—which, however, may be good for me for a while. Nothing has been found yet in the way of work, but the tension on that subject has fortunately been temporarily somewhat relaxed. —/—/

354: To LORNA DIETZ

[Chagrin Falls]   *Feb. 10th '31*

Dear Lorna: —/—/ As nothing more has been said about photography, I guess I'm to be spared the useless apprenticeship to the village baby tickler; instead I've been hammering, waxing, rubbing, painting and repairing—odd jobs—around the place, and work which is rather amusing. Once a week I generally go into Cleveland and spend some hours with my old friends, the Rychtariks (a Prague painter and his wife whom you must have heard me mention) who really "belong"—and are about the only people in this district that I enjoy seeing. I can be more or less myself with them, and that's a great relief after the unmitigated rigor of the parental regime. (Poetry or anything like that is an offense to mention here, as something belonging in the category with "youthful errors," "wild oats," et cetera, and the "reform" that has been inaugurated has brought me back to just that pleasantly vegetable state of mind that can read Coolidge's daily advice without a tremor of protest.) My father, you can visualize his type, is "enjoying" the depression, or at least his incessant howls about it. Despite the losses personally involved, I think he will actually be disappointed if matters improve in less than five years. From his standpoint at any rate, anything that disproved his doleful prediction would prove a calamity. His great reiteration being that every one has been spending too much money. He is willing to admit, however, that it hasn't been spent on candy! (which is among the luxuries, too, if I am not mistaken). All of which makes very stimulating conversation, of course, especially when you are obliged to agree on each and every occasion and reiteration, ad infinitum. . . .

The possibility of a Guggenheim keeps me restive. That failing, I may hike back east in March anyway. Too prolonged a stay here at my present age isn't sensible, whatever the alternatives may be right now, and however generously my father might feel.

You've been awfully generous in writing. Sounds as though your winter were being rather pleasant after all. — — — — Partying seems to continue unabated as well as discussions of Communism. But Eda Lou Walton writes me that nobody is writing anything. Certainly I'm not either. Some reading, however. No wonder F—— liked *The Story of San Michele* so much; it's almost as full of dog sentiment as she is. But in some ways a marvelous book. A friend of mine on *Fortune,* Russell Davenport, has written a good book, *Through Traffic,* on a combined business and love theme. I'll send it to you to keep for me and read. I've just gotten around to read *Jurgen!* Always resented the pow-wow about it, but rather like it. Dos Passos' *42nd Parallel* is good—as far as it goes. But Dos has yet to create a full portrait. What did you think of Mumford's series of leaders in the *Tribune,* just concluded? I find myself agreeing pretty thoroughly with him. —/—/

355: To Waldo Frank

Chagrin Falls, Ohio   *Feb. 19th*

Dear Waldo: —/—/ These are bewildering times for everyone, I suppose. I can't muster much of anything to say to anyone. I seem to have lost the faculty to even feel tension. A bad sign, I'm sure. When they all get it decided, Capitalism or Communism, then I'll probably be able to resume a few intensities; meanwhile there seems to be no sap in anything. I'd love to fight for—almost anything, but there seems to be no longer any real resistance. Maybe I'm only a disappointed romantic, after all. Or perhaps I've made too many affable compromises. I hope to discover the fault, whatever it is, before long.

Since you seem to have retired completely from any journalistic appearances I'm completely ignorant of your current opinions or reactions. Do write me soon and tell me what you're engaged in. And such of your plans as you care to divulge. I'd like to have heard your recent lecture mentioning *The Bridge,* as I gather. Present day America seems a long way off from the destiny I fancied when I wrote that poem. In some ways Spengler must have been right.

On the water wagon two months now. . . . If abstinence is clarifying to the vision, as they claim, then give me back the blindness of my will. It needs a fresh baptism.

356: TO HENRY ALLEN MOE

Chagrin Falls, Ohio   *March 16, 1931*

Dear Mr. Moe: My appointment as a Fellow of the John Simon Guggenheim Memorial Foundation is appreciated greatly, not only as a welcome opportunity to continue my creative endeavors, but also as a distinguished honor conferred upon me as a poet. In accepting this Fellowship for 1931-32 I feel a stimulating sense of pride and gratitude. Needless to say, this evidence of trust in my abilities and character, alone and quite apart from my instinctive response to such good fortune, would prompt me to my utmost efforts to justify such confidence as the liberal terms and the generous conditions of the Fellowship imply. I fully subscribe to all these conditions as detailed in your announcement,—not, however, without realizing that I am assuming some serious responsibilities.

As I am at present among the vast horde of the unemployed—and with nothing of consequence to detain me, I should like to situate myself definitely as soon as possible in a favorable environment for constructive work and study. It will therefore be most gratifying to hear from you regarding the propriety and feasibility of taking up my projected foreign residence at an early date. To be specific, I should like to sail for France by the middle part of April, provided such proposal meets the unreserved approval of the Trustees of the Foundation. A statement from a local physician regarding my state of health will be sent you very shortly. —/—/

357: TO CHARLOTTE AND RICHARD RYCHTARIK

New York, New York   *March 30th*

Dear Lotte & Ricardo: I am to sail to *Mexico* (damn the gendarmes!) next Saturday. The change [in Guggenheim Fellowship plans] was made without any trouble and I am too happy at change to a *really* (for *me*) creative locality to be anything but pregnant.

Have been having too wonderful a time to breathe—and it still goes on. Will write you more when I know my permanent address. First a week in Mexico City with my old and wonderful friend, Katherine Anne Porter (whom you will notice *also* was awarded)—and then on to some country location. —/—/

358: TO SAMUEL LOVEMAN

México, D.F. [Mexico City]   *April 12, 1931*

Dear Sambo: Got here last night (I always seem to arrive in cities on Sat. nights) and have just had a Sunday dinner a la Mexicano. I begin to feel at home here already, despite my complete ignorance of the language. But kindly people and generous faces have a way of compensating for one's lack of palabra. The peons are the marvel of the place, just as Lawrence said. So lovable, and although picturesque, not in any way consciously so. What faces, and the suffering in them—but so little evidence of bitterness.

We had one evening in Havana, and one night in Vera Cruz on the way, the latter not to be repeated if I can help it. I had better than usual luck by meeting on the second day out the great Dr. Hans Zinsser, of Harvard, who is probably the world's greatest bacteriologist. And what a man besides! He arrived along with me last night with letters from the state and war departments and a half dozen rats in the hold loaded with the deadly typhus. He is to conduct some local experiments and then return to Harvard in two weeks, leaving his assistant, Dr. Maximiliano Castaneda here for 3 more months to complete the experiment. Castaneda, being a native Mexican and very much a gentleman, has and will continue to do all kinds of favors for me—and one thing is assured: I shall not lack proper attendance here if I ever get sick. "Max" as I call him, knows everyone from the president down.

Zinsser, a product of Heidelberg, the Sorbonne, Pasteur Institute and other places besides American Universities, knows and has more interesting ideas about literature than almost anyone I have ever met. What conversations we had!—He's about 51, bandy legged from riding fast horses, looks about 40 at most, writes damn good poetry (which he claims he'd rather do than excel as he does in the scientific world) and in carelessness and largesse is a thoroughbred if I ever saw one. . . . But I could write ten books about him and his incredible adventures in the war and in various parts of the world. Next year he's going to Abyssinia to fight hook worm and other complaints. Well—and what is the best of it—I guess I've made a friend who will be a perennial stimulus to the best that I can do.

The ride up from Vera Cruz was marvelous, not alone the scenery, but the country people all along the way who swarmed around the train selling fruits, cakes, tortillas, serapes, canes, flowers, pulque, beer and what have you! One rides up, up along incredible ledges over valleys filled with tropical vegetation, waterfalls, etc., for about 5 hours. Then in front of Orizaba everything suddenly begins to change. This is the great plateau that in some ways seems even more splendid. Very austere—and with the mountains rising in the distance on each side, here and there the feudal walls of some old rancho—and the burros and brown natives jogging along dry roads. How I wish you were here to witness it. But you will come sometime. I know. —/—/

359: To KATHERINE ANNE PORTER

[Mixcoac] *[April 28]*

DEAR KATHERINE ANNE: HAVE GONE TO THE MANCERA[1] UNTIL THE FIRST. EXCUSE MY WAKEFULNESS PLEASE.

P.S. NO. HAVEN'T BEEN BUSY WITH "LOVERS." JUST YEOWLS AND FLEAS. LYSOL ISN'T NECESSARY IN THE BATHTUB. HAVEN'T GOT "ANYTHING" YET. —/—/

360: To KATHERINE ANNE PORTER

[Mixcoac] *[April 30]*

Dear Katherine Anne: This is as near as I dare come to you today. Shame and chagrin overwhelm me. I hope you can sometime forgive.

361: To KATHERINE ANNE PORTER

[Mixcoac] *[May 1]*

Darling Katherine Anne: I'm too jittery to write a straight sentence but am coming out of my recent messiness with at least as much consistency as total abstinence can offer.

Your two notes were so kind and gave me so much more cheer than I deserve that I'm overcome all over again. God bless you!!! I've got myself in a fix with a hell of [a] bill at the Mancera—but I'll get out of it somehow. My father is sending me some money—meanwhile Hazel Cazes is going to advance some.

This house is a love—and I'm glad to know that it won't be ruined for me now by any absence on your part—and — — — —. The recent

1. A hotel. Crane had been living in Miss Porter's home.

cyclone is my last—at least for a year. Love and a thousand thanks.
When I get D.T.'s again I'll just take it out on police. . . . They'll
have at least a cell for me—or a straitjacket.

362: To Malcolm Cowley

Mixcoac,DF   *June 2nd, 1931*

Dear Malcolm: —/—/ Don't expect much more from me about
Mexico for awhile. Maybe it's the altitude (which *is* a tremendous
strain at times), maybe my favorite drink, Tequila; maybe my b——s
and the beautiful people; or maybe just the flowers that I'm growing
or fostering in my garden . . . but it's all too good, so far, to be
true. I've been too preoccupied, so far, with furnishing, from every
little nail, griddle, bowl and pillow, to look around much outside
the fascinating city markets and streets and bars. No chance to
stretch pennies—just to spend them. Ran out long ago on my Guggenheim installment. But a house just can't be lived in without a
few essentials. And the main "standard American" essentials in
Mexico cost like hell.

Lorna [Dietz] will have to relay to you the more complete details
of my house, should such matters interest you. I found, by advice,
that single mozos weren't apt to be much good. Pulque sprees three
times a day, and the evenings never certain. Besides I needed a
woman to cook. Consequently I have a delightful hide and seek
combination—of both functions (page Mormon be sneezed BUnson)
besides a new installation of electric lights with just enough "glim"—
not to say Klim—to be pleasant.

Moisés [Sáenz] has been swell to me. His innate Aztec refinement;
his quiet daring; his generosity (one should avoid an *et cetera* in
such exceptional cases!) has made me love him very much. He was
very instrumental in my accidental possession of a real decoration:
an ancient silver pony bridle (bells and all!) from the period of the
Conquest, about my neck in a photo taken by Katherine Anne
[Porter]—you shall soon see, like it,—believe it, or not!

I have a quilty, besides a guilty conscience! Haven't yet even
written to Waldo [Frank], whose letters gave me a wonderful send-
off with certain writers here. But Latin American manners, I have
discovered, are rather baffling. Great dinners are planned, but never
come off! If Katherine Anne couldn't explain it all away with
references to certain previous experiences of her own, I'd feel quite
crushed. As it is, I don't mind in the least. Because . . . Mexico

has incredibly fine native painters. (You should see the new Diegos [Rivera] in the Palace!) But all her pretenders to poesy have just read about orchids in Baudelaire, apparently. I have my most pleasant literary moments with an Irish revolutionary, red haired friend of Liam O'Flaherty, shot (and not missed) seventeen times in one conflict and another; the most quietly sincere and appreciative person, in many ways, whom I've ever met. It's a big regret that he's Dublin bound again after three years from home, in a few weeks. Ernest O'Malley by name. And we drink a lot together—look at frescos—and agree! —/—/

363: TO WALDO FRANK

Mixcoac, D.F.   *June 13th, 1931*

Dear Waldo: It seems to require much more determination to write a letter, so far, than to fuss around in my flower garden that skirts three sides of the house I have taken here in Mixcoac for a year. My long-suppressed passion for a few plants and a "philosopher's walk," however, is far from being the sole reason for my neglectfulness of you. The novelty and turmoil incident to the first few weeks; then locating a house; then furnishing it with the indispensables, from broom to teakettle, from mop to mattress; then "breaking in" a native couple to cook and sweep—all with my limited native vocabulary! Well, it's been a good deal to have undertaken, freshly lifted, as I am, to this high altitude.

Despite this delay in getting down to work, I haven't any regrets. You may remember that I spoke of establishing a headquarters as soon as possible on my arrival. I've had to squirm for money temporarily, but corresponding later savings and the creative advantages of having a place of my own—really for the first time in my life— ought to justify my action.

As for Mexico—I'm not frothing over quite so much as I did for awhile, but I'm still so fascinated and impressed by the people that I want to stay much longer than one year, if I can manage to. You were right, it's a sick country; and God knows if it ever has been, or will be otherwise. I doubt if I will ever be able to fathom the Indian really. It may be a dangerous quest, also. I'm pretty sure it is, in fact. But humanity is so unmechanized here still, so immediate and really dignified (I'm speaking of the Indians, peons, country people—not the average mestizo) that it is giving me an entirely fresh perspective. And whether immediately creative or not, more

profound than Europe gave me. . . . This is truly "another world."
There isn't much use for the present in describing my reactions
beyond saying that I find them all expressed in my emphatic agreement with nearly everything said by Anita Brenner in her *Idols
Behind Altars* which I've just finished reading. It would take me, I
imagine, a long residence here to be able to contradict any of her
statements, besides which I am so sympathetic to her attitude, reactions and general thesis as not to care to court divergencies of
opinion.

A few days after my arrival I took a taxi and delivered the letters
of introduction that you so generously provided. I immediately
heard from Leon Felipe [Camino], and a few days later had an audience with Estrada. The former I saw a couple of times later—and
was introduced to a flock of writers, doctors, etc., one afternoon at
the Café Colon. Camino seemed very cordial, but suddenly
"dropped" me. Latin-Americans, I've been told (and now I *know*)
have a way of inviting you out on some specific day, and then "letting you down" most beautifully—without notice or subsequent
apology or explanation. I've got so that I take it quite for granted,
and if any other more tempting occasion offers itself in the meantime, I, too, humor my whim.

Estrada gave me two de luxe volumes of his poetry in response
to the copy of *The Bridge* (Paris edition) I brought up to him. I
can't read Spanish well enough yet to even attempt his books, nor
any other "Mexican" poetry; but off-hand I've more spontaneous
respect for him than for Camino, who, as soon as he heard I was
about to call on Estrada, began to ridicule both the man and his
work in high glee. What makes me rather indifferent to all of them
is the fact that not one of them is really interested one iota in expressing anything indigenous; rather they are busy aping (as though
it could be done in Spanish!) Paul Valéry, Eliot,—or more intensely,
the Parnassians of 35 years ago. And they are all "bored"—or at least
pleased to point the reference. Estrada spoke very warmly of you,
and after what some of the others said, I should consider him a real
friend of yours. In contrast to their general directions and preoccupations, however, I still (to date, at any rate) harbor the illusion that
there is a soil, a mythology, a people and a spirit here that are capable of unique and magnificent utterance.

Moisés Sáenz, who has had me out to his place at Taxco, and who
has treated me as hospitably and generously as anyone I ever remember, has the same conviction. And he says that Casanova, whom I
have merely met, has a more natural attitude than the typical Mexi-

can *litterateur*. I hope to see more of Casanova later; he's been ill most of the time since I got here. I've not yet had a reply from Montéllano. Camino asked to do some translations from *White Bldgs* for *Contemporaneos*. I gave him the book—and offered assistance. But since he found me out of the stiff black round-shouldered "elegance" —in fact in my usual household white sailor pants and shirt—he hasn't been heard from—by mail or otherwise. One must appear in veritable Wall Street gear to impress the Mexican hidalgo!

He said that he was translating your new Latin Am. book, as I remember. Will you tell me something about its publication date, etc.—since I can't get any reply from Camino? And now, how about your new work, your novel? And your plans for this summer, etc.? I hope you are having a smooth road toward some really individual expression. Hope you'll approve of my reference to you in the enclosed interview, from *Excelsior. El Universal* was also very kindly. Their feature writer, Rafael Valle, is a very decent and intelligent and constant friend of mine. — — — —

Katherine Anne Porter and I are neighbors here in Mixcoac. You really ought to get hold of her book *Flowering Judas*. The title story, and another called "María Concepción," are very profound comments on Mexico.

364: To Morton Dauwen Zabel

Mixcoac, D.F., Mexico   *June 20th, 1931*

Dear Mr. Zabel: The post (for books, etc. 2nd class) is apt to be very slow to Mexico,—at any rate unreliable. If this be not too great an impediment to either my reception or return of review books from *Poetry*—then let me ask for the two books suggested by you for review in your very kind letter of June 11th.

Further, I realize that my facilities for adequate reviewing of books are somewhat restricted here, there being no library handy for consultation on recent or even near-recent works on American poetry, etc. But if you are willing to take the risk—then so am I. And if you find the resultant estimates too biased or unfounded, you certainly need be under no compulsion to print them.

Didn't Roy Helton compile an anthology, or rather a study interspersed with very good quotations, on Negro folk songs, spirituals, etc.? I suppose the jacket of his book will contain whatever reference to his earlier works are notable. But if not, please give me some word about the above.

Allow me to thank you and Miss Monroe for the copy of *Poetry* recently received. I hope, and very earnestly, that I shall soon have something worthy to submit to you. Since leaving the pattern of *The Bridge* the "new freedom" (call it rather a new restriction) has left me, at least momentarily, rather speechless. I'm too attached to the consciousness of my own land to write "tourist sketches" elsewhere. Mexico is well enough. But I'd rather be in my favorite corner of Connecticut. The first requirement of a scholarship, however, is to leave the U.S.A. It doesn't matter much whither. It wouldn't so much matter if the entire outside world didn't positively hate us Americans so much. To create in such an atmosphere isn't so easy however!

365: To Selden Rodman

Mixcoac, D.F.   *June 20th, 1931*

Dear Selden Rodman: —/—/ I hope you will not forsake the Muse, or her pursuit. For in the light of your "Departure" it seems to me, you ought certainly to write that "Unwritten Poem" mentioned in the subtitle; for there are lines and passages in its "Prologue" that I like immensely. I hope I can mention a few points without offense; the first six stanzas, I think, present the longest solid stretch of sustained intention, some of the rest seeming to me diffuse in patches, or at least susceptible of condensation. But when I speak of condensation I am presumably alluding as much to my own craze or weakness for that characteristic. For I've carried that element to the extreme point of unintelligibility more than once, as I well know. Here are a few of my favorite lines anyway:

> I must leave, said the traveler, everything behind me:
> The place that watched when no one else was by

> The worth of life is the single shrill protesting
> Voice; come near, listen but do not learn, he said.

> What has the flashing train in a gorge at midnight
> Carried from peace that a million years withstood?

Then there seems (to me) a rather blank or vague piling of lines until one comes to the splendidly concentrated lines beginning:
Yes, for the ink, etc., and continuing for 16 lines of real intensity that reminds me in the best sense of Rimbaud. And although you

are still a long way from the ending, I can't so far see that between there and the final stanza you gain much more than a few implications and the statement of a few opinions (which statements, etc., don't seem to rise to the same level as the passages that I've already mentioned as being so good). Please take my opinions as lightly as thistle down, however, as I'm a cripple already to my own fetishes in style, and probably as blind as a bat in any broad sense of criticism. Beyond that, I'll have to blame you, as you asked me for my opinion on that poem.

Hale's article on the Future of the Novel is the only other thing in this number I've had time to read. Hale rather frightens me: he's so declamatory and so sure. He must be a good sort to talk with; at least I'd like the chance sometimes. I agree so much with some of his statements, his keenness on the scent of such men as Thomas Wolfe, whose *Look Homeward, Angel* was one of the real experiences of life. But I imagine that some of Hale's very laudable intensity will have to take a less declamatory form of expression if he wants to exert the influence as a critic which is really his due. I don't mean that this involves any compromises, either.

Are you taking up some special studies in Europe? I hope you have such intentions; for without such anchorage, I found that Europe had a very debilitating effect on me. Not that I could have been so privileged as to have had that chance, since I have never had a day in school beyond my junior year in high school; but the case is considerably different with you.

You mentioned MacLeish and the Conquistador poem in *The Yale Review*. I wish I had bought the copy of that—the one I hastily glanced at in Brentano's basement months and months ago! I hope that he is well along with the rest of that poem, so fine was the opening. MacLeish has a more flexible literary genius than anyone writing in America today, and he'll probably be the most noteworthy poet of our times. His sensibility isn't as prodigal and startling as Cummings'; but then, Cummings will never take the trouble to prune anything or discipline his genius. —/—/

366: To Katherine Anne Porter

[*Mixcoac*]   [*June 22*]

Dear Katherine Anne: My apologies are becoming so mechanical as (through repetition) to savour of the most negligible insincerity. So I have to leave most of this to your judgment of the potency and malfeasance of an overdose of tequila.

Let Theodora[1] know—if I have any chance of talking with you and explaining. Otherwise I'll know that you don't want to be molested even to that point of endurance.

I spent the night in jail—as Theodora has probably told you. That was, in its way, sufficient punishment. Besides having made a fool of myself in Town. . . . However I was arrested for nothing more than challenging the taxi driver for an excessive rate. But if it hadn't been for waiting for you—hour on hour, and trying to keep food warm, cream sweet, and my damnable disposition—don't suppose I'd have yelled out at you so horribly en route to doom!

I don't ask you to forgive. Because that's probably past hope. But since Peggy [Baird] will be here in a few days—I'd rather, for her sake as well as mine, that she didn't step into a truly Greenwich Village scene.

367: To WILLIAM WRIGHT

Chagrin Falls, Ohio   *July 15th, 1931*

Dear Bill: —/—/ I'm very glad that you spoke about the check I sent you early in April. I couldn't figure it out any other way than that you had waited until the following month before turning it in; and if that wasn't exactly the case I still can't understand why it was returned as invalid. For my account, at least until the last of May, stood well in excess of the amount of your check. I was on the point of writing you an inquiry about all this when I was called north. The check enclosed, however, will not be at all questionable. I'm very sorry you've had to wait so long, and let me repeat my profound thanks to you for your very generous help.

As to my father's business; certain branches and departments of it (that is, several of its corporate entities in which he had controlling interest) will undoubtedly be carried on. Inventories are now in progress, statements regarding the net estate, etc., are in preparation; and as yet it is, of course, impossible to know exactly what course will be taken. Mrs. Crane was left with the authorization of deciding practically everything. Which was right and proper, since I have never taken any active part in any branch of my father's concerns. I am left in reasonably secure circumstances, at least for a few years, however, and if I so choose I can probably pursue my own literary studies with a somewhat free-er mind than formerly.

It is a real consolation to me now that I made the long stay here

1. Miss Porter's cook.

with my father that I did last winter. As you already know, our relations for many years, had been somewhat confused by general family disturbances which were most unfortunate and which resulted in a great many misunderstandings. Father and I had recently got acquainted all over again. It made both of us very much happier. And if my father had to go thus early in life—I'm very grateful that at least I am left with a fuller appreciation of his fine qualities and of his genuine love for me than might have been possible without the course of some recent events. I can say that his character and the impress of it that I lately received will be a real inspiration to me. That is the finest kind of bequest that one can leave, I'm sure. —/—/

368: To Lorna Dietz

Chagrin Falls, Ohio   *July 15th, 1931*

Dearest Lorna: To begin with the same subject which you did in your last—and to continue with what has been almost an obsession with me for the last month—I want to say a few words about Katherine Anne Porter. Not that I can possibly give even the outline of the whole queer situation, but since she has done so much announcing, just a hint at the circumstances.

Katherine Anne's disposition, as I knew her initially in NY was considerably different than I found it to be since — — — — in Mexico. —/—/ Katherine Anne was quite lovely to me on more than one occasion, and since I have always liked her a lot, it was hard to relinquish her company.

The continuance, however,—and this is the only way I can put it —resulted in some very strained situations and outbreaks on my part—generally at times when I had had too much to drink. Since I have no very clear recollection of everything said during those times I presume I must have been pretty awful. Everything had been going very smoothly for some time, however; Katherine Anne frequently dropping into my place for afternoon chats, beer, etc., when the apparently decisive moment occurred.

I had asked them both to have dinner with me on a certain day at my house. It was well understood, etc. I made extensive preparations—and was left to keep things warm the entire afternoon, nipping at a bottle of tequila meanwhile, and going through the usual fretful crescendo of sentiments that such conduct incurs. Toward evening, having fed most of the natives in the vicinity and being rather upset, I went to town, where more drinks were downed. But in an argument with the taxi driver at my gate later in the evening I challenged him to arbitration at the local police station. Result: a night in jail; for feeling is so high against Americans in Mexico since the recent Oklahoma affair, that any pretext is sufficient to embarrass one.

K.A.'s place is just around the corner from the house I took, so on the way to the station I passed her gate. She and — — — — happened to be within speaking distance. I remember having announced my predicament and of having said, in anger at her response to the dinner engagement, "Katherine Anne, I have my opinion of you." I was furious, of course, and I still have no reason for doubting that — — — — simply devised that insult deliberately. I haven't seen Katherine Anne since, nor has she ever offered the slightest explanation of her absence. She told a mutual friend that I said something particularly outrageous to her that evening at the gate; but what it may have been beyond what I have just mentioned I don't know. I wrote her a very humble apology a few days later, but there was no response.

It's all very sad and disagreeable. But one imputation I won't stand for. That is the obvious and usual one: that my presence in the neighborhood was responsible for a break or discontinuance of Katherine Anne's creative work.—/—/ I'm tired of being made into a bogey or ogre rampant in Mexico and tearing the flesh of delicate ladies. I'm also tired of a certain rather southern type of female vanity. And that's about all I ever want to say about Katherine Anne again personally.

My father was buried last Saturday. Mrs. Crane, despite the fact that the delay was really a great strain on her endurance, insisted on awaiting my arrival, which wasn't until late Friday, as I couldn't get airplane reservations beyond Albuquerque. She was so grief-stricken that I've been worried about her. I'm more impressed by her sincerity and dignity than I can tell you, however, and her feelings toward me make me feel that I have a real home whenever I want to claim it here with her. She had a room and bath all ready for me—and it's to be regarded as permanently mine.

I'm glad that I've already been able to be of some help to her in matters of the estate. It will be some time before all inventories are taken of various departments of my father's business and I'll certainly be here beyond the time of your trip west, in August. You must plan on stopping over at least a day. You really ought to see this country place, for I think it's worth more than a passing glance. And above and beyond such considerations, I have a great yen to look you over, as you might guess. Certainly you can "make it," and I'm sure that a day's break in that long trip would be refreshing. Let me know.

My father's will left very modest provisions for me, but they are as good as an annual Guggenheim, anyway, and that is all I really require. Quite properly, Mrs. Crane was left with the direction of most of his property and concerns—along with two other executors. The chocolate business will probably be discontinued, as it should have been anyway, as soon as one or two expensive leases can be disposed of. I may or may not take a hand in the picture business—but probably not. Nothing can be definitely decided until we know more about the total status of the estate.

As I just wrote Bill [Brown]—who surprised me by writing a very thoughtful note—I'm increasingly glad that I had those three months with my father last winter. The enormous advance in mutual understanding and affection that was achieved has left me with a better and truer picture of my father than I had ever had before. It's good to remember, too, that he was unusually contented and optimistic during the last few months, about his business and all other concerns. And when he went he had no more than a passing flash of recognition of the event before complete unconsciousness supervened. —/—/

369: To SAMUEL LOVEMAN

Mixcoac, D.F.   *Sept. 11th, 1931*

Dear Sam: —/—/ I have had the pleasure to meet a young archeologist from Wisconsin, who is studying in the University here and who thinks he has discovered a buried Aztec pyramid right in the vicinity of my house. Yesterday we took pick and shovel and worked our heads off digging into the side of a small hill, itself on a vast elevation overlooking the entire valley of Anahuac. Except for a few flocks of goats and sheep the entire neighborhood has been abandoned since the Conquest. A marvelous stillness and grassy perfume pervade the district; one sees the two great volcanoes in the distance and a part of the horizon glazed by Lake Texcoco, seemingly below which floats, as in a dream, the City of Mexico. It was an arduous and rich afternoon. I have a lame back today, but also some very interesting chips and pieces of the true Aztec pottery picked up here and there on the surface and from our little excavation. The experience is haunting, melancholy too. But such "first hand" contact beats the more artificial contacts that museums proffer. We also ran across one of those incredibly sharp fragments of obsidian, part of a knife blade used either to carve stone and other materials or human flesh. It is still a mystery as to how they cut obsidian—but this shard was perfectly edged and graded as though it had been as conformable as wood. —/—/

370: To William Wright

Mixcoac, D.F. Mexico *Sept. 21, 1931*

Dear Bill: — — — — Vera Cruz was a hissing cauldron when I got there; in fact the last two days on the boat were Turkish baths. But once here on the plateau—I went back to my nightly blankets and recovered quickly. The aforesaid port has had a pretty little hurricane since my debarkation. I knew it couldn't help but happen.

I felt awfully diffident about leaving the U.S., but I'm beginning to be entirely glad that I came back here after all. In the first place there was no settling down this time to be accomplished. I found my house in good order, the servants joyful to see me, and my garden a perfect miracle of growth and colorful profusion. I could begin "living" right away without a moment in a hotel, a blanket or kitchen implement to buy—having spent about three months in such preoccupations on my previous visit. The rainy season is lasting unusually long, but it keeps all the verdure so miraculously green that the countryside will hold its colors all the longer into the long months of drowth to come.

During the mere two weeks since my return I've already had the most interesting adventure that I think I ever remember. I came back with the resolution to get out more into the smaller cities and pueblos, to get as thoroughly acquainted with the native Indian population as possible. So when I met a young archeologist from Wisconsin who asked me to go along with him on a five days' trip to Tepoztlan I didn't linger. Though two books and a dozen articles have been written about Tepoztlan (see Stuart Chase's *Mexico* and Carleton Beals' *Mexican Maze*) it has never been invaded by tourists. And isn't likely to be, either, for some time. As there is nothing remotely resembling a hotel or lodging house in the place I went prepared to sleep on the floor of the Monastery. One can sleep soundly almost anywhere and be thankful for the limited diet of beans and tortillas if one has spent the whole day walking, scrambling over dizzy crags or hunting fragments of old Aztec idols, of which the surrounding cornfields of Tepoztlan are full.

The town is practically surrounded by cliffs as high as 800 feet, basalt ledges with a perilous sheer drop sometimes of 300 feet, covered with dense tropical foliage and veritable hanging gardens—with cascades and waterfalls galore. The descent begins about 3 miles from El Parque where the train leaves one—about 4 hours from Mixcoac.

(Distances in linear miles are so deceptive here, since mountainous country necessitates such inclines and devious windings. One can watch the engine from the rear most of the way.)

But I'm not going to give an exhaustive description of the town as you can read that, and better formulated too in Chase's book, which everyone seems to be reading now anyway. The most exciting feature of our trip and visit was the rare luck of arriving on the eve of the yearly festival (fiesta) of Tepozteco, the ancient Aztec god of pulque, whose temple, partially ruined by the Spaniards and recent revolutions, still hangs on one of the perilous cliffs confronting the town.

Only a small fraction of the populace (they are all pure unadulterated Aztec) took part or even attended this ceremony; but we found those that did, largely elderly, the finest and kindliest of all the lovely people of the place. Aside from those who had climbed up to spend the night in watch at the temple, there were only about twenty-five. These, divided into several groups around lanterns (of all places!) on the roof of the Cathedral and Monastery which dominates the town, made a wonderful sight with their dark faces, white "pyjama" suits and enormous white hats. A drummer and a flute player standing facing the dark temple on the heights, alternated their barbaric service at ten minute intervals with loud ringing of all the church bells by the sextons of the church. Two voices, still in conflict here in Mexico, the idol's and the Cross. Yet there really did not seem to be a real conflict that amazing night. Nearly all of these "elders" I have been describing go to mass!

And so kindly and interested in explaining the old myths of their gods to us! Fortunately my archeologist friend speaks perfect Spanish —besides knowing some Aztec and some local mythology. Meanwhile, if you can possibly imagine such a night, the lightning flickered over the eastern horizon while a crescent moon fell into the west. And between the two a trillion stars glittered overhead! It was truly the Land of Oz, with the high valley walls in the Wizard's circle. Rockets were sent whizzing up—to be answered by other rockets far up and over from the lofty temple. After nine, when the playing stopped, we asked the "elders" to a stall in the town market and served them each with a glass of tequila. We were invited to join them again at 3 A.M. atop the church again, for the conclusion of the watch.

I'm sorry to say I didn't awake until five. But it was still pitch dark. And to hear those weird notes of drum and fife in the dark valley, refreshed as we were with sleep, it was even more compelling. We rushed from the baker's house (where we had found a bamboo bed and exquisite hospitality) over the rough stone streets into the church yard, stumbling up the dark corridors and narrow stairs of the monastery just as a faint light emerged over the eastern break in the cliffs. There was the same bundle of elders welcoming us and serving us delicious coffee, all the hotter for a generous infusion of pulque, straight pulque alcohol in each cup.

But most enthralling of all was the addition of another drum— this being the ancient Aztec drum, pre-Conquest and guarded year after year from the destruction of the priests and conquerors, that how many hundreds of times had been beaten to propitiate the god, Tepozteco, the patron and protector of these people. A large wooden cylinder, exquisitely carved and showing a figure with animal head, upright, and walking through thick woods,—it lay horizontally on the floor of the roof, resounding to two heavily padded drum sticks before the folded knees of one of the Indians. The people at the temple had played it up there the night before, and now someone had brought it down to be played to the rising sun in the valley.

Suddenly, as it was getting lighter and lighter and excitement was growing more and more intense, one of the Indians who had been playing it put the drum sticks into my hands and nodded toward the amazing instrument. It seemed too good to be true, really, that I, who had expected to be thrown off the roof when I entered the evening before, should now be invited to actually participate. And actually I did! I not only beat the exact rhythm with all due accents, which they had been keeping up for hours; I even worked in an elaboration, based on the lighter tattoo of the more modern drum of the evening before. This, with such ponderous sticks, was exhaust- ing to the muscles of the forearm; but I had the pleasure of pleasing them so that they almost embraced me. They did, in fact, several of them—put their arms around our shoulders and walk back and forth the whole length of the roof, when at the astronomical hour of six the whole place seemed to go mad in the refulgence of full day. It is something to hear bells rung, but it is inestimably better to see the sextons wield the hammers, swinging on them with the

full weight of their entire bodies like frantic acrobats—while a whole
bevy of rockets shower into such a vocal sunrise!

Well, after that there was the whole series of tableaus and performances incident to the Mexican Independence Day celebration
(Sept. 15-16-17) in which everybody took part. But of that another
time. You can see how I am enthusiastic about Tepoztlan. I went
bathing in mountain streams with a young Indian, gorged on beans
and tortillas, found idols in the surrounding cornfields and finally,
the morning I was leaving, met the Vicar at stool in the Cathedral.
On the climb back to the station we visited the ancient temple. It
still has fragments of remarkable relief and is staunchly and beautifully constructed. I may go back to Tepoztlan for two weeks in
October. I never left a town feeling so mellow and in such pleasant
relations with everybody in the place. —/—/

371: To Malcolm Cowley

Mixcoac, D.F.   *Oct. 5th, 1931*

Dear Malcolm: —/—/ Yes, Peggy [Baird] must have been pretty close
to danger for awhile judging by what she said about her symptoms.
She stayed in bed for a week or so, but went to Puebla over last
weekend and looked very well this morning when I called. I think
she's to keep pretty quiet, however, if relapses aren't to be expected.
Bill Spratling wired me to bring her along with me to Taxco tomorrow for a few days, and I think she's planning on joining me since
I've had no word to the contrary this afternoon. She was going to
ask her doctor about it. . . . —/—/

As Bill [Brown] has probably told you, the Katherine Anne [Por-
ter] upset accounted for my more than diffidence about seeing most
of our mutual friends when I passed through NY. Sometime I may
say more about it, but I'm sick of the subject just now; and since
Mexico is proving to be so much more pleasant and absorbing to me
during this second sojourn, I don't want to stir up any more un-
neighborly dust here in Mixcoac this evening than matches a pleasant mood.

—/—/ I'm glad to be of any help I can to Peggy, love her as always,
and enjoy her company (and we see quite a lot of each other) immensely. Old friends are a God-send anywhere! Especially when
they're as good sports as Peggy is. . . . She's pretty fragile, but I
think she's happy here, possibly more so than anywhere else right
now. —/—/

372: TO MORTON DAUWEN ZABEL
(Postcard)

[*Mixcoac*]   [*ca. October 10*]

Your letter this morning—and now the books. Putnam is more surprising and magnificent than ever! Am glad to have such a challenge
of a review.

373: TO SLATER BROWN

[*Mixcoac*]   *Oct. 22nd*

Dear Bill: Please tell Malcolm that his article on the Munson-
Josephson "debate" has delayed my dinner by two hours of sore
sides! "Old Nick" (Jamaica) Rum *may* have contributed a little to
some pleasant distress, but I still owe a debt. . . . I wish I had the
two previous articles of the series at hand; can't you get Betty to sort
them out and send them to me?

From cock-crow to sunset, here in Mixcoac, my life is extremely
jolly. And then beyond. . . . How I wish you and Sue [Jenkins]
were here sometimes! Guitars and *corridas* galore. Even *I* am learning how to sing! One thing I can't seem to get around to do—and
that's the reviews I contracted to do for *Poetry*. Have you seen Putnam's new book of poems, *The Five Seasons?* I've got to "do" that,
and it's almost too big a job.

"Old Nick" and Nicotine keep me too occupied.

PS—Allen's note on Milton was one of the best things in modern
criticism I expect to anticipate!

374: TO CHARLOTTE AND RICHARD RYCHTARIK

[*Mixcoac*]   *Nov. 4, 1931*

Dear Charlotte & Richard: —/—/ Then there have been two rather
extensive visits to Taxco, pictures of which you've seen. David
Siqueiros, whom I consider to be the greatest of contemporary Mexican painters, is living out there. He's painted a portrait of me that
is astounding. When photographs are made I'll have to send you
one, and for heaven's sake don't lose it, whether you like it or not.
I don't know yet how I'm going to get the original up north.
Siqueiros is the one who painted the picture of that train flying

along, that we took particular notice of in the Carnegie exhibit at the Art Amusement last spring. Remember? But that wasn't a fair example of his vast power and scope at all. He's fundamentally a mural painter, and even his smaller paintings have a tremendous *scale*. I bought a small water color of his, a Mexican boy's head, which you will be quite wild about. I've never seen anything of Gauguin's which was better. Indeed the two have a certain plastic quality in common as well as the use of heavy pigments. Siqueiros, however, is always *most* Mexican and himself. The very soil of Mexico seems spread on his canvasses.

The last two days have been important on the native Indian calendar: the Day of the Dead. All over the country, and right here in this metropolitan city, you will find the cemeteries full of dark-skinned men and women, whole families in fact, sitting on tomb-stones day and night holding lighted candles to the spirits of the dead. They bring their food and drink with them. Far from being sad, it's very merry. They drink and eat much—and it all ends up by setting off firecrackers made in the image of Judas. You must re-member some of the amazing skeleton toys and paper and clay skulls that we saw at that Mexican exhibition. Well, they are for sale everywhere right now—and such a variety of other beautiful trays, crockery, serapes, toys, etc., from all the provinces as would drive you wild. A certain park in the city is set apart for the *puestas,* or booths, that form this special market. A walk through there beats the ex-citement of any museum I've ever been in. —/—/

I've had some nice parties here in my house. I know more people than I did before, and as far as space goes I might have sixty here at a time. My servant plays the guitar and sings beautifully. Mexi-cans are always bursting into song and strum away for hours. When I have a party it's easy to get him to bring in two or three of his friends, equally gifted, and the result is such music, my friends, as would make your feet dance and your eyes shine brightly all the night! The results were a little too lively, in fact, one day last week when I gave a party to two American boys who are touring down here in a big Lincoln car. One of them suddenly climbed up on my roof, drawing the ladder after him, and began pelting tiles down into the courtyard of my neighbor. I nearly had heart failure before we got him down, since my neighbor is a crack shot, and the provo-cations for shooting are much less here in Mexico than anywhere I know. The kid had just drunk about a quart of *tequila,* so of course it was only partly due to his response to the music! —/—/

375: To SOLOMON GRUNBERG
(Postcard)

[Mixcoac]   *[November 10, 1931]*

Haven't heard since that long letter I wrote you. And wonder if you
got it. Mail is sometimes opened here and not forwarded. I never
know. If I'm tampered with any more I intend to object, to the
Secretary of State who is a poet and knows me.

376: To PEGGY BAIRD

[Mixcoac]   *Nov. 13th*

Dear Peggy: I don't think you need bother to consider me a friend
any more.

377: To PEGGY BAIRD

[Mixcoac]   *Thursday [ca. Nov. 14]*

Dear Peggy: I don't know why I felt impelled to write you that
gracious note of yesterday, except perhaps on account of the heeby-
jeebies—and the fact that when I called with Daniel[1] in the morning
I was refused admittance.

Of course, if you really feel that strongly about it, for whatever
causes I don't know, then we'll have to remain apart. Please let me
contradict that note of yesterday, anyway.

378: To SAMUEL LOVEMAN

Mixcoac, DF   *Nov. 17th*

Dear Sam: —/—/ I haven't been any too well lately. First a week's
spell of the grippe—then lately a kind of half relapse, bad cold, back
ache, etc. All this in spite of heavenly weather, but not, I'm afraid,
despite a strenuous program of dancing, *tequila* and amor. I'm on
the water wagon for awhile. . . . Meanwhile my house is in considerable tumult. David Siqueiros (who is certainly the greatest painter
in Mexico) arrived Sunday night from his house in Taxco, with his
wife and doctors—so deathly ill from malaria that he had to be

1. Crane's Mexican servant.

carried into the house. No really expert medical attention being available in a town so small as Taxco—and after 8 days of mounting fever—there was nothing to do but rush to Mexico City. He contracted it during a long trip through the *tierra caliente,* or "hot country" which is the wild jungleland of Mexico near Acapulco along the Pacific coast. It is a marvelous trip, but very strenuous and dangerous, through native villages where a tax collector has never dared venture, and where the people wear the same Aztec costume that Cortez found them in, there being several towns entirely of Negroes (escaped slaves) who wear nothing but the slender loin cloths of Africa and who shoot with bow and arrows. It seems incredible, but Mexico is more vast than you can ever realize by looking at a map and more various in its population than any country on earth. Layer on layer of various races and cultures scattered in the million gorges and valleys which make the scenery so plastic and superb. Siqueiros is going to pull through all right, but I shall probably have him here with me for a couple of months. Malaria takes a long time. I'm glad to be of help in such a crisis, however, and since I had three rooms which I never used the house really isn't crowded.

I bought two fine paintings of S. which I hope someday you will see. I guess I wrote you that he painted a portrait of me (about 4 by 2½ ft) which is causing much favorable comment. Besides which I have a splendid watercolor of an Indian boy's head. You have never seen anything better by Gauguin, which, however, doesn't describe the originality and authenticity of these works. Then I have about a dozen small watercolors, mostly landscapes, painted by Mexican children none of whom are older than eight—these for about 20¢ apiece!

Of course the Siqueiros works cost me *considerably,* so much, in fact, that I've been worried about making ends meet until my next quarterly from the Guggenheims falls due Jan. 1st. For what was my great shock after buying them to be notified that none of the income that I had been assured of from the estate would be paid, and would continue unpaid indefinitely! This meant that the paintings had to be paid for out of the Guggenheim allowance—and in consequence I'm stranded excepting for a few dollars remaining in my personal N.Y. account—until January 1st. And it will be hard to cash personal checks hereabouts. And if business doesn't pick up before next May it probably means that I can't continue to stay in Mexico for awhile longer, as I had hoped to do.

Those masks that you bought last fall are undoubtedly Mexican.

Even the neo-Greek mask that puzzled me so. I am sure about them all being Mexican because I've seen dozens in private collections and museums here that have the same variety of stylizations. There is a great tradition of masks here, and while those of yours may not be extremely old they are decidedly not new nor sold around in the shops here, and are really valuable. You have to go out to some of the most remote settlements to get that sort, and they're seldom to be bought because of their religious significance.

I haven't been able to resist buying some other things like serapes, giant hats, embroideries, lacquer trays and Guadalajara pottery. You've never seen such beautiful arts and crafts as the Indian element here has perpetuated. Wm. Spratling's collection at Taxco is one of the best, and when his book comes out, called *Little Mexico* (Cape & Smith), for heaven's sake read it. Its illustrations are many and will give you more detail than I could squeeze into twenty letters.

This letter is becoming ungodly long—and I haven't been able to tell one fragment of all there is to tell. I'm not upset about the Eastman and Mencken notices. There *was* a quite serviceable editorial in *The New Republic* on the former a couple of weeks back. And if it provides something for Burke and Cowley to write about—then so much the better. They're bound to be fairly loyal to my *style,* even if not to my "personality." It is even more consoling that a few people like yourself maintain a constancy to both.

379: To His Stepmother

[*Mixcoac*]   *Nov. 23rd*

—/—/ Last Friday the situation [Siqueiros' visit] got so on my nerves that I bolted for Tepoztlan. It proved to be the best of all remedies. Long strenuous walks over rocks and mountains with my pack on my back, pleasant encounters with some of the natives who remembered me from my former visit, and baths in nearby streams —there's really nothing like getting out in the wilds occasionally to clear one's head. I was invited to a very sociable weekend party at a lovely house in Taxco, but I preferred to be absolutely alone for a change. Deciding to walk from Tepoztlan to Cuernavaca Sunday I got lost on a false trail through a dense forest and stumbled about, not knowing where on earth I was for hours. Thirsty!!! and blistered feet!!! Finally I came upon the railroad track, miles from where I should have been, but was so glad to find something *definite* that

I walked the ties for about four hours more until I came [to] a small station outside Cuernavaca, a filling station for locomotives. And there wasn't much water left in the tank for future trains when I got through drinking there, I can tell you. I didn't attempt any further exploits, but took the next train through to Mexico [City]. I must have walked about 35 miles at least that day. But I've really felt swell ever since. Next time, however, I won't carry so much in my pack!

380: To Eda Lou Walton

Mixcoac, D.F.   *Nov. 27th '31*

Dear Eda Lou: I'm very glad to hear that you are applying for a Guggenheim. You certainly deserve it and would make splendid use of it. Mr. Moe, the Secretary, has sent me a copy of your proposed program (this being part of the usual routine regarding references) and I shall be greatly disappointed if you do not have a chance to carry it out. Naturally my response to Moe will be very warm in your favor. However slight your hopes may be there is evidence that at least you are being considered seriously.

These are dull times for poetry, even as Mr. Mencken says, and I must admit that with all my present salutary circumstances my impulses in that direction are surprisingly low. A beautiful environment and economic security are far from compensating for a world of chaotic values and frightful spiritual depression. And I can't derive any satisfaction in the spinning out of mere personal moods and attitudes.

Meanwhile, I am, however,—or at least I feel I am—penetrating to a new kind of world in the psychology of the Indians, hereabouts, though it hasn't taken on any real outline as yet. Everyone says that it takes a long time to make an adjustment here. The infinite variety of climate, vegetation, and the distraction of a new language as well as thousands of fascinating sights and speculations, all combine to uproot one and hold one in a strange suspension. At least I feel that I am living fully and absorbing a great deal, whatever else. And that, I suppose, is a considerably better state to be in than the dubious tenure some office job would provide, if such indeed were even accessible! I like Mexico and the Mexicans (Indians) so much that I'd like to remain here permanently. I'm even thinking of attempting some work like teaching (English Lit.) in one of the many private colleges if I can locate such work before my Guggenheim fellowship expires. —/—/

381: To ——

Mixcoac, D.F.   *Nov. 30th*

Dear ——: The nature of the Mexican Indian, as Lawrence said, isn't exactly "sunny," but he is more stirred by the moon, if you get what I mean, than any type I've ever known. The fluttering gait and the powder puff are unheard of here, but that doesn't matter in the least. Ambidexterity is all in the fullest masculine tradition. I assure you from many trials and observations. The pure Indian type is decidedly the most beautiful animal imaginable, including the Polynesian—to which he often bears a close resemblance. And the various depths of rich coffee brown, always so clear and silken smooth, are anything but Negroid. Add to that—voices whose particular pitch will make the welkin ring—and you have a rather tempting setting for an odd evening. Even Lawrence, with all his "blood-fear" of them, couldn't resist some lavish descriptions of their fine proportions.

—/—/ I have a project of a poetic drama on Cortes and Montezuma, but the more I see the more I realize how intricate the subject is—and how much longer it is going to take me than I anticipated. —/—/

382: To His Stepmother

[*Mixcoac*]   *December 12th, '31*

Dear Bess: There is a distinct smell of powder in the air this evening. But that isn't all! Rockets are whizzing up sporadically for miles around, and the sound of church bells far and near, has been incessant since dawn. All of which is to say that this is an important day in the Mexican calendar—nothing less, in fact, than the annual Feast of the Virgin of Guadalupe, the particular Patroness of all Mexicans. This year's celebration is all the more extravagant, as she is reputed to have "appeared" here (before a humble peon named Juan Diego) just four hundred years ago today.

For weeks the influx of Indians and pilgrims of all types from all the provinces and tribes of Mexico has been in progress. It is probably no exaggeration to say that there are two hundred thousand extra souls, pious and near-pious, who have flocked here to continue the *fiesta* until New Year's. But today—all of them, including the majority of Mexico City's population of one million—went to the little town of Guadalupe Hidalgo, practically a suburb now, of Mexico City, where a great cathedral has been erected near the spot where the Virgin is reputed to have made her first appearance.

I engaged a cab the night before, and got up at four this morning to get an early start, arriving before the Cathedral just at dawn. Even then one couldn't elbow one's way into the church without waiting in line for an hour. I gave that up, having come more to see some of the native Indian dances that take place here and there throughout the town—some, in fact, right in front of the cathedral. The whole business is simply indescribable without ten reams of paper; but suffice to say that the dances were wonderful. Certain people are picked from each district or tribe for their marked ability—and there is quite a rivalry between districts in the excellence of their performance. There are from 24 to 45 in a group, generally in circular formation, with banners, guitars which they play as they sway and turn, and elaborate pantaloons, skirts, feather crests, etc. Death and the Devil weave in and out among them— and other masked figures, like wild boars and old man-of-the-mountain.

I pushed and prodded from one group to the other, until by 9:30 I was ready to come home; and did. I had taken Daniel along, and was glad of it, since I just missed causing a riot by attempting to photograph some of the dancers in action, which is, it seems, forbidden. The dancing is all very serious and very set and formal; it generally derives from very ancient tribal rites. It isn't any sort of Mardi-Gras mood at all that the Indians express, despite the flamboyant colors of their costumes.

Well, when I consider that the Indians, all of those, at least, that I saw—had been dancing the same measure for practically all the night before—continued all day after I left and WILL continue on the same schedule for practically two weeks more—and ALL for the sake of a ritual and *not a cent of money*—I must say I admire their devotion to custom and tradition. The figure of the Virgin of Guadalupe miraculously unites the teachings of the early Catholic missionaries with many survivals of the old Indian myths and pagan cults. She is a typical Mexican product, a strange blend of Christian and pagan strains. What a country and people! The most illogical and baffling on earth; but how appealing! I enclose the authoritative portrait of this Virgin, who, I think, is quite beautiful. She is really the Goddess of the Mexican masses, and you will find her image or picture everywhere, even when you can't see it—as for instance, inside the hat bands of wide *sombreros*. It is rare to escape the sight of her—on a postcard or stencil above the windshield facing half the taxi drivers of Mexico. For protection and good luck! I think I shall have to "wear" her around with me for awhile—likewise for "Protection and good luck" against the wiles and extortions of some of those same drivers!

I haven't heard from you in a long while—no answer yet to my last. But I'm not complaining. I know the season, the other trials— and how filled your time is. Thank you very much, by the way, for having arranged the money payment for me through the Chase bank. It saved me many pesos on the "exchange." I won't need to bother you again this month—nor next. Matters go more smoothly with me as I get myself more acclimated to Mexico, its habits and the peculiar strain of the high altitude here. I'm feeling very well, and am even accused of getting fat.

As Christmas draws near I think much of the Season's loss in all it can give to you and me this year. Christmas always probes the deepest memories, and the fondest; and I know what you will be thinking about this Christmas, and how apt it will be to make the hearth seem cold. I know your fortitude also, Bess,— and your natural, spontaneous response to all that is good and enduring. And I'm sure, therefore, that surrounded as you are by the loyalty and love of those whose names need no particular mention, you'll still find many reasons for gratitude and even a bit of seasonal merriment. —/—/

1 9 3 2

383: To Peggy Baird

[*Mixcoac*]   *January 6th*

Dearest Peggy: I hope you got the $75. I sent yesterday afternoon. I went first to the Mancera where I ate like a horse; then rushed to the bank in time to get all I wanted. Daniel I found as drunk as usual when I got home, but he did manage to get me a hot bath before eight, after which I really began to enjoy my weariness. Slept fairly well—waking to find old Mizzentop flaunting the colors still in valiant dreams of you.

M—— was here, besides the family box of goodies and about a million letters. I'll just never catch up, I'm sure. M., as I expected, is as settled as ever. . . . I can foresee a number of needs, or rather uses for him in the next fortnight.

Lesley [Simpson] is coming to lunch with me at the Mancera this noon. All things considered, I am hoping that he, rather than anyone else, will want to take over the house. For one thing it would mean that I could trust *all* my belongings to the premises—and be freer than ever to move about as I took a notion to. I wouldn't lose any more money in the end than storage costs and transportation otherwise necessitated.

I'm in such a hectic rush this morning that I can't do more than remind you that you already know the depth of my love for you. The ride back yesterday was psychologically so strange and new a meditation to me that it seemed almost like sheer delirium. When I get more of the pressure of events eased and a moment for a little personal thinking, I'll write you a more decent expression of my gratitude. I'm dying now to be off to Acapulco with you in two weeks time, and almost every moment must be bent to that end.

I'll see Mary [Doherty] today or tomorrow about your clothes. Has Malcolm replied yet? Let me know when to write him if he hasn't. DAMN that Putnam review! Of all times, now, to sharpen the critical blade! But that's what I get for procrastinating. Mexico [City] doesn't look any more tempting and reassuring than I expected. It's cold, bloody cold, of course, too.

I'm expecting a letter from you tomorrow, and often afterwards, dear Twidget! Apply yourself well; don't forget the toilet paper, the water wagon, your typewriter, nor your Hart. — — — —

384: To Malcolm Cowley

Mixcoac, DF   *January 9th, 1932*

Dear Malcolm: I've just returned Maddow's poems to him with a brief note of appreciation, tempered by some objections to his chaotic structural tendencies, etc. It's hard to say much against a person who has so obviously experienced one's own temper and angle of vision. Furthermore, I suspect that he is no more obscure to me (at his *worst*) than I have been to hundreds of others. But what the hell! I don't pretend to excuse myself for a lot of things. He has power and original vision, though—if he's got the conscience and brains to channel them. . . .

Peggy and I had the pleasantest Christmas and New Years together that I remember for ages. Peggy's usual mixed crowd appeared for

the former date; but I stayed long enough to enjoy a week alone
with her. Taxco is so extremely beautiful—and the townsfolk still
so affable—that whatever one has to say about the Yankee occupation
(and that ultimately seals its doom) it's still one of the pleasantest
places to be. Peggy has probably written you about encounters with
Brett, Bynner, King, et al. Lewd limericks were shouted from the
rooftops—your collection being more than ever in demand. A mad
crowd, though. — — — —

I enjoyed your attack on Munson very much—that is, the initial
broadside that appeared in *The N.R.* But having read answers and
replies since then in *Contempo,* I've lived to regret those later readings—from both sides of the battle line. Of course it was a great
mistake for Munson to have replied at all. No dignity could be
saved that way—and in the end it put you, too, into a rather apologetic position. Your advantage rests—not chiefly, but partially—in
the fact that you initiated the fracas—and in a journal of vastly
greater circulation and weight than that little receptacle on Chapel
Hill. Now people are beginning to accuse you of being a successful
politician. But I hardly agree with that; I think that greater conquests are necessary for that title, even though Mr. Boyd lay flaccid
under the same swipe. —/—/

385: TO PEGGY BAIRD

[*Mixcoac*]   [*January ?*]

Dearest: In case I don't get off tomorrow morning for Taxco—and
hence anticipate this letter by kisses and much contentment—I want
you at least to know that it won't be long before we are together
again, for I shall be with you certainly before Sunday.

Your letter of this morning makes me ache for you. Why is it you
love me so? I don't deserve it. I'm just a careening idiot, with a talent for humor at times, and for insult and desecration at others. But
I can, and must say that your love is very precious to me. For one
thing it seems to give me an assurance that I thought long buried.
You can give me many things besides—if time proves me fit to receive them: the independence of my mind and soul again, and perhaps a real wholeness to my body.

Do you remember me saying that I would *not* fall in love with
you, or with anyone again? But I find that though I like to perpetuate that statement, I have really overruled it in a thousand thoughts
and emotions.

(The period on that last sentence was accompanied by a convulsion under the table from Palomo. Rather horrible, in fact. I roused M——, we called a policeman; but though the dog has resumed all the appearances of his normality—we've relegated him to the shed-room in back of the kitchen. Rabies are common here, so M—— says, and I shouldn't wonder if we'll have to shoot the "dove.")

Since there seems to be such a slight chance of renting the house, and since I really can't welsh on Eyler Simpson (who is equally responsible, since he signed the lease with me) by just walking out— I've decided to pay the $70. odd dollars difference by just keeping it—wherever else I spend my time during the next three months. The family will just have to fork up a loan or something for me, and I feel sure they will. I'm going to try and avoid spoiling my remaining time in Mexico; and much more worry about the house and my few items of possession would succeed in doing so. Don't you think I'm right?

Besides, M——will be in on weekends, and will watch over the servant's care of things, and forward my mail wherever I am. I want you to go to Acapulco with me—and after that I'm going to spend some time up in Michoacan, Morelia, Lake Chapala, etc. I may end up in Jalapa (which is very near Vera Cruz) but by that time I rather expect you'll be with me. I feel serene and happy in your love today, mad dogs and convulsions notwithstanding!.

386: To — —

Mexico, D.F.   [*January 15*]

Dear — —: —/—/ Your Christmas gift was a great surprise—and an inspiration. Lawrence never wrote a greater story, nor one which provoked less divided feelings. It was a great revelation to me, and I shall read "The Man Who Died" more than once again. In all honesty—it has more to tell me—at least in my present state of mind —than any book in the Bible. It was originally published by the same people in Paris who brought out my *Bridge*—under the title of, "The Escaped Cock"; but I never happened to have read it before. I remember that they had a terrible time with the customs, getting it into this country—and largely on account of that title! Imagine! —/—/

387: To Solomon Grunberg

Mixcoac, D.F., Mexico   *Feb. 8th, '32*

Dear Mony: As usual, I'm ignoring all the questions of your last letter. . . . Don't know how long I'm going to remain here, etc. Hate it and love it alternately, but am not, as you surmise, in a constant Bacchic state. Not by any means. However, I happen to be in something approximating it at this present moment, since I've got to work on the first impressive poem I've started on in the last two years.[1] I feel the old confidence again; and you may know what that means to one of my stripe!

The servants are all asleep—and I'm in that pleasant state of beginning all over again. Especially as I'm in love again—and as never quite before. Love is always much more important than locality; and this is the newest adventure I ever had. I won't say much more than that I seem to have broken ranks with my much advertised "brotherhood"—and a woman whom I have known for years—suddenly seems to "have claimed her own." I can't say that I'm sorry. It has given me new perspectives, and after many tears and groans—something of a reason for living.

So much for "Mexico." I'm not able to write tourist sketches any more. They take too long—and are only the more incomplete. I've lots to tell you about all that some other day. And they needn't be the less stirring for a little delay. Meantime let me say that you are one of the few heroes I know. I love your steadfastness and uncompromising attitude, Mony. Have we the patience to endure? I say YES! —/—/

388: To Peggy Baird

[Mixcoac]   Feb. 10th

Dearest: So glad to hear from you this morning! I have been up late for the past two nights, writing countless letters—and with a little tequila (a very little!) walking back and forth the length of the room to the tune of the records that we enjoyed so together. I haven't really seen anyone since you left; even M—— hasn't shown up for 48 hours again. The version of the beginning of "The Broken Tower" that I sent you early this morning is probably to be changed a good deal yet. But you seemed to hanker for it—and so I let 'er fly.

I could be doing a lot these days, since I feel so much like working, if the tension were less, around here. Sr. Daniel Hernandez is morose and very threatening indeed, despite the fact that I haven't even reprimanded him for his recent drunkenness. Lisa is scared to death of him, and warns me that there may be all kinds of trouble in store if I fire him, since he knows about half the Police in Mixcoac,

1. "The Broken Tower."

knows I have no firearms on the place, etc. Well, neither can I bring myself to endure his insolence and complete disregard of services much more. Sr. Lepine, my landlord, is going to try to corner and talk to him this afternoon, but Daniel won't be around at the time, as Lepine, who called this morning when D. was out, told his wife the hour when he'd return this afternoon.

Oh Hell! I say. I'm getting so damned tired of the whole problem. Lisa thinks she won't dare remain after Daniel leaves on account of his probably exposing her political affiliations. If you can't find someone from Taxco I shall probably be left here a perfect prisoner —without even a telephone, and afraid to leave the place a minute. Well, don't see how I'm going to get any work done *this* afternoon, nor probably tomorrow. Damned outrageous, I think. Daniel will probably come lurching in about 8 tonight and begin to flirt a knife and pistol about. Such a quiet life in this pretty retreat!

It's too bad you have to move so preemptorily—on the exact 15th. But those scorpions worry me—especially their generous numbers. That house will always attract them—being so on the side of a hill. I miss you a lot, dear. Somehow we have such a lot to talk about together. I am getting more and more serious and dignified day by day—getting maybe back into myself—as well as into you.

389: To Peggy Baird

[*Mixcoac*]   *Feb 11th*

Dearest: I was so tremulous and distracted with the domestic situation as described yesterday to you, that last night I went on a mild tare with Lisa here in the salon. I finally came to the decision of packing up and leaving for the States within a week; there just didn't seem to be any other way of proceeding. I certainly felt fed up! Lepine didn't come round until this morning, and if he hadn't offered me a new servant who he swears is reliable, I think I should be sending you the telegram I typed out last night, announcing my departure.

Lepine is sending me an old man he has known for 14 years, the most honest soul, he declares, he has ever met. Lisa will stay, she says, and cook. The combination will be perfect, and will result in little more expense than I have been under right along. Lepine says that Daniel has been wanting to work for "the general" for some time. I think they will leave within a few days—and without umbrage. Certainly they have no reason to resent my simple objec-

tion to constant drunkenness. Daniel came home stewed again last
night, after working all day at "the general's." But I was too gay
with Lisa and tequila and dancing—and my secret resolution to pull
out, to mind very much. I have a notion that this rearrangement
will be satisfactory. Certainly I'm lucky to have Lisa here—so intelligent, generous, neat and efficient in a thousand ways. She doesn't ask
for anything but her board and keep, but I shall try to induce her
into some sort of salary.

These photographs, I think, are perfectly splendid. I especially
love those of you with the goat! And you *ought* to like the one of
me. Remember, I was looking at you—and the expression seems to be-
speak a lot of love and happiness. And what a scrumptious and
monumental pose that is of Lisa's! Siqueiros really ought to see it.

Of course I'm anxious about your plans after leaving Natalia's.
You know you're welcome—more than that, my dear, to make this
your future headquarters. I miss you *mucho, mucho, mucho!* But I
don't think that either of us ought to urge the other into anything
but the most spontaneous and mutually liberal arrangements. I am
bound to you more than I ever dreamed of being, and in the most
pleasant and deep way. I think I have wandered back to some of my
early idealism, and in the proper sort of way—without any arbitrary
forcing or conscious reckoning. You're a great little "rouser," my
dear! — — — —

390: To Peggy Baird

[*Mixcoac*]   *Feb 13th*

Dear Peggy: I just can't make up my mind to go traveling or even
visiting until I get through some real work here in Mixcoac. Somehow, it seems to me that the time is ripe even though circumstances
are difficult; and if I can't do any better I think I'll just try to let
the domestic situation here "ride" as best possible—so long as there is
no pistol twirling. The place seems to run itself fairly smoothly with
Daniel away until 7-8-or-9 at night, and for the moment, at least, relations are back again on a fairly friendly basis. I'm doing my best
not to think or worry too much about it. Certainly I shall avoid
any rows in the future. And it's lucky—if I do finally dismiss Daniel—
that he can immediately go to work at a place such as the "general's,"
where he has said for some time he wanted to remove, anyway.
Under such conditions I don't see how he can possibly harbor much
resentment.

I had a very enjoyable lunch and afternoon yesterday with Lesley and Marion [Simpson]. She's fundamentally very likable, I think. But I should imagine that Lesley would welcome a little warmer company. He seems more than satisfied, however, and is looking even better than usual. In the morning I had been to the glass factory with Anita [Brenner]. A very gratifying experience. I couldn't resist buying a half dozen wine glasses, of a smoky rose-purple transparency that set one dreaming even when empty. Then some exquisite hand-woven textiles (table and pillow covers, cotton) in the afternoon from Davis's—made in Oaxaca, and quite unique. I almost bought myself a turquoise and silver ring; but Lesley and Marion dragged me out in time. It's dangerous for me to hang around town very long.

The strangest rumors circulate about Natalie's house. She seems to have written someone, I forgot whom, that she hasn't sold it at all, and doesn't intend to. Then Davis, who seems to hear everything, reports to me that "the Kings are leaving Taxco and intend to settle somewhere up in northern New York." I had to smile at this, recognizing the source, etc. But I didn't know that the plan had ripened to such a decided and public extent as yet. If they aren't coming in until Tuesday I wish they would wire me to that effect by noon on Monday. I'll expect them overnight Monday otherwise. I want to have provisions on hand, too, and fresh at the proper time.

I'm going to make a stab again at the Putnam review this afternoon. I'm feeling shabbier and shabbier about my delay. . . . Must send up *something* anyway. And maybe later I'll catch up the creative thread of my poem again. After all I've been through lately, it just doesn't seem to exist any more.

So glad to hear you've finished your story! Where do you inten sending it? Lots of love, dear! — — — —

391: To Peggy Baird

[*Mixcoac*]   *Feb 16th*

Dearest: I was in the mood for swearing last night that I wouldn't write you for at least a week. My blast at the Kings, I felt, needed some very definite and concrete "substantiation"—such as a long, glum silence; which I hoped might worry you. But, really, I find daily communication with you quite irresistible. Especially when your reciprocation is so regular and—need I say? charming. And then, besides, the entire household has been in such a perfectly delightful mood all day,—I can't really be sad or important.

True to my word last night, I got very lit. Daniel had come home that way anyhow, and I took the opportunity to talk to him about sobriety—meanwhile pouring him glass after glass of the Tenampa I'd bought for the Kings. The more he drank the more he talked of "his" or "our" Pegguié—accent on the penult;—but you will be able to pronounce that without the acquaintance of Quintilian anyway, I'm sure. You're very popular around here, and I'm sure that if you care to come and stay with me for awhile you will be regarded as the pet of the place—since Elise and Conrada both dote on you—as well as myself. M—— just isn't around for days and days any more.

Daniel is not drunk tonight; rather he appeared at 6 PM with a large bush of *buena de noche,* from the *jardine del general,* as well as a large bouquet of heliotrope. Judge what the sala smells like with a large bunch of tuberoses also, which I purchased yesterday in honor of the Kings! Some times I think this house is the nicest place in the world. It certainly could be—in a not ambitious way. My temperamental reversals of opinion regarding Mexico are a joke. I now regard myself as a confirmed idiot who can't make up his mind about anything whatever any more.

I can't yet figger how Tommy [Robert Thompson] could say we looked like "two waifs" sitting on a strange doorstep. Yes, that letter was distinctly below his usual level. Got a fine long letter from Peggy Robson yesterday, which hints at the same relations with — — — — that you mentioned. Well, well, and *como no!* She also said that Malcolm (in long underwear) and Waldo left together in the same truck for the scene of action. Perhaps common suffering will weld a friendship there, after all. By the way, I don't believe a thing of your wagon wagon, water wagon story. Especially with Luz around, who Lisa says is a great little tanker. I have my own ideas about the sobriety of those nights of yours in such company, and how "lonely" they are. Just as long as you don't let your right hand know what your left hand doeth, as they say. I'll keep the same code, at least with my index finger. —/—/

392: To Peggy Baird

[Mixcoac]   [Feb ?]

Dearest Peggy: Everything is very much at loose ends again since Daniel appeared dead drunk again yesterday afternoon—and I had to spend the rest of the day and evening cogitating and recogitating just what was to be done about it. I'm very near firing him (the case seems to be hopeless, and I just can't stand being "run" by servants to such an extent). Also, I've lost a lot of confidence in him since Lisa has discovered that he has my watch and fob in his cabin, which Conrada unwittingly showed her the other day. Whether Filemon took it or not in the first place makes very little difference. . . .

So, will you squint around—and ask Bill [Spratling] also to keep an open eye for a mozo for me there in Taxco. There are plenty of honest youngsters there who are known to be honest and would welcome the idea of coming to Mexico for a few months. Lisa (and everybody else) says that you're sure to pick a thief no matter who you hire here in Mexico. I would never have a peaceful moment with one of them around; whereas a boy from Taxco [would] behave differently, especially if his family could be referred to there. I don't say send anyone at present, but I wish you would be ready to immediately if I should wire you to one of these days. Maria Luisa's brother (not the goblin midget), or Raphael, I'm sure, would be glad to come. Cleaning and gardening and errands—you know the slight requirements. I would pay them 10-15 pesos a month with board. I'm hoping to keep Lisa as cook, but she isn't enough by herself on account of having to remain constantly with her child. She's done more spontaneous cleaning around the place in the last two days than I can tell you. Ask Bill to find out if Santiago is satisfied at the Taxqueno. When I last talked to him he was very keen to come to Mexico—at almost any cost. If I should wire for immediate action I'm sure you wouldn't mind advancing the bus and taxi fare, would you? You know this house simply cannot be left alone a minute. And I don't see how I can possibly stand it much longer in its present equivocal state.

I worked late on my poem[1] last night despite all the disturbance, and willy-nilly shall get some work accomplished, at least correspondence, today. The enclosed was delivered by a man from Taxco last evening, and I think it's the money from Leslie that failed of being enclosed in his letter to you of yesterday. M——absent another night! —/—/

Clinton [King] wrote me a long letter of apology—which was more than sufficient. I haven't much ground to stand on myself when it comes to drunken outbreaks and melodramatic abuse of my friends, so it makes it very easy indeed for me to forgive and forget. They are

1. "The Broken Tower."

two very decent and lovable people and I'm glad they like me enough to speak as they do. If Clinton ever bombs and bombards me again in the same manner I'll know better how to take it. I'm looking forward to some pleasant times together when they come to Town. Please convince them of my affection and hope of seeing them. —/—/

Don't forget about my servant problem, dear. You know it's yours in a way, too. I want things to be smoother than before on your next "visit" to Mixcoac, besides which I want to get my mind free for work as soon as possible. I'm really in extraordinarily good condition and do hope you also feel more settled and industrious.

I hope to send you more of the poem in a few days.

393: To His Stepmother

Mixcoac, DF   *Feb. 17th, 1932*

Dear Bess: —/—/ I get so aggravated at times that I swear I'll pack up and leave for the States on the first available boat. Then the next clear and glorious morning comes around, with fresh flowers in the garden, good coffee on the stove—and the renewed vision that sleep brings. . . . Then I change my mind all over again. For I know that as soon as I go back I'll regret it—and long and long for Mexico again. Not that I plan on staying here forever; but for the time being the business situation in the States is zero. There's nothing I can really do there. And although I have found that living here is far from being as cheap as it's cracked up to be, it *is* less, on the whole, and when one learns—and how long it takes!—to wade around and learn one's depth and altitude—one can make a good deal of a lame proposition. At least Mexico affords me time and space. I'm not so giddy as I once was about *all* its features; but a very pleasant residue remains. And I'm just getting to know it well enough to get down to work on my poetry and other creative work.

Bess, you certainly have given a demonstration of real heroism in handling the factory rent problem as you have. I sense a certain amount of weariness in your letter; and I can well understand the causes and the justifications. The sheer day-to-day strain of management, complicated as it is, I know to be a burden—a real cross to bear. You're one of the finest people I've ever met or expect to meet. I've always been so glad that Father found someone at last who really took the pains to understand him; because he was certainly a difficult person to comprehend. He had many faults, too. I only regret that I was so late in realizing his many virtues. [The rest of this letter is lost.]

394: To Samuel Loveman

Mixcoac, DF   *March 10th, 1932*

Dear Sambo: —/—/ Rather amazing things have happened to me since Xmas. Peggy Cowley [Baird], whom you certainly remember as Malcolm's wife, and who is — — — — here in Mexico, is mainly responsible. You may have heard that we are now living together, and I must admit that I find conjugal life, however unofficial, a great consolation to a loneliness that had about eaten me up. Maybe I am fulfilling some of your theories and predictions. —/—/

Just about 20 more days before my scholarship is officially terminated. But I have my doubts about coming back before six months, and maybe not that soon. I can't hope to find any interesting work in the States for some time, meanwhile the estate has guaranteed me at least a portion of the yearly allowance left me by my father, which will go farther here than in the north. Besides I'm just getting to work on a few things—and Peggy and I enjoy Mexico more than ever, being together.

How I wish you could step into our house here some afternoon! Week by week I've collected more and more beautiful Mexican serapes, leather work, pottery, embroideries, lacquers, etc. Fresh bunches of lilies, tuberoses, violets, nasturtiums, etc., every day from the garden. The white iris is just coming out, too. When my lease on this house expires—6 weeks from now—we're going to do more traveling. There are at least twenty wonderful towns and places I haven't yet visited. Last week we went to Puebla. I only visited 2 of its 365 churches and chapels (one for every day of the year) and what gold and decorations and carvings I saw defies description. We came back laden down with gorgeous pottery and serapes, etc., from the superb market there. —/—/

395: To Solomon Grunberg

Mixcoac, D.F.   *March 20th '32*

Dear Mony: What a fine, understanding and spirited letter that was from you! Proving not only your friendship again but the clean and heroic attitude you hold toward life also. . . . Not that I have ever doubted either one, but fresh reassertions of that kind are always highly gratifying. —/—/

Peggy and I are still very happy together here. — — — — We've known each other for nearly 12 years, intimately—but never dreamed, of course, of our present happy relationship. How permanent that will be is far from settled; but we have learned to enjoy the present moment without too much romanticizing—which I think is wisdom.

Wish you could see—and smell—all the delicious flowers that surround our house: calla lilies, freesia, roses, calendulas, white iris, violets, cannas, a dozen colors of geraniums, pansies, feverfew, candy tuft, morning glories, etc. The days are getting warmer and all the deciduous trees are back again in fresh leaf. My fellowship is about terminated, but I expect to stay on here for several months longer if the income from my father's estate seems to warrant. Am even thinking of making my permanent home here. Mexico gets into your veins. Beautiful people, manners, scenery, speech and climate.

The poem ("Broken Tower") has undergone considerable change and extension since the version I sent you. I'm so glad that you liked it. I'm not sending any more of it to you, however, until it's quite finished.

There is a small group of quite interesting compatriots here which gathers occasionally at one or the other of our houses—most of whom are Guggenheim fellows like myself. Carleton Beals and wife; Anita Brenner; Marsden Hartley, the painter, who has just arrived and who is wildly enthusiastic; Lesley Simpson (University of California) and wife; Pierre & Caroline Durieux, head of General Motors here; Wm. Spratling, whose book *Little Mexico* (just out) you ought to read, etc. Plenty of good company, in fact, for one like myself who doesn't care for a great many people.

A way, way back you asked me a question about what I thought of *Moby Dick*. It has passages, I admit, of seeming innuendo that seem to block the action. But on third or fourth reading I've found that some of those very passages are much to be valued in themselves— minor and subsidiary forms that augment the final climacteric quite a bit. No work as tremendous and tragic as *Moby Dick* can be expected to build up its ultimate tension and impact without manipulating our time sense to a great extent. Even the suspense of the usual mystery story utilizes that device. In *Moby Dick* the whale is a metaphysical image of the Universe, and every detail of his habits and anatomy has its importance in swelling his proportions to the cosmic rôle he plays. You may find other objections to the book in mind, but I've assumed the above to be among them, at least, as I among others that I know, found the same fault at first. —/—/

396: To Caresse Crosby

Mixcoac, D.F.   *March 31st, 1932*

Dear Caresse:—/—/ As I have not been near that Bank, c/o which you wrote me, for months and months until yesterday, your message and gift remained in complete limbo! Judge my surprise and pleasure at what appeared—practically from limbo!

The poems for Harry [Crosby] are an everlasting litany of chivalry and love. The whole collection achieves a power in repose, a renunciation-plus, that is very rare. I hope you are writing more and more, Caresse; for the sheer vision of your nature deserves an ever branching extension and expression. You really come up to the great themes of Love and Tragedy, as very few women can, at least in words.

My Guggenheim Fellowship terminates today. But I am remaining a while longer in Mexico on the modest income afforded me from my father's estate, since his death last July. At that time I came North for two months, but was very glad to get back here again as soon as possible. Mexico with its volcanoes, endless ranges, countless flowers, dances, villages, lovely brown-skinned Indians with simple courtesies, and constant sunlight—it enthralls me more than any other spot I've ever known. It *is* and isn't an easy place to live. Altogether more strange to us than even the orient. . . . But it would take volumes to even hint at all I have seen and felt. Have rung bells and beaten pre-Conquistadorial drums in firelit circles at ancient ceremonies, while rockets went zooming up into the dawn over Tepoztlan; have picked up obsidian arrows and terra-cotta idols from the furrows of corn-fields in far valleys; bathed with creatures more beautiful than the inhabitants of Bali in mountain streams and been in the friendliest jails that ever man got thrown in. There is never an end to dancing, singing, rockets and the rather lurking and suave dangers that gives the same edge to life here that the mountains give to the horizon. Harry would have adored it—past expression—and I am sure you would. I should like to stay indefinitely.

My Spanish is still as lame as my French when I left France. Of the "Epic"—I haven't yet written a line. Only a few lyrics. But then, what did I actually write while in Europe—an environment not half so strange and distractingly new-old curious as this? Besides I'm nearly two miles above you here in the air—at least while I remain in these headquarters of mine in the suburbs of Mexico City,—an old-fashioned Mexican residence of 8 rooms, 3 servants, a luxurious garden—with a goat, fighting cock, cat, Spitz dog and an occasional scorpion—all for $50. a month. But I've about made my adjustment now and am beginning to rap the typewriter a good deal lately. With the world all going to hell—what can one gather together with any confidence these days anyway? But I'm realizing responsibilities—or doubtless should have written quite a bit of trash, which might have been better mentioned than perused.

Do you see Kay [Boyle] and Lawrence [Vail] any more? Kay's novel *Plagued by the Nightingale* (and how they please over here!) impressed and delighted me immensely. —/—/

397: To Malcolm Cowley

[*Mixcoac*]   *Easter '32*

Dear Malcolm: Peggy and I think and talk a great deal about you. That means in a very fond way, or it wouldn't be mentioned. I'm wondering whether or not you'll like the above poem ["The Broken Tower"]—about the 1st I've written in two years. . . . I'm getting too damned self-critical to write at all any more. More than ever, however, do I implore your honest appraisal of this verse, prose or nonsense—whatever it may seem. Please let me know.

And because I congratulate you most vehemently on your recent account of the Kentucky expedition—please don't tell me anything you don't honestly mean. This has already been submitted to *Poetry* —so don't worry about that angle.

I miss seeing you a great deal. Peggy is writing you some sort of account of the Easter celebrations here. We're very happy together— and send you lots of love!

398: To Samuel Loveman

[*Mixcoac*]   *Easter '32*

What a jolly long letter from you, Sam! I can't get time to answer immediately, but here's a poem ["The Broken Tower"]—about the first in 2 years—tell me if you like it or not. Happiness continues, with also all of the gay incidentals of a Mexican Easter—exploding Judases, rockets, flowers, pappas (excuse me, that's the spelling for

Mexican potatoes!), mammas, delicious and infinitesimal children wearing masks and firemen's helmets, flowers galore and a sky that carries you ever upward! More anon, and soon!

399: To Solomon Grunberg

Mixcoac, DF   *April 12th, 1932*

Dear Mony: So glad to hear that the lacquer box reached you—and I hope there wasn't duty on it. Things often get through (small articles) I'm told—if not sent by registered mail. The cutter is awaiting me at the main post office. At least I take the notice just rec'd to indicate *that* as the article, as I'm not expecting anything else of late. — — — —

I'm in a dull mood today, trying to get back into harness after a couple of feverish weeks spent in running thither and yon every day or so to borrow enough money to keep us going until my check from the estate finally arrived. Somehow I can't get people to understand that any break in schedule regarding remittances in a foreign country like Mexico is quite catastrophic, especially when, like myself, you're asking for a mere minimum for all expenses, and when the first of each month finds you with less than a shoe string to meet all obligations. Finally after borrowing money for wires, writing a dozen letters, etc., the check arrived; but I hope for a little more consistent treatment in the future. After all, it isn't like asking for a favor; the money was left me in the will, and the least the executors can do is to send it to me on the schedule agreed on.

Through the son-in-law of the President I'm acquiring a permanent passport; something damned hard to get here these days. Peggy and I shall probably stay here at least until next fall, and maybe longer. We like our isolation from mutual friends there in the north and our domestic life here with a house, servants, garden, pets, etc., proves more satisfying every day. If I can avoid drinking too much I'm expecting to get nearer solid earth than I have for several years. Sheer loneliness had nearly eaten me up. Peggy has sufficient sportsmanship, mentality, taste and sensuality to meet me on practically every level. And I think I'm learning considerable that would hardly be possible from any other person.

—/—/ Most all the letters we get from the north are pretty damned blue and dubious in tone. Well, no wonder, of course. I sometimes wonder if I shouldn't go back and wail around the grave of capitalism myself, adopting sackcloth and ashes too, instead of the beautiful bright woolen serape worn around here on cold evenings. All my friends are turning at least a violent pink lately, and I'm almost convinced myself. In fact, by all the laws of logic I *am* convinced. But it goes so against my native grain—seeing nothing but red on the horizon. —/—/

Speaking of music, did you ever hear any *real* Mexican songs and dances? Some of the best of them are now on disks which can be ordered, if not in stock, at least from the factory through your dealer: *Las Mañanitas* (Brunswick #40397) might have been composed by Bach. It's a ceremonial song played to one or another Mexican in honor of his birthday. Very solemn and eloquent. *La Marihuana* (Victor 46107-A), a wild jargon about the native drug of the same name (generally smoked in cigarettes) and its effects. *Capulin* (Victor 30323-A). A wild and throbbing native canción that will set you prancing.

The Mexican singer uses a part of his throat or larynx never used elsewhere that I know of, except in the Orient or Arabia. It has great range, is generally shrill but capable of heart-wringing vibrations. Has the old Hawaiian gargling backed off the map. It is nothing to have four or five singers (masons, plumbers or pickslingers during the day) drop in here for an evening's singing. And to my mind they're generally preferable to all the trained and professional strummers and whoopers-up I've ever heard. Tequila is passed around; or beer; or coffee. And the corridas (endless ballads) and seranatas go on for hours and hours. There are endless corridas about "poor Pancho Villa," Zapata and other dead revolutionaries. And then, if we're drunk enough, someone dances a *jarabe,* a dance that is all vibrant gristle, emphasis and exhausting grace. — — — —

400: TO SAMUEL LOVEMAN

Mixcoac, DF   *April 13th, 1932*

Dear Sam: —/—/ Marsden Hartley, the painter, is here on his Guggenheim, as well as Andrew Dasburg. I don't know the latter, but Hartley is delightful company and has brought a young nephew from Cleveland along with him who paints, on canvas, I mean. . . . Then I got a letter from Charlotte [Rychtarik] saying that she and Richard expected to motor down with some of their wealthy Cleveland friends—only to hear just yesterday, that a relative had died suddenly in Europe, money had to be sent—and therefore the trip had to be abandoned. Charlotte is philosophical enough, but I'm sorry not to see her refreshed by Mexico. Well . . . maybe later. My biggest surprise in a long while, however, has been a note from dear old D—— C——. Don't tell me you've forgotten our old Cleveland hero! Who is still trying to write novelettes and best sellers in Des Moines. At least he says he's still trying. Is also the friend of some fellows who are trying to start up a quarterly, and wouldn't I kindly send them some poems of mine. . . . I must write him a picture card at least in answer; but I'm damned if I want to continue any correspondence of that kind.

That last of yours was a bang up letter, Sam. Say what you will, you certainly haven't lost your old good humor and sympathy. I love to think of my "Ka" as you and the Egyptians call it, still haunting my basement basinette on Col. Hts. Good lord, but how I jumped to my feet right into a perfect salute yesterday when suddenly—over the neighbor's radio—I caught the chorus of that old favorite of mine, "The Navy Blues" . . . which certainly you can't have forgotten either. Which reminds me that I still haven't heard from B—— S—— since the recent fatal cyclones that swept right across his home town in A——. I wrote immediately for assurances of his welfare and safety. But no word yet. I can never forget that sweet boy; and his letters to me for the last two years have been so consistently affectionate and nostalgic that they sometimes bring tears to my eyes.

—/—/ Peggy and I have each of us written Tommy [Thompson] a letter today. I hope they cheer him up a little. He's so shy he almost never writes any tangible news about himself. Just wise cracks, burlesque slogans, oblique hints: all very witty and amusing, but not quite explicit enough about himself to really fully satisfy. He's probably having his worries these days. —/—/

Dos Passos has written a very important record of the war and the "war mind" in *1919*. Do read it, Sam. My old friend (though an "enemy for awhile") Claire (Spencer) Smith, who wrote *Gallows Orchard,* and another friend of Peggy's, Wm. Seabrook's wife, barged in on us the other day on the way to Cuernavaca, and loaned me the book to read. Claire has just finished her second novel, which Hal Smith is bringing out in May. We had a great reconciliation and I've decided that I'm not the only one who has improved since our ancient misunderstandings. —/—/

401: TO SOLOMON GRUNBERG

Mixcoac   *April 20th*

Dear Mony: Just a hasty note in the fever of packing and final arrangements. . . . My plans for staying in Mexico have been completely reversed by a suit against the estate which may cut me off from any income for years. Since I'm having to depend even now entirely on loans from my stepmother's salary the only thing possible to do is return to Chagrin Falls and try to work some of it out in service to the organization, several branches of which are approaching bankruptcy. Not a very happy prospect. . . .

Am sailing for NY on the *Orizaba* from Vera Cruz on the 24th. Shall probably land in NY without a penny. Could you send me a small loan of some kind c/o Hotel Lafayette, University Place & 11th St.? It would be wonderful if you could happen to be in NY sometime during the three or four days I hope to be there before going into my middle western exile. This crash has prevented my collecting the cutter as yet, but I hope to get it before leaving if I have anything like the pesos to pay the duty charges. If not it may come back to you. I've had an awful time all round lately . . . will tell you later. — — —

402: TO MORTON DAUWEN ZABEL

Mixcoac, DF   *April 20th, 1932*

Dear Morton Zabel: I've suddenly been called north on account of business. Sailing immediately and probably won't return to Mexico. Will you kindly have my subscription address [changed] to my permanent residence; *Box 604, Chagrin Falls, Ohio.* . . .

About a month ago I sent you a poem, for possible use in *Poetry*, but have not as yet heard from you about it. The letter may have gone astray for all I know, as service isn't any too reliable here.[1]

I hope I may hear from you soon after my arrival in Ohio. — — —

403: TO *Contempo*[2]

Mixcoac, Mexico   *April 20, 1932*

Dear Contempo: Delighted to hear that you like the "Bacardi" poem and are using it.

I'm leaving for the States in a few days and can't write you a de-

1. The manuscript of "The Broken Tower" alluded to here was apparently never received by Mr. Zabel or *Poetry* (Chicago), of which he was an editor. A letter from Mr. Zabel, dated April 24, 1932, in response to this note from Crane, has been found; it explicitly states that the poem in question was not received either by Harriet Monroe or himself. It is of interest that Crane's ms. copy of the poem is dated March 25, 1932.

2. *Contempo* (July 5, 1932).

cent response at the moment. But I hope you meant what you said about sending me *Contempo* regularly. And I should like to do reviews when I get settled in the north again.

Please address me from now on at Box 604, Chagrin Falls, Ohio, where I shall probably be after May 10th.

P.S. I should love to review MacLeish's *Conquistador* for you if you haven't already assigned it elsewhere.

404: To His Stepmother

Mixcoac   *April 22nd '32*

Dear Bess: Pardon me for wiring Byron [Madden] about money, but so many difficulties came to a head at once here, and with myself weak from a fever and dysentery I had to use every way of impressing on you the urgency of my immediate needs. And I imagine that you may well have been too preoccupied to realize the situation here anyway—even in part.

Altogether I've had a terrible time lately. I can't begin to write the details now in the finalities of packing. I leave for Vera Cruz tomorrow night and sail Sunday morning on the *Orizaba* for New York. I was planning to return to Ohio even before the shocking news came about the W—— matter. But with that having happened I wouldn't have thought of staying here another minute anyway. I may be able to be of some help to you this summer. Anyway I want to make the effort, especially since you must be quite crippled (at least at the Cottage) without Dorothy's help.

You can't imagine how difficult the Mexicans make it for any foreigners to remain here—comfortably. I love the country and the people (Indians) but certainly have had my fill of passport difficulties, servant problems and other complications for awhile. I have been not only ill—but frightened nearly out of my wits because I happened, in all innocence, to put my passport-renewal problem in the hands of a lawyer-crook. It's all right; I have clearance papers; but it involved me in a lot of expense, consultations with innumerable people and just endless worry. Then at the last moment my servant got roaring drunk and left, and came back and shook the gate to its foundations, yelling threats against my life, terrorizing us for days, until we had to call on the American Embassy for special police service, etc., and so on. Do you wonder I've been anxious to get off as soon as possible. Thank God the lease on my house is already expired—and there can be no further complications that I know.

I hated to draw on you so heavily for money lately, but after all, I had no way of knowing how matters would turn out with the estate; and the expense of coming home now certainly seems justified in view of the possibility of economizing later on. There are many things highly important for us to discuss together, and besides that I am looking forward to seeing you and the rest of our friends and relatives again. I am bringing back a lot of very interesting things, some very beautiful, that you'll enjoy seeing, I'm sure.

A case of books had to be sent collect (Wells Fargo) direct to the factory. Please be on the watch for it. The other things are all in a large hamper which will go with me on the boat and will be expressed to the factory later on from New York. I'll be in New York a couple of days as I simply must see some of my old friends after so long a time. I'll telephone you on the first night of my arrival around 10 o'clock when rates are reduced.

Please give my love to poor little Dorothy. I haven't had a moment to write to anyone lately or I should have written her long ago. Had to spend all day yesterday running around trying to get the telegraphed money cashed. Wasn't your fault, nor mine. Peggy nearly went crazy with hers, sent from her former husband, too. The telegraph office paid us off in six hundred and some odd "Tostons" (about like getting it all in dimes) and neither the Ward Line office nor the official Banco de Mexico would accept them. . . . It seems there's a law against paying out any such currency beyond a certain small amount. But how should we know—and besides what does a government agency like the telegraph here mean by paying you in currency which the government itself, through its own official bank, turns around and refuses! We finally had to arrange a special interview with the president of the bank himself. I was all ready to complain to the embassy. So you see how slow things move here and what incessant obstacles one has to fight for the simplest sort of transactions. It certainly has about made a nervous wreck of me. But I'll rest up on the boat.

405: To Mrs. T. W. Simpson
(Postcard)

[*Havana, Cuba*]   [*April 26, 1932*]

Off here for a few hours on my way north. Will write you soon. Am going back to Cleveland to help in the business crisis. Permanent address—Box 604, Chagrin Falls, Ohio.

LIST OF CORRESPONDENTS

(Numbers are those of the letters)

— —: 55, 103, 105, 121, 136, 245, 250, 267, 381, 386

— and —: 242, 273, 292, 300

Anderson, Sherwood: 54, 85

Baird, Peggy: 376, 377, 383, 385, 388, 389, 390, 391, 392

Baird, Peggy and Malcolm Cowley: 295

Brown, Slater: 216, 294, 298, 303, 323, 373

Bubb, Charles C.: 15

Contempo: 403

Cowley, Malcolm: 225, 237, 310, 311, 319, 328, 362, 371, 384, 397

Cowley, Malcolm and Peggy Baird: 255

Crosby, Caresse: 329, 331, 332, 333, 335, 396

Crosby, Harry and Caresse: 330

Dietz, Lorna: 334, 354, 368

Father (Clarence A. Crane): 3, 4, 8, 9, 173, 219, 221, 283, 286, 288, 291, 306, 307

Frank, Waldo: 119, 131, 137, 140, 182, 188, 211, 212, 213, 217, 228, 236, 244, 247, 248, 249, 253, 254, 257, 259, 260, 261, 262, 263, 265, 272, 296, 299, 304, 315, 320, 327, 337, 355, 363

Grandmother (Elizabeth B. Hart): 1, 2, 165, 209, 226, 230

Grunberg, Solomon: 346, 352, 375, 387, 395, 399, 401

Guggenheim Memorial Foundation: 344

Josephson, Matthew: 40, 57

Kahn, Otto H.: 222, 235, 289

Lachaise, Gaston: 231

Lachaise, Isabel and Gaston: 171, 258

Loveman, Samuel: 290, 297, 312, 313, 316, 322, 351, 353, 358, 369, 378, 394, 398, 400

Moe, Henry Allen: 356

Mother (Grace Hart Crane): 5, 6, 7, 10, 11, 12, 13, 16, 17, 18, 19, 20, 23, 25, 26, 146, 151, 153, 155, 157, 158, 159, 162, 163, 169, 174, 175, 176, 177, 180, 181, 183, 184, 186, 187, 189, 190, 191, 192, 193, 194, 197, 198, 199, 201, 202, 205, 206, 207, 208, 210, 223, 227, 229, 238, 240, 243, 246, 251, 256, 268, 271, 278, 284

Munson, Gorham B.: 27, 29, 30, 31, 32, 33, 34, 35, 36, 39, 41, 42, 43, 44, 45, 46, 47, 48, 49, 50, 51, 52, 53, 56, 58, 59, 60, 61, 62, 63, 64, 65, 66, 67, 68, 69, 70, 71, 72, 73, 75, 76, 77, 79, 80, 81, 82, 83, 84, 86, 88, 90, 91, 92, 94, 96, 97, 99, 101, 102, 106, 108, 109, 110, 111, 112, 114, 115, 116, 117, 118, 120, 122, 124, 125, 126, 128, 129, 132, 135, 138, 161, 167, 168, 172, 185, 195, 196, 233, 234, 239, 302

Porter, Katherine Anne: 359, 360, 361, 366

Rickword, Edgell: 270

Rodman, Selden: 341, 347, 365

Rosenfeld, Paul: 338

Rychtarik, Charlotte: 141, 143, 149, 156, 166, 170, 264, 309, 336

Rychtarik, Charlotte and Richard: 139, 145, 152, 179, 200, 203, 214, 215, 220, 224, 232, 241, 293, 308, 321, 357, 374

Rychtarik, Richard: 147

Schneider, Isidor: 274, 301, 325, 34 350

Schneider, Isidor and Helen: 305

Seltzer, Thomas: 204

Simpson, Mrs. T. W.: 266, 287, 405

Sommer, William: 144, 218

Stein, Gertrude: 318, 324

Stella, Joseph: 317

Stepmother (Bessie M. Hise): 379, 382, 393, 404

Stieglitz, Alfred: 142, 148, 150, 154, 160, 164

Tate, Allen: 98, 100, 104, 130, 133, 134, 178, 269, 275, 276, 277, 279, 280, 281, 282, 326, 343, 345

Walton, Eda Lou: 340, 380

Wiegand, Charmion: 28, 74, 95, 107, 113, 127, 314

Weinstock, Herbert: 339

Winters, Yvor: 285

Wright, William: 14, 21, 22, 24, 37, 38, 78, 87, 89, 93, 123, 252, 348, 349, 367, 370

Zabel, Morton Dauwen: 364, 372, 402

INDEX

(Asterisks denote works of Hart Crane)

"Abbott, Dorian" (J. B. Wheelwright), 125

Abraham Lincoln: The Prairie Years (Sandburg), 272

Aeneid, The (Virgil), 309

Aeschylus, 235

Aesop, 58

Aesthete, 1925, 196

*"Again" ("The Wine Menagerie"), 255

Aiken, Conrad, 69, 294 f.

Akron, Ohio, 23 ff.

Alden, Priscilla, 306

Aldington, Richard, 12, 341

All God's Chillun Got Wings (O'Neill), 177

Alleghany College, xi

American, The (James), 41

American Caravan, The, 291

*"America's Plutonic Ecstasies," 120, 126

Anarchism Is Not Enough (Riding), 321

Anderson, Margaret, 10, 30, 45 ff., 56-57, 61, 64, 70, 174

Anderson, Sherwood, 23, 26 ff., 34 ff., 37-38, 40, 47, 53, 56, 58 f., 62, 65-66, 69, 73, 75, 83 ff., 95 ff., 103, 187, 208, 287, 364

Anthology of Magazine Verse (ed. Braithwaite), 104

Annunzio, d', Gabriele, 41

Apollinaire, Guillaume, 84 f.

Apuleius, 36

Aquinas, Saint Thomas, 313

Aragon, Louis, 84

Aristotle, 139, 311

Atlantic Monthly, 75

*"Atlantis," 268, 270

Atlantis in America (Lewis Spence), 255

*"At Melville's Tomb," 218, 259

*"Ave Maria," 242, 268, 291 ff., 305 f.

*"Bacardi Spreads the Eagle's Wings," 315, 410

Bach, J. S., 408

Back to Methuselah (Shaw), 66, 104

Baird, Peggy, 232, 330, 376, 383, 393-394, 396, 403 f., 406 f., 409, 412

Barnes, Djuna, 28

Barney, Alice, 325

Barney, Nathalie Clifford, 325

Barrie, Sir James, 25

Barrymore, John, 38

Bartholomew Fair (Jonson), 71

Bartók, Béla, 177

Baudelaire, Charles, 56, 58, 67, 88, 91, 115, 213, 358, 371

Bax, Arnold, 177

Beach, Rex, 73

Beals, Carleton, 404

Beardsley, Aubrey, 105

Beethoven, van, Ludwig, 109, 316

Benét, William Rose, 243, 324

Berners, Lord, 177

Better Sort, The (James), 41

Biggers, Earl Derr, 5-6

Binet, Jean, 66

*"Black Tambourine," 54, 58, 60, 63, 70, 72, 77

Blair, Mary, 195

Blake, William, 39, 88, 90, 100, 115, 132, 138, 176, 260, 288, 291, 294, 301, 322, 324, 364

Bloch, Ernest, 66, 78, 82, 129, 177

Blue Juniata (Cowley), 330-331, 343

Blume, Peter, 349

Bodenheim, Maxwell, 9, 75, 295

Boni, Albert and Charles, 254

Boni and Liveright, 14, 136

Boone, Daniel, 307

*"Bottom of the Sea Is Cruel, The" ("Voyages I"), 69, 96, 99

Boyd, Ernest, 75, 243, 394

Boyle, Kay, 321, 335, 341, 406
Bradley, F. H., 322
Brahms, Johannes, 316
Braithwaite, William Stanley, 104
Brancusi, Constantin, 70
Braque, Georges, 177
Brenner, Anita, 399, 404
Breughel, 314
*Bridge, The, vii, ix f., xviii, 118, 119-120, 123, 124-125, 127 f., 135 ff., 145, 148, 153, 178, 184, 191 f., 201, 222-223, 231-233, 236, 240-242, 248 ff., 254 f., 259, 261 f., 265, 267 f., 268-269, 269-270, 271 f., 273, 274-275, 276 ff., 280, 285, 293, 296 f., 302 f., 304-308, 309 f., 318, 322, 325, 334 ff., 338 f., 342, 343-349, 350 ff., 364, 366, 374
*"Bridge of Estador, The," 55
Brody, Alter, 40
*"Broken Tower, The," viii, x, 396, 401, 404, 406, 410
Brookhaven, Long Island, 20 f.
Brooklyn Bridge, ix f., 181, 183, 232, 240, 261, 270, 283, 307, 334, 363
*"Brooklyn Bridge, To," 267, 347
Brooklyn Heights, 181 ff.
Brooks, Charles S., 13, 56
Brooks, Mrs. Charles S., 13
Brooks, Van Wyck, 28, 47, 178, 195, 291
Broom, 76, 95, 101, 103 f., 106, 113, 117 ff., 123, 154 f., 161 f., 185
Brothers Karamazov, The (Dostoievsky), 49 f.
Browning, Elizabeth Barrett, 67
Brown, John, 61 f., 241
Brown, (William) Slater, vi, 85, 133 ff., 155 ff., 160 ff., 167, 197, 205 f., 208 f., 214, 217, 226, 244, 268, 290, 293, 303, 321, 355, 379, 383
Bruno's Weekly, xvii
Bullus, Leonard, 292
Burchfield, Charles, 56
Burke, Kenneth, 36, 63, 70, 99, 103-104, 106, 108, 135, 155, 158, 160, 162, 166, 185, 218, 388

Burleson, Albert S. (Postmaster General), 29, 47
Butler, Samuel, 98-99
Bynner, Witter, 37, 394
Byron, Lord, 67

Cabell, James Branch, 105, 108
Cabinet of Dr. Caligari, 65
Calendar, The, 259, 281
Calhoun, Alice, 14-15, 311
California, 311 ff.
Calles, Plutarco, 293, 319
Camino, Leon Felipe, 372 f.
Campbell, Roy, 342
Canby, Henry Seidel, 345
Candee, Harry, 29-30, 32, 43, 141
Cannan, Gilbert, 85
*"Cape Hatteras," 308, 344 ff.
Casanova, 372-373
Casella, Alfredo, 177
Castaneda, Dr. Maximiliano, 368
Catel, Jean, 194 f.
Catullus, 29, 33
Cavalcanti, Guido, 67
Cazes, Hazel, 369
Cervantes Saavedra, de, Miguel, 17
Cezanne, Paul, 86, 342
Chagrin Falls, Ohio, 359 ff.
Chaplin, Charlie, 65 f., 68 f., 85, 149-150, 170, 311, 326
*"Chaplinesque," 65 f., 68 ff., 74, 85, 195, 313
Chapman, George–Homer, 287
Chartreuse de Parme, La (Stendhal), 39, 64
Chase, William Merritt, 7
Chatterton, Thomas, 67
Chaucer, Geoffrey, 17, 78, 299
Chekhov, Anton, 39
Chirico, de, Giorgio, 87, 251
Chopin, Frédéric, 59
Christian Science, xvii, 3, 12, 15-16, 33-34, 161, 180, 280
City Block (Frank), 124, 128, 130, 132-133
Clarke, Donald, 292

Cleveland, Ohio, xvii, 30 ff., 45 ff.
Cleveland *Plain Dealer*, 12
Coburn, Alvin Langdon, 30
Cocteau, Jean, 72, 86
Coleridge, Samuel Taylor, 67, 215, 314, 343, 353
Collected Poems of Hart Crane, The, v
Collioure, France, 339 ff.
Columbia Heights, Brooklyn, 181 ff.
Columbia University, 19-20, 21
Columbus, Christopher,232, 234, 240 f., 268, 305
Colum, Mary, 6 f.
Colum, Padraic, 6 f., 14, 51, 63, 95, 149
Commedia (Dante), 356
Comstock, Anthony, 30
Conrad, Joseph, 41, 187
Conquistador (MacLeish), 375, 411
Contact, 51, 53
Contempo, 394
Coolidge, Calvin, 365
Copeau, Jacques, 85, 178
Copland, Aaron, 195
*Cortez-Montezuma epic, 276, 390, 405
Coué, Emile, 109
Counterfeiters, The (Gide), 316, 322
Cowley, Malcolm, vi, 42, 75, 84 f., 97, 113, 135, 155, 160-161, 162, 166, 182, 184, 231 n., 244, 252, 256, 294, 321, 325, 327, 340, 384, 388, 393, 400
Craig, Gordon, 66-67
Crane, Bessie (aunt), 3
Crane, Bessie M. (stepmother, II), *see* Hise, Bessie M.
Crane, Clarence Arthur (father), x-xii, xvii f., 3, 9, 18, 20-21, 22 f., 27 f., 32 f., 35, 41, 45, 48, 50-51, 55, 57, 82, 108, 167 f., 173-174, 175, 179 ff., 186, 207 f., 214, 219 n., 226, 284, 292, 296-297, 337 f., 360, 363 ff., 376-377, 378 f., 402-403, 404
Crane, Frances (stepmother, I), 173, 283-284
Crane, Grace Hart (mother), vi, x, xvii, 3, 7 f., 19, 24, 32, 33-34, 36, 48 f., 57, 82, 107-108, 110, 134, 140-141,

143, 153 f., 162, 169, 212, 214, 219, 226-227, 231, 234 f., 250, 252, 256, 276, 278, 303-304, 316, 320-321, 327, 337-338
Crevel, René, 341
Crime and Punishment (Dostoievsky), 46
Criterion, The, 218, 308
Critique of Humanism, The (ed. C. H. Grattan), 352, 354
Crome Yellow (A. Huxley), 82
Crosby, Caresse, xviii, 340, 342, 348
Crosby, Harry, xviii, 335 f.,' 338-339, 340, 342, 344, 346, 348, 405
*"C 33," xvii
Cummings, Anne, 310-311, 324
Cummings, E. E., 85, 96, 108, 120, 133, 167, 182, 213, 251, 307, 310-311, 321, 324, 349, 354 f., 375
Curtis, Charles, 188, 198, 224, 226, 243, 252, 284
*"Cutty Sark," 268, 283, 294, 307, 346

Dadaism, 52, 70, 72
Daly, James, 123
Damon, S. Foster, 100
*"Dance, The," 288-289, 292, 307
Dante Alighieri, ix, 67
Dark Mother, The (Frank), 47
Dasburg, Andrew, 408
Davenport, Russell, 366
Davidson, Donald, 294
Davies, Sir John, 213
Debussy, Claude, 78, 108
Decline of the West, The (Spengler), 267
Deming, Zell Hart (aunt), 14, 188, 226
Democratic Vistas (Whitman), 354
Derain, Andre, 87, 90
Destinations (Munson), 178, 323-324
Deutsch, Babette, 63
Dial, The, 27, 32, 35 f., 36, 40, 42 f., 47, 54, 55 f., 65, 70, 73, 75, 92, 94, 97, 101, 103, 115, 117 f., 124, 133, 135, 136-137, 154, 160, 162, 178, 180, 191, 218, 220, 289, 292

Dickinson, Emily, 213, 324
Dietz, Howard, 325
Dietz, Lorna, 370
D'Indy, Vincent, 129
Dio Cassius, 32
Dionysios, 91
Dr. Transit (Schneider), 231, 287
Doherty, Mary, 393
Don Quixote, 261
Don Quixote (Cervantes), 263
Donne, John, 25, 66 ff., 71, 73, 77, 86, 88, 176, 213, 301
Dos Passos, John, 213, 324, 366
Dostoievsky, Feodor, 46 f., 50, 52-53
Double Dealer, The, 58 f., 61 f., 66, 74, 87 f., 104, 115, 129
Douglas, Lord Alfred, 43
Drayton, Michael, 78, 86, 286
Dreiser, Theodore, 27, 69, 324
Duchamp, Marcel, 52, 177
Duchess of Malfi, The (Webster), 90
Duncan, Isadora, 108 f., 322
Durieux, Caroline and Pierre, 404

Eames, Claire, 174
East High School, Cleveland, xvii, 4, 359
Eastman, Max, 388
Egoist, The, 91
Einstein, Albert, 311
El Greco, 114, 267, 333
El Universal, 373
Eliot, T. S., 24, 26, 28, 34, 36, 44, 66, 86, 88, 90, 102, 104 f., 114-115, 117 f., 121, 123, 261, 308, 311, 313, 323, 345, 351, 355 f., 359, 372
Ely, 3, 14
Emerson, Ralph Waldo, 73
*"Emily Dickinson, To," 277
Enormous Room, The (Cummings), 96 f., 133
Enters, Angna, 349
*"Episode of Hands," 37, 38-39, 40
Epstein, Jacob, 46, 95
Erik Dorn (Hecht), 66, 68 ff., 73
Estrada, Genaro, 372

Evans, Walker, 347
Excelsior, 373

Faust (Goethe), 94
*"Faustus and Helen, For the Marriage of," 87, 89, 92-93, 96, 98, 100-101, 102 f., 113 ff., 120-121, 123-124, 125, 127 ff., 131, 135-136, 140, 154, 178, 181, 184, 195, 301
Fawcett, James Waldo, 24-25, 27
Fernandez, Ramon, 319, 322 f.
Field, Eugene, 29
Fielding, Henry, 300
Fisher, William Murrell, 107, 161 ff., 167
Fitts, Norman, 119 f., 126
Fitzgerald, Eleanor, 224, 303, 311, 354
Fitzgerald, F. Scott, 78
Five Seasons, The (Phelps Putnam), 384, 393, 399
Flaubert, Gustave, 75
Fletcher, Herbert, 25-26, 63
Fletcher, John Gould, 63, 295
Fleurs du Mal, Les (Baudelaire), 33
Florida land boom, 209-210
Flowering Judas (Porter), 373
Flynn, Bina, 216 f., 248, 252
Ford, Ford Madox, 285, 341
Fortune, 357 ff.
42nd Parallel (Dos Passos), 366
Frank, Thomas, 263
Frank, Waldo, vii, 26-27, 28, 34-35, 95 f., 98-99, 104, 107 f., 113, 118 f., 124, 128 ff., 132-133, 136 f., 140 f., 145, 149 f., 154 f., 162, 170, 178, 186 f., 193, 195 f., 199 f., 203, 206, 208, 218-219, 223 ff., 236, 251 f., 255 f., 269 f., 278, 284, 291, 312, 322 ff., 370, 400
Freeman, G. W., 204, 211
Freeman, The, 40, 58-59, 125
Freud, Sigmund, 268
Freytag-Loringhoven, von, Baroness Elsa, 23, 30, 52, 56, 62
From Ritual to Romance (Jessie L. Weston), 314

Friedman, Dr. Paul, viii
Frost, Robert, 17, 27
Fugitive, The, 88, 123, 155, 161
Fyodor Dostoyevsky (J. Middleton Murry), 53

Gale, Zona, 66
Garden, Mary, 65
*"Garden Abstract," 31, 37, 39 f., 51-52
Gargoyle, 70, 79-80
Garman, Douglas, 281
Garrettsville, Ohio, xvii
Gauguin, Paul, 29, 36, 55, 385
Gide, André, 66, 85, 294, 317, 336
Gilmore, Louis, 290
Goethe, 240
Gogh, van, Vincent, 55
Gogol, Nikolai, 34
Gold, Michael, 357
Golden Ass, The (Apuleius), 44
Goldman, Emma, 341
Gordon (Tate), Caroline, 225 f., 245-247, 283, 294, 341 ff.
Gorman, Herbert, 295
Gourmont, de, Rémy, 66, 73, 78 f., 123
    Marginalia on Poe and Baudelaire, 64
Goya, Francisco, 114
Graechische Vasenmalerei (Ernst Buschor), 116
Grand Cayman, West Indies, 257-258, 264-266, 293
Grandmothers, The (Wescott), 316
Graves, Robert, 333
Gregory, Alyse, 136, 160
Green, Sonia, 187
Greenberg, Samuel B., 162-163
Grey, Zane, 73
Gris, Juan, 341
Grosz, George, 87
Grunberg, Solomon, 331
Guardian, The, 215, 218
Guest, Edgar A., 73
Guggenheim Fellowship, xviii, 358, 365, 367, 374
Gurdjieff, George Ivanovitch, 174, 298

Habicht, Charmion. *See* Wiegand, Charmion
Habicht, Hermann, 22, 131, 180
Hackett, Francis, 28
Hale, William Harlan, 357, 375
Hamlet of A. MacLeish, The, 343
Hampden, Walter, 44-45
Harbor, The (Ernest Poole), 256
*"Harbor Dawn, The," 283, 306
Harcourt, Brace, 155, 213
Hardy, Thomas, 289, 300, 357
Harkness Hoot, The, 356-357
Harris, Charles, 121
Harris, Frank, 50
Hart, Clinton (grandfather), 249
Hart Crane (Philip Horton), v, 240 n.
Hart, Elizabeth Belden (grandmother), xvii f., 10, 14, 23 f., 34, 140, 162 ff., 188, 214, 219, 224 f., 227, 233, 243, 270, 303, 321, 328, 337
Harte, Bret, 23
Hartley, Marsden, 27, 30, 75, 342, 404, 408
Havana, Cuba, 10, 251, 275, 412
Hays, Arthur Garfield, 330
Heap, Jane, 46 f., 61, 64, 100, 224
Hecht, 69 f., 104
Heine, Heinrich, 59, 71, 117
Heliogabalus (Mencken & Nathan), 32
Helton, Roy, 373
Hemingway, Ernest, 287 f., 294
Hertha, 305
Hints to Pilgrims (Charles S. Brooks), 56
Hise, Bessie M. (stepmother, II), 364, 377, 378 f., 410
History of American Poetry, A (Gregory and Zaturenska), v
History of Ferdinand and Isabella (W. H. Prescott), 235
Hoboken, New Jersey, 286
Hofmann, Josef, 177
Hollywood, California, 324-325
Homer, 120
Hopkins, Gerard Manley, 317, 319, 340, 359

Hoppé, E. O., 30
Hound & Horn, The, 352
Howells, William Dean, 47
Huebsch, B. W., 85, 96-97, 125, 171 f.,
    175
*"Hurricane, The," 316, 363
Huxley, Aldous, 72, 90
Huysmans, Joris Karl, 69, 78

Ibsen, Henrik, 9
Idols Behind Altars (Brenner), 372
Imperial Purple (Saltus), 32, 49
Iliad, The (Homer), 81
In Our Time (Hemingway), 219
In the American Grain (Williams),
    277-278
*"Indiana," 307, 345, 357-358
Instigations (Pound), 51
*"Interludium," 166
International Studio, 30
Isle of Pines, Cuba, vii, xvii f., 10, 151
    ff., 210, 234, 248-249, 251 ff., 293

Jacobs, S. A., 201, 202-203, 205
James, Henry, 17, 41, 90, 106
Jammes, Francis, 104
Jenkins, Sue, 135, 174, 182, 197, 205,
    209, 217, 262, 384
Jimenez, Juan Ramon, 187, 212
John Brown (Oswald Garrison Villard),
    61
Jolas, Eugene, 293 f., 334, 336, 338, 341
Jolson, Al, 32, 290
Jones, Robert Edmond, 166, 177
Jonson, Ben, 71, 78, 88, 129
Jordan, Virgil, 53
Josephson, Hannah, 63, 330
Josephson, Matthew, 23 f., 26 f., 35,
    37, 48, 63, 64-65, 71 f., 74-75, 78-79,
    84 f., 87, 95-96, 97, 100 ff., 104, 105-
    106, 113 f., 118 ff., 135, 162, 166, 285,
    384
Journal of First Voyage to America
    (Columbus), 234 f.
Joyce, James, 47, 58, 61, 66, 69, 94 f.,
    99, 104 f., 108, 288

Judge, The (Rebecca West), 102
Jurgen (Cabell), 73, 366

Kahn, Otto H., xviii, 221, 225, 227,
    232 f., 247 f., 250, 254, 259, 262 ff.,
    267, 274, 286, 310, 321, 351
Kafka, Franz, viii
Keats, John, 67, 353
Kid, The (Charlie Chaplin), 65, 68 f.
*"Kidd's Cove" ("O Carib Isle"), 259
King, Clinton, 394, 399 ff.
Kirkham, Hall, 292
Kling, Joseph, 25, 31-32
Knopf, Alfred A., 26, 125
Kreymborg, Alfred, 194 f., 244, 291
Kunitz, Stanley J., 353
Kuniyoshi, Yasuo, 107

Lachaise, Gaston, 135, 149, 159, 170,
    205, 252, 258
Lachaise, Isabel, 159, 205, 252, 258
*"Lachrymae Christi," 183
Ladies Home Journal, 75
Laforgue, Jules, 45, 67, 71, 85 f., 88, 90,
    104, 123, 163, 261, 282
Landor, Walter Savage, 39, 73
Larbaud, Valery, 95, 294, 336
Lasky, Jesse, 325
Laukhuff, Richard, 12, 23, 277, 280
Laurencin, Marie, 87
Lawrence, D. H., 17, 52, 63, 390, 395
Leaves of Grass (Whitman), 109
LeBlanc, Georgette, 174
Leda (Huxley), 44
Leffingwell, 167
Leonardo da Vinci, 300
Lescaze, William, 56, 62-63, 66-67, 70,
    77, 85, 91 f., 104
Letters of Henry James, The, 41
Lewis (Winters), Janet, 313
Lewis, Sinclair, 66
Lewis, Wyndham, 55, 196, 313, 319,
    322 f.
Liberator, The, 31, 91
Light, James, 155, 166, 174, 213-214,
    215, 224, 262, 267

Light, Sue. *See* Jenkins, Sue
Limbo (Huxley), 41
Lincoln, Abraham, 27
Lindsay, Vachel, 7, 295
Li Po, 67
Literary Digest, 68
Little Mexico (Spratling), 388, 404
Little Review, The, 10, 12, 16-17, 18,
    20-21, 23 f., 27 f., 30, 45-46, 47, 51,
    56, 61, 64, 68, 70, 75, 117, 126, 191
Liveright, Horace, 125, 128, 171, 206,
    218, 220, 254, 259, 262-263, 281, 292,
    296, 340
Lives of the Caesars (Suetonius), 49
"Locations des Pierrots," 87
Loeb, Harold, 113
London, 332-333, 338, 341
London *Times*, 295
Long, Haniel, 63
Look Homeward, Angel (Wolfe), 375
Los Angeles, California, 314-315
Lovecraft, Howard, 187
Lovell, Wheeler, 267
Loveman, Samuel, x, 91, 100, 104, 106,
    187 f., 190-191, 200, 201-202, 206, 331
Love of Three Kings, The (Italo Mon-
    temezzi), 65
Lowell, Amy, 26, 89, 125
Lowenfels, Walter, 341

McAlmon, Robert, 53, 80
Macaulay Company, 291
MacCown, Eugene, 341
McFee, William, 256
Macgowan, Kenneth, 166
Machinery, 167
Mackenzie, Compton, 52
MacLeish, Archibald, 285, 294, 351,
    357, 375
McPherson, Aimee, 314-315, 322
Macy, John, 105
Madden, N. Byron (uncle), 15, 411
Maddow, Ben, 393
Maeterlinck, Maurice, 174
Magellan (A. S. Hildebrand), 235
Maillol, Aristide, 177

Mallarmé, Stéphane, 78
Man Who Died, The (D. H. Lawrence),
    395
"Mango Tree, The," 254 f., 259
Mann, Klaus, 341
Many Marriages (S. Anderson), 103
Marching Men (S. Anderson), 56
Maria Chapdelaine (Louis Hémon), 81
Marichalar, Antonio, 313-314
Marin, John, 102, 177, 349
Marks, Harry L., 344
Marlowe, Christopher, 25, 67, 71, 86,
    88, 300, 353
Marseille, France, 342 ff.
Martinique, West Indies, 310
Masses, The, 91
Massis, Henri, 313
Masters, Edgar Lee, 28, 295
Matisse, Henry, 87, 171
Maugham, W. Somerset, 29
Maupassant, de, Guy, 24
Maurras, Charles, 313
Measure, The, 64
Meleager, 100
Melville, Herman, 252, 331
Mencken, H. L., 26, 30, 32, 388 f.
Menorah Journal, The, 359
Merchant of Venice, The (Shakes-
    peare), 44-45
Mercure de France, 194
Messages (Fernandez), 317, 319
Mexican Maze (Beals), 380
Mexico, xviii, 368 ff.
Mexico (Stuart Chase), 380 f.
Michelangelo, 114
Millay, Edna St. Vincent, 67-68
Milton, John, 67, 384
Minns, Hervey W., 30, 46, 52, 54
Mitchell, Stewart, 182, 313, 321
Moby Dick (Melville), 86, 258, 260,
    404-405
Modernist, The, 22 f., 24-25, 27
Moe, Henry Allen, 389
Monroe, Harriet, 294, 374, 410 n.
Montéllano, 373
Moody, William Vaughn, 89

Moon and Sixpence, The (Maugham),
    29
Moore, George, 354
Moore, Marianne, 37, 85, 194 f., 215,
    218, 220, 224, 255, 259, 275, 289 f.,
    294, 324
Moore, Thomas, 67
Morris, William, 333
Mumford, Lewis, 195, 366
Munson, Elizabeth, vi, 126, 133, 143-
    144, 146 f., 155, 166, 180, 184
Munson, Gorham, vi f., ix, 85, 88, 94
    f., 97, 101, 106 ff., 117, 119, 127, 130
    ff., 143-144, 146 f., 153-154, 158, 171 f.,
    176, 178, 180, 182, 184 ff., 201, 213 f.,
    224, 251, 270 f., 273-274, 275, 282,
    298, 300, 330, 335, 353, 384, 394
Murry, J. Middleton, 75
*"My Grandmother's Love Letters,"
    22 f., 25 f., 32, 37, 39
My Heart and My Flesh (Elizabeth
    Madox Roberts), 314

Nagle, Edward, 135, 155 ff., 159 ff.
Nathan, George Jean, 32
Nation, The, 49, 58-59, 283
Natural Philosophy of Love, The (de
    Gourmont, trans. Pound), 73, 91
Naumburg, Margaret, 150, 154, 162,
    166, 336
Negri, Pola, 149
Nelson, Ernest, 75, 93
New American Caravan, The, 351
New Criterion, The, 240
New Masses, The, 240
New Orleans, Louisiana, 303, 326
New Republic, The, 28, 40, 58-59, 108,
    219, 290, 292, 388, 394
New York City, xvii, 4 ff., 130 ff., 165 ff.
New York *Evening Journal,* 24
New York *Times,* 36, 100
Newton, Sir Isaac, 238
Nietzsche, Friedrich, 67, 75, 93, 99, 358
Nigger of the Narcissus, The (Conrad),
    41
1919 (John Dos Passos), 409

1924, 185, 191 f.
Noa Noa (Paul Gauguin), 39
Nouvelle Revue Française, La, 78, 85

"O Carib Isle," 283, 293
O'Flaherty, Liam, 371
O'Keeffe, Georgia, 114, 177, 195, 349
O'Malley, Ernest, 371
O'Neill, Eugene, 155-156, 166, 170, 174,
    177, 180, 184, 190, 193, 203, 208, 211-
    212, 214-215, 216, 218, 220 ff., 224 f.,
    240, 254, 258-259, 262-263, 270
Orage, A. R., 282
Ordeal of Mark Twain, The (Van
    Wyck Brooks), 28
Oresteia of Aeschylus, The (trans. G.
    Warr), 235
Ornstein, Leo, 271
Others, 7, 9
Our America (Frank), 26-27, 28, 34-35,
    131

Pagan, The, xvii, 7, 12, 23, 31
"Paraphrase," 195
Paris, 333 ff.
Parker, Dorothy, 322
Parrish, Maxfield, 21
Parsifal (Wagner), 35
Pascal, Blaise, 48
"Passage," 215, 218, 259
"Pastorale," 64, 69, 71
Pater, Walter, 108, 117, 161
Patterson, New York, xviii, 208 ff.,
    224 ff., 277 ff.
Pavannes and Divisions (Pound), 24
Pelléas et Mélisande (Debussy), 339
"Persuasion, A," 58, 64
Petits Poèmes en Prose, Les (Baude-
    laire), 274
Petrouchka (Stravinsky), 200
Phibbs, Geoffrey, 340
Picabia, Francis, 64
Picasso, Pablo, 55, 87, 146, 171, 177,
    336, 341
Picture of Dorian Gray, The (Wilde),
    38

Pindar, 129
Pinski, David, 47
Plagued by the Nightingale (Boyle), 406
Plato, 17, 238
Plato and Platonism (Pater), 161
Plowshare, The, 34
Plumed Serpent, The (D. H. Lawrence), 236
Pocahontas, 232, 241, 305, 307
Poe, Edgar Allen, 67, 231, 278, 290, 331
Poetry (Chicago), 25, 51, 289, 373 f., 410 n.
Poetry Society of America, 7
Pollard, Percival, 44
Polo, Marco, 242
Poor White (S. Anderson), 47, 53
*"Porphyro in Akron," 40, 42 f., 51, 64
Porter, Katherine Anne, 367, 370, 373, 377-378, 383
Port of New York (Rosenfeld), 202
Portrait of the Artist (Joyce), 99, 313
Possessed, The (Dostoievsky), 46 f., 49 f.
*"Possessions," 176
Potamkin, Harry Alan, 240
Potapovitch, Stan, 8
Pound, Ezra, 28, 41, 44, 51, 54, 61 ff., 64, 66, 70, 86, 88, 96
*"Powhatan's Daughter," 305
Powitzki, Mrs., 286
Powys, John Cowper, 136
*"Praise for an Urn," 93, 104, 259
Principles of Literary Criticism (I. A. Richards), 314
Proust, Marcel, 66
Provincetown Theatre, 40, 174, 177, 214
Psychoanalytic Quarterly, viii

*"Quaker Hill," 345, 347
Quinn, John, 47
Rabelais, 30, 36, 56
Rahab (Waldo Frank), 98-99, 108
Rainbow, The (D. H. Lawrence), 43
Ransom, John Crowe, 100, 289
Rauh, Ida, 28

Ravel, Maurice, 66, 108, 129, 139-140
Ray, Man, 52, 94-95
*"Recitative," 161, 176
Reeck, Emil, 84, 97
Re-discovery of America, The (Waldo Frank), 318-319, 322 f., 326, 335
Rembrandt, 54
Renaissance, The (Pater), 161
Revista de Occidente, 313 n., 314
Rickword, Edgell, 259, 281, 333
Riding, Laura, 217, 291, 294, 321, 333 f., 341
Rimbaud (E. Rickword), 283
Rimbaud, Arthur, 43, 45, 85, 162, 213, 252, 260 f., 270, 272, 317, 359, 374
*"River, The," 303, 306-307
Rivera, Diego, 371
Robeson, Paul and Essie, 333
Robinson, Boardman, 54
Robinson, Edwin Arlington, 89, 93
Robson, Peggy, 400
Rodin, Auguste, 46
Roebling, Washington, 293-294
Romains, Jules, 24
Rorty, James, 244
Rosenfeld, Paul, 75, 77, 95, 97 f., 102, 105, 126, 166, 178, 193-194, 202, 224, 291 f.
Rouge et le Noir, Le (Stendhal), 64
Rousseau, Henri, 177
Russell, Bertrand, 240
Rychtarik, Charlotte, 106, 144-145, 247, 364 f., 408
Rychtarik, Richard, 106, 131, 132-133, 139, 141, 144-145, 147, 160, 247, 364 f.

Sacre du Printemps, Le (Stravinsky), 200
Sacred Wood, The (Eliot), 71
Sáenz, Moisés, 370, 372
Salmon, André, 66
Saltus, Edgar, 29, 44, 106, 187
Salvos (Frank), 178
Sandburg, Carl, 69
San Pedro, California, 315, 319-320
Santayana, George, 240

Saphier, William, 70
Satie, Erik, 66
Saturday Evening Post, The, 284, 345
Saturday Review of Literature, The, 345
Satyricon (Petronius Arbiter), 44, 105
Schmitt, Carl, 4 ff., 8
Schneider, Isidor, 231, 281
Schoenberg, Arnold, 177
Schopenhauer, Arthur, 41
Science and the Modern World (A. N. Whitehead), 235
Scientific American, The, 271
Scriabin, Alexander, 63, 109, 129
Seaver, Edwin, 185, 218
Secession, 82, 84 f., 88, 94 f., 97, 100 f., 103, 105 ff., 108, 117, 121, 123 ff., 154 f., 178, 185
Second April (Millay), 6
S4N, 120, 126
Seiberling, F. H., 30
Seldes, Gilbert, 70, 103
Seligmann, Herbert J., 195, 285
Seltzer, Thomas, 206
Service, Robert W., 73
Seven Arts, The, 9
Seltzer, Thomas, 206
Shadowland, 61, 63, 75
Shakespeare, 67, 129, 289, 299 f.
Shelley, P. B., 67
"Sherwood Anderson," 59-60, 61 ff.
Simpson, Eyler, 395
Simpson, Lesley, 393, 399, 404
Simpson, Marion, 399
Simpson, Mrs. T. W. ("Aunt Sally"), 152, 248-249, 251 ff., 286
Since Cézanne (Clive Bell), 96
Siqueros, David Alfaro, 384-385, 386-387, 388
Sistine Chapel, 305
Sitwell, Edith, 44
1601 (Mark Twain), 26, 28, 30
Smart Set, The, 10 n., 25, 34
Smith, Captain John, 306
Smith, Claire. *See* Spencer, Claire
Smith, Elizabeth, 172-173

Smith, Harrison, 17, 19 f., 22, 128, 155, 167, 180, 224, 334-335
Sodome et Gomorrhe (Proust), 316, 322
Sommer, William, 54 ff., 58 ff., 71, 75, 78, 83, 86, 89-90, 92, 95, 98, 101 f., 105, 107, 113-114, 115, 119, 137, 233, 363-364
Soupault, Philippe, 104, 294, 336, 341
South Wind (Norman Douglas), 280
Spencer, Claire, 12, 17, 19 f., 22, 136, 180, 409
Spencer, Jessie, 12 f.
Spencer, Pat, 12
Spengler, Oswald, 158, 259 f., 267, 285, 293, 313, 319, 322, 357, 366
Speyer, Leonora, 67
Spoon River Anthology (Masters), 28
Spinoza, Baruch, 363
Spratling, William, 388, 401, 404
Springhorn, Carl, 63
"Stark Major," 117-118, 121, 124, 126
Starved Rock (Masters), 28
Stein, Gertrude, 121 f., 167, 294, 311, 321, 336, 341
Stella, Joseph, 335, 339, 345
Stendhal, 64, 79
Stevens, Emily, 43
Stevens, Wallace, 25, 37, 53, 71, 88, 289
Stieglitz, Alfred, 95, 107, 113-114, 128 f., 141, 166 f., 170, 177, 195, 202
Story of San Michele, The (Axel Munthe), 366
Strand, Paul, 195
Strauss, Richard, 108, 129
Stravinsky, 200, 238
Success, 284
Sun Also Rises, The (Hemingway), 286-288
"Sunday Morning Apples," 96, 195
Swann's Way (Marcel Proust), 263
Swinburne, A. C., 332
Synge, John M., 71
Szold, Bernadine, 341
Szymanowski, Karol, 177

Taggard, Genevieve, 353 f.

*"Tampa Schooner" ("Repose of Rivers"), 259

Taras Bulba (N. Gogol), 80-81

Tarr (Wyndham Lewis), 69

Tate, Allen, 87, 100 ff., 104, 107, 118, 121 f., 126, 131, 185, 195, 197, 211, 215, 224 ff., 237, 239 f., 244, 245-249, 267 f., 270 f., 273, 284 f., 296, 313, 321, 341, 384

Tate, Caroline. *See* Gordon, Caroline

Teagle, J. Walter, 357 ff., 363

Teasdale, Sara, 67

Tempest, The (Shakespeare), 317

Temptation of Anthony, The (Schneider), 287

Tennyson, Lord, 67

Tepoztlan, Mexico, 380-383, 388

Tertium Organum (P. D. Ouspensky), 124

Théâtre du Vieux Colombier, 178

Their Day in Court (Percival Pollard), 105

Thomas, Edward, 72, 88

Thomas, Harold, 6

Thompson, Basil, 59

Thompson, Francis, 67

Thompson, Robert, 400, 409

Three Soldiers (Dos Passos), 68

Through Traffic (Russell Davenport), 366

Tiberius, 52, 63

Time and Western Man (Wyndham Lewis), 317, 319

Toomer, Jean, 149 f., 155, 162, 166 f., 185, 195, 214

Torrence, Ridgely, 289

transition, 294, 334

Tristram Shandy (Laurence Sterne), 91

Triumph of the Egg, The (S. Anderson), 65, 73, 76

Trois Poèmes Juifs (Bloch), 82

Trans-Atlantic Review, The, 185

Tschaikowsky, P. I., 109

*"Tunnel, The," 274-275, 278

Turbyfill, Mark, 125

Turner, Addie M., 224, 242, 245 ff., 255, 286, 292 f., 354

Turner, W. J., 330

Twain, Mark, 17, 26 f., 30

Tzara, Tristan, 84

Ulysses (Joyce), 62, 69, 72-73, 94 ff., 101, 127, 143 f., 288

Un Coeur Virginal (R. de Gourmont), 73, 79 f.

Underwood, Wilbur, 43-44, 155, 325

Untermeyer, Louis, 104, 107 f., 118, 244

Vail, Lawrence, 335, 406

Valéry, Paul, 195, 213, 300, 325, 372

Valle, Rafael, 373

Van Doren, Mark, 285

Vanity Fair, 61, 94, 345

Van Vuren, Floyd, 350

*"Van Winkle," 290, 306

Varèse, Edgar, 177, 334, 341

Vaughan, Henry, 88, 301

Vedanta, 242

Verlaine, Paul, 239

Vielé-Griffin, Francis, 104

Vildrac, Charles, 37, 45, 60

Villon, François, 36

Virgil, ix

*"Virginia," 272

Virgin Spain (Frank), 235-236, 242, 274

Vision and Design (Roger Fry), 57

Vlaminck, de, Maurice, 87, 90

*"Voyages," viii, 187, 192, 215, 218, 224, 244

Wagner, Richard, 108, 135

Waldo Frank (Munson), 104, 115, 119, 125, 128 f.

Walton, Mrs., 10

Walton, Eda Lou, 366

Wall Street Journal, The, 324

Warren, Ohio, xvii, 292

Warren, Robert Penn, 321

Washington, D.C., 42 ff.

Waste Land, The (Eliot), 105, 127, 271 f., 350 f.

Way of All Flesh, The (Samuel Butler), 39

Webster, John, 25, 67, 71, 86, 88, 129

Wells, H. G., 319

Wescott, Glenway, 125, 166, 316, 341

Watson, J. Sibley, 103, 136-137

Whale Ships and Whaling (G. F. Dow), 235

Wheeler, Monroe, 125

Wheelwright, John B., 125-126, 154

*White Buildings, xviii, 199 ff., 202-203, 205, 213 f., 218 ff., 254, 258-259, 262-263, 267, 270, 277, 280 f., 284 f., 290-291, 292, 294-295, 340, 345, 353

White, Hervey, 34 f.

Whitehead, A. N., 321

White-Jacket (Melville), 235

Whitman, Walt, 67, 73, 128, 184, 223, 241, 261-262, 284, 290, 308, 352, 353-354

Wiegand, Charmion, 131, 180, 333-334

Wilcox, Walter, 10

Wilde, Oscar, 38, 44

Wilder, Thornton, viii, 357

Wilkinson, Marguerite, 67, 104

Williams, William Carlos, 37, 51, 53, 102, 105, 114, 278, 294, 324

Wilson, Edmund, 195, 298, 301

*"Wine Menagerie, The," 218, 220

Winesburg, Ohio (S. Anderson), 34, 47, 75

*"Winesburg, Ohio" (review), 23

Winters, Yvor, 278, 284 f., 288 f., 294, 313 f., 317, 321, 348, 352 ff.

Wise, Herbert, 316, 318, 322, 324, 326, 331

Wolfe, Thomas, 375

Woodstock, New York, xvii, 154, 156 ff.

Wright, Cuthbert, 100

Wuthering Heights (Emily Brontë), 316-317

Wylie, Elinor, 243

Yale Review, The, 375

Yeats, W. B., 86, 88, 95, 300

Young Visitors, The (Daisy Ashford), 25

Zabel, Monroe Dauwen, 410 n.

Zigrosser, Carl, 158

Zinsser, Dr. Hans, 368

Zwaska, Caesar, 27, 96